The Arc of Due Process in American Constitutional Law

The Arc of Due Process in American Constitutional Law

E. Thomas Sullivan, President, University of Vermont
and
Toni M. Massaro, Regent's Professor and
Milton O. Riepe Chair in Constitutional Law,
University of Arizona

OXFORD
UNIVERSITY PRESS

OXFORD
UNIVERSITY PRESS

Oxford University Press is a department of the University of Oxford. It furthers the University's objective of excellence in research, scholarship, and education by publishing worldwide.

Oxford New York
Auckland Cape Town Dar es Salaam Hong Kong Karachi Kuala Lumpur Madrid
Melbourne Mexico City Nairobi New Delhi Shanghai Taipei Toronto

With offices in
Argentina Austria Brazil Chile Czech Republic France Greece Guatemala Hungary
Italy Japan Poland Portugal Singapore South Korea Switzerland Thailand
Turkey Ukraine Vietnam

Published in the United States of America by
Oxford University Press
198 Madison Avenue, New York, NY 10016

Library of Congress Cataloging-in-Publication Data
Sullivan, E. Thomas.
The arc of due process in American constitutional law/E. Thomas Sullivan and Toni M. Massaro.
pages cm
Includes bibliographical references and index.
ISBN 978-0-19-999080-1 (hardback : alk. paper)
1. Due process of law—United States. I. Massaro, Toni Marie, 1955—II. Title.
KF4765.S85 2013
347.73'5—dc23

2012042268

Note to Readers
This publication is designed to provide accurate and authoritative information in regard to the subject matter covered. It is based upon sources believed to be accurate and reliable and is intended to be current as of the time it was written. It is sold with the understanding that the publisher is not engaged in rendering legal, accounting, or other professional services. If legal advice or other expert assistance is required, the services of a competent professional person should be sought. Also, to confirm that the information has not been affected or changed by recent developments, traditional legal research techniques should be used, including checking primary sources where appropriate.

(Based on the Declaration of Principles jointly adopted by a Committee of the American Bar Association and a Committee of Publishers and Associations.)

To
Leslie Black Sullivan (ETS)
and
Genevieve Leavitt (TMM)

{CONTENTS}

{ACKNOWLEDGMENTS}

Tom Sullivan would like to acknowledge with appreciation the University of Minnesota, which provided him with a leave for the winter semester 2012 to finish this book. He also acknowledges with appreciation the University of Minnesota Law School, including Dean David Wippman and the faculty, especially Professors Robert Stein and Brian Bix, who gave comments on portions of this book. He also would like to recognize and extend a special appreciation to his research assistants Tom Pryor (Class of 2013), Emily Puchalski (Class of 2013), Eric Friske (Class of 2013), Daniel Schiff (Class of 2011), Cicely Miltich (Class of 2011), and Mary Alice Schumacher, his administrative assistant. Also, he would like to express deep appreciation to colleagues at New York University Law School who hosted him as a Visiting Professor for the winter 2012 semester, including Dean Richard Revesz and Vice Dean Randy Hertz, and Robert Anselmi, his administrative assistant at NYU.

Toni Massaro would like to acknowledge with appreciation the University of Arizona James E. Rogers College of Law for research and ongoing intellectual support. Special thanks go to Professor Barbara Atwood, for her characteristically wise comments and warm support; her excellent research assistants Joseph Ezzo (Class of 2012), Emily Peiffer (Class of 2014), Michael Shumway (Class of 2013), Nick Verderame (Class of 2013), and Matt A. Walker (Class of 2013); Ms. Sandy Davis, Ms. Judith Parker, Ms. Barbara Lopez and Ms. Carol Ward for superb administrative and secretarial support; and Ms. Maureen Garmon—world's best research librarian. Finally, she wishes to acknowledge the enormous intellectual debt she owes to her Arizona faculty colleagues and to her Stanford co-authors and colleagues, Barbara Allen Babcock and Norman Spaulding. All give meaningful substance to the professional process—through "thick and thin."

This work builds on our prior work, including writings in the following publications:

- E. Thomas Sullivan and Richard S. Frase, PROPORTIONALITY PRINCIPLES IN AMERICAN LAW (2009).
- E. Thomas Sullivan and Toni M. Massaro, *Due Process Exceptionalism*, 46 THE IRISH JURIST (2011).
- Toni M. Massaro, *Constitutional Law as "Normal Science,"* 21 CONST. COMMENT. 547 (2004).
- Toni M. Massaro, *Substantive Due Process, Black Swans, and Innovation*, UTAH L. REV. 987 (2011).

{PREFACE}

What do the contemporary issues of military tribunals, same-sex marriage, informational privacy, and reproductive rights have in common? All of them raise constitutional issues that fall under the umbrella of the Due Process Clauses of the United States Constitution. The resolution of all of them hinges, to a dramatic degree, upon ever-evolving judicial interpretations of that "due process of law" mandate.

Few Americans understand the common constitutional source of these rights, its ancient history, or the ornate set of rights that today fall within the due process embrace. Even many scholarly debates about judicial activism and the need to return to "original meaning" of constitutional rights—especially original meaning of due process of law—fail to apprehend the full due process terrain. Instead they often cherry-pick issues within the doctrine to criticize or praise specific pieces of the law, and are unmindful of the implications of these critiques for other rights that flow from the same due process artery. In particular, many critics who insist that the phrase *due process* historically and logically embraces only procedural, not substantive rights, ignore the multiple ways in which procedural rights flow from substantive rights and depend upon them. More fundamentally, the arguments against substantive due process rights simply blink too much doctrinal reality: Americans' settled expectations of ordered liberty and baseline sense of what constitutes a legitimate exercise of government power now include a complex set of procedural and substantive rights that emerged since the late 1800s under the due process framework.

In this book, we outline this history and argue that modern constitutional theory and practice must come to grips with it. We examine the origins and contemporary uses of due process principles in American constitutional law, and offer an overarching description of the factors and normative concepts that permit courts to invalidate a government action on the grounds of "due process."

Given the expanse of the doctrine, however, the common factors and normative concepts are general ones, subject to multiple interpretations as applied to particular due process contexts. Moreover, they trigger different legal standards in different contexts. For example, a "gross disproportionality" standard is used when courts review civil or criminal forfeitures of property; "undue burden" is the standard applied to measures that regulate abortion rights during the early stages of a woman's pregnancy; claims that legislative or executive measures unduly impinge on First Amendment rights are subject to varying levels of judicial "scrutiny" (strict, intermediate, and rational basis). Yet they have in common liberal democratic expectations of what counts as government "rationality" and proper obedience to expectations about the limits of government power over individual liberties.

When, for example, government seeks to punish an American citizen without a proper trial, to deny a same-sex couple the right to marry, to place new restrictions on early term abortions, or to insist on disclosure of private information as a condition to government employment, due process sensitivities and arguments surface. In each of these scenarios, there is a sense that government has "gone too far" and failed to observe procedural and substantive constraints on government power that ring due process bells. That we disagree—sometimes vehemently—upon where the line between legitimate government power and "goes too far" should be drawn does not mean we lack a common vocabulary for analyzing the issues or that due process notions become irrelevant to the resolution of the dispute simply because government power is upheld. Nor does the fact that the due process principles are quite general ones subject to immense contextual and temporal variations mean that they are meaningless or incapable of judicial interpretation and expression. On the contrary, the evolving judicial interpretations and expressions are the most powerful ways in which the general principles have taken form in American law, and thus the most significant source of what due process, in practice, means.

We illustrate these points in four steps. First, we identify the historical underpinnings of due process. Constitutional meanings always have begun with the historical problems and debates that gave rise to them. We therefore regard the deep roots of due process as relevant and illuminating to its contemporary expressions; but we do not agree with those who would tether modern due process solely to its historical underpinnings.

In the United States, as in all developed legal systems subscribing to the rule of law, courts are called upon in a wide variety of contexts to determine whether a particular government action excessively impinges on settled expectations of fundamental justice and individual autonomy. Many of these issues are matters of policy that are more properly resolved by the legislative and executive branches. Courts have limited ability to gather and weigh empirical data, limited legitimacy in making complex policy choices, and limited power to enforce their judgments. Legislative and executive officials and private actors are the primary decision makers, and they must be accorded substantial deference and allowed a considerable margin for error or difference of view. But courts still can, and do, impose meaningful limits on these decisions. One of the most important and controversial limits is imposed by *due process*.

The constitutional language is open-ended and designed to apply to a world that is ever-evolving. Moreover, the legal practice in the United States is based on a common law model of judicial interpretation, which too is ever-evolving. As long as this remains the judicial practice, constitutional principles will continue to evolve and morph, even as they are measured against, and understood in relation to, their particular historical backdrops.

Second, we chart the evolution of American due process doctrine. In particular, we identify three categories of due process rights that the United States Supreme Court has located within due process: procedural, substantive, and hybrid rights. We outline the elements of each strand and their interrelationships.

Third, we describe the judicial analysis of rights within each category. In these sections, we seek not to be exhaustive—each would properly be the subject of its own book or series of books—but illustrative. We show the arc of due process cases, due process principles, and due process themes across time and subject matter. This panoptic view makes crystal clear that due process embraces both process and substance, and springs from fundamental liberal democratic notions about the importance of procedural regularity, jurisdictional and structural restraints on government actors, and protection of individual liberty and equality. This is especially true as due process has evolved since the late nineteenth century, as courts confronted a rapidly changing world armed with constitutional language adopted during Reconstruction.

Finally, we identify several fundamental norms that span these disparate threads of due process and the most salient principles that animate due process doctrine across this broad expanse. Specifically, American due process doctrine reflects the following principles, which more generally promote the notion that government exists to promote the public good in ways that respect shared notions of rationality, order, and a legitimate "rule of law" as this is understood in a liberal democratic order:

- fair procedures, especially notice and opportunity to be heard, but also political process integrity
- impartial decision makers
- respect for settled expectations and traditions
- prospective, rather than retrospective, lawmaking
- transparency and accessibility of government processes
- proportionality, in terms of avoiding excessive government measures
- respect for individual autonomy and liberty in making fundamental life decisions
- respect for individual equality
- respect for separation of powers, geographical, and other structural and jurisdictional limits on government authority

In criminal justice and civil liberties contexts, the principles cited above usually have been used by courts to protect citizens from arbitrary or unduly invasive government measures. Due process principles today also cover freedom of expression, religious freedom, the right to bear arms, and right to compensation for takings—to name but a few of the substantive rights that have been deemed to be incorporated into the due process clause over time.

Those who condemn due process doctrine—especially the "substantive due process" strand of this doctrine—as an undue, judge-made intrusion into representative officials' lawmaking authority ignore that the due process framework was designed to channel that authority toward the public good. The doctrinal parameters are most directive when they map strong cultural consensus about rationality and rights. They impose vastly looser, but still significant constraints in areas in which consensus is more tentative, emerging, or eroding.

Those who believe that due process doctrine should be defined exclusively by past practices or strictly historical interpretations of liberty and justice underplay the importance of the modern due process framework. The current doctrine anticipates and restrains new forms of government irrationality, no less than historical forms. Even if such interpretive dynamism were not the original intent of the drafters of the due process clauses, however, this interpretive practice has been a mainstay of the United States Supreme Court. As we will show, the Court has engaged in a gradual and inherently conservative form of evolutionary constitutionalism that nevertheless recognizes that fundamental notions of ordered liberty are not static but are instead living principles that continue to inform due process doctrine as well as other areas of constitutional rights and liberties.

The task of identifying and applying traditional and evolving due process principles requires sound judgment, proper respect for the rule of law, and a sober recognition that government can violate due process in innovative as well as familiar ways. Although people can—and do—disagree about whether the Court has "gotten it right" in specific due process cases, they should recognize that the process of articulating and refining due process principles is a legitimate judicial enterprise with a long and proud constitutional pedigree. They should also acknowledge the ways in which the arc of due process, over time, has been expanded to cover a broader span of rights as our notion of rights-bearing "persons" has expanded. When the franchise was extended to African-Americans, to women, and to younger voters, the "settled expectations" that frame the due process baseline came to enfold wider sensibilities and experiences. These aspects of constitutional reconstruction too are profoundly important pieces of the due process story. "Liberty" is not only a context-dependent, but a human perception-dependent principle.

Finally, even if the due process ideal is fixed, its expressions should be provisional to assure that this ideal is best realized in the real and changing world to which it must be applied, and to account for the imperfections of those who pursue it. In other words, judicial humility both requires restraint and the acceptance of responsibility for effecting change. This is the inescapable paradox of judicial power to interpret the Constitution.

{1}

English History and Rule of Law Roots of American Due Process

I. Introduction

As totalitarian regimes are being challenged by prodemocratic forces, fundamental issues arise about how laws should govern the conduct of the citizenry. But do we understand the underpinnings of liberal democracy and what gives it legitimacy? What are the central differences between totalitarian governments and majoritarian desires to dominate over individual rights? A reprise of history, both ancient and modern, suggests that a primary feature of a liberal democratic regime is respect for the rule of law as it is expressed in its modern formulation of American due process of law.

Rule of law is a doctrine with roots in ancient philosophy. It is also the backdrop to modern American due process jurisprudence. Rule of law principles can be traced back to the Greeks through the British system. The original sealing of the Magna Carta was a historically significant codification of centuries of thinking and writing about the concept that an individual should be governed equally by general laws rather than by the arbitrary will of rulers. The Magna Carta also gave rise to a more modern variant and specific application of rule of law ideals in leading to the enunciation of the concept of due process of law.[1]

---

[1] Some scholars tend to speak of rule of law and due process somewhat interchangeably. However, for purposes of this discussion it is critical to separate the general abstract notion of "due process of law" from the Due Process Clauses in the United States Constitution and their resulting interpretations. For example "[i]t is chiefly the combination of the principles of due process and equality that enables the rule of law to be properly characterized as a 'rule of reason': they amount to a basic requirement of justification, or condition of legitimacy, whereby the legality of a person's treatment, at the hands of the state, depends on its being shown to serve a defensible view of the common good[.] ... It is not sufficient for laws or government policies to be accurately applied to particular persons, in accordance with their true meaning or proper interpretation; the associated distinctions made between persons, or groups of persons, must also be capable of justification." T. R. S. ALLAN, CONSTITUTIONAL JUSTICE: A LIBERAL THEORY OF THE RULE OF LAW 2 (2001). American due process provides more to the individual than an opportunity for government justification; additionally, due process is not the only structure in American government and law that provides a check on government legitimacy and justification or guarantees fundamental liberties.

The eighteenth-century framers of the American Constitution relied heavily on the writings and experiences of political and legal philosophers who had expounded on principles of rule of law. From the separation of powers to an independent judiciary, the United States government embodies many of the institutions and structures called for by proponents of a strong rule of law foundation as a prerequisite to any high-functioning government. When the Bill of Rights was amended to the Constitution, traditional rule of law language influenced the inclusion of a Due Process Clause.[2]

History reveals a number of unique circumstances and concerns that played an important role in shaping America's current due process jurisprudence as a protection of both substantive and procedural rights. This chapter describes these events and conflicts and identifies ways in which due process jurisprudence both reflects and has deviated from its rule of law roots.

Tracing the history of due process from these early conceptions of the rule of law provides a useful benchmark from which to measure the evolution and development of modern doctrine. It likewise responds to the growing interest in the rule of law among contemporary legal and political scholars.[3] The current global climate, combined with the increased efforts to measure developing governments against the rubric of traditional rule of law principles, presents a particularly important time to examine America's own system.[4] By exploring the historical origins of rule of law principles, we can understand how and to what extent debates over the rule of law influenced the formation and development of the American government and its due process jurisprudence. We also can better understand the justifications for and tensions within the current state of this jurisprudence.

After defining rule of law, we trace its path from ancient Greece through England to demonstrate how it influenced the formation of the American Constitution and the Due Process Clauses in particular. Special attention is paid to early and pivotal case law on due process and the formation of two distinct, though interdependent branches of due process jurisprudence: procedural and substantive.

---

[2] *See* RHONDA WASSERMAN, PROCEDURAL DUE PROCESS: A REFERENCE GUIDE TO THE UNITED STATES CONSTITUTION 4–5 (2004) (noting that Anti-federalist advocates for a bill of rights steeped their arguments in principles of liberty and law, which resulted ultimately in the inclusion of the Bill of Rights, which was influenced by rule of law principles).

[3] Robert A. Stein, *Rule of Law: What Does it Mean?*, 18 MINN. J. INTL. L. 293, 293 (2009) (referring to the extensive activity of the American Bar Association in the past two decades, the International Legal Assistance Consortium, and a host of United States Supreme Court Justices as "the rule of law movement.").

[4] *See* THE RULE OF LAW IN COMPARATIVE PERSPECTIVE (Mortimer Sellers and Tadeusz Tomaszewski eds., 2010) (providing more insight into the international role that rule of law has recently come to play); GLOBAL PERSPECTIVES ON THE RULE OF LAW (James J. Heckman, Robert L. Nelson, and Lee Cabatingan eds., 2010); RULE OF LAW PROMOTION: GLOBAL PERSPECTIVE, LOCAL APPLICATIONS (Per Bergling, Jenny Ederlof, and Veronica Taylor eds., 2009).

II. Rule of Law Defined

The definition of the "Rule of Law" is often debated.[5] For some the term has been so broadly and frequently used and abused that it has been deprived of any useful meaning.[6] As elusive as the term and notion may be,[7] however, the idea of the rule of law can usefully be reduced to the principle that law should be known, just, and enforceable.[8] The rule of law marks a fundamental move away from "the rule of men,"[9] and requires that laws be publicly known prior to their enforcement.[10] In this manner citizens of a government can conform their behavior to the known

---

[5] *See* Richard H. Fallon, *"The Rule of Law" as a Concept in Constitutional Discourse*, 97 COLUM. L. REV. 1, 1 (1997) ("The Rule of Law is a historic ideal, and appeals to the Rule of Law remain rhetorically powerful. Yet the precise meaning of the Rule of Law is perhaps less clear than ever before.").

[6] *See* TOM BINGHAM, THE RULE OF LAW 5 (2010) (citing Judith N. Shklar, *Political Theory and the Rule of Law, in* THE RULE OF LAW: IDEAL OR IDEOLOGY 1 (Allan C. Hutchinson and Patrick Monahan eds. 1987). "It would not be very difficult to show that the phrase 'the Rule of Law' has become meaningless thanks to ideological abuse and general over-use. It may well have become just another one of those self-congratulatory rhetorical devices that grace the public utterances of Anglo-American politicians. No intellectual effort need therefore be wasted on this bit of ruling-class chatter." Shklar, *supra*, at 21.

[7] BRIAN TAMANAHA, ON THE RULE OF LAW: HISTORY, POLITICS, THEORY 3 (2004) (describing rule of law as an "exceedingly elusive notion" giving rise to "rampant divergence of understandings.").

[8] *See* Rich Cassidy, *The Rule of Law: Supreme Court Justice Anthony Kennedy Tells Us What It Means and Why It Counts*, ON LAWYERING (May 4, 2010), http://onlawyering.com/2010/05/the-rule-of-law-supreme-court-justice-anthony-kennedy-tells-us-what-it-means-and-why-it-counts/ (quoting Justice Anthony M. Kennedy's speech at "the ABA Annual Meeting in August of 2006") ("He suggests a provisional definition of The Rule of Law with three key elements: '[(1)]The Law is superior to, and thus binds, the government and all its officials.' '[(2)] The Law must respect and preserve the dignity, equality, and human rights of all persons. To these ends the Law must establish and safeguard the constitutional structures necessary to build a free society in which all citizens have a meaningful voice in shaping and enacting the rules that govern them.' '[(3)] The Law must devise and maintain systems to advise all persons of their rights, and it must empower them to fulfill just expectations and seek redress of grievances without fear of penalty or retaliation.'"). The World Justice Project, focusing on the structures of emerging and developing governments created an index in 2010 which reflects the basic factors whose presence they consider essential to constitute a rule of law: "The government and its officials and agents are accountable under the law[;] [t]he laws are clear, publicized, stable and fair, and protect fundamental rights, including the security of persons and property[;] ... laws are enacted, administered and enforced ... [through] accessible, fair and efficient [processes;] [a]ccess to justice is provided by competent, independent, and ethical adjudicators, attorneys or representatives, and judicial officers who are of sufficient number, have adequate resources, and reflect the makeup of the communities they serve." World Justice Project, *World Justice Project, Rule of Law Index*, (2010), http://worldjusticeproject.org/rule-of-law-index/; *see also* Randall Peerenboom, *Let One Hundred Flowers Bloom, One Hundred Schools Contend: Debating Rule of Law in China*, 23 MICH. J. INT'L L. 471, 472 (2002) ("At its most basic [level] rule of law refers to a system in which law is able to impose meaningful restraints on the State and individual members of the ruling elite, as captured in the rhetorically powerful if overly simplistic notions of a government of laws, the supremacy of the law, and equality of all before the law.").

[9] *See* Marbury v. Madison, 5 U.S. 137, 163 (1803) (referring to the American government as one "of laws, and not of men.").

[10] *See* Fallon, *supra* note 5, at 2 ("If courts (or the officials of any other institution) could make law in the guise of applying it, we would have the very 'rule of men' with which the Rule of Law is supposed to contrast.").

law and can check potential abuses of authority by those in power.[11] In a more elaborate articulation, the rule of law requires first that the law be superior to and binding on government and its officials. Second, it requires that, by providing the necessary safeguards, the law "must respect and preserve the dignity, equality, and human rights of all persons."[12] Finally, the law must "devise and maintain systems to advise all persons of their rights, and it must empower them to fulfill just expectations and seek redress of grievances without fear of penalty or retaliation."[13] Rule of law is ultimately a combination of the multiple values it is meant to preserve, the principles by which governmental institutions must operate in order to preserve those values, the institutions "responsible for doing the safeguarding," and the procedures through which the institutions effectuate the principles.[14]

Regardless of how one defines it, the rule of law in most of its conceptions contains both procedural[15] and substantive elements.[16] The procedural component is organized around the idea that certain institutional arrangements and rules are required to ensure that governments operate through laws, not caprice.

---

[11] Randy E. Barnett, *Foreword: Unenumerated Constitutional Rights and the Rule of Law*, 14 HARV. J.L. & PUB. POL'Y 615, 615–16 (1991).

[12] Cassidy, *supra* note 8.

[13] *Id.*; *see also* BINGHAM, *supra* note 6, at 7; Joseph Raz, *The Rule of Law and Its Virtue in* LIBERTY AND THE RULE OF LAW 3, 5 (Robert L. Cunningham ed., 1979). "Stripped of all technicalities, this means that government in all its actions is bound by rules fixed and announced beforehand—rules which make it possible to foresee with fair certainty how the authority will use its coercive powers in given circumstances and to plan one's individual affairs on the basis of this knowledge." FRIEDRICH HAYEK, THE ROAD TO SERFDOM 112 (1944).

[14] GEOFFREY DE Q. WALKER, THE RULE OF LAW: FOUNDATION OF CONSTITUTIONAL DEMOCRACY 9 (1988).

[15] *See* Antonin Scalia, *The Rule of Law as a Law of Rules*, 56 U. CHI. L. REV. 1175, 1178–80 (1989) (discussing the advantages of a procedural, rule-based approach to rule of law over a common law approach); Stephen R. Munzer, *A Theory of Retroactive Legislation*, 61 TEX. L. REV. 425, 471 (1982) ("The rule of law ... is a defeasible entitlement of persons to have their behavior governed by rules publicly fixed in advance. This entitlement frowns on retroactivity. But this entitlement can be defeated when following the rule of law will be heavily counter to utility or justice."). Though some scholars have emphasized the procedural components of a rule of law doctrine with less acceptance of the role the principle can play in moral judgements, these views, grounded in originalism, perhaps reflect more of an aspirational narrowing of the principle than is currently found in practice, or was contemplated in the writings of ancient philosophers.

[16] *See* Frank Michelman, *Law's Republic*, 97 YALE L.J. 1493, 1510–13 (1988) (discussing the Constitution's enactment in terms of pluralism). The "substantive" component of the rule of law is by no means consistent across differing conceptions of rule of law. Hayek, for example postulated that "any policy aiming directly at a substantive ideal of distributive justice must lead to the destruction of the Rule of Law." HAYEK, *supra* note 13, at 87–88 as cited in Brian Z. Tamanaha, *The Dark Side of the Relationship Between the Rule of Law and Liberalism*, 3 N.Y.U. J. L. & LIBERTY 516, 535 (2008). "Attempts at achieving substantive equality and distributive justice are inconsistent with the rule of law, according to Hayek, because both require context specific adjustments in social distributions of opportunities and wealth, which cannot be accomplished through the application of general rules set forth in advance." *Id.* Substantively, Hayek argued that natural law theory must form the basis of rule of law, and that legislation "is the chief instrument of oppression." FRIEDRICH HAYEK, *supra* note 13, at 155–56 as cited in Tamanaha, *supra*, at 536. Dicey and Hayek together linked this understanding of rule of law to liberal ideas, whereas other liberals advocating the prohibition on redistributions of wealth tied their ideas to concepts of protection of property and the free market. Tamanaha, *supra*, at 536.

The substantive component stipulates, however, that individual laws made by a government can be deemed unjust if they violate ideas of natural law or accepted traditions, even if they were passed by institutions that otherwise adhered to the structural requirements of the rule of law.[17] Borrowing terminology, it can be useful to think about the procedural and substantive components of different versions of rule of law theories as existing on a continuum in which a particular version is "thin" or "thick" in the sense that it may have few or many requirements.[18] A "thin" version might require merely that a government rule, procedurally, by laws as opposed to through informal actions and, substantively, that it respect some bare minimum of individual rights. As we will later explain, this thin version of rights manifests itself in American constitutional law as a form of "rational basis" review, under which courts afford representative branches broad discretion to shape rules. A "thicker" version of rights might require, procedurally, some form of rule by democratic consent to law making and, substantively, actively advancing social welfare and protecting citizens' dignity.[19] This latter sense of thicker rights is reflected in the modern due process case law that identifies so-called fundamental rights that receive particularly strong substantive and procedural protection.

The American government structure in general, and its due process jurisprudence in particular, align closely to these general definitions of rule of law.[20] Stemming from the Fifth Amendment assurance that no person shall be deprived of "life, liberty, or property, without due process of law," the post-bellum United States Supreme Court has established and elaborated on a myriad of procedural and substantive due process protections. Procedural due process protections today include rules on administering trials, hearings for denying government benefits, and generally ensuring the proper administration of justice and reducing the arbitrary abuse of power. Substantive due process rulings, in contrast, strike down laws that, while enacted by a democratically elected government of limited powers, are nonetheless found invalid according to broader principles of fairness, justice, and individual rights. Yet the line between these two categories is fuzzy, and hybrid rights exist that capture important aspects of both categories. Moreover, the nature of process that is due is heavily dependent on the substance of the right

---

[17] *See* Ernest J. Weinrib, *The Intelligibility of the Rule of Law, in* THE RULE OF LAW: IDEAL OR IDEOLOGY, at 59–63.

[18] TAMANAHA, *supra* note 7, at 91; *see also* Peerenboom, *supra* note 8, at 472 (defining thin theories of rule of law as those which stress "the formal or instrumental aspects of rule of law" as contrasted from thick conceptions which "incorporate elements of political morality."). *See generally* LON FULLER, THE MORALITY OF LAW (1976).

[19] TAMANAHA, *supra* note 7, at 91.

[20] The great breadth of rule of law definitions, however, belies the creation of any single concept that could in fact "align closely" to all of these disparate views. To the extent that the American tradition reflects a system of legislative and constitutional support for redistributive efforts and basic equality, due process is at odds with the classic liberal construct of the substantive underpinnings of rule of law. *See, e.g.*, TAMANAHA, *supra* note 7, at 534–35 (citing KARL POLANYI, THE GREAT TRANSFORMATION: THE POLITICAL AND ECONOMIC ORIGINS OF OUR TIME 146–47 (2001)); *Id.* at 535 (citing FRIEDRICH HAYEK, THE ROAD TO SERFDOM 90 (1944)).

being burdened. Modern American due process jurisprudence allows the courts to check the legislative and executive actions of the government on procedural and substantive grounds, as opposed to simply enforcing "the law of the land."[21]

III. History of the Rule of Law

No definitive definition exists of the rule of law nor precise manner in which to distinguish it from due process. This can be demonstrated by briefly tracing the origins and development of the concept throughout the ages. The three-word phrase is a deceptively simple representation of an amalgamation of enormously complex political and legal thought. Although the near ubiquitous and constant reference to rule of law principles across continents and millennia explains why current definitional debates about these principles persist, it also sheds light on the history and context of American due process jurisprudence.

ANCIENT ORIGINS

The concept of rule of law first appeared in ancient Greece, and was embodied by the term "isonomia" meaning "equality of laws to all manner of persons."[22] The principle of rule of law was more important to the Greeks than a system of democratic government.[23] Aristotle observed:

> [H]e who asks Law to rule is asking God and Intelligence and no others to rule; while he who asks for the rule of a human being is bringing in a wild beast; for human passions are like a wild beast and strong feelings lead astray the very best of men. In law you have the intellect without the passions.[24]

Aristotle emphasized the importance of separate legislative and judicial bodies.[25] The Greek conception of rule of law was later inherited by Republican Rome, which similarly subscribed to the idea that laws should be applied equally to all citizens and that all men are ruled by a supreme law of the land.[26] Cicero, for example, agreed that the judiciary should be separate from any law-making function, and should have limited discretion.[27] On a conceptual level, both the Greeks and

---

[21] Edward S. Corwin, *The "Higher Law" Background of American Constitutional Law*, 42 Harv. L. Rev. 149 *passim* (1928).

[22] F.A. Hayek, The Constitution of Liberty: The Definitive Edition 238–39 (University of Chicago Press 2011) (1960).

[23] Walker, *supra* note 14, at 93.

[24] *Id.* (quoting Aristotle, The Politics Book IV 161; Book III 143 (Penguin 1962)).

[25] Stein, *supra* note 3, at 297 (citing Aristotle, Rhetoric 32 (George A. Kennedy trans., 2d ed. 2007)).

[26] Walker, *supra* note 14, at 93–94.

[27] Stein, *supra* note 3, at 298 (citing Cicero, On the Laws bk. III, *in* Cicero: On the Commonwealth & On the Laws 157 (James E.G. Zetzel ed., 1999); *see also* Franz Neumann, The Rule of Law: Political Theory and the Legal System in Modern Society 51 (1986).

Romans argued that there was a natural law or higher principles that can conflict with human laws. This is exemplified in the story of Antigone or through the words of Cicero when he wrote that "[t]rue law is right reason in agreement with nature; it is of universal application, unchanging and everlasting."[28]

Medieval writings from various European countries also referenced principles of universal law, when application of a single law should be made to both king and subjects.[29] Religious scholars in the Middle Ages referenced higher principles of justice and natural law as derived from scriptures, noting that adherence to such principles separates princes from tyrants.[30] The Reformation and subsequent lack of one religious power on the continent, combined with the rise of the nation-state, shifted emphasis from the idea of universalistic law and justice to positive law. But this occurred after important seeds of rule of law principles were planted in England.[31]

ENGLISH DEVELOPMENTS IN RULE OF LAW AND DUE PROCESS

Although rule of law principles underlie the structures of many governments, the "rule of law" has been described as a distinctive characteristic of English constitutional law.[32] The concepts that trace back to the writings of Greek, Roman, and medieval philosophers were ultimately incorporated into the Magna Carta; but the English document "was not a sudden intrusion into English society and politics. On the contrary, it grew out of them... Laymen had been assuming, discussing and applying the principles of Magna Carta long before 1215."[33] Both the origins of due process[34] and the rule of law can be linked to chapters 39 and 40 of the Magna Carta.[35] Whether or not the drafters of the Charter intended the meanings given to these chapters, the Charter became the basis for many constitutions, and has been cited countless times for the theoretical underpinnings of the rule of law and due process.[36] Chapter 39 provides that:

---

[28] W. Burnett Harvey, *The Rule of Law in Historical Perspective*, 59 MICH. L. REV. 487, 488 (1961) (citing Cicero, DE RE PUBLICA, bk. III, XXII (Keyes transl. 1928)). In defiance of the King's decree, Antigone followed her conscience and buried her brother according to religious custom. *Id.*; *see also* Corwin, *supra* note 21, at 154–57.

[29] NEUMANN, *supra* note 27, at 94–95; Corwin, *supra* note 21, at 164 (citing THE STATESMAN'S BOOK OF JOHN OF SALISBURY 33 (John Dickinson trans., Alfred A. Knopf, 1927)).

[30] Harvey, *supra* note 28, 488–89 (referencing St. Thomas Aquinas); Corwin *supra* note 21, 164–65 (referencing John of Salisbury).

[31] *See* Harvey, *supra* note 28, at 489.

[32] WALKER, *supra* note 14, at 2 ("[T]he legal historian W.S. Holdsworth described ... [the rule of law] as 'the most distinctive, and certainly the most salutary, of all the characteristics of English constitutional law.'").

[33] JAMES CLARKE HOLT, MAGNA CARTA 295 (1992).

[34] *See* Charles A. Miller, *The Forest of Due Process of Law: The American Constitutional Tradition*, *in* DUE PROCESS: NOMOS XVIII 3–38 (Ronald Pennock and John W. Chapman eds., 1977) (discussing the prevalent traditions of American due process).

[35] WALKER, *supra* note 14, at 95–96.

[36] W.S. MCKECHNIE, MAGNA CARTA: A COMMENTARY ON THE GREAT CHARTER OF KING JOHN 395 (2d ed. 1914).

> No free man shall be seized or imprisoned or stripped of his rights or possessions, or outlawed or exiled, or deprived of his standing in any other way, nor will we proceed with force against him, or send others to do so, except by the lawful judgment of his equals or by the *law of the land*.[37]

Chapter 40 states that "[t]o no one will we sell, to no one deny or delay right or justice."[38]

It was not until a 1354 reissue of the charter that the phrase "due process of law" was included, but by the end of the fourteenth century the due process check against arbitrary government forces was firmly established within the charter.[39] From the outset, the Magna Carta's explicit restriction on royal power contained "the rule of law in embryo."[40] The basic protections for free men set out in the charter were dependent upon the existence of an overarching law—*legem terrae*—that existed apart from and above the whims of individual rulers or government entities. Though the Magna Carta was not seen as providing the same liberties to each class until later, the original charter did recognize the supremacy of law.[41] Importantly, the Magna Carta did not represent a radical departure from historical trends, but instead grew out of principles that had been assumed and applied by average freemen long before its creation in 1215.[42] The use of widely accepted and understandable terms helped create a strong foundation in the charter for its denunciation of unaccountable royal power.[43]

Though the Magna Carta had planted the seeds, development of a truly robust rule of law structure with due process protections did not take place after it was sealed because of the influence of divine right. The Tudor period in 1485 was characterized by "over-mighty subjects" conducting private warfare against their rivals to the detriment of the safety and prosperity of the rest of the country.[44] This practice was disfavored by both the king and the people, which resulted in a concession of "wide powers to the government if it could deliver them from internal strife, religious violence and foreign encroachment."[45] This trend of concentrating powers with royalty was exacerbated by the development of the doctrine of the divine right of kings, whereby the "secular government was not merely allowed but actu-

---

[37] BINGHAM, *supra* note 6, at 10; Miller, *supra* note 34, at 4 (emphasis added).

[38] *Id.* BINGHAM, *supra* note 6, at 10.

[39] Miller, *supra* note 34, at 5.

[40] BINGHAM, *supra* note 6, at 12.

[41] WALKER, *supra* note 14, at 97. Indeed, the original Magna Carta was a pact between the King and the feudal class wherein the former promised to respect the traditional rights of the latter with little or no reference to the population at large. *See* Corwin *supra* note 21, at 175.

[42] BINGHAM, *supra* note 6, at 12 (citing J. C. HOLT, MAGNA CARTA AND MEDIEVAL GOVERNMENT 295 (1992)).

[43] *Id.*

[44] WALKER, *supra* note 14, at 97 (citing C.H. MCILWAIN, THE HIGH COURT OF PARLIAMENT AND ITS SUPREMACY 341 (1910)).

[45] *Id.*

ally ordained by God and that the secular ruler took his title directly from the Almighty, with no intervening authority."[46]

In England, King Henry VIII embraced the theory of the divine right and declared that he was "not 'subject to the laws of any earthly creature.'"[47] Despite this hostile environment, the rule of law survived and continued to develop. Medieval institutions continued to form the basis of English monarchies, and Henry VIII continued to act under the authority of Parliament. Though Parliament was "so subservient as to offer no serious threat to royal autocracy and willingly allowed the king to clothe his most ruthless and arbitrary acts in the raiment of statute," its maintenance as an institution emphasized the ultimate rule of law system, which depended upon enacted laws for government action.[48] The English monarchy and Parliament during this period effectively eliminated reliance on private law, which further established the rule of law as a governing principle.[49]

Sir Edward Coke revolutionized the still not fully-formed principles underlying the concept of rule of law. Coke's work came at the time of a legal crossroads:

> Two paths to the future lay open. One, the "modern" model as it then appeared, was the continental system of a sovereign king, backed by a standing army and a royal career bureaucracy.... The other was the parliamentary model, which drew its inspiration from the mediaeval past, especially from the conception of the rule of law.[50]

Coke was in the minority in England, arguing that a powerful parliament should take the place of a powerful monarch[51] and that laws should be the basic and fundamental basis from which government should rule.[52] For instance, Coke's recasting of the habeas corpus writ is illustrative of the role he played in fostering and promoting the principles of rule of law. The writ was not originally used to protect the liberty of unlawfully detained individuals, however, but was used to secure the presence in court of a criminal defendant.[53] After its transformation, the writ became "'the most usual remedy by which a man is restored again to his liberty, if he have been against law deprived of it.'"[54] Use of the writ evidenced that

---

[46] *Id.* at 97–98.

[47] *Id.* at 98 (quoting W. H. Dunham, *Regal Power and the Rule of Law: a Tudor Paradox* 3 J. of British Studies 24, 34 (1964)).

[48] *Id.* at 99.

[49] *Id.* at 102.

[50] *Id.* at 104 (citing Frederic Maitland, English Law and the Renaissance 29 (Cambridge 1901)).

[51] *Id.* at 104–106.

[52] Sir Edward Coke, Commentary Upon Littleton 97b (Charles Butler ed., 18th ed., Legal Classics Library 1985) (1628). Also known as the First Part of the Institutes of the Laws of England.

[53] Bingham, *supra* note 6, at 13.

[54] *Id.* at 14 (quoting *Bushell's Case* (1670) Vaughan 135, 136).

government officials were restrained from detaining individuals without some underlying law granting them the power to do so, a fundamental tenet of a rule of law.

Coke further influenced the doctrine by explicitly introducing the need for an independent judiciary.[55] In restating the English common law, Coke gave recognition to the fact that a body of recognized law existed.

> It meant that expertise in the law, not a willingness to carry out government policy, had to be the decisive criterion for appointments to the bench; that a judge deciding a case according to law but in a way that displeased the regime had an answer to any charges of anti-government bias; and, on the other hand, it meant that the rule of law would not become the rule of the judges, since while a judge was protected by the law, he was also bound by it and could not use his position to give free rein to his own theories.[56]

Grounded in this framework, judges, not the whims of politicians and government leaders, came to be seen as applying fixed law. The extent to which this fixed law was limited to the law as passed by the government or whether it included conflicting notions of universal or natural law is discussed below.

IV. Development of American Due Process

The United States Constitution encompassed many of the principles of rule of law that had developed throughout Europe across the ages. The first framers explicitly contemplated the form of government as creating government power that was "so qualified, and so divided into different Channels, and committed to the Direction of so many different Men, with different Interests and Views, that the Majority of them could seldom or never find their Account in betraying their Trust in fundamental Instances."[57] The idea of checking judicial power "was motivated primarily by the rule of law's disdain for arbitrariness. Abhorrence of arbitrariness is a major theme that runs through all the rule of law writing through the centuries. They consistently expressed the view that individual decisions can not be trusted[.] . . ."[58]

Though it does not explicitly contain the phrase "rule of law," the Constitution embodies the principle through the enumeration of powers that limit the power

---

[55] *See* Harold Berman, *The Origins of Historical Jurisprudence: Coke, Selden, and Hale*, 103 YALE L.J. 1651, 1673–94 (1994).

[56] WALKER, *supra* note 14, at 106.

[57] John Trenchard, Cato's Letters no. 60 (Jan. 6, 1721), *in* 1 THE FOUNDERS CONSTITUTION 619–20 (Philip B. Kurland & Ralph Lerner eds., 1987), *available at* http://press-pubs.uchicago.edu/founders/documents/v1ch17s6.html.

[58] Stein, *supra* note 3, at 298.

and discretion[59] of the federal government, the structure of which separates the powers of the different branches of government, and through the Fifth and Fourteenth Amendments. The Constitution was "ground-breaking in its enlightened attempt to create a strong and effective central government while at the same time preserving the autonomy of the individual states and (in the first ten amendments) preserving the fundamental rights of the individual against … 'the form of elective despotism.'"[60] For the first time, the explicit expression of a rule of law principle emerged that bound not just the executive and judiciary, but also the legislature.[61]

The Due Process Clauses also were explicitly adapted from rule of law language that can be traced back to the Magna Carta. The clauses functioned as an early expression of the rule of law principle as a protection of citizens against arbitrary treatment by the judiciary and other government officials.[62] At first blush, due process expressly connected the concepts of rule of law with a provision of proper procedures: providing for limitations of government search and seizure, protections for criminal defendants, basic notice and hearing opportunities, and a host of other procedural protections for unfair application of the law or deprivation of life, liberty, or property without a firm base in existing law.[63]

The Due Process Clauses over time came to play a role quite different from that suggested by basic notions of rule of law. Indeed, the first judicial interpretations of American due process led to the evolution[64] of a jurisprudence that both over- and under-represents certain aspects of the rule of law principle. The structure of a government that was constrained by strong institutions and that enforced separation of powers paved the way for an independent judiciary, which provided access to and accountability for an evolving notion of due process. Due process thus has

---

[59] Alexander Hamilton, A Second Letter from Phocion (Apr. 1784), *in* 1 THE FOUNDERS CONSTITUTION, *supra* note 57, at 643, *available at* http://press-pubs.uchicago.edu/founders/documents/v1ch17s21.html. For a recent discussion of due process as primarily intended to promote separation of powers principles, see Nathan S. Chapman & Michael W. McConnell, *Due Process as Separation of Powers*, 121 YALE L.J. 1672 (2012) (arguing that there is little historical basis for modern substantive due process doctrine, or for much that falls under procedural due process doctrine). http://ssrn.com/abstract=2005406. The article responds to the compelling new work on substantive due process by Ryan C. Williams. *The One and Only Substantive Due Process Clause*, 120 YALE L.J. 408 (2010) (arguing that the original meaning of the Fourteenth Amendment, but not the Fifth Amendment, protects substantive due process in some forms).

[60] BINGHAM, *supra* note 6, at 26.

[61] *Id.* at 27.

[62] William Letwin, *Economic Due Process in the American Constitution and the Rule of Law*, *in* LIBERTY AND THE RULE OF LAW, *supra* note 13, at 23.

[63] *See id.* at 28–29 (explaining that due process was regarded as preventing the retroactive application of laws).

[64] Some scholars have argued that the evolution in American society has been of the meaning of the rule of law itself and "the specific principles that inform the rule of law." James Lanshe, *Morality and the Rule of Law in American Jurisprudence*, 11 RUTGERS J. L. & RELIGION 1, 1 (2009). This chapter instead seeks to explore the notion of rule of law as a historically moored notion and to measure the development of procedural and substantive due process from this beginning.

become a central component of the American constitutional tradition, and its evolution has "depended on the rise and decline of social interests and on society's changing perceptions of what is arbitrary, unfair, or unjust."[65]

TRACING EARLY INFLUENCES

Lord Coke, in dicta in *Dr. Bonham's Case*,[66] established a form of judicial review similar to that created much later by *Marbury v. Madison*.[67] He ruled that acts of Parliament are void when they are against "common right or reason, or repugnant or impossible to be performed."[68] Coke reiterated this principle in his *Institutes*, where he explicitly stated that the Magna Carta acts as a check against parliamentary acts.[69]

Parliament, other judges, and legal commentators (including Blackstone) rebelled against this notion and reaffirmed parliamentary supremacy over judicial review and common law procedural mandates.[70] After the Glorious Revolution in 1688, the use of common law principles as a defense against both Royal and Parliamentary acts was likely to favor the former, given the long history of legal deference to the monarch. This made a limited form of judicial review that treated Parliamentary acts as inviolable and "more tolerable than a fundamental law of which the Stuart Prerogative was so legitimate a portion."[71] While Lord Coke's arguments lost the day in England, they were more persuasive in the colonies.[72] Access to the actual document of the Magna Carta was limited, and prerevolutionary colonies lacked the number of well-trained lawyers of mainland England. But

---

[65] Miller, *supra* note 34, at 3.

[66] 8 Co. Rep. 114 (Court of Common Pleas 1610).

[67] 5 U.S. 137 (1803).

[68] Theodore F.T. Plucknett, *Bonham's Case and Judicial Review*, 40 HARV. L. REV. 30, 32–34 (1926) (explaining that in *Dr. Bonham's Case* the Royal College of Physicians was authorized by statute to imprison and fine people practicing medicine without a license. Because the College was authorized to conduct the trial *and* collect a fine it acted as both a party and a judge in violation of a settled maxim of common law); *see also* RODNEY L. MOTT, DUE PROCESS OF LAW 49–51 (1926).

[69] MOTT, *supra* note 68, at 49; *see also* WILLIAM S. MCKECHNIE, MAGNA CARTA: A COMMENTARY ON THE GREAT CHARTER OF KING JOHN, WITH AN HISTORICAL INTRODUCTION 437–43 (1905) (arguing that Coke relied on fourteenth-century statutes to create an interpretation of the original "law of the land" language to imply substantive if minimal protections. The original Magna Carta language was more likely intended to limit the practice of executing defendants before trying them and was thus less concerned with the specific requirements of the trial than it was the timing).

[70] MOTT, *supra* note 68, at 51–54. In deciding later cases in which an act by Parliament appears to create an impossibility, courts insisted that Parliament "can do no wrong" but admitted that it may do "several things that look pretty odd." Plucknett, *supra* note 68, at 55–56 (citing City of London v. Wood, 12 Mod. 669 (1701)).

[71] Plucknett, *supra* note 68, at 53–54.

[72] MOTT, *supra* note 68, at 125–27; Frank H. Easterbrook, *Substance and Due Process*, 1982 SUP. CT. REV. 85, 96–100 (1982). *But see* Gary L. McDowell, *Coke, Corwin, and the Constitution: The "Higher Law Background" Reconsidered*, 55 THE REVIEW OF POLITICS 393 *passim* (1993) (arguing that Coke's writing, specifically his dicta in *Dr. Bonham's Case*, is almost completely absent from any of the founders' writings, speeches, or cases).

the colonists still held chapter 39 in high esteem and frequently referred to it in pressing their case regarding their rights as "Englishmen."[73]

The political thinking of the colonists also was drawn from a number of sources that included the writings of classical antiquity, the writings of Enlightenment rationalism, English common law, the theories of New England Puritanism, and writers identified as being associated with the English Civil War and Commonwealth period.[74] Such writings were referenced in a host of founding documents and heavily influenced the provisions found in the Declaration of Independence, state constitutions, and most importantly the American Constitution and later Bill of Rights.

Also influential were Locke's *Two Treatises on Civil Government*, which were regarded as fundamental statements of political theory.[75] Locke's works directly referenced basic principles of rule of law, reasoning for example that:

> The great and *chief end* ... of Mens uniting into Commonwealths, and putting themselves under Government, *is the Preservation of their Property*. To which in the state of Nature there are many things wanting. *First*, There wants an *establish'd*, settled, known *Law*, received and allowed by common consent to be the standard of Right and Wrong, and the common measure to decide all Controversies between them. For though the Law of Nature be plain and intelligible to all rational creatures, yet Men, being biased by their Interest, as well as ignorant for want of study of it, are apt not to allow of it as a law binding to them in the application of it to their particular Cases.[76]

Classical references also abounded during the Founding period. Such references influenced the founders not only to structure a government around laws, but to imbue many of the founding documents with ideals of "virtue, justice, and liberty."[77]

ADDING DUE PROCESS TO THE CONSTITUTION

The inclusion of a bill of rights was hardly discussed during the writing of the Constitution in the summer of 1787.[78] Concerns raised about the lack of a bill of

---

[73] MOTT, *supra* note 68, at 91–93; *see also* Seth Thomas, *The Origin of the Power of Courts to Declare Statutes Unconstitutional*, 22 MINN. L. REV. 18,25 (1937) (arguing that judicial supremacy and Coke in particular took root in America prior to the formation of the Constitution, as evidenced by the writings of such leaders as James Otis in his "Rights of the British Colonies Asserted and Proved.").

[74] Lanshe, *supra* note 64, at 5–6 (citing a comprehensive study done by Donald Lutz published as *The Relative Influence of European Writers on Late Eighteenth-Century American Political Thought*, 78 AM. POL. SCI. REV. 189, 189 (1984)).

[75] *Id.* at 2; MOTT, *supra* note 68, at 136.

[76] JOHN LOCKE, TWO TREATISES OF GOVERNMENT Ch. IX § 124 (emphasis in original), *available at* http://press-pubs.uchicago.edu/founders/documents/v1ch16s3.html.

[77] Lanshe, *supra* note 64, at 8–10.

[78] THE BILL OF RIGHTS: ORIGINAL MEANING AND CURRENT UNDERSTANDING 1 (Eugene W. Hickok, Jr., ed., 1991).

rights were largely ignored, and the constitution sent to the states for ratification contained no enumerated individual rights.[79] The Due Process Clause, however, came to the forefront of political discussion during the ratification of the United States Constitution.[80] Indeed, "[A] major objection to the Constitution in the state-ratifying conventions came to center on the absence of a Bill of Rights."[81] The New York ratification convention in 1788 proposed that due process language be included in the federal Constitution.[82] The New York state constitution at that time contained a clause that echoed the Magna Carta and provided that "no member of this State shall be disfranchised, or deprived of any of the rights or privileges secured to the subjects of this State by this constitution, unless by the *law of the land*, or the judgment of his peers."[83] New York also had a statutory bill of rights that stated "no person shall be put to answer without presentment before justices, or matter of record, or due process of law according to the law of the land."[84] Although New York ratified the Constitution without the addition of the due process language, it indicated that the addition of such language would be consistent with the purpose and structure of the document.[85]

Upon ratification, Virginia also acknowledged the shortcomings of the Constitution without a Bill of Rights, and requested that an amendment be added that "no freeman ought to be taken, imprisoned, or disseised of his freehold, liberties, privileges or franchises, or outlawed or exiled, or in any manner destroyed or deprived of his life, liberty or property but by the law of the land."[86] Other recommendations for amendments came to the First Congress from Massachusetts, South Carolina, and New Hampshire.[87]

Many of the founders argued vigorously that enumeration of a Due Process Clause and other individual rights was unnecessary.[88] These arguments were based largely on principles of rule of law.[89] The structure of government—complete with

---

79 *Id.* (citing JAMES MADISON, NOTES OF DEBATES IN THE FEDERAL CONVENTION OF 1787 651 (A. Koch ed., 1966)).

80 PAGE SMITH, THE CONSTITUTION: A DOCUMENTARY AND NARRATIVE HISTORY 227 (1978).

81 *Id.*

82 Andrew T. Hyman, *The Little Word "Due,"* 38 AKRON L. REV. 1, 11–12 (2005).

83 *Id.* at 11 (quoting N.Y. CONST. of 1777, art. XIII).

84 *Id.* (quoting 1787 N.Y. Laws 344, 345, 10th Sess., ch. 1, § 4 (1787) (repealed 1828)).

85 *Id.* at 12.

86 *Id.* (quoting 2 DOCUMENTARY HISTORY OF THE CONSTITUTION 268, 379 (Johnson Reprint Corp. 1894)).

87 RICHARD B. BERNSTEIN, AMENDING AMERICA 33–34 (1993).

88 *See generally* THE FEDERALIST NO. 84 (Alexander Hamilton), *available at* http://press-pubs.uchicago.edu/founders/documents/bill_of_rightss7.html.

89 "[I]n truth the Constitution itself was in every rational sense, and to every useful purpose, a bill of rights for the Union. It specifies and declares the political privileges of the citizens in the structure and administration of the government. It defines certain immunities and modes of proceeding which relate to their personal, private, and public rights and concerns. It confers on them the unalienable right of electing their rules, and prohibits any tyrannical measures and vindictive prosecutions." JOSEPH STORY, CONSTITUTIONAL LAW VOLUME II 623 (5th ed. 1891); *see also* THE FEDERALIST NO. 84 (Alexander Hamilton).

an independent judiciary, strong procedural safeguards in the form of separation of powers, and a federal government of limited enumerated powers—was enough to protect the individual rights of citizens, without appending a separate list, many urged.[90] Promulgating such a list could give rise to the possibility "that a bill of rights aimed at keeping government in its place might provide the vehicle for the exercise of governmental power in areas beyond those delegated to it by the Constitution."[91] Additionally, the founders pointed to the numerous individual rights encompassed in the body of the Constitution itself, such as the Privileges and Immunities Clause and the prohibition on interference with private contracts.[92] Alexander Hamilton argued that because the origin of a bill of rights was between kings and their subjects, they functioned as "reservations of rights not surrendered to the prince."[93] As one scholar has noted,

> Here, in strictness, the people surrender nothing, and as they retain every thing they have no need of particular reservations, "We, The People of the United States, to secure the blessings of liberty to ourselves and our posterity, do ordain and establish this Constitution for the United States of America." Here is a better recognition of popular rights than volumes of those aphorisms which make the principal figure in several of our State bills of rights and which would sound much better in a treatise of ethics than in a constitution of government.[94]

If the Due Process Clause was appended to a constitution that already complied with the structural dictates of the rule of law doctrine, this is at least some evidence that the Due Process Clause was intended to accomplish more in the way of individual protection than structural elements of the rule of law could provide.

The objections to the lack of a bill of rights proved stronger than the views of the founders who believed such a listing was unnecessary. James Madison and other authors of the Bill of Rights designed its guarantees "to placate the Anti-federalists who chiefly feared the actions of the national government."[95] Madison, originally siding with Hamilton in opposition to adding a bill of rights, finally (for largely political reasons) argued that adoption of the Bill of Rights would not weaken the effect of the Constitution, and would have the positive effect of increasing popular confidence in the new Constitution.[96] Consistent with this position, Madison

---

[90] The Bill of Rights: Original meaning and Current Understanding, *supra* note 78, at 2–3.

[91] *Id.* at 2.

[92] Jack N. Rakove, Original Meanings: Politics and Ideas in the Making of the Constitution 316–17 (1996).

[93] The Bill of Rights: Original meaning and Current Understanding, *supra* note 78, at 2 (quoting The Federalist No. 84 (Alexander Hamilton)).

[94] *Id.* (quoting The Federalist Nos. 38, 238 (James Madison)).

[95] John R. Vile, A Companion to the United States Constitution and Its Amendments 124 (5th ed. 2010).

[96] The Bill of Rights: Original meaning and Current Understanding, *supra* note 78, at 3.

presented a list of amendments to the Congress that was nearly identical to the provisions found in many of the states' constitutions.[97]

The Virginia Bill of Rights is an example of the type of language contained in many of the state constitutions at the time the Bill of Rights was written and proposed.[98] In 1776, when the Virginia Convention had begun to meet, many drafters shared a concern that preference in the resulting laws or governmental structure not be given to wealthy individuals. Patrick Henry wrote to John Adams that "'among most of our opulent families' there existed 'a strong bias to aristocracy' that must be resisted."[99] Adams wrote to his Virginia friends that "[i]t was the will of the great body of the people and their leaders in every state 'that a more equal liberty than has prevailed in other parts of the earth must be established in America.'"[100] The Virginia Convention adopted The Virginia Bill of Rights as the first portion of the Virginia Constitution. The Virginia Bill of Rights included provisions that:

> all men are by nature equally free and independent, and have certain inherent rights, of which, when they enter into a state of society, they cannot by any compact deprive or divest their posterity; namely the enjoyment of life and liberty, with the means of acquiring and possessing property, and pursuing and obtaining happiness and safety ... [and that no man could be] bound by any law to which ... [he] had not ... assented for the public good.[101]

Many other state constitutions contained similar due process provisions that incorporated the principles of rule of law indicated by the "law of the land" language. Contemporary awareness and discussion of the English due process clause and the prevalence of the "law of the land" language used in state constitutions' equivalent clauses demonstrate that the Due Process Clause has its origins in the English tradition, which, in turn, was clearly steeped in notions of rule of law.[102] By 1860, eighty percent of states had adopted a due process clause of which a significant portion used the original "law of the land" language.[103]

---

[97] Smith, *supra* note 80, at 288; Akhil Reed Amar, America's Constitution: A Biography 315–21 (2005).

[98] Other examples of state constitution due process language include Pennsylvania's Constitution of 1776 declaring "every member of society hath a right to be protected in the enjoyment of life, liberty, and property ... no part of a man's property can be justly taken from him, or applied to public uses, without his own consent ... nor can any man be justly deprived of his liberty except by the laws of the land, or the judgment of his peers." Miller, *supra* note 34, at 9. In addition, Maryland and North Carolina's 1775 Constitutions also contained "law of the land" wording. *Id.*

[99] Smith, *supra* note 80, at 55.

[100] *Id.*

[101] *Id.* at 57–58 (quoting 1776 Va Bill of Rights).

[102] Miller, *supra* note 34, at 8–9. The text of the Fifth Amendment does not exactly match the text of the Magna Carta as the former refers to "due process of law" and the latter "law of the land." Scholars believe the variation is due in part to avoid confusion with the Supremacy Clause's reference to "law of the land," where law refers to positive law (statutes, etc.) in comparison to "due process of law" where law can refer also to common law. Wasserman, *supra* note 2, at 5.

[103] Mott, *supra* note 68, at 20, 26–29 (containing tables and charts on state constitutions and due process clauses).

When Madison first introduced the language, which became the Bill of Rights, he was heavily influenced by these existing state constitutions. Important changes, however, were made in the final version of the Fifth Amendment. Madison advocated the adoption of a preamble which would have stated that "Government is instituted and ought to be exercised for the benefit of the people; which consists in the enjoyment of life and liberty, with the right of acquiring and using property, and generally pursuing and obtaining happiness and safety."[104] The elimination of this preamble removed the more explicit references to natural law and instead embedded the Due Process Clause in the "context of rights for persons accused of crime." Additionally, the use of "law of the land" was changed to "due process of law."[105] This difference potentially stemmed from the fact that the Magna Carta's reference was to common law.[106]

After Madison presented the draft Bill of Rights, a Congressional committee was formed to finalize the amendments. Several provisions, not included in the final Bill of Rights, were heavily debated and faced great opposition. The major struggle occurred over the extent to which the Bill of Rights would serve as an express limit on the powers of the federal government.[107] Some Congressmen took issue with the introductory clause: "'The powers not delegated by the Constitution, nor prohibited to it by the States, are reserved to the states respectively,'"[108] arguing that the phrase should be "'all powers not expressly delegated.'"[109] The suggestion that the Bill of Rights bind both the state and national governments was also rejected.[110] Finally, a Congressman introduced seventeen amendments designed to expressly limit certain powers of the federal government; none of the amendments was included in the final Bill of Rights.[111] With increasing frustration about the Bill of Rights process as senators attempted to "rake over issues that had been debated dozens of times before," Egbert Benson of New York moved to have the amendments approved by two-thirds of Congress, immediately after which the amendments would be sent to the states for ratification.[112] Despite the struggle to include various contested provisions, the actual contents of the eventual Bill of Rights were sent to the states with almost no debate.[113] Congress sent twelve amendments on

---

[104] Miller, *supra* note 34, at 10 (quoting Perry, *Sources*, 422 *in* Gales, *Debates*, 433–34).

[105] *Id.* at 10–11.

[106] *Id.* at 11.

[107] Smith, *supra* note 80, at 289.

[108] *Id.*

[109] *Id.*

[110] *Id.* at 290. Madison was a lead proponent of including "no state shall" language in the entirety of the Bill of Rights; opponents saw this as functionally increasing the power of the federal government with respect to the states, and inconsistent with the tradition of "local self-rule." Amar, *supra* note 97, at 320.

[111] Smith, *supra* note 80, at 290.

[112] *Id.*

[113] Christopher Wolfe, *The Original Meaning of the Due Process Clause in* The Bill of Rights: Original Meaning and Current Understanding 213, 220 (Eugene W. Hickock ed., 1991) ("One of the most important facets of the historical evidence on the meaning of the Due Process Clause of the Fifth Amendment is what was not said. First, there was hardly any debate or controversy about the Due Process Clause in the congressional discussion of the Bill of Rights or in the state ratification of the Bill of Rights.").

which there had been "remarkable consensus"[114] to the states to be ratified, two of which were not ratified.[115] Thus the Fifth Amendment encompassing the Due Process Clause was accepted both on a national level and in each state with very little if no debate, largely supported by the view that it would act as a check against executive and legislative abuse.[116]

EXPLAINING AMERICA'S VARIANCE

A variety of unique concerns of the new Americans and interpretations of other clauses of the American Constitution helped contribute to the development of the robust due process jurisprudence that exists today.

First, an unwillingness to accept the fundamental notion that a "parliament" should be all-powerful drove the American due process jurisprudence in a direction different from the English conceptions of rule of law. The Due Process Clauses, stemming originally from the language of the Magna Carta and the early state constitutions, presented a marked shift away from the parliament-centric understanding of the rule of law that characterized England's government.[117] The original concerns of the founders and Americans had been the "arbitrary acts of the Crown and its colonial officials, including judges of the higher courts."[118] But Madison recognized after several years of experience with state constitutions that "the abuse of legislative power was more ominous than arbitrary acts of the executive,"[119] and "that the true problem of rights was less to protect the ruled from their rulers than to defend minorities and individuals against factious popular majorities acting through government."[120]

Second, American development of due process was heavily influenced by a unique need to manage the competing interests of a federal government, a desire for a strong tradition of state sovereignty, and a highly developed sense of individual liberties. The brief history of the founding recounted above demonstrates the particular concern that individuals' and states' rights not be superseded, even by laws duly enacted by the national government. Such concerns took on an unprecedented weight in the decisions made about the structure of the American government. The founders wanted an enumerated set of rules and laws, but were also guided by the notion of fundamental rights. Consequently, "natural rights were conceived of as possessing the same law-like status, and by implication as having

---

[114] THE BILL OF RIGHTS: ORIGINAL MEANING AND CURRENT UNDERSTANDING, *supra* note 78, at 5.

[115] VILE, *supra* note 95, at 114. One of the amendments not ratified related to the size of Congress. The other amendment, later ratified as the Twenty-seventh Amendment, prohibited Congress from enacting congressional pay raises before an election. *Id.*

[116] MOTT, *supra* note 68, at 154–56.

[117] RAKOVE, *supra* note 92, at 288–90.

[118] *Id.* at 289.

[119] *Id.* at 290.

[120] *Id.*

a similarly compelling 'scientific' style of justification, as the laws governing the behaviour of physical bodies."[121] Many of the founders viewed the Constitution as implicitly reaffirming preexisting "fundamental rights" that could not be taken away even by otherwise legitimate government action.[122]

Third, the passage of the Fourteenth Amendment after the Civil War had a profound effect upon the development of the doctrine of due process and rule of law in the United States.[123] The amendment placed explicit constitutional restraints on certain actions taken by states that, until 1868, had been imposed only on the federal government.[124] This had the effect of increasing judicial review power to curtail behaviors by states, even if their people and legislatures had duly enacted certain laws.[125] The lengthy and complicated history of the Fourteenth Amendment's passage also expressly raised the notions of individual rights and protections against abuses by the legislative or executive branches, concerns that were brushed over when the first Due Process Clause was placed in the Fifth Amendment.[126] Finally, the Fourteenth Amendment combined in a single sentence the Due Process Clause, the Privileges and Immunities Clause, and the Equal Protection Clause. Even more so than the Fifth Amendment, which surrounds its own Due Process Clause with rules-based procedures, the Fourteenth Amendment suggested a "unified reading" that more explicitly combined the individual liberty and the substantive and procedural components of a fair governmental system.[127] It thus became easier for

---

[121] Lanshe, *supra* note 64, at 12.

[122] *See, e.g.*, Edward Corwin, *The Basic Doctrine of American Constitutional Law*, 12 MICH. L. REV. 247 (1914) (discussing the general principles regarding the role of the American Constitution); Thomas C. Grey, *Do We Have an Unwritten Constitution?* 27 STAN. L. REV. 703 (1975) (discussing whether the Constitution includes, beyond its literal words, principles of liberty and justice).

[123] Though the effects and implications of the Fourteenth Amendment have been far too numerous to be listed or explained in any single work, this section highlights a few of the particularities of the Amendment that helped drive development of due process away from its original "law of the land" roots.

[124] *See* Barron v. Mayor & City Council of Baltimore, 32 U.S. 243, 250 (1833) (holding expressly before passage of the Fifth Amendment that the Bill of Rights was a restriction only of federal actions, not state and local conduct, if the Framers had intended for the Bill of Rights to apply to the states, "they would have declared this purpose in plain and intelligible language.").

[125] *See* David P. Currie, *The Constitution in the Supreme Court: Limitations on State Power*, 51 U. CHI. L. REV. 329, 346–48 (1983) (arguing that the framers of the Fourteenth Amendment intended to limit state power); *See, e.g.*, Richard L. Aynes, *Constricting the Law of Freedom: Justice Miller, the Fourteenth Amendment, and the Slaughter-House Cases*, 70 CHI-KENT L. REV. 627, 686 (1994) (discussing the interpretations of the Fourteenth Amendment).

[126] *See generally* MICHAEL CURTIS, NO STATE SHALL ABRIDGE: THE FOURTEENTH AMENDMENT AND THE BILL OF RIGHTS (1986) (providing an in-depth view of the Fourteenth Amendment's history); *see also* JOSEPH JAMES, THE FRAMING OF THE FOURTEENTH AMENDMENT (1956); WILLIAM D. GUTHRIE, LECTURES ON THE FOURTEENTH ARTICLE OF AMENDMENT TO THE CONSTITUTION OF THE UNITED STATES (1898).

[127] Jane Rutherford, *The Myth of Due Process*, 72 B.U. L. REV. 1, 5–6, 74–76 (1992). *Cf.* Ryan C. Williams, *The One and Only Substantive Due Process Clause*, 120 YALE L.J. 408 (2011) (arguing that in 1791 due process of law had a procedural meaning only, which guaranteed proper judicial procedures. But by 1868, when the Fourteenth Amendment was ratified, it was construed to embrace a substantive meaning as well).

courts later to use due process as a jumping-off point for constitutional rights of both a substantive and a procedural nature.

Integral to the development of the due process scheme was the interpretation (or misinterpretation) of other portions of the American Constitution, most notably the Privileges or Immunities Clause of the Fourteenth Amendment, and the Ninth Amendment in the Bill of Rights. The Fourteenth Amendment states "No State shall make or enforce any law which shall abridge the privileges or immunities of citizens of the United States." Though use of the Privileges or Immunities Clause as a means to apply the Bill of Rights provisions to the states was all but foreclosed in the *Slaughter-House Cases*,[128] legal scholars and professionals have continued to argue whether this clause, instead of the Fifth and Fourteenth Amendment, is the more logical home for individual rights.[129]

The Ninth Amendment was also a potential vehicle with which the Court could enforce a host of unenumerated rights. It provides that "The enumeration in the Constitution, of certain rights, shall not be construed to deny or disparage others retained by the people."[130] Yet the Supreme Court "has long dismissed the Ninth Amendment as a constitutional irrelevance."[131] A handful of opinions have based certain substantive rights on the Amendment,[132] but the Due Process Clause ultimately has become the workhorse for enforcing substantive rights. The constricted interpretation of these other rights-protecting clauses, combined with America's strong sense of individual rights, helped drive the post-Reconstruction evolution of the Due Process Clauses into both procedural and substantive directions.

V. Putting the Law of the Land into Practice

After the Bill of Rights was added to the Constitution, the task of interpreting the amendments began. As in the constitutional debates, legal and philosophical history played an important role in these interpretations. The Due Process Clause, while important, was rarely invoked in the beginning of the nation. The first due process

---

[128] 83 U.S. 36 (1873).

[129] *See* Alfred H. Kelly, *Clio and the Court: An Illicit Love Affair*, 1965 Sup. Ct. Rev. 119, 132–34 *see, e.g.*, Timothy S. Bishop, Comment, *The Privileges or Immunities Clause of the Fourteenth Amendment: The Original Intent*, 79 Nw. U. L. Rev. 142 (1984) (discussing the Privileges and Immunities Clause of the Fourteenth Amendment); *see generally* McDonald v. City of Chicago,—U.S—, 130 S. Ct. 3020 (2010) (providing the most recent discussion of this issue by the United States Supreme Court). See also discussion of substantive due process and the selective incorporation of the Bill of Rights into the Fourteenth Amendment in chapter 4, *infra*.

[130] Randy E. Barnett, *The Ninth Amendment: It Means What It Says*, 85 Tex. L. Rev. 1, 2 (2006) (citing U.S. Const. amend. IX).

[131] *Id.* (citing United Pub. Workers v. Mitchell, 330 U.S. 75, 95–96 (1947)).

[132] *See, e.g.*, Griswold v. Connecticut, 381 U.S. 479 (1965) ("The foregoing cases suggest that specific guarantees in the Bill of Rights have penumbras, formed by emanations from those guarantees that help give them life and substance.").

case did not reach the Supreme Court until sixty-five years after ratification.[133] There was much about the clause's history and its place within the Constitution to imply that it should operate as a check against legislative overreach, though the most obvious intentions related to basic separation of powers principles and insistence upon prospective, versus retrospective laws.[134] The Constitution and the Bill of Rights enumerated a substantial number of procedural guarantees. Unless the Due Process Clause was intended to be mere verbiage, it presumably created and protected an interest above and beyond those already listed.[135] Articulating that interest, however, remains a complex and contested endeavor.

Early cases on due process referred and conformed to principles derived from Coke's view of the Magna Carta. In particular, the Court ruled in *Murray's Lessee v. Hoboken Land and Improvement Company*[136] that "Due Process of Law" did not mean merely any procedures prescribed through law by Congress but instead referred to ancient practices and customs under common law and derived from the English system.[137] Additionally, the United States Supreme Court decided cases regarding issues of substantive due process dating all the way back to the founding of the country.[138]

The clause thus borrowed from the English system in particular by referring to common law to determine due process requirements and in general by being used as a check against some forms of arbitrary governmental power.[139] Similar usage of the clause was employed after the passage of the Fourteenth Amendment, when Justice Bradley and Justice Swayne referred to and quoted from the Magna Carta in their dissents in the *Slaughter-House Cases*.[140]

---

[133] Wasserman, *supra* note 2, at 6–7.

[134] Mott, *supra* note 68, at 154–56.

[135] *But see* Miller, *supra* note 34, at 11; Easterbrook, *supra* note 72, at 94–95 (arguing that because the Bill of Rights outlines specific procedural protections it is unlikely that the Due Process Clause is designed to be a general "catch-all" phrase for procedural guarantees).

[136] 59 U.S. 272 (1856).

[137] Murray's Lessee v. Hoboken Land and Improvement Co., 59 U.S. 272, 275–77 (1856).

[138] *See* Frank R. Strong, Substantive Due Process of Law: A Dichotomy of Sense and Nonsense 29 (1986) (discussing the concerns over "legislative acts expropriating from citizens title to land or to personal property."). These early expropriations cases can be compared to the Takings Clause cases seen in the modern Court. Interestingly, when faced with legislative takings without just compensation for the land, both the early and modern courts rarely supported the legislature. *Compare* Van Horne's Lessee v. Dorrance, 2 U.S. 304 (1795), *and* Bowman v. Middleton, 1 Bay 252 (1792), *with* Lugar v. Edmonson Oil Co., 457 U.S. 922 (1982), *and* Pennsylvania Coal Co. v. Mahon, 260 U.S. 396 (1922). When there has been some form of compensation discussed in the legislature, however, the modern Court has given far greater deference to the legislative action. *See, e.g.*, Kelo v. City of New London, 545 U.S. 469 (2005) (affirming a state action to take land and give it to Pfizer Corporation to build a research facility); Hawaii Housing Authority v. Midkiff, 467 U.S. 229 (1984) (allowing a redistribution of land from large landowners to their tenants and rejecting the argument this was a private rather than a public benefit).

[139] Miller, *supra* note 34, at 13–14.

[140] *Id.* at 18. These cases are also notable because the Due Process Clause was applied to property rights, outside of the criminal sphere, foreshadowing the "due process revolution" of the 1960s. Wasserman, *supra* note 2, at 10.

DEVELOPMENT OF TWO STRANDS OF DUE PROCESS

Throughout Supreme Court history, interpretations of the Due Process Clause departed from explicit ties to the English manifestation of rule of law principles and established a more modern application of the conceptual components of rule of law theory. The Court, for example, moved away from an explicit reference to the Magna Carta in the late-nineteenth century. In *Hurtado v. California*,[141] Justice Matthews paid homage to the original English charter and the intellectual debt owed to it, but claimed that the American Constitution was designed to adapt flexibly to future eras and was not constrained by an antiquated legal past.[142] According to Matthews, standards of due process should be determined and adjusted according to the customs of the age as determined by the judiciary.[143] The shift away from traditional and historical definitions of "due process of law" was further advanced in *Powell v. Alabama*,[144] where the Court ruled that common law practices were no longer sufficient and that a contemporary understanding of fairness was necessary to justify a procedure under due process.[145] This related back to the early writings of Aristotle and Cicero, which noted that when natural law and universal principles of justice conflict with the positive laws as passed by the legislature, the former take precedence. Unlike those earlier foundational philosophers, however, modern due process principles were tied less to religious or historical notions of justice and more to contemporary notions of right and wrong.[146]

Procedural due process jurisprudence also continued to change, and several major categories of case law developed that are important to mention as illustrations. These included questions of: jurisdiction; notice; and fair hearings within the administrative, criminal, civil, and military arenas. An important subcategory of procedural due process involved the identification of particular liberty and property interests that triggered procedural due process protections.

Some of the earliest and best known due process cases addressed a hybrid of procedural and substantive due process principles and involved questions of jurisdiction, in particular whether a given tribunal can properly claim jurisdiction over a case or interest.[147] For example, due process principles govern whether a court has power to compel a corporation to appear and defend a lawsuit within a given state, a decision that hinges on the corporation's general presence or specific acts in the given forum.[148] Likewise, the court's power over individuals and their property depends upon the

---

[141] 110 U.S. 516 (1884).

[142] *See* Miller, *supra* note 34, at 17–18.

[143] *See id.* at 19.

[144] 287 U.S. 45 (1932).

[145] WASSERMAN, *supra* note 2, at 14.

[146] *See* Lanshe, *supra* note 64, at 24–31.

[147] *See, e.g.*, Pennoyer v. Neff, 95 U.S. 714 (1877). We discuss the jurisdiction cases in greater detail in chapter 5, *infra*.

[148] *See* International Shoe Co. v. State of Washington, 326 U.S. 310, 316–19 (1945); World-Wide Volkswagen Corp. v. Woodson, 444 U.S. 286, 291–93 (1980); Helicopteros Nacionales de Colombia, S.A. v. Hall, 466 U.S. 408, 414–16 (1984); Arthur T. von Mehren & Donald T. Trautman, *Jurisdiction to Adjudicate: A Suggested Analysis*, 79 HARV. L. REV. 1121, 1136–44 (1966).

physical or other "presence" of either in the forum state.[149] In related cases, the Court has stipulated various rules for what constitutes giving fair notice that is "reasonably calculated, under all the circumstances, to apprise interested parties of the pendency of the action and afford them an opportunity to present their objections."[150] Although sometimes formalistic, most of the case law in this area either explicitly or implicitly requires that the outcome be "fair," "just," or "reasonable" in a fashion that harkens back to the Court's insistence in *Powell v. Alabama* that common law principles must bow to justice, as defined by contemporary standards.[151]

A separate but related avenue of due process jurisprudence deals with hearings themselves. The Court established procedural due process rules for what constitutes a fair hearing dependent upon the context. Relevant factors include whether the hearing is a civil suit or a criminal case, whether the person in question is a minor, mentally incapacitated, a prisoner, or in the military, and the nature of the interests or rights in dispute. Beginning with the last category first, the Court has undergone a marked development from a formalistic and limited conception of protected interests to a more functionalist and flexible standard. Although earlier cases made a distinction between rights and privileges, more modern jurisprudence acknowledges that conceptions of liberty and property can change with society and, as such, courts use less restrictive tests for defining protected interests.[152] Specifically, in 1982, the Court reasoned that "[t]he personal jurisdiction requirement recognizes and protects an individual liberty interest,"[153] placing "a restriction on judicial power not as a matter of sovereignty, but as a matter of individual liberty."[154] Protected interests in liberty can include freedom from restraint, freedom of contract, freedom …

> [T]o engage in any of the common occupations of life, to acquire useful knowledge, to marry, establish a home and bring up children, to worship God according to the dictates of his own conscience, and generally to enjoy those privileges long recognized … as essential to the orderly pursuit of happiness by free men.[155]

---

[149] *See, e.g.*, Pennoyer v. Neff, 95 U.S. 714, 722–24 (1877); Burnham v. Superior Court of CA, 495 U.S. 604, 617–22 (1990); Shaffer v. Heitner, 433 U.S. 186, 207–12 (1977).

[150] Mullane v. Central Hanover Bank & Trust Co., 339 U.S. 306, 314 (1950).

[151] Powell v. Alabama, 287 U.S. 45, 71–73 (1932).

[152] *See* Insurance Corp. of Ireland, Ltd. v. Compagnie des Bauxites de Guinée, 456 U.S. 694, 702–703, n.10 (1982); Burger King Corp. v. Rudzewicz, 471 U.S. 462, 472 (1985); William W. Van Alstyne, *The Demise of the Right-Privilege Distinction in Constitutional Law*, 81 HARV. L. REV. 1439, 1439–40 (1968) (citing McAuliffe v. Mayor of New Bedford, 29 N.E. 517, 517 (Mass. 1892)); Sidney A. Shapiro, *Government Benefits and the Rule of Law: Toward a Standards-Based Theory of Due Process*, 57 ADMIN. L. REV. 107, 131–32 (2005); Rodney A. Smolla, *The Reemergence of the Right-Privilege Distinction in Constitutional Law: The Price of Protesting Too Much*, 35 STAN. L. REV. 69, 70–72 (1982).

[153] *Insurance Corp. of Ireland, Ltd.*, 456 U.S. at 702.

[154] *Id.*; *see also* Mullane v. Central Hanover Bank & Trust Co., 339 U.S. 306, 314 (1950).

[155] Board of Regents of State Colleges v. Roth, 408 U.S. 564, 572 (1972) (quoting Meyer v. Nebraska, 262 U.S. 390, 399 (1923) (omissions in original)).

Protected property interests, on the other hand, can include government-created benefits or entitlements, government contract or tenured employment, and traditional property interests like ownership of real or personal property.[156]

Once the Court has determined that there is a deprivation of a protected interest that requires procedural protections, the question becomes one of determining whether the protections in place are sufficient. As we explain in detail in chapters to follow, most procedural due process cases use the *Mathews v. Eldridge* framework and those that do not constitute a "self-conscious exceptions to the general rule."[157] The *Eldridge* case, while not applying a rigid framework on procedural due process questions, clarified much of the disparate but fundamentally similar principles espoused in cases throughout the nineteenth- and twentieth-century cases.[158]

> More precisely, our prior decisions indicate that identification of the specific dictates of due process generally requires consideration of three distinct factors: First, the private interest that will be affected by the official action; second, the risk of an erroneous deprivation of such interest through the procedures used, and the probable value, if any, of additional or substitute procedural safeguards; and finally, the Government's interest, including the function involved and the fiscal and administrative burdens that the additional or substitute procedural requirement would entail.[159]

The Court explicitly cautioned that this balancing framework, like previous procedural due process cases, was to be employed flexibly and be applied to the facts at hand.[160] The Court has since used this framework to establish varying standards for procedural due process, dependent largely upon the context in which the deprivation occurred.

The three notable and self-identified exceptions to the *Eldridge* framework are notice cases (described above), criminal cases, and cases involving military personnel. The Court in *Medina v. California*[161] explicitly distinguished *Eldridge* from criminal cases, stating that the appropriate standard, as described in *Patterson v. New York*, is one in which the states are given broad deference to determine procedural rules provided that they do not offend "'some principle of justice so rooted in the traditions and conscience of our people as to be ranked as fundamental.'"[162] In *Weiss v. United States*,[163] the defendant claimed that his court martial violated

---

[156] *See id.* at 576–78; Goss v. Lopez, 419 U.S. 565, 572–74 (1975). We develop the concept of protected interests under due process in chapter 2, *infra.*

[157] Mathews v. Eldridge, 424 U.S. 319 (1976). *See* chapters 2 and 3, *infra. See also* Gary Lawson, Katherine Ferguson, & Guillermo Montero, *Rediscovering the Mathews v. Eldridge and Penn Central Frameworks*, 81 Notre Dame L. Rev.1, 7 (2005). *See* chapter 3, *infra.*

[158] *See id.* at 7–15.

[159] *Id.* at 19–20 (citing Mathews v. Eldridge, 424 U.S. 319, 333–35 (1976) (citations omitted)).

[160] *Mathews*, 424 U.S. at 333–35.

[161] 505 U.S. 437 (1992).

[162] *Id.* at 442–45 (quoting Patterson v. New York, 432 U.S. 197, 201–202 (1977)).

[163] 510 U.S. 163 (1994).

procedural due process because the judge did not have a fixed term and thus could not be considered a neutral arbiter.[164] The Court ruled that, in the military context, judicial deference is at its "apogee" and that a procedure would not violate due process unless the factors in favor of the defendant were so "'extraordinarily weighty as to overcome the balance struck by Congress.'"[165]

Finally, the evidentiary standards for different types of proceedings vary according to the interests and context involved. In civil cases, or noncriminal cases in which a natural or constitutional right like freedom from restraint is at stake, the Court typically takes an intermediate approach to the required process. In applying the *Eldridge* framework to a civil commitment hearing, for example, the Court has ruled that a "clear and convincing" evidentiary standard is sufficient because, while freedom from restraint is an important interest, the government's interest in protecting the public *and* mentally ill people make the added burden of a "beyond a reasonable doubt" standard constitutionally unnecessary.[166] The intermediate standard of "clear and convincing evidence" has also been applied to civil cases between private parties that involve a quasi-criminal charge such as fraud that risks erroneously harming the defendant's reputation.[167] In criminal cases, however, courts will apply either strict or lenient procedural requirements dependent upon whether the individual has yet to be convicted. In *Estes v. Texas*,[168] the Court found that procedures that are inherently likely to produce prejudice in a criminal trial violate procedural due process regardless of whether they *actually* produce bias or prejudice in the proceedings.[169] At the same time, the Court allows for relatively lenient processes when the individual is already in custody of the state or has been convicted of a crime, because the interests of the government are more pronounced,[170] but also because the court discounts the likelihood of lax procedures producing an erroneous deprivation.[171] In other words, the nature and degree of procedural protection that due process requires hinge in part on

---

[164] *Id.* at 164.

[165] *Id.* at 177–78 (quoting Mittendorf v. Henry, 425 U.S. 25, 44 (1976)).

[166] Addington v. Texas, 441 U.S. 418, 425–27 (1979) (indefinitely detaining a mentally ill man via civil commitment proceeding that used a "clear and convincing evidence" standard does not violate due process).

[167] *See id.* at 424.

[168] 381 U.S. 532 (1965).

[169] *Id.* at 543–44 (broadcasting of pretrial proceedings was sufficiently likely to bias potential jurors and distract the judge so as to violate procedural due process).

[170] *See* Walpole v. Hill, 472 U.S. 445, 454–56 (1985) (recognizing "legitimate institutional needs of assuring the safety of inmates and prisoners" justifies deference to prison proceedings that deprive inmates of "good time credits" provided the decision is supported by *some* evidence); Bell v. Wolfish, 441 U.S. 520, 540 (1979) (determining that government's legitimate interests in ensuring pretrial detainees are available for trial and for the proper administration of a detention facility justifies deprivations of liberty that fall short of punishment).

[171] *See, e.g.*, Jones v. United States, 463 U.S. 354, 366–68 (1983) (holding that a "preponderance of evidence" standard can be used in an automatic commitment hearing when the individual was already found not guilty by reason of insanity because such a hearing is less likely to produce erroneous results).

the substantive rights at stake: procedure and substance notions are inherently interdependent.

As we shall see in later chapters that elaborate on all of these developments, modern lines of procedural due process jurisprudence are based on balancing tests and standards of scrutiny that give proportionate weight to the individual or the state's interests to the extent that doing so would produce a fair and just decision as determined by contemporary standards.[172] Although the current methods of analysis and justifications for procedural due process cases no longer strictly rely on common law and historical precedent,[173] many of the procedural protections established by the Court likely were contemplated within the Due Process Clauses of the American Constitution and are arguably important protections from a rule of law perspective, too.[174] The Court has used these same clauses, however, to protect explicitly substantive rights under the mantle of "liberty," leading inevitably to an amorphous jurisprudence that arguably stretches the boundaries of "original intent"—particularly if by this one refers to the eighteenth-century framers' intent versus the nineteenth-century framers' intent. Yet this move beyond explicitly procedural rights further connects United States due process jurisprudence to historical conceptions of rule of law requirements.

THE BEGINNINGS OF SUBSTANTIVE DUE PROCESS

Lochner v. New York[175] is widely viewed as the Court's entrance into the subject matter of substantive due process.[176] However, the ideals and theories prevalent in substantive due process reasoning are traceable, at least in part, throughout earlier case law and all the way back to England and chapter 39 of the Magna Carta.[177]

Well before *Lochner*, the Court confronted but rejected the argument that the Due Process Clause of the Fourteenth Amendment had a substantive component that might embrace economic rights. In the *Slaughter-House Cases*, the Court

---

[172] *See generally* E. Thomas Sullivan & Richard Frase, Proportionality Principles in American Law (2009).

[173] It should be noted that Justice Scalia and Justice Thomas have signaled dissatisfaction with the current due process jurisprudence and a desire to return to a more historically based method that relies on "settled usage," similar to the approach demonstrated in Hurtado v. California. *See* Weiss v. United States, 510 U.S. 163, 197–99 (1994) (Scalia, J., concurring); Pacific Mutual Life Ins. Co. v. Haslip, 499 U.S. 1, 28–40 (1991) (Scalia, J., concurring).

[174] Justice Scalia acknowledges that a "settled usage" test would likely result in similar outcomes to the Court's current approach. Pacific Mutual Life Ins. Co. v. Haslip, 499 U.S. 1, 36 (1991) ("Even so, however, very few cases have used the Due Process Clause, without the benefit of an accompanying Bill of Rights guarantee, to strike down a procedure concededly approved by traditional and continuing American practice.").

[175] 198 U.S. 45 (1905).

[176] *See*, chapter 4, *infra*. *See also* Mattei Ion Radu, *Incompatible Theories: Natural Law and Substantive Due Process*, 54 Vill. L. Rev. 247, 249 (2009) ("*Lochner v. New York* marked the clear beginning of the Court's foray into the oxymoronic field of substantive due process.").

[177] *See* Strong, *supra* note 138, at 3. *See* chapter 4, *infra*.

concluded that due process under the Fourteenth Amendment was principally about slavery, because it was a "development of the thirteenth [amendment], and is a more comprehensive exposition of the principles which lie at the foundation of the thirteenth [amendment]."[178] Justice Field's dissent in the *Slaughter-House Cases* often is cited as the origin of substantive due process in the United States Supreme Court.[179] It would be another twenty years, however, before the term became part of the Court's lexicon.

The roots of a "substantive" component of due process, however, arguably extend back even further than Justice Field's dissent. In 1798, Justice Chase eloquently laid out many of the principles that modern substantive due process reflects, though his precise intentions obviously must be taken in their narrower, historical context.[180]

> An act of the legislature (for I cannot call it a law), contrary to the great first principles of the social compact, cannot be considered a rightful exercise of legislative authority. The obligation of a law in governments established on express compact, and on republican principles, must be determined by the nature of the power, on which it is founded.... A law that punishe[s] a citizen for an innocent action, or, in other words, for an act, which, when done, was in violation of no existing law; a law that destroys, or impairs, the lawful private contracts of citizens; a law that makes a man a Judge in his own cause; or a law that takes property from A and gives it to B ... is against all reason and justice, for a people to entrust a legislature with [such] powers; and, therefore, it cannot be presumed that they have done it.[181]

Justice Chase felt that these principles were so important that, even though they were not specifically stated in the Constitution, they were of natural law, and could supplement the deficiencies of the written Constitution.[182] This passage was dicta in the 1798 case and its original meaning has been much debated. Yet the notion that there are some principles greater than the text of the Constitution and that there are fundamental rights which cannot be taken away by legislative action lived on, and was expanded and adapted in subsequent eras.[183]

By the end of the nineteenth century and the beginning of the twentieth century, substantive due process became a basis for challenges to state or federal government actions.[184] In *Allgeyer v. Louisiana*,[185] a unanimous Court invalidated a state

---

[178] Slaughter-House Cases, 83 U.S. 36, 51 (1872).

[179] *See, e.g.*, McDonald v. Chicago, U.S. 130 S. Ct. 3020, 3029–30 (2010) (citing Justice Field's dissent in *The Slaughter-House Cases*).

[180] Calder v. Bull, 3 U.S. 386, 388–90 (1798).

[181] *Id.* at 388–89.

[182] *See* STRONG, *supra* note 138, at 31.

[183] *See id.*

[184] *See* chapters 3 and 4, *infra*..

[185] 165 U.S. 578 (1897).

statute on due process grounds, which began the use of substantive due process as both a vehicle for and an opponent of social reform.[186] At issue in *Allgeyer* was a measure enacted by the Louisiana legislature preventing the sale of marine insurance to customers within Louisiana if the company did not comply with Louisiana law.[187] Louisiana fined Allgeyer & Co. for sending a "letter of advice of certificate of marine insurance" to an insurance company in New York.[188] Allgeyer challenged the Louisiana act as unconstitutional on due process grounds, claiming that its freedom to contract had been violated.[189] In holding the statute unconstitutional, the Court focused on the freedom of the insurance company and its customers to conduct business and contract as they wished.[190]

Allgeyer led to the decision in *Lochner v. New York*,[191] in which the Court struck down a New York labor law that prohibited the employment of bakers for more than ten hours per day or sixty hours per week.[192] Lochner was fined for having an employee work more than sixty hours in one week.[193] The Court held that the statute "interferes with the right of contract between the employer and employees" and that "[t]he general right to make a contract in relation to his business is part of the liberty of the individual protected by the 14th Amendment of the Federal Constitution."[194] The Court stated that "[t]he act must have a more direct relation, as a means to an end, and the end itself must be appropriate and legitimate, before an act can be held to be valid which interferes with the general right of the individual to contract."[195] The dissents in *Lochner* criticized the decision as sweeping far too broadly and preventing a state from protecting the health of its citizens.[196] Although *Lochner* has been strongly critiqued by many scholars,[197] the Court did not repudiate it for fifty years.

---

[186] *See* STRONG, *supra* note 138, at 91 (discussing the impact of the *Allgeyer* decision).

[187] *Allgeyer*, 165 U.S. at 579.

[188] *Id.*

[189] *Id.* at 579–80.

[190] *See id.* at 591–92 ("In the privilege of pursuing an ordinary calling or trade, and of acquiring, holding, and selling property, must be embraced the right to make all proper contracts in relation thereto[.]").

[191] 198 U.S. 45 (1905).

[192] *Id.* at 45–46.

[193] *Id.* at 52.

[194] *Id.* at 53.

[195] *Id.* at 57–58; *see also* SULLIVAN & FRASE, *supra* note 172, at 54.

[196] *See* Lochner v. New York, 198 U.S. 45, 76 (1905) (Holmes J., dissenting) (arguing for a test that would uphold laws such as this, unless "a rational and fair man necessarily would admit that the statute proposed would infringe fundamental principles as they have been understood by the traditions of our people and our law."). *See also id.* at 69 (Harlan J., dissenting) ("[I]n determining the question of power to interfere with liberty of contract, the court may inquire whether the means devised by the state are germane to an end which may be lawfully accomplished and have a real or substantial relation to the protection of health.").

[197] *See, e.g.*, Anthony Page, *Has Corporate Law Failed? Addressing Proposals for Reform*, 107 MICH. L. REV. 979, 981 (2009) (discussing the balancing between the right to contract and other concerns and the rejection of *Lochner*). *See also* chapter 4 *infra* discussing critiques.

The Court was not consistent, however, in applying *Lochner* or in describing the "liberty of contract." In *Nebbia v. New York*,[198] where the Court upheld a minimum price for the retail sale of milk,[199] the Court announced a standard very different from the one in *Lochner*, stating that "the guaranty of due process ... demands only that the law shall not be unreasonable, arbitrary, or capricious, and that the means selected shall have a real and substantial relation to the object sought to be attained."[200]

In 1955 the Court officially repudiated *Lochner* in *Williamson v. Lee Optical*.[201] The Court upheld an Oklahoma law that made it unlawful for any person who was not a licensed optometrist or ophthalmologist to fit lenses to the face, or to duplicate or replace frame lenses or other optical appliances without a prescription.[202] In its opinion, the Court took an even further step back with regards to economic individual rights than it did in *Nebbia*. The Court stated that even if the law exacted a "needless, wasteful requirement in many cases" this is not for the courts to police.[203]

Even before 1955, substantive due process began to emerge in areas other than economic rights as a basis for substantive, individual rights. The Due Process Clause of the Fourteenth Amendment was used as a basis for extending the Takings Clause principles to the states in 1897.[204] Decades later, the Court grounded protection of "privacy" interests in the Fifth and Fourteenth Amendments.[205] This liberty gave rise to a host of rights related to the family that are now protected under substantive due process including: the right to marry[206] (with limitations), the right to

---

[198] 291 U.S. 502 (1934). It is important to note, however, that criticism of *Lochner*, especially in the last two decades has been anything but universal. Relying on Hayek's theory that redistributive justice, especially in the form of legislative acts, "must lead to the destruction of the Rule of Law," TAMANAHA, *supra* note 7, at 86 (discussing FRIEDRICH HAYEK, THE ROAD TO SERFDOM (1944)) scholars, largely subscribing to the liberal tradition, have called for a revitalizing of *Lochner*. *See, e.g.*, BERNARD H. SIEGAN, ECONOMIC LIBERTIES AND THE CONSTITUTION (1980) (raising a defense for the *Lochner* ruling); David E. Bernstein, Lochner *Era Revisionism, Revised:* Lochner *and the Origins of Fundamental Rights Constitutionalism*, 92 Geo. L.J. 1, 2, 60 (2003) (arguing that the bases for the *Lochner* decision have been misplaced, and that *Griswold*, *Roe*, and other due process decisions "*can* be traced back to *Lochner*") (emphasis in original); *see* Richard A. Epstein, *The Mistakes of 1937*, 41 WM. & MARY L. REV. 3, 8–10 (1999) (indicating that the Court was wrong to overrule the Lochnerian line of cases).

[199] *Nebbia*, 291 U.S. at 537 ("So far as the requirement of due process is concerned, and in the absence of other constitutional restriction, a state is free to adopt whatever economic policy may reasonably be deemed to promote public welfare, and to enforce that policy by legislation adapted to its purpose.").

[200] *Id.* at 525.

[201] 348 U.S. 483 (1955). The Court, referring to *Lochner*, said that "[t]he day is gone when this Court uses the Due Process Clause of the Fourteenth Amendment to strike down state laws, regulatory of business and industrial conditions, because they may be unwise[.]" *Id.* at 488.

[202] *See id.* at 485–87.

[203] *Id.* at 487.

[204] Chicago, Burlington & Quincy Railroad Co. v. Chicago, 166 U.S. 226, 241 (1897).

[205] *See, e.g.*, Griswold v. Connecticut, 381 U.S. 479, 480, 484–86 (1965). We develop this case law more fully in chapter 4, *infra*.

[206] *See* Loving v. Virginia, 388 U.S. 1, 12 (1967). Though *Loving v. Virginia* was decided on equal protection grounds, the Court has relied on its holding in the context of substantive due process cases.

choose how to maintain extended family relationships,[207] the right to care for one's children,[208] the right to choose when or whether to bear children,[209] and the right to be free from government intrusions into aspects of sexual autonomy.[210]

Yet the Court, in its attempts to reconcile individual rights with state sovereignty, interpreted the Due Process Clause in drastically different ways depending on the perceived nature of the right and on the individual justices. As we explain in chapters 3 and 4, several overarching and distinct categories of cases have emerged, each with its own internal complexities and analytical difficulties. In each of these due process arenas, however, the Court weighs the autonomy interest of individual

---

For example, in *Roe v. Wade*, in enumerating the "penumbras" of the Bill of Rights from which guarantees of personal privacy emanate, the court cites *Loving*, stating that earlier decisions under the Fourteenth Amendment "make it clear that the ... [guarantee of personal privacy] has some extension to activities relating to marriage[.]" Roe v. Wade, 410 U.S. 113, 152 (1973). The Court in *Loving* itself noted that "[t]hese statutes also deprive the Lovings of liberty without due process of law in violation of the Due Process Clause of the Fourteenth Amendment. The freedom to marry has long been recognized as one of the vital personal rights essential to the orderly pursuit of happiness by free men." *Loving*, 388 U.S. at 12. Though some of the language in the case has since been overruled, *Meyer v. Nebraska* provides another excellent example of the broad reading of liberty relied upon by the court in later substantive due process cases. 262 U.S. 390, 399 (1923) (reading liberty in the Due Process Clause as denoting "not merely freedom from bodily restraint but also the right of the individual to contract, to engage in any of the common occupations of life, to acquire useful knowledge, to marry, establish a home and bring up children, to worship God according to the dictates of his own conscience, and generally to enjoy those privileges long recognized at common law as essential to the orderly pursuit of happiness by free men.") For a detailed history on the Court's various constitutional holdings with regard to this right see Cass R. Sunstein, *The Right to Marry*, 26 CARDOZO L. REV. 2081 (2005). For a discussion of how the rights enunciated by the Court indicate that prohibitions on same-sex marriage are unconstitutional see WILLIAM N. ESKRIDGE, THE CASE FOR SAME-SEX MARRIAGE: FROM SEXUAL LIBERTY TO CIVILIZED COMMITMENT (2006). *See also* chapter 4, *infra*.

[207] *See generally* Moore v. East Cleveland, 431 U.S. 494 (invalidating a zoning ordinance limiting occupancy of a dwelling to members of a single "family" narrowly defined to exclude grandparents and cousins).

[208] *See, e.g.*, Troxel v. Granville, 530 U.S. 57 (2000) (concluding that a state decision to grant grandparents visiting rights to their grandchildren over the objections of the sole surviving parent had violated the mother's substantive due process rights).

[209] *See, e.g.*, Griswold v. Connecticut, 381 U.S. 479 (1965) (declaring unconstitutional a state law prohibiting the use and distribution of contraceptives); Roe v. Wade, 410 U.S. 113 (1973) (recognizing a constitutional right to abortion in the "liberty" of the Due Process Clause); Casey v. Population Services International, 431 U.S. 678, 685–86 (1977) ("That the constitutionally protected right of privacy extends to an individual's liberty to make choices regarding contraception does not, however, automatically invalidate every state regulation in this area. The business of manufacturing and selling contraceptives may be regulated in ways that do not infringe protected individual choices. And even a burdensome regulation may be validated by a sufficiently compelling state interest."); *see generally* John Hart Ely, *The Wages of Crying Wolf: A Comment on Roe v. Wade*, 82 YALE L.J. 920 (1973) (providing an in-depth discussion of *Roe*); Richard A. Epstein, *Substantive Due Process by Any Other Name: The Abortion Cases*, 1973 SUP. CT. REV. 159 (discussing substantive due process principles in abortion cases).

[210] *See* Lawrence v. Texas, 539 U.S. 558, 562 (2003) ("Freedom extends beyond spatial bounds. Liberty presumes an autonomy of self that includes freedom of thought, belief, expression, and certain intimate conduct.").

citizens against the police power of the state or federal government,[211] though it affords greatly varying degrees of deference to the representative branches under each strand of substantive due process.

The first strand of cases involves socioeconomic liberties, an idea championed by *Lochner*,[212] but later greatly curtailed.[213] Tracking the socioeconomic liberty cases, one can see the Court's views on where governmental power trumps individual liberty, from almost never in *Lochner*, to almost always in *Lee Optical*, even if the law is considered by the Court to be ill-advised and very poorly constructed.

A second strand of substantive due process cases deals with the government's taking land from private citizens and either using the land or transferring it to third parties for use. This strand technically stands apart from the Due Process Clause per se, but has now been incorporated into due process through judicial interpretation of the Fourteenth Amendment.[214] For example, the right of an individual to be compensated under the Takings Clause has often been subverted to the interests of government in undertaking almost any purpose.[215] The Court has consistently

---

[211] In *Lochner*, the Court characterized this weighing of rights by saying "[i]t is a question of which of two powers or rights shall prevail, the power of the state to legislate or the right of the individual to liberty of person and freedom of contract." Lochner v. New York, 198 U.S. 45, 57 (1905).

[212] *See generally id.*

[213] *See* Williamson v. Lee Optical, 348 U.S. 483, 487–88 (1955).

[214] It should not be forgotten that the constraints on states from the Takings Clause are technically not a matter of substantive due process jurisprudence, but rather the protections of the Fifth Amendment's Takings Clause have been incorporated against the states through the Fourteenth Amendment. *See* Chicago, Burlington & Quincy R.R. Co. v. City of Chicago, 166 U.S. 226 (1897) (enforcing the provisions of the Fifth Amendment's Takings Clause against the states). However, the Court's modern incorporation analysis has many of the hallmarks of substantive due process analysis. The recent case of *McDonald v. Chicago* provides an excellent example of this intertwinedness, U.S. 130 S. Ct. 3020 (2010). In *McDonald* the Court considered whether the individual right to keep and bear arms under the Second Amendment, as defined in *District of Columbia v. Heller*, 554 U.S. 570 (2008), was incorporated against the states through the Fourteenth Amendment. 130 S. Ct. at 3028. In finding that the Second Amendment right is fundamental to America's scheme of ordered liberty, and thus incorporated through the Fourteenth Amendment, the majority looked to whether the right to keep and bear arms is "deeply rooted in this Nation's history and tradition," *id.* citing *Washington v. Glucksberg*, 521 U.S. 702 (1997), a case decided on substantive due process lines. 130 S. Ct. at 3036. Further emphasizing the fine line between a substantive due process inquiry and incorporation analysis, Justice Stevens dissented in *McDonald*, arguing that the case was not one of incorporation, but rather a substantive due process case. *Id.* at 3090–92 (Stevens, J., dissenting) ("It follows that the term 'incorporation,' like the term 'unenumerated rights,' is something of a misnomer. Whether an asserted substantive due process interest is explicitly named in one of the first eight Amendments to the Constitution or is not mentioned, *the underlying inquiry is the same*: We must ask whether the interest is 'comprised within the term of liberty.'") (emphasis added). Despite its technical status as an "incorporated" right, the Takings Clause jurisprudence mirrors the considerations made in substantive due process cases and provides a crucial commentary on the Court's protection of economic rights in the post-*Lochner* world—as a fundamental balancing between state interests and the rights of individuals.

[215] The line of takings cases exemplifies the trend of state "interests" superseding the rights of individuals to their private property. *See, e.g.*, Berman v. Parker, 348 U.S. 26, 32, 35–36 (1954) (upholding the condemnation of property under the District of Columbia Redevelopment Act—"it is not for the courts to oversee the choice of the boundary line nor to sit in review on the size of a particular project." In analyzing whether a project has a public purpose or not, the Court exercised its power in a very narrow capacity.); Hawaii Housing Authority v. Midkiff, 467 U.S. 229, 231–32, 41 (1984) (upholding the

upheld the right of the states to use their power of eminent domain assuming that certain conditions are met. Takings Clause cases protect fairly robust government power. Unless there is a serious flaw in the taking—e.g., the citizens are not reasonably compensated or there is no public purpose whatsoever to justify the taking—the Court typically will defer to the legislature.

The third, most significant strand of substantive due process cases involves fundamental rights that trigger close judicial scrutiny. As we explain in chapter 4, the Court has described these liberties in various ways over the years, but generally they include liberties that by tradition and evolving shared sensibilities occupy a privileged position in a liberal democracy. For example, individual privacy is an area in which the rights of the individual have changed from being a low constitutional priority to a paramount due process concern over the past sixty years. Most notably, fundamental liberties based on a notion of "privacy" include marital rights, reproductive rights, and sexual autonomy. This area of due process protection emerged in the mid-twentieth century and has seen an ebb and flow as the Court has sought a balance between the rights of the individual and the power of the government.[216] When compared to the socioeconomic liberties cases, the fundamental rights cases evolved in exactly the opposite way. In the socioeconomic cases, the Court moved from valuing individual autonomy above all else, to valuing the judgment of the legislature more heavily. In the fundamental rights cases, the Court moved from deference toward the state to greater protection of individual autonomy.

The Court has not harmonized these different approaches to substantive due process across categories. Rather, it has continued to carve out separate categories of rights in which a different balance between autonomy and government power plays out. All three areas of substantive due process jurisprudence share an absence of bright line rules, which invites litigants to assess ever-evolving notions of "fundamental" rights against ever-evolving notions of compelling or important governmental interests. We nevertheless believe that there are shared, however general, characteristics of due process concern that surface across all of these categories, as well as procedural due process. We identify these baseline due process concerns in

---

ability of the state of Hawaii to take the title of real property from lessors and transfer it to lessees as a means of reducing the concentration of ownership. The Court emphasized that it would not substitute its judgment for that of the legislature's as to what constitutes a public use unless the use is palpably without reasonable foundation); Kelo v. City of New London, 545 U.S. 469, 477–83 (2005) (upholding a development plan that took land from private citizens in order for a redevelopment program, including building a compound for the Pfizer corporation, where the Court remained deferential to legislative judgments).

216 *See, e.g.*, Griswold v. Connecticut, 381 U.S. 479, 484–85 (1965) (declaring unconstitutional a state law prohibiting the use and distribution of contraceptives, finding the right in the First, Third, Fourth, Fifth, Ninth, Fourteenth, and "penumbras, formed by emanations from those guarantees that help give them life and substance"); Roe v. Wade, 410 U.S. 113, 152–56 (1973) (recognizing a constitutional right to abortion and grounding it in the "liberty" portion of the Due Process Clause).

chapter 6, and explain why they necessarily have very different expressions in the varied contexts to which they have been applied over time.

VI. How American Due Process Jurisprudence Fares under Traditional Rule of Law Principles

American due process jurisprudence does not map neatly onto traditional rule of law principles, but continues to be informed by them. Given the many differing definitions and manifestations of rule of law, the framework of a "thin" or "thick" rule of law is useful for evaluating the American system.[217] Again, the many contexts to which due process is applied helps to explain the thin-to-thick progression of protection within the modern doctrine and the absence of bright line rules invoked to protect evolving interests.

The American system in general and its due process jurisprudence, in particular, can be said to have a relatively "thick," robust procedural rule of law—though the thickness of these rights varies greatly with the thickness of the substantive right in question. On the procedural side, the Court has established numerous procedural requirements that protect people's rights in the civil, criminal, and administrative context. Personal jurisdiction rules limit a court's ability to unfairly force defendants to represent themselves in foreign jurisdictions and establish detailed rules on providing sufficient notice and adequate hearings.[218] Criminal procedures are closely guarded with judicial rulings that span issues like what and how evidence can be admitted and whether and how much public media can be present at a trial.[219] Courts have, administratively, established a range of procedures required before the government can discontinue employing or even providing public benefits to particular individuals.[220] In sum, these procedural guarantees protect individuals' ability to receive notice and a proper hearing before their rights are abrogated through government processes. This fulfills an important aspect of rule of law principles by ensuring citizens can properly predict and adapt to governmental decisions.

---

[217] *See* TAMANAHA, *supra* note 7, at 91.

[218] *See, e.g.*, World-Wide Volkswagen Co. v. Woodson, 444 U.S. 286 (1980) (placing limits on whether a long-arm statute had the ability to claim jurisdiction over a foreign corporation that sold an automobile in New York that was involved in an accident in Oklahoma); *In re* Murchison, 349 U.S. 133 (1955) (finding that being convicted of contempt of court by a "one-man grand jury" by the same judge that levied the accusation in the first place is a violation of due process).

[219] *See, e.g.*, Snyder v. Com. of Mass., 291 U.S. 97 (1934) (finding that the defendant was not allowed to be present when the jury was shown the scene of the crime scene was not a violation of due process and did not thwart ability to receive a fair hearing); Estes v. State of Tex., 381 U.S. 532 (1965) (determining that due process rights were violated by a highly publicized criminal trial).

[220] *See, e.g.*, Perry v. Sindermann, 408 U.S. 593 (1972) (due process rights were violated when a college fired without process a professor who had claim to "de facto" tenure); Mathews v. Eldridge, 424 U.S. 319 (1976) (proper notice and hearing required before social security disability benefits can be terminated).

Similarly, American due process jurisprudence has many elements of "thick" substantive rule of law principles given the Court's expansive reading of the substantive due process rights derived from the Fourteenth Amendment and the incorporation of the Bill of Rights. Again, however, the protection ranges from a very thin, "rational basis" level of protection in cases that involve nonfundamental rights, to a thick, "strict scrutiny" level of protection for certain fundamental rights. In particular, the Court's jurisprudence offers thicker protection to rights to privacy, reproduction, and other named fundamental rights.[221] The Court has thus ensured that majoritarian preferences, as translated through democratic processes, do not burden unduly the liberties of citizens, but has done so on a constitutional continuum that has evolved over time and is still evolving.

These procedural and substantive protections were developed in large part, however, through judicial review. This has two-fold implications for rule of law principles. First, the courts are changing laws and rules and sometimes their own jurisprudence in a way that implicates a citizen's ability to predict and adapt to the law.[222] For example, in *Hewitt v. Helms*,[223] the Court ruled that repeated and explicit mandatory language with regard to prison regulations on segregated confinement created a protected liberty interest.[224] But in *Sandin v. Connor*[225] the Court ruled that mandatory language was not a sufficient basis for creating a protected liberty interest.[226] A prisoner, relying on the first ruling, would have been dismayed to find that his or her rights were changed by the Court's subsequent ruling. Being able to predict new rules and regulations is always difficult, but a judicially driven change in rules can retroactively impact the rights of at least the individual litigants to the case in which the rule was altered.

Judicially driven changes to procedural rule of law's "predictability" element are indicative of a larger rule of law problem with the American system of due process and judicial review. A feature in many formulations of rule of law theory is a system of checks and balances that ensure a democratically accountable government.[227] Such a system can be important if for no other reason than it is an efficient method of ensuring that government actors cannot act capriciously or without some sort of external check from the populace. A very "thin" version of rule of law, for example, can be described as "rule *by* law," wherein the government passes and changes authoritarian decrees, but does so through formally adopted laws.[228] There is still some semblance of a procedural rule of law, but the difference

---

[221] *See supra* notes 206–10.

[222] *See, e.g.*, John Harrison, *Substantive Due Process and the Constitutional Text*, 83 VA. L. REV. 493 (1997) (arguing that substantive due process jurisprudence is unmoored from the text of the Constitution).

[223] 459 U.S. 460 (1983).

[224] *Id.* at 471–72.

[225] 515 U.S. 472 (1995).

[226] *Id.* at 480–84.

[227] *See* TAMANAHA, *supra* note 7, at 99–101.

[228] *See id.* at 92–93.

between such a regime and a totalitarian government might be merely academic. A "thicker" version of rule of law requires some sort of democratic check on the formulation of laws.

While America fulfills this requirement, the Court's ability to strike down and sometimes unilaterally create new policy through judicial review and due process jurisprudence stands in stark contrast to this democratic requirement.[229] Moreover, unlike the rationale set forth for judicial review in *Marbury v. Madison*,[230] due process jurisprudence is not based explicitly on specific terms of a written Constitution, but instead on evolving authority such as social mores, conceptions of morality, and shifts in legal rules. Putting aside political checks on the judiciary—such as the nomination process, impeachment, or jurisdiction-stripping powers of Congress—this unelected institution has power over law that can produce an obvious potential conflict with the rule of law principle.[231] Yet this inherent tension between judicially-regulated notions of due process and democratic notions of a rule of law was almost exactly what the founders had in mind.[232]

This undemocratic aspect of due process was thus a "necessary evil," not just for American democracy but for rule of law theory in general.[233] The more democratic a nation is, the less formal the barriers become between majoritarian desires and individual rights protection. The creation of constitutional rights and the empowerment of a branch designed to protect them is an important step in protecting the procedural and substantive rights of citizens, even as it limits citizens' and elected officials' ability to create policy. The Court's decisions on procedural and substantive due process questions demonstrate sensitivity to this tension. When ruling on procedural issues, for example, the Court will typically determine whether the procedures designed adequately protect the interest of the individual given the

---

[229] *See generally* Robert Bork, *Neutral Principles and Some First Amendment Problems*, 47 Ind. L.J. 1 (1971) (expounding that when judges fail to adhere closely to the text and history of the Constitution rights are arbitrarily constructed based on the whims and moralities of those on the bench); Hans A. Linde, *Judges, Critics, and the Realist Tradition*, 82 Yale L.J. 227 (1972).

[230] 5 U.S. 137 (1803).

[231] Justice Black indicated his disquiet with the democratic implications of the courts due process jurisprudence when he wrote "that the 'natural law' formula which the Court uses to reach its conclusion in this case should be abandoned as an incongruous excrescence on our Constitution. I believe that formula to be itself a violation of our Constitution, in that it subtly conveys to courts, at the expense of legislatures, ultimate power over public policies in fields where no specific provision of the Constitution limits legislative power." Adamson v. California, 332 U.S. 46, 75 (1947) (Black, J., dissenting); *see also* Pacific Mutual Life Insurance Co., 499 U.S. 1, 35–36 (1991) (Scalia, J., dissenting).

[232] *See, e.g.*, The Federalist No. 78 (Alexander Hamilton) ("Limitations of this kind can be preserved in practice no other way than through the medium of courts of justice, whose duty it must be to declare all acts contrary to the manifest tenor of the Constitution void. Without this, all the reservations of particular rights or privileges would amount to nothing."). *But see* McDowell, *supra* note 72, at 414–20 (discussing the anti-federalist and other founders' opposition to a powerful and independent judiciary and to the use of natural law as a check against the legislature in particular).

[233] *See* Allan C. Hutchinson & Patrick Monahan, *Democracy and the Rule of Law*, *in* The Rule of Law: Ideal of Ideology, *supra* note 6, at 97–99.

countervailing interests of the government and using current social norms and a prudential cost-benefit analysis as a kind of weighing mechanism.

Although it may find some democratically enacted legislation inadequate, the Court usually does so through a balancing of the interests at stake. The challenging issue for modern courts is to maintain this balance, in an increasingly partisan atmosphere, while dealing with cases that are increasingly complex. The rule of law may be advanced in some respects, due to the procedural protections and fundamental rights established by the Court, but the higher question of democratically enacted law and community-based morality may suffer as a result. More importantly, America's moderately "thick," or robust form of rule of law as related to due process jurisprudence is heavily dependent on the changing composition of a principled but nonetheless human, and hence imperfect, institution.

VII. Conclusion

The rule of law stands for the idea that laws, not individuals, should govern behavior and that they should do so in a fair and just manner. This implies both that certain governmental structures, institutions, and procedures are necessary to protect against arbitrary action, and that some laws are by their nature just or unjust. The entire structure of the American government, including the independent judiciary, is a consequence of these principles.

More specifically, American due process jurisprudence owes an intellectual debt to rule of law concepts that date back to the ancient Greeks but more directly to England, through the Magna Carta. The American version of the rule of law, as manifested in the due process, departed from its English antecedents in several ways, but the most important difference is that American courts are allowed to check legislation. Due process also has evolved to embrace substantive rights and not just to check judicial procedures. The sources of authority for the law of the land evolved differently in English and American governmental structures and jurisprudence, as the founders of the United States Constitution struggled to incorporate a balance of federal and state power that could be wielded without obliterating the rights of individual citizens. These balances and tensions obviously continue today, and are unlikely to disappear as long as the constitutional commitment to liberal democratic principles endures.

In the following chapters, we analyze the architecture of modern due process in greater detail. We begin with an overview of the basic division between procedural and substantive notions of due process, and the rights that fall under each category. We then elaborate on the protections offered under each, and the debates about the proper scope and content of due process—especially substantive due process. We note, however, that the division between "procedure" and "substance" is a hazy one, and offer examples of rights that are better described as hybrids than as either pure procedural or substantive rights per se. And again, we recognize that procedural rights are never defined independently of the substantive interests being burdened. The weightier the latter interests become, the more elaborate the former rights often become as well.

We conclude with a discussion of whether these disparate strands of modern due process share common features that might be described as core due process values. We conclude that such common features exist, though they are quite general and are given varying weight across due process contexts and across time. We discuss the future of these due process fundamentals in light of the current call to "original intent" and tradition as the anchors of constitutional rights. In our view, the long and distinguished history of due process *in practice* clearly demonstrates that the actual judicial approach to due process has been evolutionary, as courts have applied the enduring basic due process values to a changing human landscape. That case law, we maintain, will remain the most important piece of the due process "furniture," even as it is influenced by scholarly critiques, new historical insights, sociopolitical events, economic and technological developments, and evolving notions of fair play and substantial justice. Consequently, our primary focus here is on the post-bellum, evolutionary case law that has most powerfully defined the content of modern due process.

Finally, we commend the Court's evolutionary approach to due process on normative and practical grounds. Only a "living" Constitution can address the due process needs of an ever-evolving nation. Individual liberty and procedural fairness should remain the baseline due process concerns, but they should continue to morph as new insights, new technologies, and new global and domestic threats to liberty or complements to basic notions of liberty emerge. Tradition should continue to be a starting point, but not the end point, of our constitutional thinking.

As we evolve, the long arc of due process should evolve as well, and bend to meet the needs of rising generations. Indeed, the framers of both of the due process clauses—eighteenth century and nineteenth century—were visionary reformers who believed in fundamental liberties but also in the importance of thinking anew. Thus the most important question is not whether our courts should embrace change as they contemplate the future of due process, but how to best assure that the judges and other legal actors will embrace wise changes going forward. We turn now to their work thus far, with particular emphasis on the work of the United States Supreme Court during the late nineteenth century to the present moment.

{2}

The Primary Divide: Procedural versus Substantive Due Process

The constitutional guarantee against a deprivation "of life, liberty, or property, without due process of law," as provided in the Due Process Clauses of the Fifth and Fourteenth Amendments,[1] has evolved into a complex and important principle in American constitutional law, despite the relatively little space the language occupies in comparison to the entire constitutional text. Today, "due process" has come to be understood as ensuring both procedural and substantive protections.[2] Yet despite the common origin of procedural due process and substantive due process, and despite their analytical interdependence, the two strands have developed into fairly distinct doctrines.

In this chapter, we first introduce the doctrinal history of the two strands and provide a preliminary overview of their current content. We then describe the various interests that trigger the procedural due process protections. In chapter 3, we elaborate on the content of procedural rights—i.e., what process is due when the constitutional right is triggered? In chapter 4, we elaborate on the most controversial aspects of due process—i.e., what "liberties" does substantive due process protect, and how have these been justified?

I. Procedural Due Process Doctrinal Roots

The doctrinal evolution of procedural due process follows a pattern that largely mirrors changes in American society as a whole. Initially, the Court deployed a

---

[1] Note that the Due Process Clauses of the Fifth and Fourteenth Amendments have been read as providing the same protections, and thus, representing the same principles. *See* Hurtado v. California, 110 U.S. 516, 534–35 (1884) ("[W]hen the same phrase was employed in the fourteenth amendment to restrain the action of the states, it was used in the same sense and with no greater extent" than when the same language was used in the Fifth Amendment); *see also* Frank H. Easterbrook, *Substance and Due Process*, 1982 Sup. Ct. Rev. 85, 102 (explaining that the Due Process Clauses of the Fifth and Fourteenth Amendment have the same meaning).

[2] *See,* e.g., Rhonda Wasserman, Procedural Due Process: A Reference Guide to the United States Constitution 1 (Jack Stark ed., 2004) ("These Due Process Clauses [of the Fifth and Fourteenth Amendments] afford both substantive and procedural protections.").

rigid approach that was almost entirely retrospective. As American society evolved, however, so did the Court's notions of what life, liberty, and property mean, and accordingly, what process is due in a given situation.[3] Thus the rigid approach to determining what interests warrant due process protection[4] eventually was replaced by a more flexible approach to determining what qualifies for the protections of due process and what protections due process provides.[5] Just as American legal society, at large, faced challenges in applying established legal frameworks to a society that looked incredibly different from that in which the frameworks were originally conceived, so too the Court faced challenges in applying due process principles.

The rise of industrialization, the transformation of methods of commerce and transportation, other developments in science and technology, and changing political and social norms all altered the nature of government regulation in ways that had direct relevance to due process principles. Political and social movements also affected the ways in which legal actors understood the nature of constitutional rights and rights bearers, including the rights embraced by due process and the individuals to which it extended. Indeed, how due process doctrine evolved after the ratification of the Fourteenth Amendment in 1868 provides considerable insight into both the Court's general intellectual transformation during the late nineteenth and the twentieth centuries and into the transformation of American society as a whole during these eras of profound national political and social reconstruction. The due process story both reflects and helped to shape these greatly altered external social, economic, cultural, and political circumstances—perhaps especially in its shift away from legal formalism to legal pragmatism as a means of coping with the rapidly changing legal and governmental landscape.

One thing remained a constant throughout the many reformulations and expansions of the meaning of constitutional due process: at a minimum, constitutional due process is about *procedural* protection from arbitrary government action, *as it affects important individual interests*.[6] The primary interpretive conundrums—then and now—centered on determining what interests trigger these procedural

---

[3] *See generally* chapter 2(c) *infra* for a complete discussion of how the definition of protected interests has changed over time and chapter 3 *infra* for a complete discussion of how determinations of what process is due in a given context have changed.

[4] *See*, e.g., WASSERMAN, *supra* note 2, at 34 (discussing how by the 1960s American society provided the impetus for reassessing the rigid right-privilege approach to defining protected property interests; the major societal factors were the Civil Rights movement and the "Great Society governmental programs" of the 1960s, which gave the Court a chance to revisit its precedent involving the definition of protected interests).

[5] *See* chapter 2(c), *infra* for a discussion of the progression of cases leading to the Court's adoption of a more flexible approach to defining protected interests.

[6] *See, e.g.*, Martin A. Schwartz, *Section 1983 Litigation Claims and Defenses*, § 3.05, (Aspen Publishers, 2011) ("The Due Process Clause also guarantees individuals certain substantive protections. Although the language of the Due Process Clause literally imposes only procedural ('process') obligations upon government, it is settled that the Due Process Clause also imposes substantive restraints against governmental action.")

protections, defining what satisfies the requirement of "procedural protections" in a given context,[7] and resolving whether there also is a substantive component to due process that restricts government regulatory power.

The Court's post-bellum procedural due process jurisprudence centered on the first two issues: identifying these protected interests and defining what process is due in a given situation.[8] What emerged is a bifurcated framework for analyzing procedural due process cases that follows a two-step approach, asking first whether there has been a deprivation by a state actor of a protected interest,[9] and then turning to the question of what procedures due process requires under the circumstances.[10]

Initially, the Court defined the protected interests under procedural due process by determining the importance of the interest at issue. It did not attempt to categorize the interest as an interest in "life, liberty, or property" per se.[11] By the late twentieth century, it took an important turn when it began to categorize interests as "life, liberty, or property," and focused more particularly on the *nature* of the interest at issue instead of its importance.[12]

LIFE AS TRIGGERING INTEREST FOR PROCEDURAL PROTECTIONS

Procedural due process cases have centered mostly on "liberty" and "property" interests. The Court only occasionally has addressed the life interest directly in its due process jurisprudence.[13] The likely reason for the dearth of cases that address the life interest is that the importance of a life interest of a living individual is self-evident.[14]

---

[7] *See generally* chapters 2(III) and 3 *infra,* discussing procedural due process in-depth and focusing respectively on how interests warranting due process protection are defined and how adequate procedures in a given context are determined.

[8] *See* chapters 2(III) and 3 *infra* for an in-depth discussion of how the Court's approach to procedural due process has largely been focused on both defining interests warranting procedural due process protection and in determining the procedures that due process requires in a given context.

[9] *See* WASSERMAN, *supra* note 2, at 63 (explaining that before considering the question of what process is due, first "it ... [must be] determined that a protected interest in life, liberty or property is implicated.").

[10] *See, e.g., id.* at 31, 63 (explaining that after the determination that a protected interest exists the next inquiry concerns the procedures required to sufficiently protect the interest).

[11] *See* WASSERMAN, *supra* note 2, at 31 (citing to cases employing this "unitary concept").

[12] *Id.*

[13] *Id.* (stating that the Court has focused more on defining property and liberty interests than life interests); *see generally* chapter 2(III) *infra*, which outlines the Court's jurisprudence regarding each of the protected interests and illustrates by a relatively short discussion of life interests in comparison to property and liberty interests, where the Court has devoted much of its precedent.

[14] Ohio Adult Parole Auth. v. Woodard, 523 U.S. 272, 291 (1998) (Stevens, J., dissenting) ("When we are evaluating claims that the State has unfairly deprived someone of liberty or property, it is appropriate first to ask whether the state action adversely affected any constitutionally protected interest. Thus, we may conclude, for example, that a prisoner has no 'liberty interest' in the place where he is confined, or that an at-will employee has no 'property interest' in his job. There is, however, no room for legitimate debate about whether a living person has a constitutionally protected interest in life. He obviously does.") (internal citations omitted).

When government policies or practices literally end a human life, procedural concerns are the most profound and the procedural protections are the most elaborate. The high-water mark for procedural protection therefore is triggered in cases that involve capital punishment.[15] Yet the life interest also figures prominently in cases involving reproductive rights,[16] and the so-called right to die.[17] The primary focus in these cases, however, has been less on the proper procedures for burdening or terminating the applicable interests than in defining which interests that government may not burden without substantial justification, even through proper

[15] Gardner v. Florida, 430 U.S. 349, 351 (1977) ("Petitioner was convicted of first-degree murder and sentenced to death. When the trial judge imposed the death sentence he stated that he was relying in part on information in a presentence investigation report. Portions of the report were not disclosed to counsel for the parties. Without reviewing the confidential portion of the presentence report, the Supreme Court of Florida, over the dissent of two justices, affirmed the death sentence. We conclude that this procedure does not satisfy the constitutional command that no person shall be deprived of life without due process of law.") (internal citation omitted); *see also* WASSERMAN, *supra* note 2, at 32 ("Although the Court has developed much of its capital punishment jurisprudence under the Eighth Amendment ban on cruel and unusual punishment, it has also invoked the Due Process Clause, proceeding on the often unstated assumption that the defendant's interest in avoiding the death penalty is a protected life interest.") (footnotes omitted); *see also* chapter 2(c), *infra*, for a more in-depth discussion of the life interest as well as a discussion of cases finding a life interest.

[16] Roe v. Wade, 410 U.S. 113, 162–63 (1973) ("In view of all this, we do not agree that, by adopting one theory of life, Texas may override the rights of the pregnant woman that are at stake. We repeat, however, that the State does have an important and legitimate interest in preserving and protecting the health of the pregnant woman, whether she be a resident of the State or a nonresident who seeks medical consultation and treatment there, and that it has still *another* important and legitimate interest in protecting the potentiality of human life. These interests are separate and distinct. Each grows in substantiality as the woman approaches term and, at a point during pregnancy, each becomes 'compelling.'"); Planned Parenthood v. Casey, 505 U.S. 833, 876 (1992) (facing a Pennsylvania abortion statute that had various requirements, including informed consent and a mandatory 24-hour waiting period, as well as others) (holding that "[t]he very notion that the State has a substantial interest in potential life leads to the conclusion that not all regulations must be deemed unwarranted. Not all burdens on the right to decide whether to terminate a pregnancy will be undue. In our view, the undue burden standard is the appropriate means of reconciling the State's interest with the woman's constitutionally protected liberty."); *see* WASSERMAN, *supra* note 2, at 32 ("The Court has occasionally considered whether a protected life interest exists beyond the capital punishment setting. In the abortion context, for example, the Court has rejected the view that a fetus is a person who may not be deprived of life without due process of law."); *see also* chapter 4 *infra* for a discussion of the life interest in the abortion setting.

[17] *See* Cruzan v. Dir. Mo. Dep't of Health, 497 U.S. 261, 262 (1990) ("The choice between life and death is a deeply personal decision of obvious and overwhelming finality. We believe Missouri may legitimately seek to safeguard the personal element of this choice through the imposition of heightened evidentiary requirements. It cannot be disputed that the Due Process Clause protects an interest in life as well as an interest in refusing life-sustaining medical treatment.") (footnotes omitted); *see also* Washington v. Glucksburg, 521 U.S. 702, 728 (1997) ("[O]ur decisions lead us to conclude that the asserted "right" to assistance in committing suicide is not a fundamental liberty interest protected by the Due Process Clause. The Constitution also requires, however, that Washington's assisted-suicide ban be rationally related to legitimate government interests.") (footnotes omitted); *see also* WASSERMAN, *supra* note 2, at 32 ("In the context of a 'right to die' case, the Court stated that 'the Due Process Clause protects an interest in life as well as an interest in refusing life-sustaining medical treatment' and it recognized an 'unqualified [state] interest in the preservation of human life to be weighed against the constitutionally protected interests of the individual. . . .'").

procedures.[18] Again, the due process cases raise two sets of concerns: what *process* is due when government regulates various interests, and what interests trigger *substantive* limits on government regulatory power that go beyond assuring that government processes are fair and reasonable. In these "substantive due process" determinations, the boundaries of what constitutes a "life" interest under due process have been affected by advances in medical technology—among other developments—which influence the constitutional debates about when a fetus becomes a juridical "person" for purposes of the Fourteenth Amendment, or when the meaningful "life" of a terminally ill person in a persistent vegetative state has ended.[19]

PROPERTY AS TRIGGERING INTEREST FOR PROCEDURAL RIGHTS

Early cases employed a distinction between rights and privileges as a tool for classifying protected property interests. Only rights were entitled to the protections of procedural due process.[20] Thus, privileges that were created generally by statute or agency rule, "such as a government jobs or benefits[,]" were not entitled to the protection of due process.[21] Through the application of this distinction, due process was found to apply only to a relatively small subset of cases.[22] Due to the limited scope of procedural due process under this rigid framework, the doctrine, during this time, was advanced through other avenues.[23]

Later, a changing society provided the impetus for abandoning the rigidity of the right-privilege distinction in favor of a more encompassing, flexible approach. This flexible approach largely was demanded by the denial of procedural due process protection to the recipients of government benefits created by statute.[24]

---

[18] *See supra* notes 13–17 and accompanying text; *see also* chapter 4 *infra* for a deeper discussion of the "life" cases.

[19] *See generally* Roe v. Wade, 410 U.S. 113, 159–63 (1973) (discussing the differing scientific opinions as to at what point life definitively starts) ("Substantial problems for precise definition of this view are posed, however, by new embryological data that purport to indicate that conception is a 'process' over time, rather than an event, and by new medical techniques such as menstrual extraction, the 'morning-after' pill, implantation of embryos, artificial insemination, and even artificial wombs."). The Court, thus, outlined how advancing medical technologies can complicate the process of defining life interests. Although not mentioned by the *Roe* court, one can see how advancing medical technologies that prolong life, for example, life support mechanisms, can cause difficulty in the defining of life interests because the technologies blur the traditional lines of life and death. See chapter 4.

[20] *See, e.g.*, Richard J. Pierce, *The Due Process Counterrevolution of the 1990s?*, 96 COLUM. L. REV. 1973, 1974 (1996).

[21] *Id.*

[22] *Id.*

[23] *See* William W. Van Alstyne, *The Demise of the Right-Privilege Distinction in Constitutional Law*, 81 HARV. L. REV. 1439, 1445–46 (1968) (outlining the applicability of different doctrines for avoiding the right-privilege distinction including: "[t]he doctrine of unconstitutional conditions," procedural due process, equal protection, and bills of attainder).

[24] *See, e.g.*, Pierce, *supra* note 20, at 1974 ("Prior to 1970, due process applied only to a narrow class of cases in which the government sought to deprive an individual of a 'right' on the basis of a set of contested

Statutory benefits, however, were deemed "new property" by Professor Charles Reich, who is credited with providing the intellectual impetus for the dismissal of the rigid right-privilege distinction.[25] Following Professor Reich's lead, the Court changed its definition of protected property interests between 1970 and 1972, in what is known as "the due process revolution."[26]

As we will see, the results of the "due process revolution" included protections for interests formally dismissed as mere privileges, including statutorily created benefits.[27] In ruling that "new property" interests warrant procedural due process protection, the Court cited to Professor Reich's seminal articles for its reasoning that the government provides many statutory entitlements that have become essential parts of society, and accordingly, these entitlements no longer can be regarded as "gratuity;" they must be considered property interests.[28]

After this initial recognition of protection as a property interest for what was formerly regarded as mere "privilege," the protected property interest was expanded still further. The protected interests first recognized were those most closely related to an individual's ability to earn a living, followed subsequently by other types of interests.[29] After the due process revolution began to expand the protected property interests, the Court officially rejected the right-privilege distinction as the method for determining whether a given interest was a protected property interest.[30] Subsequent attempts to limit the expanded property

---

facts unique to the individual. Rights were defined narrowly to include only forms of property that are usually the fruits of an individual's labor, such as money, a house, or a license to practice law, as well as forms of liberty recognized in the Bill of Rights. An individual threatened with a deprivation of a 'right' was entitled to 'some kind of hearing.' Due process did not apply at all to mere 'privileges,' such as a government job or benefits made available pursuant to a statute or an agency rule .... [which led directly to Professor] Reich['s] ... impassioned plea for judicial recognition of what he called the 'new property,' benefits provided by the government pursuant to statutes and regulations.") (footnotes omitted).

[25] *See id.* ("Yale law professor Charles Reich can be credited with intellectual paternity for the due process revolution. In two highly influential articles published in the Yale Law Journal in 1964 and 1965, Reich made an impassioned plea for judicial recognition of what he called the 'new property,' benefits provided by the government pursuant to statutes and regulations.").

[26] *Id.* at 1973. Notably, the Court did not independently conceive of the "due process revolution." Rather, "When the Court recognized the 'new property,' it did not even bother to provide an independent explanation for its conclusion that government benefits were entitled to recognition as property rights. It simply cited and paraphrased Reich's articles to support this revolutionary change in constitutional law doctrine." *Id.* at 1974 (footnotes omitted).

[27] *Id.* at 1980.

[28] Goldberg v. Kelly, 397 U.S. 254, 262, 279 n.8 (1970); *see also id.* at 1974.

[29] WASSERMAN, *supra* note 2, at 33.

[30] The Court in *Roth* rejected the right-privileges distinction saying that it "fully and finally rejected the wooden distinction between 'rights' and 'privileges.'" Bd. of Regents of State Colls. v. Roth, 408 U.S. 564, 570–71 (1972); *see also* Rodney A. Smolla, *The Reemergence of The Right-Privilege Distinction in Constitutional Law: The Price of Protesting Too Much*, 35 STAN. L. REV. 69, 73 (1982) (citing to the *Roth* language rejecting the right-privilege distinction).

concept failed to exclude "new property" from protection.[31] Nevertheless, the "new property" concept faced additional challenges, including the expanding administrative state.[32]

LIBERTY AS TRIGGERING INTEREST FOR PROCEDURAL RIGHTS

Defining the "liberty" interest that will trigger procedural due process rights has been the most complicated interpretation issue of all. Again, it is important to distinguish between the two strands of due process interests. There are liberty interests that trigger *procedural* protection under due process, and liberty interests that are *substantive,* and restrict government regulatory power.[33] That protected liberty interests of either type can be deprived only through the application of adequate procedures[34] has been widely accepted.[35] That there are constitutionally protected liberty interests that also constrain state and federal government *regulatory* power, versus merely trigger adequate *procedural* protections when the government burdens them, has been far more contentious.[36] We develop this latter, more complex aspect of liberty in chapter 4. Our focus here is on when "life, liberty and property" interests trigger *procedural* protection, though the relevant case law on substantive and procedural dimensions of liberty overlap. As we will explain, the government-created liberty interests that trigger procedural due process may exist even when federal constitutional law does not itself create

---

[31] In a notable attempt to limit the applicability of the protected property interest, Justice Rehnquist adopted "the bitter with the sweet" theory that held "that where the grant of a substantive right [via statute] is inextricably intertwined with the limitations on the procedures which are to be employed in determining that right, a litigant in the position of appellee must take the bitter with the sweet." Arnett v. Kennedy, 416 U.S. 134, 153–54 (1974); *see* also Pierce, *supra* note 20, at 1986.

[32] Edward L. Rubin, *Due Process and the Administrative State*, 72 CAL. L. REV. 1044, 1082 (1984) ("The procedural due process cases of the post-*Roth* (or perhaps the post-*Goldberg*) era, although not impressive examples of legal reasoning, generally represent serious efforts to deal with a complex legal issue: the relationship between procedural due process and the activities of an administrative state.").

[33] *See* Sandin v. Conner, 515 U.S. 472, 483–84 (1995) ("Following *Wolff*, we recognize that States may under certain circumstances create liberty interests which are protected by the Due Process Clause. But these interests will be generally limited to freedom from restraint which, while not exceeding the sentence in such an unexpected manner as to give rise to protection by the Due Process Clause of its own force ....") (internal citations omitted). S*ee generally* Meachum v. Fano, 427 U.S. 215 (1976) (discussing whether the claimed "liberty" interest originated from state law or from the Due Process Clause, answering both questions in the negative and accordingly denying Due Process Clause protection); *see also* WASSERMAN, *supra* note 2, at 41.

[34] *See* Bd. of Regents of State Colls. v. Roth, 408 U.S. 564, 569–71 (1972) ("The requirements of procedural due process apply only to the deprivation of interests encompassed by the Fourteenth Amendment's protection of liberty and property. When protected interests are implicated, the right to some kind of prior hearing is paramount .... And a weighing process has long been a part of any determination of the form of hearing required in particular situations by procedural due process. But, to determine whether due process requirements apply in the first place, we must look not to the 'weight' but to the nature of the interest at stake.") (footnotes omitted).

[35] *See* Schwartz, *supra* note 6.

[36] *See infra* note 53 and accompanying text.

that interest. These liberty interests may arise from many federal, state. and local government sources, such as regulations, statutes, and official practices. Where the United States Constitution does create a liberty interest, it also triggers procedural due process protection.

The due process revolution that overhauled the definition of protected property interests also changed the determination of what "liberty" includes as a matter of procedural due process.[37] Even before the due process revolution, however, the understanding of "liberty" encompassed much more than just being physically free.[38] Liberty was expanded to include any classification of an individual in a manner that could potentially stigmatize the person.[39] This level of protection afforded reputation represents a relatively high level of protection that has been tempered by subsequent decisions.[40] The Court, for example, retreated partially from this broad notion of liberty and recognized that an individual's reputation warranted procedural due process protection only when accompanied by a "more tangible interest."[41]

Liberty also was expanded to include protection of prisoners' procedural rights.[42] Historically, a valid criminal conviction was thought to eliminate any former liberty interests an individual possessed.[43] Subsequent cases, however, found that inmates maintain a residual liberty interest.[44] This limited interest protects only

---

[37] *See,* e.g., Pierce, *supra* note 20, at 1979 ("The Court also expanded the scope of the 'liberty' interests protected by due process dramatically in the final decisions of the due process revolution.").

[38] *See,* e.g., Charles H. Koch, Jr., *Finding a "Due Process Interest,"* 1 ADMIN. L. & PRAC. § 2:21 (3d ed. 2011) ("The liberty interest has long reached well beyond traditional restraint on freedom. Early in twentieth century, the Supreme Court observed: '[The liberty interest] denotes not merely freedom from bodily restraint but also the right of the individual to contract, to engage in any of the common occupations of life, to acquire useful knowledge, to marry, establish a home and bring up children, to worship God according to the dictates of his own conscience, and generally to enjoy those privileges long recognized ... as essential to the orderly pursuit of happiness by free men.'") (footnotes omitted); *see also* WASSERMAN, *supra* note 2, at 41.

[39] *See* Pierce, *supra* note 20, at 1979; *see also* Wisconsin v. Constantineau, 400 U.S. 433, 437 (1971) ("Where a person's good name, reputation, honor, or integrity is at stake because of what the government is doing to him, notice and an opportunity to be heard are essential.").

[40] Pierce, *supra* note 20, at 1983–84.

[41] Koch, *supra* note 38 ("The Supreme Court's subsequent opinion in Paul v. Davis signaled a retreat from *Constantineau.* The facts were similar. Paul, a chief of police, distributed a list of 'active shoplifters' with Davis' name on it. The Supreme Court held that 'reputation alone' was not a sufficient basis for a constitutionally protected liberty interest. Davis instead required that the due process claimant show harm to 'reputation plus;' that is, to 'some more tangible interest' in addition to reputation.") (footnotes omitted) (citing Paul v. Davis, 424 U.S. 693, 701 (1976)).

[42] *See, e.g.,* Wolff v. McDonnell, 418 U.S. 539, 555–58 (1974) (holding that prisoners deserve due process protection of their property and liberty, and that by granting good time credits to prisoners, the State created a statutorily created liberty interest).

[43] Ruffin v. Virginia, 62 Va. 790, 796 (1871) ("The bill of rights is a declaration of general principles to govern a society of freemen, and not of convicted felons and men civilly dead. Such men have some rights it is true, such as the law in its benignity accords to them, but not the rights of freemen. They are the slaves of the State undergoing punishment for heinous crimes committed against the laws of the land."); *see also,* e.g., WASSERMAN, *supra* note 2, at 45.

[44] Wolff v. McDonnell, 418 U.S. 539, 594 (1974) ("Every prisoner's liberty is, of course, circumscribed by the very fact of his confinement, but his interest in the limited liberty left to him is then only the more substantial."); *see also* WASSERMAN, *supra* note 2, at 45.

the fundamental aspects of liberty.[45] Despite the limited nature of the liberty interest, the Court has recognized the existence of a prisoner's protected liberty interest in some cases.[46]

We further develop the nature of "triggering interests" for procedural due process below. Before turning to this elaboration, however, we first introduce the second strand of due process: substantive due process.

II. Substantive Due Process Doctrinal Roots

The second major strand of due process is substantive due process, which refers to due process limits on government regulatory authority.[47] This approach is associated with the Court's famous decision in *Lochner v. New York*,[48] but the idea that the Due Process Clause protection encompasses certain substantive protections can be traced back much further than *Lochner*.[49] Despite this history, critics have argued[50] that the Due Process Clause only ensures that adequate procedural

---

[45] Hewitt v. Helms, 459 U.S. 460, 466 (1983) ("Prison officials have broad administrative and discretionary authority over the institutions they manage, and lawfully incarcerated persons retain only a narrow range of protected liberty interests."); *see also* WASSERMAN, *supra* note 2 at 45.

[46] *See, e.g.*, Vitek v. Jones, 445 U.S. 480, 480 (1980) ("The involuntary transfer of appellee to a mental hospital implicates a liberty interest that is protected by the Due Process Clause of the Fourteenth Amendment."); Washington v. Harper, 494 U.S. 210, 210 (1990) (holding that a mentally ill prisoner had a protected liberty interest in being free from the arbitrary administration of drugs to treat his mental illness); *see also* WASSERMAN, *supra* note 2, at 45.

[47] *See* Peter J. Rubin, *Square Pegs and Round Holes: Substantive Due Process, Procedural Due Process, and the Bill of Rights*, 103 COLUM. L. REV. 833, 847 (2003) ("Like all substantive due process rights, this right's infringement violates the Fourteenth Amendment 'regardless of the fairness of the procedures' attendant upon it.") (footnote omitted). States and the federal government alike are prevented from implementing legislation that deprives substantive due process rights. *See* chapter 4 *infra*.

[48] *See, e.g.*, Mattei Ion Radu, *Incompatible Theories: Natural Law and Substantive Due Process*, 54 VILL. L. REV. 247, 249 (2009) ("*Lochner v. New York* marked the clear beginning of the Court's foray into the oxymoronic field of substantive due process . . . .").

[49] *See* chapter 1, *supra*.

[50] *See e.g.*, James W. Ely, Jr., *The Oxymoron Reconsidered: Myth and Reality in the Origins of Substantive Due Process*, 16 CONST. COMMENT, 315, 315 (1999) ("The view that the due process clauses of the Constitution impose substantive restraints on governmental power has long been a subject of contention. It has become an article of faith in some quarters that due process pertains entirely to matters of procedure. Thus, John Hart Ely maintained: '[W]e apparently need periodic reminding that "substantive due process" is a contradiction in terms—sort of like "green pastel redness."' Other observers have also derided substantive due process as an 'oxymoron.' Similarly, Robert H. Bork considers substantive due process to be 'a momentous sham' that 'has been used countless times since by judges who want to write their personal beliefs into a document.'" (footnotes omitted); *see generally* John Harrison, *Substantive Due Process and the Constitutional Text*, 83 VA. L. REV. 493 (1997) (discussing in great detail the possible textual and historical justifications for substantive due process and finding no satisfactory link). Harrison concluded that reference to the text "may seem misconceived in connection with a doctrine that these days usually rests on the claim that the language is vague and open-ended, when it rests on any claim about the language at all. Dismissal of the text, however, cannot be completely satisfying as long as it is a criticism of a doctrine to say that it has no *Marbury*, as that case rests on the notion that judicial review is based on the Constitution. Whatever one's conclusion may be in the end, in the beginning there is the word." *Id.* at 558.

guidelines are followed when government burdens constitutionally protected liberties.[51] Two other major criticisms of substantive due process, particular to the fundamental rights strand, include federalism concerns[52] and separation of powers.[53] Finally, some observers criticize the Constitution itself for protecting individuals' procedural rights while largely leaving substantive rights unprotected.[54]

Yet the theoretical and textual arguments against infusing due process with substantive content have not prevailed. Instead, the due process clauses have been construed to embrace powerful substantive protections that have endured over time.

An important precondition to the development of substantive due process occurred in 1872, when the Court held that the Privileges or Immunities Clause should be read very narrowly, thus excluding coverage of substantive rights.[55] This narrow reading of what some regard as the more plausible Fourteenth Amendment home for substantive rights has faced stiff opposition,[56] but still applies today.[57]

---

[51] *See, e.g.*, Albright v. Oliver, 510 U.S. 266, 275 (1994) (Scalia, J., concurring) ("I reject the proposition that the Due Process Clause guarantees certain (unspecified) liberties, rather than merely guarantees certain procedures as a prerequisite to deprivation of liberty.").

[52] *See* Rubin, *supra* note 47, at 837–38 ("The history of the *Lochner* era, and two well-placed concerns about the doctrine ensure that judicial invocation of substantive due process remains a less-than-comfortable process. The first is a concern about the legitimacy of judicial invalidation of democratically-enacted legislation, a concern that may appear to be at its zenith when the Court is called upon to interpret broad language with only limited intermediate premises upon which to rely.") (footnotes omitted).

[53] *Id.* ("The second [concern] is a concern about the risk that, in interpreting broad language, the Court's Members will impose their own personal preferences instead of engaging in the proper judicial role of determining the meaning of that language through the accepted process of judicial analysis. Yet while the Court's opinions show reluctance to recognize 'new' substantive due process rights, its decisions do also describe a continuing expansion under the substantive due process heading of autonomy- or personhood-related rights.") (footnotes omitted).

[54] John Paul Stevens, *Our "Broken System" of Criminal Justice*, N.Y. Rev. Books, Nov. 10, 2011, at 413 (reviewing William J. Stuntz, The Collapse of American Criminal Justice (2011)) (describing Stuntz as "believ[ing] that our Constitution overprotects procedural rights and underprotects substantive rights."). We address the many critiques of substantive due process in chapter 4.

[55] *Slaughter-House Cases*, 83 U.S. 36, 77–81 (1872) ("[The Privileges and Immunities clause] sole purpose was to declare to the several States, that whatever those rights, as you grant or establish them to your own citizens, or as you limit or qualify, or impose restrictions on their exercise, the same, neither more nor less, shall be the measure of the rights of citizens of other States within your jurisdiction.").

[56] *See, e.g.*, McDonald v. City of Chicago, 130 S. Ct. 3020, 3029–30 (2010) ("Today, many legal scholars dispute the correctness of the narrow *Slaughter-House* interpretation.") (citing cases and other authorities that criticize the holding of the *Slaughter-House* cases); *see also* William J. Rich, *Taking "Privileges Or Immunities" Seriously: A Call To Expand The Constitutional Canon*, 87 Minn. L. Rev. 153, 154 (2002) ("dissenting Justices and critical scholars have ridiculed the Court's majority for rendering the Clause 'superfluous and redundant' and merely reinforcing a Supremacy Clause that had no need for additional support. In often cited dissents, Justice Field accused the Court of turning the Clause into a 'vain and idle enactment, which accomplished nothing,' and Justice Swayne argued that the majority had 'turn[ed] … what was meant for bread into a stone.' William Crosskey agreed, labeling judicial interpretation of the clause 'completely nugatory and useless.' Charles Black blamed the Supreme Court for 'annihilat[ing]' the Clause and transforming it into a 'cost-free blown kiss.' Robert Bork compared the Clause to a provision 'written in Sanskrit' or 'obliterated past deciphering by an ink blot.'") (footnotes omitted).

[57] *See, e.g.*, Rich, *supra* note 56, at 154 ("Today, almost everyone agrees that the Privileges or Immunities Clause in the Fourteenth Amendment, as authoritatively construed, belongs on the insignificant list."); *see also McDonald*, 130 S.Ct. at 3030–31 (2010) (reaffirming the *Slaughter-House* holding).

The Court thus either had to look beyond the Privileges or Immunities Clause, or overrule its earlier narrow reading of that clause, if it wished to anchor substantive rights in the Fourteenth Amendment. It chose to do the former, and the Due Process Clause became that constitutional anchor.[58]

As we explain more fully in chapter 4, the development of substantive due process case law, in turn, produced three subcategories of rights. The first subcategory included "non-fundamental" rights that trigger low-level, rational basis judicial review.[59] The second covered unenumerated substantive rights that the Court identified as fundamental, which trigger elevated judicial scrutiny.[60] The final subcategory included enumerated fundamental rights that the Court derived selectively from the Bill of Rights.[61] All of these categories of substantive due process trigger procedural due process protection.

Socioeconomic rights today fall into the first category of "non-fundamental rights," but they began on a much higher perch. The Court in *Lochner v. New York*[62] held that liberty included the "right to contract."[63] Thus, it struck down a New York law that regulated the hours of bakers,[64] on the theory that there are no reasonable grounds to interfere with the right of the employee to contract with an employer.[65] *Lochner* went to one end of the due process spectrum, drastically limiting government involvement in redistributing resources and regulating economic activity.[66] The other major development from *Lochner* was the elevated scrutiny given to the relationship between the ends invoked by the state and the means the state

[58] *See McDonald*, 130 S.Ct. at 3030–31 ("For many decades, the question of the rights protected by the Fourteenth Amendment against state infringement has been analyzed under the Due Process Clause of that Amendment and not under the Privileges or Immunities Clause. We therefore decline to disturb the *Slaughter-House* holding.").

[59] *See, e.g.*, Washington v. Glucksberg, 521 U.S. 702, 767 n.9 (1997) ("Justice Harlan thus recognized just what the Court today assumes, that by insisting on a threshold requirement that the interest (or, as the Court puts it, the right) be fundamental before anything more than rational basis justification is required, the Court ensures that not every case will require the 'complex balancing' that heightened scrutiny entails.").

[60] *See, e.g., id.* at 719–20 ("The Due Process Clause guarantees more than fair process, and the "liberty" it protects includes more than the absence of physical restraint.... The Clause also provides heightened protection against government interference with certain fundamental rights and liberty interests.") (internal citations omitted).

[61] *See, e.g.*, Rubin, *supra* note 47, at 835 (describing the incorporation of Bill of Rights provisions as a "subspecies of substantive due process.").

[62] 198 U.S. 45 (1905).

[63] *See id.* at 53 ("The general right to make a contract in relation to his business is part of the liberty of the individual protected by the 14th Amendment of the Federal Constitution."). *See* chapter 4, *infra* for an elaboration of socioeconomic liberty.

[64] 198 U.S. at 45–52.

[65] *Id.* at 57 ("The question whether this act is valid as a labor law, pure and simple, may be dismissed in a few words. There is no reasonable ground for interfering with the liberty of person or the right of free contract, by determining the hours of labor, in the occupation of a baker.").

[66] *See* Cass. R. Sunstein, *Lochner's Legacy*, 87 Colum. L. Rev. 873, 877 (1987) (noting the effects of the *Lochner* decision as "[ruling out] most forms of redistribution and paternalism.").

used to achieve its stated ends.[67] In dissent, Justice Holmes argued that due process requires only that "a rational and fair man necessarily would admit that the statute proposed would infringe fundamental principles as they have been understood by the traditions of our people and our law."[68] His due process test was a low threshold for states to surmount, and offered greater leeway for state and federal government experimentation in addressing the perceived social and economic problems.[69]

The Court eventually retreated from the *Lochner*'s judicial close scrutiny of socioeconomic legislation in favor of Holmes's rational basis review.[70] *Lochner* was overruled,[71] and the case today stands as an example of a laissez-faire Court attempting to protect as many liberties as possible from government interference. The official end to *Lochner* came in 1937, when the Court retreated from its strongly libertarian approach to socioeconomic rights, and stated that liberty in this realm must be thought of in its broader social context, and required only a reasonable

---

[67] *Lochner*, 198 U.S. at 57 ("Viewed in the light of a purely labor law, with no reference whatever to the question of health, we think that a law like the one before us involves neither the safety, the morals, nor the welfare, of the public, and that the interest of the public is not in the slightest degree affected by such an act. The law must be upheld, if at all, as a law pertaining to the health of the individual engaged in the occupation of a baker. It does not affect any other portion of the public than those who are engaged in that occupation. Clean and wholesome bread does not depend upon whether the baker works but ten hours per day or only sixty hours a week. The limitation of the hours of labor does not come within the police power on that ground."); *see also* E. THOMAS SULLIVAN & RICHARD S. FRASE, PROPORTIONALITY PRINCIPLES IN AMERICAN LAW 61–63 (2009) ("Under *Lochner v. New York*, the Court showed little or no deference to the states' political and economic judgment. Economic and social laws were overturned on the finding that they were not reasonably related to the declared end. The principle of rational relation of regulatory means to the desire objectives proclaimed in *Lochner* bears some notion of proportionality in that it was intended to protect the freedom of individuals from government interference with their economic activity.").

[68] *Lochner*, 198 U.S. at 76 (Holmes, J., dissenting).

[69] *See generally id.* (describing the application of the rational basis test to the facts of *Lochner*) ("It does not need research to show that no such sweeping condemnation can be passed upon the statute before us. A reasonable man might think it a proper measure on the score of health. Men whom I certainly could not pronounce unreasonable would uphold it as a first instalment of a general regulation of the hours of work. Whether in the latter aspect it would be open to the charge of inequality I think it unnecessary to discuss.").

[70] *See, e.g.*, Note, *Resurrecting Economic Rights: The Doctrine of Economic Due Process Reconsidered*, 103 HARV. L. REV. 1363, 1367 (1990) [hereinafter *Resurrecting Economic*] ("Once the Court had reconceptualized economic liberty in this fashion, it never looked back, not once striking down a law on economic due process grounds. Economic and social legislation must now survive only a rational basis test—that is, the law must bear a 'reasonable relation' to a 'legitimate purpose.'") (footnotes omitted)

[71] *But see* Sunstein, *supra* note 66, at 917–18 ("If the *Lochner* era is thought to embody less [of] an active judicial role and more particular conceptions of baseline, neutrality, and action, it has not been entirely overruled. Numerous modern decisions reflect similar understandings. Cases distinguishing between 'positive' and 'negative' rights are built on *Lochner*-like premises that take the common law as the baseline for decision. Much of the law of racial discrimination can be understood similarly, though here the baseline is the status quo rather than the common law. The constitutional attack on affirmative action, indeed the very term, suggests that the current distribution of benefits and burdens along racial lines is simply 'there.' The state action doctrine borrows heavily from common law understandings about the proper role of government. Some of first amendment doctrine, especially that involving campaign financing, is based on similar premises.").

relationship.[72] The new test required only minimal rationality, an exceedingly easy test to satisfy.[73] The Court's change of heart came at a time in history when it was becoming clear that certain socioeconomic situations may require new forms of regulation, and a rigid judicial approach would thwart innovation.[74] Today, the Court continues to subject the laws at issue to rational basis review, allowing for flexibility in a society that is continuously advancing.

The key cases under substantive due process, post-1937, thus became those in which the Court was willing to find a right to be sufficiently "fundamental" to trigger elevated judicial scrutiny. These fell into two categories: rights that were derived from specific guarantees under the original Bill of Rights and deemed to be "incorporated" into Fourteenth Amendment due process, and "unenumerated" fundamental rights derived directly from due process liberty. In developing the latter concept, the Court identified certain interests as "privacy" rights that triggered increased judicial protection for individuals.[75]

The Court's protection of so-called privacy interests through substantive due process owes an enormous intellectual debt to one law review article that has been credited as the origin of the individual privacy interests.[76] Samuel D. Warren and

---

[72] West Coast Hotel Co. v. Parrish, 300 U.S. 379, 391 (1937) ("The Constitution does not speak of freedom of contract. It speaks of liberty and prohibits the deprivation of liberty without due process of law. In prohibiting that deprivation, the Constitution does not recognize an absolute and uncontrollable liberty. Liberty in each of its phases has its history and connotation. But the liberty safeguarded is liberty in a social organization which requires the protection of law against the evils which menace the health, safety, morals, and welfare of the people. Liberty under the Constitution is thus necessarily subject to the restraints of due process, and regulation which is *reasonable in relation* to its subject and is adopted in the interests of the community is due process.") (emphasis added).

[73] *See Resurrecting Economic Rights*, *supra* note 70, at 1367 ("[The rational basis test for economic liberties] is applied 'so tolerantly that no law [is] ever likely to violate it.'") (footnotes omitted).

[74] *See*, e.g., Ely, *supra* note 50, at 315–16 (discussing how the Supreme Court changed the level of review it afforded to socioeconomic substantive due process cases following the "political triumph of the New Deal.").

[75] *See* Grisvold v. Connecticut, 381 U.S. 479, 485 (1965) ("The present case, then concerns a relationship lying within the zone of privacy created by several fundamental constitutional guarantees. And it concerns a law which, in forbidding the use of contraceptives rather than regulating their manufacture or sale, seeks to achieve its goals by means having of a maximum destructive impact upon that relationship. Such a law cannot stand in light of the familiar principle, so often applied by this Court, that a 'governmental purpose to control or prevent activities constitutionally subject to state regulation may not be achieved by means which sweep unnecessarily broadly and thereby invade the area of protected freedoms.'") *See generally* Meyer v. Nebraska, 262 U.S. 390 (1923) (striking down a law preventing the teaching of the German Language to a student who had not yet passed the eighth grade at least in part because it violated a parent's right to direct the education of their minor children); Pierce v. Society of the Sisters, 268 U.S. 510 (1925) (ruling that a state law requiring every parent or guardian send their children to public school unreasonably interfered with the liberty of parents and guardians to direct the upbringing of their children); Skinner v. Oklahoma, 316 U.S. 535, 541 (1942) (striking down an Oklahoma statute that required sterilization for criminals with three felony convictions involving moral turpitude and stating that the case dealt with "one of the basic civil rights of man," i.e., the fundamental rights of marriage and procreation).

[76] *See, e.g.*, Irwin R. Kramer, *The Birth of Privacy Law: A Century Since Warren and Brandeis*, 39 CATH. U. L. REV. 703, 703–706 (1990) ("Although the law did provide some protection for privacy before Warren and Brandeis wrote their famous article, the protection consisted of limited legal theories

Louis D. Brandeis penned this article in 1890 as young lawyers in response to their concerns about the intrusion into individual privacy by nineteenth-century journalists who employed ever-advancing technology to capture stories and images.[77] The article has become "perhaps the most influential law journal piece ever published"[78] and today is canonical.[79] It begins with the proposition "[that] the individual shall have full protection in person and in property is a principle as old as the common law; but it has been found necessary from time to time to define anew the exact nature and extent of such protection."[80] Warren and Brandeis endeavored to "consider whether the existing law affords a principle which can properly be invoked to protect the privacy of the individual; and, if it does, what the nature and extent of such protection is."[81] In their analysis of existing law, they argued that privacy was inherently protected under what seemed to be remote legal theories including intellectual property and contract laws.[82] After supporting their assertion through an analysis of precedent, the authors stated that the protection of privacy through intellectual property and contract law was "nothing more [or] less than a judicial declaration that public morality, private justice, and general convenience demand the recognition of such a rule, and that the publication under similar circumstances would be considered an intolerable abuse."[83]

---

whose shortcomings outweighed their usefulness. Rather than protecting individuals through legal doctrine specifically designed to safeguard their privacy interests, nineteenth century American courts and legislatures provided remedies for only a limited number of intrusions and left individuals with incomplete and inadequate protection."). *Contra* Diane L. Zimmerman, *Requiem For A Heavyweight: A Farewell to Warren and Brandeis's Privacy Tort*, 68 CORNELL L. REV. 291, 293 (1983) ("[O]ne can argue that the Warren-Brandeis contribution has actually had a pernicious influence on modern tort law because it created a cause of action that, however formulated, cannot coexist with constitutional protections for freedom of speech and press.").

[77] Kramer, *supra* note 76, at 703 (citing Samuel D. Warren & Louis D. Brandeis, *The Right to Privacy*, 4 HARV. L. REV. 193 (1890)).

[78] *Id.* (citing P. DIONISOPOULOS & C. DUCAT, THE RIGHT TO PRIVACY 20 (1976)). A Westlaw KeyCite search shows that *The Right to Privacy* has been cited about 3000 times at the time of this writing.

[79] Samuel D. Warren & Louis D. Brandeis, *The Right to Privacy*, 4 HARV. L. REV. 193, 210 (1890).

[80] *Id.* at 193.

[81] *Id.* at 197.

[82] *See generally id.* at 197–213 (discussing how intellectual property and contract law impliedly recognize privacy rights); *see also id.* at 213 ("We must therefore conclude that the rights, so protected, whatever their exact nature, are not rights arising from contract or from special trust, but are rights as against the world; and, as above stated, the principle which has been applied to protect these rights is in reality not the principle of private property, unless that word be used in an extended and unusual sense. The principle which protects personal writings and any other productions of the intellect or of the emotions, is the right to privacy, and the law has no new principle to formulate when it extends this protection to the personal appearance, sayings, acts, and to personal relations, domestic or otherwise."); *see also* Kramer, *supra* note 76, at 710 ("In advocating a right to be let alone, or a "right to privacy," Warren and Brandeis relied primarily on English precedents to demonstrate that courts have long protected privacy under the guise of seemingly remote legal theories. These theories were based upon the laws of intellectual property and of contract.").

[83] Kramer, *supra* note 76, at 713 (citing Warren & Brandeis, *supra note 79*, at 210).

Accordingly, the two authors advocated for direct protection of privacy through tort law, while also recognizing that the right was limited.[84]

Brandeis, of course, later became a Supreme Court Justice, and during his tenure on the Court set out in 1928 in *Olmstead v. United States*[85] a constitutional basis for the right of privacy he and Warren envisioned years earlier:

> The protection guaranteed by the (Fourth and Fifth) amendments is much broader in scope. The makers of our Constitution undertook to secure conditions favorable to the pursuit of happiness. They recognized the significance of man's spiritual nature, of his feelings and of his intellect. They knew that only a part of the pain, pleasure and satisfactions of life are to be found in material things. They sought to protect Americans in their beliefs, their thoughts, their emotions and their sensations. They conferred, as against the government, the right to be let alone—the most comprehensive of rights and the right most valued by civilized men.[86]

This development, first emanating in *The Right of Privacy* article, brought the Court to its important privacy case, *Griswold v. Connecticut*.[87] However, even before its *Griswold* decision the Court was faced with "many controversies over these penumbral rights of 'privacy and repose.'"[88] In *Public Utilities Comm'n v. Pollak*,[89] for example, the Court was faced with the question "whether ... the Constitution of the United States precludes a street railway company from receiving and amplifying radio programs through loud speakers in its passenger vehicles" when the programs were played "in a streetcar and in a bus.... operated on various lines at various hours."[90] The Court held that "[t]he liberty of each individual in a public vehicle or public place is subject to reasonable limitations in relation to the rights of others."[91] Consequently, radio programs "containing music, commercial advertising and other announcements are constitutionally permissible."[92] Recently the

---

[84] Warren & Brandeis, *supra* note 79, at 211, 213–14 ("[T]he doctrines of contract and of trust are inadequate to support the required protection, and the law of tort must be resorted to. The right of property in its widest sense, including all possession, including all rights and privileges, and hence embracing the right to an inviolate personality, affords alone that broad basis upon which the protection which the individual demands can be rested.... It remains to consider what are the limitations of this right to privacy, and what remedies may be granted for the enforcement of the right."); *see* Kramer, *supra* note 76 at 714 ("Warren and Brandeis urged courts to discard such legal fictions and to protect privacy directly by providing tort remedies for its unwarranted invasion.... While advocating both monetary and injunctive relief for violations of the right to privacy, Warren and Brandeis did not regard this right as absolute.") (footnotes omitted).

[85] 277 U.S. 438 (1928).

[86] Griswold v. Connecticut, 381 U.S. 479, 494 (1965) (Goldberg, J., concurring) (quoting Olmstead v. United States, 277 U.S. 438, 478 (1928) (Brandeis, J. dissenting)).

[87] 381 U.S. 479 (1965).

[88] *Id.* at 485 (internal citations omitted).

[89] 343 U.S. 451 (1952).

[90] *Id.* at 453–55.

[91] *Id.* at 465.

[92] *Id.* at 465–66.

Court faced a Fourth Amendment case in which it was challenged with the issue of "whether the attachment of a Global-Positioning-System (GPS) tracking device to an individual's vehicle, and subsequent use of that device to monitor the vehicle's movements on public streets, constitutes a search or seizure within the meaning of the Fourth Amendment."[93] In an argument reminiscent of the Court's holding in *Pollak*, the Government argued that "no search occurred ... since Jones had no 'reasonable expectation of privacy' in the area of the Jeep accessed by Government agents (its underbody) and in the locations of the Jeep on the public roads, which were visible to all."[94] The Court, however, deemed it unnecessary to address the Government's argument, because the case could be decided on narrower grounds.[95]

In *Griswold*, the Court had ruled that the right to privacy existed in a "penumbra" of the Bill of Rights provisions.[96] Notably, Justice Black's dissent cited *The Right of Privacy* as the origin of the concept of privacy, and stated that the majority incorrectly "appears to be exalting a phrase which Warren and Brandeis used in discussing grounds for tort relief, to the level of a constitutional rule which prevents state legislatures from passing any law deemed by this Court to interfere with 'privacy.'"[97] As we explain in chapter 4, the Court nevertheless continued on the substantive due process path and identified a wide range of important unenumerated fundamental rights that protect individuals from government interference based on this originally contested notion of privacy and substantive due process.

A less controversial category of liberty-based substantive due process includes the Bill of Rights provisions that have been "selectively incorporated" into the Fourteenth Amendment.[98] Overall, incorporation triggers less criticism for being unsupported in the constitutional text than other categories of substantive due process rights because these rights, at the least, derive from express constitutional text and historical protection—though the text in question clearly anticipated that the rights applied to the federal government and not the states.[99]

The incorporation process began in 1897, when the Court concluded that a violation of the Takings Clause of the Fifth Amendment also violated the Due

---

[93] United States v. Jones, 132 S.Ct. 945, 948 (2012).

[94] *Id.* at 950.

[95] *Id.* ("But we need not address the Government's contentions [regarding Jones' reasonable expectation of privacy in his vehicle and on public roads], because Jones's Fourth Amendment rights do not rise or fall with the *Katz* formulation. At bottom, we must 'assur[e] preservation of that degree of privacy against government that existed when the Fourth Amendment was adopted.'") (internal citations omitted).

[96] Griswold v. Connecticut, 381 U.S. 479, 484–86 (1965) ("The foregoing cases suggest that specific guarantees in the Bill of Rights have penumbras, formed by emanations from those guarantees that help give them life and substance.").

[97] *Id.* at 510 n.1 (Black, J. dissenting).

[98] *See, e.g.*, Rubin, *supra* note 47, at 862 (describing selective incorporation of certain Bill of Rights provisions as a "'subspecies' of substantive due process."). *See* chapter 4 *infra*.

[99] *See* Rubin, *supra* note 47, at 842 ("The most commonplace form of fundamental rights analysis—so commonplace that it is often treated as though it were not substantive due process at all—is the incorporation of the Bill of Rights provisions against the states.").

Process Clause of the Fourteenth Amendment.[100] The Court held that an unconstitutional taking violated fundamental principles that the Fourteenth Amendment was designed to protect.[101] The Court thus adopted a selective incorporation approach in which each right would be assessed separately.[102] The test for which rights would be incorporated initially centered on whether the right at issues was "of such a *nature*" that it would be "included in the conception of due process of law."[103] However, the Court elaborated on the standard for incorporation by adopting the question whether the right at issue was "of the very *essence* of a scheme of ordered liberty."[104] In a more recent enunciation of the incorporation standard, the Court explained that only those rights that are "fundamental to *our* scheme of ordered liberty or ... [are] 'deeply rooted in this Nation's history and tradition'" should be incorporated.[105] This standard recalls the historical right-privilege distinction that was employed in defining property interests warranting procedural due process protection,[106] as it denies the incorporation of certain Bill of Rights provisions against the states, thus protecting certain state governmental action from due process review.[107]

In both the Court's procedural and substantive due process jurisprudence, the technological and social advancements of the American society caused the Court

---

[100] *See* Chicago, Burlington & Quincy R.R. Co. v. Chicago, 166 U.S. 226, 241 (1897) ("In our opinion, a judgment of a state court, even if it be authorized by statute, whereby private property is taken for the state or under its direction for public use, without compensation made or secured to the owner, is, upon principle and authority, wanting in the due process of law required by the fourteenth amendment of the constitution of the United States, and the affirmance of such judgment by the highest court of the state is a denial by that state of a right secured to the owner by that instrument.").

[101] *Id.*

[102] *See* McDonald v. City of Chicago, 130 S. Ct. 3020, 3034 (2010) ("While Justice Black's theory was never adopted, the Court eventually moved in that direction by initiating what has been called a process of 'selective incorporation,' i.e., the Court began to hold that the Due Process Clause fully incorporates particular rights contained in the first eight Amendments. The decisions during this time abandoned three of the previously noted characteristics of the earlier period. The Court made it clear that the governing standard is not whether any 'civilized system [can] be imagined that would not accord the particular protection.' Instead, the Court inquired whether a particular Bill of Rights guarantee is fundamental to our scheme of ordered liberty and system of justice.") (citations and footnotes omitted).

[103] Twining v. New Jersey, 211 U.S. 78, 99 (1908) (emphasis added).

[104] Palko v. Connecticut, 302 U.S. 319, 325 (1937) (emphasis added).

[105] *McDonald*, 130 S. Ct. at 3036 (citations omitted).

[106] *See supra* note 24 and accompanying text; *see also* Joel Hugenburger, Note, *Redefining Property Under the Due Process Clause:* Town of Castle Rock v. Gonzales *and the Demise of the Positive Law Approach*, 47 B.C. L. REV. 773, 780 n.31 (2006) ("[The right-privilege distinction] had been famously set out by Justice Holmes in a Massachusetts case involving a policeman who challenged being fired for political activities: '[t]he petitioner may have a constitutional right to talk politics, but he has no constitutional right to be a policeman.'") (citing McAuliffe v. Mayor of New Bedford, 29 N.E. 517, 517 (Mass. 1892)).

[107] *See, e.g.*, Henry Paul Monaghan, *Of "Liberty" and "Property,"* 62 CORNELL L. REV. 405, 407 (1977) ("[The right-privilege doctrine] had been invoked to justify a denial of due process scrutiny of some types of governmental conduct in the public sector; for example, since there was no independent 'right' to welfare payments, their denial, standing alone, did not implicate any constitutional value."). *See* chapter 4 *infra* for a fuller discussion of the incorporation process.

to adopt more flexibility in its due process decisions.[108] In procedural due process, this increased flexibility is apparent in the Court's adoption of expanded definitions of protected interests as well as the balancing approach to determining what procedures due process requires in a given context.[109] The Court's subjecting of economic interests to rational basis, rather than a more exacting form of judicial review, evidences the Court's trend toward flexibility in its substantive due process jurisprudence.[110] Rational basis review provides the government with the ability to deal with changing socioeconomic conditions, which was prevented during the New Deal era under the *Lochner* framework.[111]

Although societal changes are partially responsible for the historical development of due process jurisprudence that animates and unites both procedure and substance, there are also substantive themes in the progress. Perhaps the most prevalent of these is the Court's attempt to protect individual autonomy.[112] In both procedural and substantive due process the overarching goal has been to protect individuals from arbitrary deprivations at the hands of the government.[113] As the historical roots of both procedural and substantive due process illustrate, the challenge in these cases is to strike a sensible balance between the power and interests of the government on the one hand and the liberty or autonomy interests of the individual on the other.[114] Across time and different contexts, the balance struck

---

[108] The Court has recognized that the evolving American society in which due process operates demands some flexibility in the application of due process over time. *See* District Attorney's Office for Third Judicial Dist. v. Osborne, 557 U.S. 52, 104 (2009) (Souter, J., dissenting) ("We recognize the value and lessons of continuity with the past, but as Justice Harlan pointed out, society finds reasons to modify some of its traditional practices ... and the accumulation of new empirical knowledge can turn yesterday's reasonable range of the government's options into a due process anomaly over time.") (citations omitted).

[109] For an in-depth explanation of the development of the evolution of the more flexible definition of protected interests *see* chapter 2 (c) *infra*, and for a deeper dive into the development of the more flexible balancing approach for determining the procedures required by due process *see* chapter 3, *infra*.

[110] For a complete discussion of the Court's progression towards flexibility in its treatment of socioeconomic interests under substantive due process *see infra* chapter 4.

[111] *See, e.g.*, Wayne McCormack, *Economic Substantive Due Process and the Right of Livelihood*, 82 KY. L.J. 397, 400 (1993–1994) ("Certainly, the lack of substantive judicial review of government regulation and subsidization during the post-New Deal era has made imposition of social programs and economic regulation much easier.").

[112] *See* McDonald v. City of Chicago, 130 S. Ct. 3020, 3090–91 (2010) (Stevens, J., dissenting) (arguing that the Due Process Clause contains a substantive component "consonant with the venerable 'notion that governmental authority has implied limits which preserve private autonomy'") (footnote omitted).

[113] Wolff v. McDonnell, 418 U.S. 539, 558 (1974) ("The touchstone of due process is protection of the individual against arbitrary action of government.") (internal citations omitted); *see also* Rubin, *supra* note 47, at 841 ("Ultimately, the substantive due process clause is a 'bulwark [] ... against arbitrary' government action. But action can be arbitrary in more than one sense—and the Due Process Clause has been construed to provide protection against more than one type of arbitrary government action.") (footnotes omitted).

[114] Washington v. Glucksburg, 521 U.S. 702, 765 (1997) ("'Due Process has not been reduced to any formula; its content cannot be determined by reference to any code. The best that can be said is that through the course of this Court's decisions it has represented the balance which our Nation, built upon postulates of respect for the liberty of the individual, has struck between that liberty and the demands of organized society.'") (quoting Poe v. Ullman, 367 U.S. 497, 542 (1961)).

in either procedural or substantive due process between government power and individual autonomy has varied according to context.[115] In each context, the Court has attempted to harmonize the competing interests.[116] The utility of this balancing approach allows the Court, in both procedural and substantive cases, to consider the breadth of the circumstances and context involved in the given cases. The result is that the Court is able to reach decisions based more on the evolving and contextualized notions of "fairness" and liberty, than on formalistic, bounded, bright-line rules.[117]

III. Defining "Protected Interests" under Modern Due Process

The foregoing history of protected interests under procedural due process shows that the interests that trigger substantive due process—textually, this is "life, liberty or property"— were initially defined rigidly. During the early period, protected interests were defined by whether the interest involved in a given case was important enough to require the protection afforded by due process, without attempting to categorize the interest as an interest in life, liberty, or property per se.[118] The Court employed a distinction between rights and privileges as a tool for classifying protected interests; only rights were entitled to the protections of procedural due process.[119] Consequently, privileges that were created generally by statute or agency rule, "such as a government job or benefits[,]" were not entitled to the protection of due process.[120] Through the application of this distinction, due process was found to apply only to a relatively small subset of cases.[121]

---

[115] For example, in procedural due process cases the government was initially given more power in cases involving statutorily created benefits, as they were deemed privileges not worthy of procedural due process protection. However, over time, the Court abandoned the right-privilege distinction, and accordingly, struck a balance more in favor of individual autonomy by protecting statutorily-created benefits as property interests under the Due Process Clause. In substantive due process in economic interests cases, the balance was initially struck in favor of the individual and then later the balance shifted to favor the individual. While, in the privacy (fundamental, unenumerated) strand of substantive due process the government initially won the balance, and subsequently the individual was favored. *See* chapter 4, *infra*.

[116] *See* Youngberg v. Romeo, 457 U.S. 307, 320–21 (1982) ("In determining whether a substantive right protected by the Due Process Clause has been violated, it is necessary to balance 'the liberty of the individual' and 'the demands of an organized society.' … In determining that procedural due process did not mandate an adversarial hearing, we weighed the liberty interest of the individual against the legitimate interests of the State, including the fiscal and administrative burdens additional procedures would entail.") (internal citations omitted) (footnotes omitted).

[117] *See*, e.g., Mathews v. Eldridge, 424 U.S. 319, 334–35 (1976) (describing due process as a flexible inquiry that requires the consideration of the different interests involved in a given circumstance for decision-making).

[118] Wasserman, *supra* note 2 (citing to cases employing this "unitary concept").

[119] *See, e.g.*, Richard J. Pierce, *The Due Process Counterrevolution of the 1990s?*, 96 Colum. L. Rev. 1973, 1974 (1996).

[120] *Id.*

[121] *Id.*

Yet despite the limited applicability of this rigid framework for defining interests, principles of procedural due process also developed through other constitutional doctrines. For example, in the first half of the twentieth century a series of cases established fundamental rules of procedural due process in areas of law that were not directly related to government-created property and liberty interests.[122] The Court also found other avenues to protect important "privileges," such as employing the Equal Protection Clause or establishing the doctrine of "unconstitutional conditions."[123] Still other safeguards were established by insisting on minimal procedural protections to ensure that whatever regulations included in the statute in the first place were in fact followed.[124] Thus, even if a police officer could be fired for exercising his or her free speech, the government had to have an adequate hearing to ensure that the officer did in fact engage in the prohibited speech.[125] In other words, procedural integrity matters even when the underlying interest is not constitutionally protected, or its status is unclear. We turn now to the modern development of procedural rights, in relation to still-evolving notions of the property, liberty, and life interests that trigger them.

---

[122] For example, *Mullane v. Central Hanover Bank & Trust Co.*, 339 U.S. 306 (1950), and Justice Frankfurter's concurrence in *Joint Anti-Fascist Refugee Committee v. McGrath*, 341 U.S. 123 (1951), are both frequently cited in later cases dealing with procedural due process and entitlement-as-property even though the former dealt with personal jurisdiction and the latter decision involved protections against defamation. *See, e.g.*, Mathews v. Eldridge, 424 U.S. 319, 348–49 (1976) (citing *Joint Anti-Fascist*); Arnett v. Kennedy, 416 U.S. 134, 178 (1974) (citing Justice Frankfurter's *Joint Anti-Fascist* concurrence for the principle that there is a right to be heard before "suffer[ing] a grievous loss of any kind"); Hanson v. Denckla, 357 U.S. 235, 245 (1958) (citing *Mullane* for the proposition that a "court … [must] employ a means of notice reasonably calculated to inform nonresident defendants of the pending proceedings."); Walker v. City of Hutchinson, Kan., 352 U.S. 112, 115 (1956) ("In *Mullane v. Central Hanover Bank & Trust Co.*…, we gave thorough consideration to the problem of adequate notice under the Due Process Clause. That case establishes the rule that, if feasible, notice must be reasonably calculated to inform parties of proceedings which may directly and adversely affect their legally protected interests.") (citations and footnotes omitted).

[123] *See* William W. Van Alstyne, *The Demise of the Right-Privilege Distinction in Constitutional Law*, 81 HARV. L. REV. 1439, 1445–46 (1968) ("[T]his doctrine [of unconstitutional conditions] declares that whatever an express constitutional provision forbids government to do directly it equally forbids government to do indirectly.… The net effect is to enable an individual to challenge certain conditions imposed upon his public employment without disturbing the presupposition that he has no 'right' to that employment."); *See id.* at 1454–57 (discussing the application of the Equal Protection Clause as a means to get around the rights-privilege distinction).

[124] *See id.* at 1451–52 ("Although there are only a few cases in which a procedural argument is clearly featured, a person may sometimes successfully rely on an independent right to procedural due process to avoid some of the harsh consequences of the right-privilege distinction.… In the first instance, a requirement of a minimally fair hearing holds only that whenever the legislature has seen fit to limit the grounds for terminating or denying certain benefits, the administering agency must still observe certain minimum procedural standards to provide reasonable assurance that the petitioner did in fact offend one of the specified grounds; but the power of Congress or a state legislature to set substantive standards without constitutional restriction is not denied.").

[125] *See id.* at 1452.

By the 1960s the stage was set for the Court to reject the right-privilege distinction as the key to whether a "property" interest merited procedural due process concern.[126] The Court changed its analysis through five landmark opinions handed down between 1970 and 1972, during "the due process revolution" described above.[127] These decisions "expand[ed] the scope of due process protection to encompass hundreds of new 'property' and 'liberty' interests that previously were considered mere unprotected 'privileges.'"[128] The Court adopted the less formulaic system for defining protected interests that now governs due process cases.[129]

The major expansion in the definition of protected property interests began when statutory benefits were included. For the first time, in *Goldberg v. Kelly*,[130] the Court recognized a protected interest in a benefit defined by statute.[131] The Court concluded that a state's termination of an individual's public assistance payments from the federally-assisted program of Aid to Families with Dependent Children (AFDC) without opportunity for a hearing prior to the deprivation violated the Due Process Clause of the Fourteenth Amendment.[132] The first step toward this conclusion was to characterize the benefits provided by the agency as a property interest protected by the Constitution.[133] The Court found that termination of the benefits provided by AFDC "involves state action that adjudicates important rights," which in turn triggered constitutional protections within the meaning of the Due Process Clause.[134] Welfare entitlements were more like "property" than "gratuity" because

---

[126] *See* Wasserman, *supra* note 2, at 34 (discussing how the Civil Rights movement as well as the "Great Society governmental programs" of the 1960s gave the Court a chance to revisit its precedent involving the definition of protected interests).

[127] Pierce, *supra* note 20, at 1973. Notably, the Court did not independently conceive of the "due process revolution."

> Yale law professor Charles Reich can be credited with intellectual paternity for the due process revolution. In two highly influential articles published in the Yale Law Journal in 1964 and 1965, Reich made an impassioned plea for judicial recognition of what he called the "new property," benefits provided by the government pursuant to statutes and regulations. When the Court recognized the "new property," it did not even bother to provide an independent explanation for its conclusion that government benefits were entitled to recognition as property rights. It simply cited and paraphrased Reich's articles to support this revolutionary change in constitutional law doctrine.

Id. at 1974 (footnotes omitted).

[128] *Id.* at 1980.

[129] *See, e.g.*, Wasserman, *supra* note 2, at 35–36 (discussing the Court's rejection of the "wooden" rights-privilege distinction and its application of a less rigid approach in subsequent cases).

[130] 397 U.S. 254 (1970). *See supra*, text accompanying notes 28–30.

[131] *See* Pierce *supra* note 20, at 1977 ("The *Goldberg* court first held that welfare benefits that are made available by statute to all individuals with specified characteristics are a form of property subject to due process protections.") (citing *Goldberg*, 397 U.S. at 262).

[132] *Goldberg*, 397 U.S. at 255.

[133] *Id.* at 262; *see also* Pierce, *supra* note 20, at 1977–78.

[134] *Goldberg*, 397 U.S. at 262. The court further states that "[t]he constitutional challenge cannot be answered by an argument that public assistance benefits are a 'privilege' and not a 'right.'" *Id.* (citing Shapiro v. Thompson, 392 U.S. 618, 627 n.6 (1969)); *see also* Pierce, *supra* note 20, at 1977–78.

much of the country's wealth takes the form of rights not falling within the traditional common-law concepts of property.[135] Thus, the benefits were protectable, which opened the range of cases in which procedural due process applied.

Post-*Goldberg*,[136] the Court continued to move away from right-privilege distinction and added other protected interests to those covered by the Due Process Clause. Examples included "Medicare and Medicaid benefits ... [,] Social Security benefits ... [,] food stamps ... [,] and veteran's benefits for death or disability...."[137] The protected interests first recognized were those that were most closely related to an individual's ability to earn a living, followed subsequently by other types of benefits.[138]

Much of the development of the entitlement doctrine initially resulted from a series of employment cases.[139] The most important of these were *Perry v. Sindermann*[140] and *Board of Regents of State Colleges v. Roth*.[141] *Roth* established that property, as entitlement, could be rooted in positive law.[142] Notably, *Roth* and *Sindermann* established the Court's current bifurcated analysis.[143] In *Roth*, the Court formally receded from the right-privilege distinction saying that it "fully and finally rejected the wooden distinction between 'rights' and 'privileges'...."[144] *Roth* also established that in its initial inquiry, the Court should look to the nature of the interest and not its weight or importance to ascertain whether it must be afforded due process protection.[145] Although the Court acknowledged a broader conception of the meaning of liberty and property, it recognized explicitly that certain boundaries do exist, and "the range of interests protected by procedural due process is not infinite."[146] Critics claimed that the Court's attempt to define

---

[135] *See Goldberg*, 397 U.S. at 262 n.8; *see also*, e.g., Pierce, *supra* note 20, at 1974–75 (noting that the Court, in adopting the "new property" concept, borrowed from the scholarship of Professor Charles Reich, who advocated for the recognition of "new property" interest, in part because government entitlements were increasingly central to modern society).

[136] Goldberg v. Kelly, 397 U.S. 254 (1970).

[137] WASSERMAN, *supra* note 2, at 37–38 (stating also that, "[u]nlike professional licenses, government benefits have been treated as protected property interests only since the early 1970s. Before then, the Court treated benefits as privileges, or 'unaccrued' property rights, not entitled to due process protection. In a single paragraph of the path-breaking case of *Goldberg v. Kelly* (1970), the Supreme Court dramatically departed from that course, holding that welfare benefits qualify as a property interest entitled to due process protection") (citations omitted).

[138] *See id.* at 33.

[139] *See*, e.g., Pierce, *supra* note 20, at 1978 ("*Goldberg* was followed in 1972 by a pair of government employee cases—*Perry v. Sindermann* and *Board of Regents v. Roth*.") (footnotes omitted).

[140] 408 U.S. 593 (1972).

[141] 408 U.S. 564 (1972).

[142] *See* WASSERMAN, *supra* note 2, at 39 ("[U]nder *Roth*, a property interest is created when positive law constrains the discretion of a disbursing agency....").

[143] *See* Rodney A. Smolla, *The Reemergence of The Right-Privilege Distinction in Constitutional Law: The Price of Protesting Too Much*, 35 STAN. L. REV. 69, 77 (1982).

[144] Bd. of Regents of State Colls. v. Roth, 408 U.S. 564, 571 (1972); *see also* Smolla, *supra* note 143, at 73 (citing to the *Roth* court's language rejecting the right-privilege distinction).

[145] *Roth*, 408 U.S. at 570–71; *see also* Smolla, *supra* note 143, at 81 (citing to the same language of the *Roth* court in discussing how an interest will be analyzed).

[146] *Id.* at 570; *see also* Smolla, *supra* note 143, at 81 (citing *Roth v. Board of Regents*, 408 U.S. 564, 570–71 (1972)).

limiting principles during this period was nothing more than a resurrection of the right-privilege distinction of the early twentieth century because the Court employed the same "contract and property analogies" in these cases that were part of the right-privilege analysis.[147] Yet the search for limiting principles was an inevitable consequence of the more open-ended approach to procedural due process begun by *Goldberg*.

The Court's procedural due process revolution was tamed by subsequent cases.[148] Efforts to rein the doctrine in included Justice Rehnquist's "attempted due process counterrevolution," which occurred between 1974 and 1985.[149] In his plurality opinion in *Arnett v. Kennedy*,[150] Justice Rehnquist adopted a "bitter with the sweet" theory for resolution of statutorily created benefits cases:[151] " [W]here the grant of a substantive right [via statute] is inextricably intertwined with the limitations on the procedures which are to be employed in determining that right, a litigant in the position of appellee must take the bitter with the sweet."[152] Under the "bitter with the sweet theory," because the legislature holds the power both to establish a benefit and to limit its scope, including the accompanying procedures for terminating the benefit, the Court cannot require additional procedures when statutes both establish the benefit and its limitation on means of termination.[153]

Justice Rehnquist continued his opposition to the "nature of the interest" approach, but his theory eventually lost favor with the rest of the justices on the Court. In *Bishop v. Wood*,[154] Justice Rehnquist seemed to have garnered a five-justice majority for his approach; however, the opinion was not explicitly clear on this point as it also referred to the principles of federalism.[155] In subsequent cases, the Court seemed to refer approvingly to the "bitter with the sweet" theory,[156] but then explicitly rejected the theory in 1985 in *Cleveland Board of Education v. Loudermill*.[157] This ended the "counterrevolution" as it was known.[158] Despite this defeat, Justice Rehnquist stayed true to his theory until the end, writing the lone dissent in *Loudermill*.[159] Expanded principles of protected interests

---

[147] *See* Smolla, *supra* note 143, at 82–83 (explaining how the Court's use of contract and property principles in defining interests were the same inquiries used in the rights-privilege distinction that the Court was rejecting).

[148] Pierce, *supra* note 20, at 1981.

[149] *Id.* at 1986.

[150] 416 U.S. 134 (1974).

[151] Pierce, *supra* note 20, at 1986.

[152] Arnett v. Kennedy, 416 U.S. 134, 153–54 (1974).

[153] *See* Pierce, *supra* note 20, at 1986 (citing *Kennedy*, 416 U.S. at 152–54).

[154] 426 U.S. 341 (1976).

[155] *See* Pierce, *supra* note 20, at 1986–87 (citing Bishop v. Wood, 426 U.S. 341, 345, 344–47 (1976)).

[156] *Id.* at 1987 (citing cases after *Bishop* discussing "the bitter with the sweet" theory in a positive manner).

[157] 470 U.S. 532 (1985).

[158] Pierce, *supra* note 20, at 1987 (citing *Loudermill*, 470 U.S. at 538–41).

[159] 470 U.S. 532 (1985).

under due process thus survived Justice Rehnquist's challenge, but this would not be the only obstacle to their progress.

Another barrier stemmed from the complexities of defining protected property interests in the expanding administrative state.[160] Historically, the Court attempted to separate procedural due process and the administrative state by "insulating traditional common law issues from definitive determination by administrative agencies, and otherwise leaving agency rulemaking and adjudication free from due process control."[161] The Court has since attempted to apply the principles of procedural due process to administrative adjudications, and ultimately to limit the applicability of procedural due process in favor of greater administrative discretion.[162]

Today, defining what constitutes an interest warranting due process protection still presents a challenge. As society continues to evolve, the novel property interests the Court must designate as protected or unprotected become more difficult to categorize, and precedent becomes a struggle to apply.

Nevertheless, the Court still employs a two-prong analysis: first, whether a protected interest of life, liberty, or property exists, and, second, what procedural safeguards are required to prevent erroneous or arbitrary interference with that interest.[163] Moreover, the Due Process Clauses only check state or federal action.[164] Accordingly, for the Court to find a deprivation of a protected interest, there must have been some governmental action.[165] The so-called "state action requirement" mandates that "the claimed deprivation result[s] from the exercise of a right or privilege having its source in state authority, and … [that] the party charged with the deprivation [is] a state actor … ."[166] Procedural due process is implicated, therefore, only when the Court has determined that there has been deprivation of a protected interest through government action. When the Court limits the

---

[160] Rubin, *supra* note 32, at 1082 (1984) ("The procedural due process cases of the post-*Roth* (or perhaps the post-*Goldberg*) era, although not impressive examples of legal reasoning, generally represent serious efforts to deal with a complex legal issue: the relationship between procedural due process and the activities of an administrative state."). A complete discussion of due process and the administrative state is beyond the scope of this book and its overview of the due process landscape, as is the issue of proper deference to agency rulemaking.

[161] *Id.* at 1082–83.

[162] *Id.* at 1983 (discussing the development of application of procedural due process principles to administrative decisions) ("The loyalty-security cases, however hesitant their tone, represent the Court's first comprehensive effort to adapt procedural due process doctrine to administrative actions. The rationale of these cases was significant but imprecise, as became apparent when courts began to apply it to the broader range of actions implicated by the welfare rights movement. In response to this imprecision, *Roth* and its successors have sought to limit the breadth of the due process clause's application, and ultimately have come to grapple with the crucial issue of administrative discretion. This is a necessary and important issue, and the results the Court has reached—while often debatable—are rarely beyond the bounds of reasonable opinion.").

[163] *See* Morrissey v. Brewer, 408 U.S. 471, 481 (1972).

[164] *See* WASSERMAN, *supra* note 2, at 27.

[165] *See id.*

[166] *See id.* (citing Am. Mfrs. Mut. Ins. Co. v. Sullivan, 526 U.S. 40 (1999); Lugar v. Edmondson Oil Co., 457 U.S. 922 (1982)).

application of the state action doctrine, it likewise limits the range of conduct to which due process principles apply. The next sections examine in more detail how the Court has defined the protected interests of property, liberty, and life.

PROPERTY INTERESTS

An important feature of the modern property interests that are afforded due process protections is worth underscoring: these property interests themselves are not constitutionally derived.[167] Instead, these property interests are created through a variety of other sources, which include statutory entitlements, operation of institutional common law, or contract law.[168] Property interests may be traditional types of property, such as real property, as well as certain statutory entitlements. These entitlements have been found in areas including public employment,[169] public education,[170] social security benefits,[171] and public assistance.[172] Government is not constitutionally required to provide any of these forms of property. Once it does provide them, however, government may be required to respect procedural due process principles when it burdens or terminates these benefits.

In *Goldberg v. Kelly*,[173] as discussed above, the Court "confirmed [its] unwillingness to limit its review by traditional notions of property interests ... [and] that the Court was prepared to assume a highly interventionist posture" that produced "a flood of cases seeking to extend, or simply to apply, *Goldberg's* precepts."[174] The basis for the Court's subsequent expansion of due process property interests was its recognition of the relationship between property rights as an integral component of an individual's economic well-being and the importance of governmentally-conferred benefits as an essential aspect of that well-being.

Recent case law suggests that the Court may be attempting anew to narrow the boundaries of due process protection for state-created property. In *Town of Castle Rock, Colorado v. Gonzales*,[175] the Court rejected a plaintiff's claim of a property interest in the execution of a restraining order against her husband.[176] The Court

[167] Cleveland Bd. of Educ. v. Loudermill, 470 U.S. 532, 538 (1985) ("Property interests are not created by the Constitution, 'they are created and their dimensions are defined by existing rules or understandings that stem from an independent source such as state law .... '") (quoting Bd. of Regents of State Colls. v. Roth, 408 U.S. 564 (1972)).

[168] *See* Perry v. Sindermann, 408 U.S. 593, 599–603 (1972); Bd. of Regents of State Colleges v. Roth, 408 U.S. 564, 576–78 (1972).

[169] *See Cleveland Bd. of Educ.*, 470 U.S. at 538–39; *Sindermann*, 408 U.S. at 596–98 (public employment).

[170] Goss v. Lopez, 419 U.S. 565 (1975).

[171] Mathews v. Eldridge, 424 U.S. 319, 332–32 (1976)

[172] Goldberg v. Kelly, 397 U.S. 254, 261–63 (1970).

[173] 397 U.S. 254 (1970).

[174] Jerry L. Mashaw, *The Supreme Court's Due Process Calculus for Administrative Adjudication in* Mathews v. Eldridge: *Three Factors in Search of a Theory of Value*, 44 U. CHI. L. REV. 28, 28–29 (1976).

[175] 545 U.S. 748 (2005).

[176] *Id.* at 768.

narrowly read the statute on restraining orders and introduced, for the first time, a requirement that a protected property interest must have some type of monetary value.[177] Further, the Court noted that state-created benefits would not be protected as a property interest under the due process clause if "government officials may grant or deny it in their discretion."[178] According to the Court, the traditional discretion necessarily afforded to police in executing arrest statutes undermined any legitimate claim to entitlement of a property interest in the police enforcement of a restraining order.[179] The Court noted that the "indeterminacy" of the statute's language was "not the hallmark of a duty that is mandatory."[180] In *American Manufacturers Mutual Insurance Co. v. Sullivan*,[181] the Court similarly took a narrow view on the definition of a due process property interest. In *Sullivan*, injured employees challenged worker's compensation procedures that permitted suspension of medical benefits without notice or opportunity to be heard, subject to a "utilization review" process.[182] The Court found that injured workers did not have a property interest in receiving medical payments prior to establishing that such benefits were "reasonable and necessary" as required by state statute.[183] The plaintiff's argument also fell short of satisfying the state action requirement of *both*

---

[177] *See id.* at 766–67 ("[T]he right to have a restraining order enforced does not 'have some ascertainable monetary value,' as even our '*Roth*-type property-as-entitlement' cases have implicitly required." And, "[p]erhaps most radically, the alleged property interest here arises incidentally … out of a function that government actors have always performed …") (quoting Thomas W. Merrill, *The Landscape of Constitutional Property*, 86 VA. L. REV. 885, 964 (2000)); *See also* Joel Hugenberger, *Redefining Property Under the Due Process Clause:* Town of Castle Rock v. Gonzales *and the Demise of the Positive Law Approach*, 47 B.C. L. Rev. 773 (2006).

[178] *Id.* at 756.

[179] *Id.* at 760 (stating that there exists a "well established tradition of police discretion [that] has long coexisted with apparently mandatory arrest statutes. 'In each and every state there are long-standing statutes that, by their terms, seem to preclude nonenforcement by the police …. However, for a number of reasons, including their legislative history, insufficient resources, and sheer physical impossibility, it has been recognized that such statutes cannot be interpreted literally …. [T]hey clearly do not mean that a police officer may not lawfully decline to, … make an arrest.'") (quoting STANDARDS FOR CRIMINAL JUSTICE § 14.5, cmt 1-124 to 1-125 (1980)); *see also* Chicago v. Morales, 527 U.S. 41, 62 n.32 (1999) (dismissing the notion that the mandatory language of a statute prevented police discretion) (as cited by *Castle Rock*, 545 U.S. at 761).

[180] *Castle Rock*, 545 U.S. at 763–64. The restraining-order statute appeared to contemplate that the police officer's statutory duty was to "seek a warrant" rather than an arrest, and that an individual cannot be "safely deemed 'entitled' to something when the identity of the alleged entitlement is vague." *Id.* (quoting Bd. of Regents of State Colls. v. Roth, 408 U.S. 564, 577 (1972)). The "seeking of an arrest warrant would be an entitlement to nothing but procedure—which we have held inadequate even to support standing." *Id.* at 764 (citing Lujan v. Defenders of Wildlife, 504 U.S. 555 (1992)); *see also* Michael L. Wells & Alice E. Snedeker, *State-created Property and Due Process of Law: Filling the Void Left by* Enquist v. Oregon Department of Agriculture, 44 GA. L. REV. 161, 174 (2009).

[181] 526 U.S. 40 (1999).

[182] *Id.* at 44–48.

[183] *Id.* at 60–61. The Court noted that an employee has to clear "two hurdles" for his interest in medical payments to parallel the interests at stake in *Goldberg* and *Mathews*: prove that the employer is liable for a work-related injury and prove that the medical treatment is necessary and reasonable. *Id.* at 61. Because the plaintiffs could not prove their treatment was "reasonable and necessary," they did not clear the second hurdle. *Id.* "To state the argument is to refute it, for what respondents ask in this case

> an alleged constitutional deprivation "caused by the exercise of some right or privilege created by the State or by a rule of conduct imposed by the State or by a person for whom the State is responsible," *and* that "the party charged with the deprivation must be a person who may fairly be said to be a state actor."[184]

The decision by the private insurers to withhold benefits for the disputed medical treatment could not be attributed fairly to the State.[185]

Several appellate court cases also have embraced the new turn toward a more constricted approach to property interests. They have denied due process protections to traditionally protected benefits where the legislature drafted the entitlement statute in such a way so as to make the conferral of the benefit discretionary.[186] Supporters of this more conservative view of procedural due process argue that the original understanding of the Fifth and Fourteenth Amendments required only that there be compliance with the "law of the land" as created by the legislature and to do otherwise would provide the judiciary with "broad and boundless authority."[187] A statute conferring welfare benefits may avoid constitutional scrutiny by explicitly stating that the statute does not create nor confer an entitlement.[188] In the *Arnett* era the Court provided a drafting guide to the legislative branch by allowing it to create a protected interest while defining the methods by which it was protected, whereas the modern drafting guidelines caution legislators to avoid creating a protected interest in the first place simply by stylistic alterations to the prose or legalistic disclaimers.

---

is that insurers be required to pay for patently unreasonable, unnecessary, and even fraudulent medical care without any right, under state law, to seek reimbursement from providers. Unsurprisingly, the Due Process Clause does not require such a result."

[184] *Id.* at 50 (quoting Lugar v. Edmonson Oil, Co., 457 U.S. 922, 937 (1982)); *see also* WASSERMAN, *supra* note 118, at 29.

[185] *Id.* at 52 ("[t]he mere fact that a business is subject to state regulation does not by itself convert its action into that of the State for purposes of the Fourteenth Amendment.") (quoting Jackson v. Metro. Edison Co., 419 U.S. 345, 350 (1974). To ensure that regulation of private enterprises does not fall to the court, there must be a strict application of the state-action requirement, and "private insurers … will not be held to constitutional standards unless 'there is a sufficiently close nexus between the State and the challenged action of the regulated entity so that the action of the latter may be fairly treated as that of the State itself.'" *Id.* (quoting *Jackson*, 419 U.S. at 351).

[186] *See* Sidney A. Shapiro & Richard E. Levy, *Government Benefits and the Rule of Law: Toward a Standards-Based Theory of Due Process*, 57 ADMIN L. REV. 107, 113–15 (2005).

[187] Martin H. Redish & Lawrence C. Marshall, *Adjudicatory Independence and the Values of Procedural Due Process*, 95 YALE L.J. 455, 458 (1986). Supporters of the positivist approach have also argued that it would be contradictory to grant the legislature the ability to "define substantive entitlements but not allow that same body to define the procedures required to terminate those entitlements." *Id.* For further discussion about why the framers' choice of constitutional language might not necessarily support the positivist approach, see generally *id.*

[188] *See* Shapiro & Levy, *supra* note 186, at 113–15 ("Since the Supreme Court has also made clear that the Constitution does not normally impose affirmative duties on the government, a legislature has the power to control the nature and extent of any benefits it creates, including whether there is an 'entitlement' to that benefit.… Although it is not entirely clear whether an express disclaimer, standing alone, is sufficient to defeat an entitlement if the statute otherwise creates one, the combination of a disclaimer with other factors appears to be sufficient.").

These newer cases present a tension between the current doctrinal trend and some of the older cases that provided a less constrained view on what types of entitlements might create protection of a property interest. In *Goss v. Lopez*,[189] for example, the Court held that a state's statutory guarantee to educational access was sufficient to create a property interest in education.[190] The case involved a class action brought by Ohio public school system students against school officials to challenge suspensions given to the students without a hearing.[191] The Court declared that by "[h]aving chosen to extend the right to an education to people of appellees' class generally, Ohio may not withdraw that right on grounds of misconduct, absent fundamentally fair procedures to determine whether the misconduct has occurred."[192] Once the property interest had been conferred, the minimum procedural protections guaranteed by due process became effective.[193]

In other cases, however, the Court has placed significant emphasis on the presence of decision-making criteria and discretion of the agency in determining if the relevant statute created a property interest.[194] For example, in *Memphis Light, Gas, and Water Division v. Craft*, the Court found that the existence of "local-law remedies" to "enjoin a wrongful threat to terminate [utility services], or to bring a subsequent action for damages or a refund" is sufficient "evidence of the State's recognition of a protected interest."[195]

The Court in *Logan v. Zimmerman Brush Co.*[196] held that the right to use adjudicatory procedures under the Illinois State Fair Employment Practices Act (FEPA) to appeal an employment termination, as guaranteed by the state, was a property interest constitutionally protected by the Due Process Clause.[197] The case involved an employee who filed timely charge of unlawful termination with the Illinois Fair Employment Commission.[198] The Commission failed to convene on the charge

[189] 419 U.S. 565 (1975).

[190] *See id.* at 572–75.

[191] *Id.* at 567–71.

[192] *Id.* at 574 (quoting Tinker v. Des Moines Indep. Cmty. Sch. Dist., 393 U.S. 503, 506 (1969)). The Court went on to argue that "[a]lthough Ohio may not be constitutionally obligated to establish and maintain a public school system, it has nevertheless done so and has required its children to attend. Those young people do not 'shed their constitutional rights' at the schoolhouse door" and that "neither the property interest in educational benefits temporarily denied nor the liberty interest in reputation, which is also implicated, is so insubstantial that suspensions may constitutionally be imposed by any procedure the school chooses, no matter how arbitrary." *Id.* at 574, 576.

[193] *Id.* at 574.

[194] *See* Rubin, *supra* note 32, at 1079–80.

[195] Memphis Light, Gas and Water Div. v. Craft, 436 U.S. 1, 11 (1978) ("Although the customer's right to continued service is conditioned upon payment of the charges due, '[t]he Fourteenth Amendment's protection of "property" ... has never been interpreted to safeguard only the rights of undisputed ownership.' Because petitioners may terminate service only 'for cause,' respondents assert a 'legitimate claim of entitlement' within the protection of the Due Process Clause.")

[196] 455 U.S. 422 (1982).

[197] *See id.* at 428–33.

[198] *Id.*

within the 120-day requirement and the employer moved to dismiss the charge.[199] The Court concluded that the cause of action founded in state law was a property interest that could not be arbitrarily deprived by an agency's action.[200] The employee's right to utilize FEPA's adjudicatory procedures was "a species of property protected by the Fourteenth Amendment's Due Process Clause."[201] The FEPA claim

> which presumably can be surrendered for value, is at least as substantial as the right to an education labeled as property in *Goss v. Lopez*. Certainly, it would require a remarkable reading of a 'broad and majestic ter[m],' to conclude that a horse trainer's license is a protected property interest under the Fourteenth Amendment, while a state-created right to redress discrimination is not.[202]

Prior to *Zimmerman Brush*, the Court only once raised the issue of whether "causes of action" could effectively be property protected by the Due Process Clause.[203] The Court in *Martinez v. California*[204] tangentially considered the issue whether a cause of action could create a property interest, stating "[a]rguably, the cause of action for wrongful death that the State has created is a species of 'property' protected by the Due Process Clause," though ultimately the issue was left mostly unresolved until *Zimmerman Brush*.[205]

The Court's approach toward property in *Memphis Light* and *Logan* was to create a balanced definition that is simultaneously broad enough to include "old property" rights recognized under common law and "new property" rights articulated in *Goldberg*, while still remaining sufficiently narrow to remain consistent with case law that requires that reasons be stated for termination of property interests.[206]

The protections of the Due Process Clause also extend to other intangible rights, including intellectual property. For example, in *Florida Prepaid v. College Savings Banks*,[207] the Court noted that patents may be considered "property" for the purposes of due process analysis and that a "State's infringement of a patent ... where

---

199 *Id.*

200 *Id.* at 428–29.

201 *Id.* at 428. The right to the adjudicatory procedure shares the characteristic hallmarks of property by being grounded in state law and that it cannot be removed except "for cause." "Once that characteristic is found, the types of interests protected as 'property' are varied and, as often as not, intangible, relating 'to the whole domain of social and economic fact.'" *Id.* at 428, 430 (quoting Nat'l Mut. Ins. Co. v. Tidewater Transfer Co., 337 U.S. 582, 646 (1949)) (Frankfurter, J., dissenting).

202 *Id.* at 431 (citations omitted).

203 Timothy P. Terrell, *Causes of Action as Property:* Logan v. Zimmerman Brush Co. *and the "Government-As-Monopolist" Theory of the Due Process Clause*, 31 Emory L.J. 491, 502 (1982) (citing Martinez v. California, 444 U.S. 277 (1980)).

204 444 U.S. 277 (1980).

205 *Id.* at 281–82.

206 Merrill, *supra* note 177, at 960. ("Third, the definition is couched so as to exclude nonconstitutional procedural rules associated with statutory entitlements, and hence avoids the positivist trap associated with the bitter-with-the-sweet thesis.").

207 527 U.S. 627 (1999).

the State provides no remedy, or only inadequate remedies, to the injured patent owners for its infringement of their patent could [result in] a deprivation of property without due process. . . ."[208]

Government actions might also lead to the expropriation of land or other property rights through the power of eminent domain or regulatory takings. Although challenges to these governmental appropriations generally constitute takings and may trigger substantive due process claims, property owners could also bring procedural due process claims and challenge the procedure afforded to the owner.[209] For example, a claimant may choose to challenge the adequacy of notice and other procedures provided to the litigant for contesting the legitimacy of the government action.[210] Failure to provide the affected individual with adequate procedures to challenge the government action could itself be violative of procedural due process protections, irrespective of substantive due process and takings considerations.

Although the Court has struggled continuously to identify and define the elements of protected property interests, the shared element of "'new property' interests since *Roth* is the recognition of a benefit rooted in a source of law independent from the Constitution that is conferred on a specific class subject to specific conditions and terminable only under specific conditions."[211] The attribute most commonly recognized in defining a property interest within the Due Process Clause is that the source of law is *independent* of the Constitution, and is sufficiently concrete to anchor the procedural due process requirement.[212] Yet the problems inherent in creating a "workable framework that incorporates a person's subjective expectation of or reliance on a benefit without grounding that reasonable expectation in a source of law has made the Court wary of straying from *Roth*'s positivist approach."[213] The Court thus has instituted further requirements that the benefit be directly "conferred on the claimant"[214] and sometimes "impliedly required" that the benefit be provided to a specific class.[215]

---

[208] *Id.* at 642–43 (citing Parratt v. Taylor, 451 U.S. 527, 539–31 (1981); Hudson v. Palmer, 468 U.S. 517, 532–33, 539 (1984)).

[209] Stuart Minor Benjamin, Note, *The Applicability of Just Compensation to Substantive Due Process Claims*, 100 YALE L. J. 2667, 2669 n.12 (1991).

[210] *See id.*

[211] Hugenberger, *supra* note 177, at 808.

[212] *See,* e.g., Bd. of Regents of State Colls. v. Roth, 408 U.S. 564, 577 (1972); Memphis Light, Gas & Water Div. v. Craft, 436 U.S.1, 11 (1978) (finding a protected property interest derived from state common law); Bishop v. Wood, 426 U.S. 341, 344–47 (1976) (refusing to find a protected interest in an ordinance which failed to provide conditions where individuals could be deprived of their job); Arnett v. Kennedy, 416 U.S. 134, 153–54 (1974) (plurality opinion) (finding that a statute which afforded employee right to be discharged only for cause created a property interest). *See also* Hugenberger, *supra* note 85, at 781–83, 808–809.

[213] Hugenberger, *supra* note 177, at 809.

[214] *Id.* at 810 ("*Castle Rock* seemed to suggest that even if the enforcement of a restraining order constituted an entitlement under state law, the indirect nature of the benefit on a claimant could bar constitutional recognition of that entitlement.").

[215] *See id.* at 811.

The naming of a "new property" interest therefore depends on the existence of some mandatory, nondiscretionary standard.[216] When such a standard exists and unqualified discretion has not been left with officials, then a "legitimate expectation has been created that [a] decision [will] be based on that standard."[217] The requirement of a nondiscretionary standard for the creation of a legitimate expectation has, at least in part, a pragmatic basis. Such a standard confers a right onto the individual to assert the use of procedures in guaranteeing its appropriate application. Where officials are provided with an expansive discretion in the application of the law, however, the existence of an official hearing or alternative procedures may be a waste of resources, because the individual generally would have less basis to contest a discretionary decision.

MODERN LIBERTY INTERESTS

Although liberty interests traditionally were associated with protections against punishment and physical restraint, the Supreme Court later determined that liberty includes a much more extensive range of issues:

> [The liberty interest] denotes not merely freedom from bodily restraint but also the right of the individual to contract, to engage in any of the common occupations of life, to acquire useful knowledge, to marry, establish a home and bring up children, to worship god according to the dictates of his own conscience, and generally to enjoy those privileges long recognized ... as essential to the orderly pursuit of happiness by freemen.[218]

By one account, liberty is the "right to define one's own concept of existence, of meaning, of the universe, and of the mystery of human life."[219] Liberty interests may be derived directly from the Due Process Clause or from state law.[220] In order for state law to create a protected liberty interest, however, it generally must utilize mandatory language and limit government discretion.

---

[216] Charles H. Koch, Jr., Administrative Law and Practice § 2:21 (3d ed. 2011).

[217] *See id.*

[218] Meyer v. Nebraska, 262 U.S. 390, 399 (1923), quoted in *Finding a "Due Process Interest,"* 32 Fed. Prac. & Proc. Judicial Review § 8127 (1st ed.).

[219] Planned Parenthood of Se. Pa. v. Casey, 505 U.S. 833, 851 (1992).

[220] *See, e.g.*, Sandin v. Connor, 515 U.S. 472 (1995); Meachum v. Fano, 427 U.S. 215 (1976). Others have argued that:

> *Meachum* is notable for its clear refusal to give the liberty notion any independent force. The state may eliminate any liberty interest, and thus escape any minimum procedures requirement, by statutory negation or by not specifying positive criteria for decision. To be sure, the result is less controversial in relation to prison inmates—which is the way subsequent cases deal with *Meachum*—but the language of the opinion suggests no such qualification. *Meachum* treated liberty just like property; both interests had to be created by positive state law of an independent constitutional provision.

Rubin, *supra* note 32, at 1076 (1984) (citations omitted).

As with property interests, statutes that permit officials a broad range of discretion, without constraint, are unlikely to create protected liberty interests. Moreover, the body of law defining liberty interests similarly has experienced considerable extension, from original protections in being free from physical restraint to the more recent safeguarding against more abstract liberties, such as reputational injury and privacy, protection of certain liberties for incarcerated persons, and for aliens.

a) Reputation[221]

Beginning in 1971, the Court in *Wisconsin v. Constantineau*[222] expanded the recognized liberty interests to governmental actions that may cause damage to one's reputation, finding that the potential threat of stigmatization may be sufficient to implicate due process protection.[223] In *Constantineau*, the police of Hartford posted the plaintiff's name in liquor outlets, notifying the owners not to sell alcohol to the plaintiff because of her alleged conduct while intoxicated.[224] The Court found that a liberty interest existed and "where a person's good name, reputation, honor or integrity is at stake because of what the government is doing to him, notice and opportunity to be heard [are] essential."[225] In the following year, the *Roth* decision merged the existing concept of liberty in employment with that of the reputational interest, holding that an employer is prevented from dismissing an employee when such termination might result in "serious damage" or "stigma" to the individual's standing.[226]

A few years later, however, the Court began a retreat from the broad holding of *Constantineau*, eventually requiring that the protection of a liberty interest should necessitate loss of an existing statutory entitlement, in addition to reputational harm. In *Paul v. Davis*,[227] respondent's "mug shot" appeared on a flyer distributed to merchants, labeling him as an "active shoplifter" due to a previous arrest.[228] The respondent subsequently brought an action that the posting of the flyers had deprived him of his constitutional rights.[229] The Court held that an employee must experience both (1) reputational harm and (2) a tangible loss, in order to implicate

---

[221] For a summary of the Court's treatment of reputational interests, *see* WASSERMAN, *supra* note 2, at 42–45.

[222] 400 U.S. 433 (1971).

[223] *See* WASSERMAN, *supra* note 2, at 42–43; *see also supra* notes 39–41.

[224] *See Constantineau*, 400 U.S. at 434–35.

[225] *See id.* at 435; *see also* WASSERMAN, *supra* note 2, at 42.

[226] Bd. of Regents of State Colls. v. Roth, 408 U.S. 564, 572–76 (1972) (ruling that "[t]he State, in declining to rehire the respondent, did not make any charge against him that might seriously damage his standing and associations in his community. It did not base the nonrenewal of his contract on a charge, for example, that he had been guilty of dishonesty, or immorality. Had it done so, this would be a different case."); *see also* WASSERMAN, *supra* note 2, at 42–43.

[227] 424 U.S. 693 (1976); *see also* WASSERMAN, *supra* note 2, at 43.

[228] *Id.* at 695–96.

[229] *Id.* at 696.

the due process protections.[230] The Court determined that no liberty interest existed when police officers distributed flyers to merchants that warned them that the plaintiff was a "shoplifter," despite not being convicted of any offense.[231] The government's actions must result in the deprivation of a liberty interest "recognized by state or federal law"[232] and, because an interest in reputation was not recognized by the state's law, it therefore was not a protected liberty under the Due Process Clause.[233] This is known as the "reputation-plus" requirement.[234]

Subsequent decisions often have refused to find a liberty interest based on either the failure of the plaintiff to demonstrate adequate reputational damage or the inability to prove a substantial, tangible loss.[235] The Court's requirement in *Paul* that the state action must alter or extinguish "a right or status previously recognized by state law" in order to invoke procedural protections of the Due Process Clause of the Fourteenth Amendment is not dissimilar from the positivist tests applied under the entitlement doctrine of property interests or, as discussed subsequently, in several prisoners' rights cases.[236]

Adding to the *Roth* line of cases and acting to constrain the protections afforded to reputational damage, the decision of *Bishop v. Wood*[237] found that harmful or stigmatizing allegations must be made available by "public disclosure" in conjunction with the termination in order to implicate a due process occupational liberty claim.[238] Consistent with the views of Justices Rehnquist and Stewart in *Arnett*, the *Bishop* opinion appeared to be an attempt at stemming the definitional expansion of due process protections.[239] Subsequent cases also have required that the claimant allege that the government's charges be false and occur in conjunction with the termination of employment.[240] Further, in the modern era, increasing government activities, including the maintenance of registries for "suspected terrorists,

---

[230] *Id.* at 701–10; *see also* WASSERMAN, *supra* note 2, at 43.

[231] *Davis*, 424 U.S. at 695–96. The Court appeared reluctant to allow respondent's claim to prevail for fear that there did not appear to be "any logical stopping place to such a line of reasoning." *Id.* at 698–99. "Respondent's construction would seem almost necessarily to result in every legally cognizable injury which may have been inflicted by a state official acting under 'color of law' establishing a violation of the Fourteenth Amendment. We think it would come as a great surprise to those who drafted and shepherded the adoption of that Amendment to learn that it worked such a result, and a study of our decisions convinces us they do not support the construction urged by respondent." *Id.* at 699.

[232] *Id.* at 711–12.

[233] *Id.* at 708–709 (stating that the tangible loss in *Constantineau* was the plaintiff's legal right to purchase alcohol.).

[234] Eric J. Mitnick, *Procedural Due Process and Reputational Harm: Liberty as Self-Invention*, 43 U.C. DAVIS L. REV. 79, 81 (2009).

[235] *See* Siegert v. Gilley, 500 U.S. 226 (1991); O'Connor v. Pierson, 426 F.3d 187 (2d. Cir. 2005); Patterson v. City of Utica, 370 F.3d 322, 332–34 (2d Cir. 2004).

[236] *See, e.g.*, Hewitt v. Helms, 459 U.S. 460 (1983); Olim v. Wakinekona, 461 U.S. 238 (1983).

[237] 426 U.S. 341 (1976).

[238] *Id.* at 348; *see also* WASSERMAN, *supra* note 2, at 43.

[239] *Arnett*, 416 U.S. 152–55.

[240] Siegert v. Gilley, 500 U.S. 226 (1991); Codd v. Velger, 429 U.S. 624 (1977); *see also* WASSERMAN, *supra* note 2, at 44.

sex offenders, gang members, prostitution patrons, and perpetrators of domestic abuse are increasingly common," have created an environment rife with the potential for reputational injury.[241]

b) Privacy

Although there is no explicit mention of a protected right to privacy within the United States Constitution, the Supreme Court has on several occasions recognized such a right, predominantly through substantive due process analysis.[242] Among the sources from which a right to privacy may be derived is the Fourteenth Amendment, and government actions that intrude upon this fundamental liberty-based right must necessarily meet certain due process requirements, predicated on the factors provided in *Mathews v. Eldridge*.[243]

c) Prisoners' Liberty Interests[244]

The Supreme Court has recognized that "a valid criminal conviction and sentence extinguish a defendant's otherwise protected right to be free from confinement."[245] Also, "although prison inmates retain a residuum of liberty, this liberty is not infringed by conditions of confinement that are 'within the normal limits or range of custody which the conviction has authorized the State to impose.'"[246] When a state chooses to provide inmates with state-created liberty interests through statutory or regulatory enactments, governmental acts that deprive inmates of those interests may infringe upon recognized and protected liberty interest.

In the 1970s, the Court examined a prisoner's liberty interest on the basis of the "nature" and importance of the interest allegedly threatened. In *Morrissey v. Brewer*,[247] the Court held that the revocation of an inmate's parole constituted

---

[241] Mitnick, *supra* note 234, at 82 (Not only has the "quantitative" risk of harm increased since cases like *Paul* and *Siegert*, but also "the qualitative depth of the resulting harm has increased as well. As we have moved from lists of suspected shoplifters, as in *Paul*, or alleged employment misconduct, as in *Siegert*, to assertions of involvement in terrorism, gang violence, sex offenses, child abuse, and prostitution, the reputational stakes have risen to levels not seen perhaps since the McCarthy era."). Some scholars have argued that the "time is ripe to reconsider the stigma-plus doctrine," in light of the emerging contemporary contexts which create risk for reputational injury. *Id.*

[242] Roe v. Wade, 410 U.S. 113, 152 (1973) ("In a line of decisions ... going back perhaps as far as *Union Pacific R. Co. v. Botsford*, 141 U.S. 250, 251 (1891), the Court has recognized that a right of personal privacy, or a guarantee of certain areas or zones of privacy, does exist under the Constitution." Among the sources from which these privacy rights may be derived is "the concept of liberty guaranteed by the first section of the Fourteenth Amendment.") *See also* Steven C. Bennett, *Privacy and the Procedural Due Process Rights of Hunger Striking Prisoners*, 58 N.Y.U. L. REV. 1157, 1165 (1983).

[243] 424 U.S. 319 (1976). *See* chapter 3 for in-depth analysis of what process is due once a protected interest has been found, and chapter 4 for a more detailed examination of privacy and its due process implications.

[244] *See generally* WASSERMAN, *supra* note 2, at 45–50.

[245] WASSERMAN, *supra* note 2, at 45 (quoting Hewitt v. Helms, 459 U.S. 460, 478 (1983) (quoting Wolff v. McDonnell, 418 U.S. 539, 555–56; Meachum v. Fano, 427 U.S. 215, 225 (1976))).

[246] *Hewitt*, 459 U.S. at 478 (quoting *Meachum*, 427 U.S. at 225) (citations omitted).

[247] 408 U.S. 471 (1972).

deprivation of a protected liberty interest, stating that the Court must consider whether the "weight" and the "nature" of the interest made it such that it falls under the protections of the Fourteenth Amendment.[248] The deprivation caused by revoking the individual's parole was of sufficient quality and weight that it implicated a liberty interest because "its termination inflicts a 'grievous loss' on the parolee and often on others."[249]

The Court historically has recognized two sources of protected liberty interests: the Due Process Clause, and state laws or regulations.[250] For instance, in *Vitek v. Jones*,[251] the Court found the Due Process Clause to be the source of prisoner's liberty interests, protecting a prisoner from involuntary commitment into a mental hospital that would constitute "a major change in the conditions of confinement amounting to a 'grievous loss.'"[252] Similarly, in *Washington v. Harper*,[253] the prisoner's liberty interest was violated when he was involuntarily administered anti-psychotropic drugs. In so doing, the Court found the existence of a protected liberty interest that was distinct from any regulatory or statutory enactment and, as such, necessarily derived from the Due Process Clause itself.[254]

A prisoner's liberty interest also may be a product of statutory creation or regulation. In *Wolff v. McDonnell*,[255] the State of Nebraska provided "a statutory right to

---

[248] *Id.* at 481; *see also* WASSERMAN, *supra* note 2, at 49.

[249] *Id.* at 482; *see also* WASSERMAN, *supra* note 2, at 49–50 (citing Young v. Harper, 520 U.S. 143 (1997) (pre-parole program constitutes a protected liberty interest); Gagnon v. Scarpelli, 411 U.S. 778 (1973) (revocation of probation elicits due process protections); Greenholtz v. Inmates of the Nebraska Penal & Correction Complex (1979) (On the issue of whether an initial parole determination created a protected interest, the Court held that "a reasonable entitlement to due process is not created merely because a State provides for the *possibility* of parole, such possibility providing no more than a mere hope that the benefit will be obtained."); Bd. of Pardons v. Allen, 482 U.S. 369, (1987) (following the holding of *Greenholtz*)).

[250] *See* WASSERMAN, *supra* note 2, at 45. Nevertheless, Justice Stevens has argued that "neither the Bill of Rights nor the laws of sovereign States create the liberty which the Due Process Clause protects. [Instead,] [t]he relevant constitutional provisions are limitations on the power of the sovereign to infringe on the [innate] liberty of the citizen. The relevant state laws either create property rights, or they curtail the freedom of the citizen who must live in an ordered society … [b]ut it is not the source of liberty, and surely not the exclusive source." Meachum v. Fano, 427 U.S. 215, 230 (1976) (Stevens, J., dissenting).

[251] 445 U.S. 480 (1990).

[252] *Id.* at 488 (1980).

> This 'objective expectation, firmly fixed in state law and official penal complex practice,' that a prisoner would not be transferred unless he suffered from a mental disease or defect that could not be adequately treated in prison, gave Jones a liberty interest that entitled him to benefits of appropriate procedures in connection with determining the conditions that warranted his transfer to a mental hospital.

Id. at 489–491; *see also* WASSERMAN, *supra* note 2, at 45.

[253] Washington v. Harper, 494 U.S. 210 (1990) as cited by WASSERMAN, *supra* note 2, at 45.

[254] *Id.* at 221–22 ("We have no doubt that, in addition to the liberty interest created by the State's Policy, respondent possesses a significant liberty interest in avoiding the unwanted administration of antipsychotic drugs under the Due Process Clause of the Fourteenth Amendment.").

[255] 418 U.S. 539 (1974).

good time ... that it is to be forfeited only for serious misbehavior."[256] The Court held that refusal to grant good-time credits deprived the prisoner of a liberty interest, stating that a person's liberty is protected even when it is a statutory creation of the State, since the interest was of "real substance" and the "touchstone of due process" is to protect individuals against arbitrary action of government.[257]

This positivist construal of the liberty interest continued in *Greenholtz v. Nebraska Penal and Correctional Complex*,[258] which addressed whether inmates had a constitutionally protected interest in the initial grant of parole. The Court held that the Nebraska parole-determination provision created an expectancy of release that entitled inmates to a measure of constitutional protection under the Due Process Clause.[259] Although the Court determined that some constitutional protection existed as a result of the statute, it also noted that the "unique structure and language" of the Nebraska statute did not necessarily imply that other state parole statutes would create a protectable entitlement and any such determination would therefore require a "case-by-case" analysis.[260] In the Court's words, "There is no constitutional or inherent right of a convicted person to be conditionally released before the expiration of a valid sentence": such a right must implicitly be rooted in positive law.[261]

The nature or type of standard provided in a statute may be determinative of whether there has been a creation of a liberty interest. In *Olim v. Wakinekona*,[262] the Court noted that while a state statute conditioned prisoner transfer on whether it "jeopardizes the safety, security, or welfare" of other prisoners or prison staff members, this condition was not sufficient to create a liberty interest because there is no "justifiable expectation that [the prisoner] will be incarcerated in any particular State."[263] Confinement of prisoners within another State, "unlike confinement in a mental institution" as in *Vitek*, is "'within the normal limits or range of custody which the conviction has authorized the State to impose.'"[264] Although the transfer in the present case involved "long distances and an ocean crossing," the determinative factor was the "'nature of the interest involved rather than its weight.'"[265]

The Court's elucidation of its positivist conception of due process protection led to greater emphasis on the specific language contained within the statute in

---

[256] *Id.* at 557.

[257] *Id.* at 557–58; *see also* WASSERMAN, *supra* note 2, at 46.

[258] 442 U.S. 1 (1979). *See also* Karen H. Flax, *Liberty, Property, and the Burger Court: The Entitlement Doctrine in Transition*, 60 TUL. L. REV. 889, 899 (1986).

[259] *Greenholtz*, 442 U.S. 1, 12 (1979).

[260] *Id.*

[261] *Id.* at 7.

[262] 461 U.S. 238 (1983).

[263] *Id.* at 242–43, 245–46. "Often, confinement in the inmate's home State will not be possible.... [and] [s]tatutes and interstate agreements recognize that, from time to time, it is necessary to transfer inmates to prisons in other States." *Id.* at 245–46. *See also* WASSERMAN, *supra* note 2, at 47.

[264] 461 U.S. at 248 (quoting Meachum v. Fano, 427 U.S. 215, 225 (1976)).

[265] *Id.* at 247–48 (quoting *Meachum*, 427 U.S. at 224).

determining the existence of a liberty interest. The eventual move toward emphasizing statutory analysis in finding an existing liberty interest in state law was evident in 1983 with *Hewitt v. Helms.*[266] In *Hewitt*, the Court determined that a statute's use of "mandatory language" and "substantive predicates" that constrain the discretion afforded to prison officers created the reasonable expectation that a liberty interest will not be arbitrarily deprived.[267] The case involved an inmate who was confined to administrative segregation following a Pennsylvania State Prison riot, pending further investigation of his role in the event. The inmate brought a claim for violation of his Due Process rights under the Fourteenth Amendment, arguing that Pennsylvania regulations governing state prisons had created a protected liberty interest in his continued residence in the general population. The Court determined that the regulatory language had an "unmistakably mandatory character" that required that procedures "shall," "will," or "must" be employed, as well as "substantive predicates" including "the need for control," or "the threat of a serious disturbance."[268] According to the Court, the "repeated use" of this language in the regulation and employment of administrative segregation "demand[ed] a conclusion that the State has created a protected liberty interest."[269] Thus, states could create liberty interests through mandatory language possessing specific standards for deprivation, paralleling the manner in which new property interests derived from state law could be created.[270]

In the later case of *Sandin v. Connor*,[271] the Court made a significant doctrinal shift away from the *Hewitt* approach of statutory analysis and rejected the search for "mandatory" language. Instead, the Court acted to curtail state-created liberty interests by requiring that prisoners show that prison operators "impose[d] atypical and significant hardship on the inmate in relation to the ordinary incidents of prison life."[272] The Court stated that the state's action in placing the prison in thirty

---

[266] 459 U.S. 460 (1983).

[267] *Id.* at 471–72. (The Court indicates the regulatory language had an "unmistakably mandatory character" which required that procedures "shall," "will," or "must" be employed, as well as "substantive predicates" including "the need for control," or "the threat of a serious disturbance." The "repeated use" of this language in the regulation and employment of administrative segregation "demand[ed] a conclusion that the State has created a protected liberty interest.").

[268] *Id.* at 471–72.

[269] *Id.* Other cases where the Court has refused to find the existence of a liberty interest generally have involved instances where officials effectively possessed "unfettered discretion" or subject to "no conditions on [their] discretionary power" under the relevant statutes or regulations. *Id.* at 479 (citing Conn. Bd. of Pardons v. Dumschat, 452 U.S. 458, 466 (1981) and Montanye v. Haymes, 427 U.S. 236, 243 (1976)). *Compare Hewitt*, 459 U.S. at 471–72 (mandatory regulatory language sufficient to create a protected liberty interest in against administrative segregation), *with* Ky. Dept. of Corr. v. Thompson, 490 U.S. 454, 457 (1989) (ruling that expansive discretion of officials to prevent visits based on "reasonable grounds" resulted in no creation of a protected liberty interest).

[270] *See id.*; *see also* Ky. Dep't of Corr. v. Thompson, 490 U.S. 454 (1989) (finding that setting categories for prison visitors who could be excluded did not create a liberty interest protectable by the due process clause); Wasserman, *supra* note 2, at 46.

[271] 515 U.S. 472 (1995).

[272] Wasserman, *supra* note 2, at 47 (quoting *Conner*, 515 U.S. at 484).

days of segregation did not constitute deprivation of any existing liberty interest, because it did not affect the duration of his sentence.[273] A liberty interest is implicated only when there is "a dramatic departure from the basic conditions of [the] sentence"[274] in "such an unexpected manner as to give rise to protection by the Due Process Clause of its own force."[275]

The apparent purpose of *Sandin* was to retreat from the existing positivist approach for defining the existence of prisoner liberty interests through state law and back toward the 1970s approach that examined the nature of the interest.[276] The Court's decision was, in part, a self-driven pragmatic attempt to address concerns that its gradual shift toward defining liberty based on expectation had created in state law .[277] Following *Sandin*'s constrained definition of liberty, a prisoner must establish that the state has increased the negative consequences on the inmate to a degree sufficient to evoke the protection of the Due Process Clause itself, or that state law has created an interest that was deprived to create an "atypical and significant hardship. . . ."[278] The Court later confirmed the *Sandin* approach in *Wilkinson v. Austin*,[279] although it acknowledged there may be some difficulty in finding the "appropriate baseline" for determining when actions impose "atypical and significant" burdens.[280]

d) Aliens' Liberty Interests

The Court historically has sought to protect the liberty interests of nonresident aliens from arbitrary deprivation without opportunity to be heard.[281] In *Yamataya v. Fisher*, the Court stated

> this court has never held, nor must we now be understood as holding, that administrative officers ... may disregard the fundamental principles that inhere in 'due process of law' ... [to] arbitrarily cause an alien, who has entered the country ... to be taken into custody and deported without

---

[273] *See Sandin*, 515 U.S. at 485–87.

[274] *Id.* at 485; WASSERMAN, *supra* note 2, at 47.

[275] *Sandin*, 515 U.S. at 484.

[276] *Id.* at 481–84.

[277] *Id.* at 481 ("[B]y shifting the focus of the liberty interest inquiry to one based on the language of a particular regulation, and not the nature of the deprivation, the Court encouraged prisoners to comb regulations in search of mandatory language on which to base entitlements to various state-conferred privileges."); *see also* Julia M. Glencer, *An "Atypical and Significant" Barrier to Prisoners' Procedural Due Process Claims Based on State-Created Liberty Interests*, 100 DICK. L. REV. 861, 914 (1996) ("By failing to define the new standard's dimensions, the *Sandin* decision invites litigation over the meaning of the terms 'atypical and significant.'") (arguing that *Sandin* may actually create more litigation).

[278] *Sandin*, 515 U.S. at 480 (quoting Morrissey v. Brewer, 408 U.S. 471, 484 (1972)).

[279] 545 U.S. 209 (2005).

[280] *Id.* at 222–23.

[281] *See, e.g.*, Yamataya v. Fisher, 189 U.S. 86, 100–101 (1903); *see also* Bradley J. Wyatt, Note, *Even Aliens Are Entitled to Due Process: Extending Mathews v. Eldridge Balancing to Board of Immigration Appeals Procedural Reforms*, 12 WM. & MARY BILL RTS. J. 605, 610 (2004).

giving him all opportunity to be heard upon the questions involving his right to be and remain in the United States.[282]

However, over the last century, the Court has established that the rights of aliens vary depending on whether they are inside or outside the borders of the United States.[283] The Supreme Court has stated that "an alien seeking initial admission to the United States requests a privilege and has no constitutional rights regarding his application . . ." but "once an alien gains admission to our country . . . his constitutional status changes accordingly."[284]

When an alien has entered the United States, even through illegal means, he "may be expelled only after proceedings conforming to traditional standards of fairness encompassed in due process of law" and is entitled to immigration proceedings.[285] However, "an alien on the threshold of initial entry stands on a different footing: 'Whatever the procedure authorized by Congress is, it is due process as far as an alien denied entry is concerned.'"[286] Although there has been substantial scholarly criticism regarding the ostensibly contradictory outcome that aliens who illegally enter into the country may obtain greater protections than those attempting to comply with the law at the border, the Court has upheld consistently this position on the basis that individuals within the country inherently develop stronger ties to the country.[287] As a result of the stark line drawn on the basis of physical presence within the country, aliens subject to potential deportation have significantly greater constitutional protection than aliens who are subject to exclusion.[288]

Procedural due process issues can exist in a variety of immigration contexts.[289] Consistent with the contemporary test for determining procedural due process requirements in administrative settings, most commonly procedural due process issues arise when the Board of Immigration Appeals (BIA) or other

---

[282] *Yamataya*, 189 U.S. at 100–101.

[283] Dulce Foster, Note, *Judge, Jury and Executioner: INS Summary-Exclusion Power under the Illegal Immigration Reform and Immigrant Responsibility Act of 1996*, 82 MINN. L. REV. 209, 218 (1997).

[284] Landon v. Plasencia, 459 U.S. 21, 32 (1982).

[285] Shaughnessy v. United States ex rel. Mezei, 345 U.S. 206, 212 (1953) (citing *Yamataya*, 189 U.S. at 100–101).

[286] *Id.* (citing Knauff v. Shaughnessy, 338 U.S. 537, 544 (1950); Ekiu v. United States, 142 U.S. 651, 660 (1892)).

[287] *See* Foster, *supra* note 283, at 218 & n.54 (citing commentators that critique the Court's "entry doctrine").

[288] In the 1950s, the Court reversed a trend toward expanding procedural rights to both deportable and excludable aliens in *Knauff v. Shaughnessy*, 338 U.S. 537 (1950). *See* Foster, *supra* note 283, at 222. *Knauff* asserted that the "government had unlimited, unreviewable power to regulate procedure in exclusion cases" while upholding the exclusion of an alien whom was married abroad to an American citizen. *Id.*

[289] As compared with the Supreme Court's less frequent adjudication of procedural due process cases, due process issues within the immigration context occur more regularly in the Third, Fifth, and Ninth Circuit Courts of Appeals cases. ANNA O. LAW, THE IMMIGRATION BATTLE IN AMERICAN COURTS 215 (2010). "In immigration cases between 1881 and 2002, the Supreme Court used procedural due process in 9 percent of its majority decisions." *Id.* at 217.

administrative agencies fail to follow the general procedures that they, themselves, have created.[290] In addition to an immigration agency failing to follow its own rules, procedural due process violations in the immigration context have also included failure to provide a competent interpreter or the use of a "boilerplate" judicial decision that facially does not appear to consider the circumstances of the case before the court.[291]

Due process violations also may occur when there is an apparent abuse of discretion by an immigration agency in adjudication or prior processing of a case.[292] In *Diaz-Resendez v. Immigration and Naturalization Service*,[293] the Fifth Circuit held that the BIA's "decision may be reversed as an abuse of discretion when it is made without rational explanation, or inexplicably departs from established policies" without a reasoned explanation.[294] Additionally, the Courts of Appeals have repeatedly recognized the procedural right to the availability of a competent interpreter and demonstrated a broader recognition of the importance that aliens who do not speak English are aware of the charges brought against them.[295]

As compared with the less frequent appearance of procedural due process issues in the Supreme Court, where such issues arise seemingly only in "egregious situations of government excess and error," procedural due process has taken a more significant role in immigration appeals for the Third, Fifth, and Ninth Circuit Courts.[296]

---

[290] *Id.* at 211. The BIA is the "highest administrative body for interpreting and applying immigration laws" and has "nationwide jurisdiction to hear appeals from certain decisions rendered by immigration judges and by district directors of the Department of Homeland Security ... in which the Government of the United States is one party and the other party is an alien, a citizen, or a business firm." *Board of Immigration Appeals*, United States Department of Justice, www.justice.gov/eoir/biainfo.htm (last visited Feb. 14, 2012).

[291] *Id.*

[292] *Id.* at 212.

[293] 960 F.2d 493 (1992).

[294] *Id.* at 495. Diaz-Resendez, a lawful-resident alien, was arrested at a checkpoint with approximately twenty-one pounds of marijuana in his vehicle and pled guilty to possession, triggering deportation proceedings in which he petitioned for discretionary relief from deportation under section 212(c) of the Immigration and Nationality Act. *Id.* at 494–95.

[295] Law, *supra* note 289, at 214. For example, in *Hernandez-Garza v. Immigration and Naturalization Service*, 882 F.2d 945 (5th Cir. 1989), an alien, Hernandez-Garza, was charged with aiding and abetting an undocumented alien and signed two affidavits written in English. Hernandez-Garza's attorney argued that his client was not aware of the contents of the affidavit nor did he understand them when they were signed. The issue at stake was determining if the border agents had sufficient command of Spanish to competently relay the contents of the affidavits to Hernandez-Garza prior to his signing of the documents. *See* Law, *supra* note 289, at 214.

[296] Law, supra note 289, at 215. "[T]he use of due process as a mode of legal reasoning by the Courts of Appeals is motivated and reinforced not just by a general judicial commitment to fair process but by the specific institutional role expectation of these courts to continue their function as error correctors.... In the U.S. Courts of Appeals cases where aliens won their appeals, the most common mode of legal reasoning used was procedural due process." *Id.*

MODERN LIFE INTERESTS[297]

Although the Court has made references to a life interest in the context of capital punishment cases,[298] abortion cases,[299] and "right to die" cases,[300] the life interest has been seldom explored by the Court in its development of due process jurisprudence, particularly in civil cases.

Within the criminal context of capital punishment, an individual's life interest is subject to a variety of stringent procedural protections.[301] Unlike the inquiries applied by the Court in determining whether a protected property or liberty interest exists, the existence of a life interest of a living individual appears to be axiomatic.[302] In *Ohio Adult Parole Auth. v. Woodard*,[303] Justice Stevens stated that

> [t]he text of the Due Process Clause properly directs our attention to state action that may "deprive" a person of life, liberty, or property. When we are evaluating claims that the State has unfairly deprived someone of liberty or property, it is appropriate first to ask whether the state action adversely affected any constitutionally protected interest. Thus, we may conclude, for example, that a prisoner has no "liberty interest" in the place where he is confined, or that an at-will employee has no "property interest" in his job. There is, however, no room for legitimate debate about whether a living person has a constitutionally protected interest in life. He obviously does.[304]

As Justice Stevens wrote in the dissent, this conception appeared to be well-received by the majority of Justices and is consistent with the notion that there is an enduring protected interest in life simply by virtue of being alive.

Although the Court appears to agree that there is a persistent life interest, the extent to which that interest may be legally relevant is not clear. Chief Justice Rehnquist suggested that following a conviction, in some instances it may be little more than that of a "residual life interest ... in not being summarily executed by prison guards."[305] Under this view, even though a prisoner may technically still possess a residual interest, he effectively has minimal legal right in that interest. This conception differs greatly from the notion articulated by Justice O'Connor in

---

[297] *See generally* Wasserman, *supra* note 2, at 32–33.

[298] *Id.* (citing Shafer v. South Carolina, 532 U.S. 36 (2001); Gardner v. Florida, 431 U.S. 953 (1977)).

[299] *See* Roe v. Wade, 410 U.S. 113 (1973).

[300] *See* Cruzan v. Mo. Dept. of Health, 497 U.S. 261 (1990).

[301] Wasserman, *supra* note 2, at 32 ("Although the Court has developed much of its capital punishment jurisprudence under the Eighth Amendment ban on cruel and unusual punishment, it has also invoked the Due Process Clause, proceeding on the often unstated assumption that the defendant's interest in avoiding the death penalty is a protected life interest.").

[302] Ohio Adult Parole Auth. v. Woodard, 523 U.S. 272, 291 (1998) (Steven, J. dissenting).

[303] *Id.*

[304] *Id.*

[305] *Id.* at 281. (While the Court in *Woodard* agreed that a residual life interest exists, respondent in the present case could not "use his interest in not being executed in accord with his sentence to challenge [a] clemency determination by requiring the procedural protections he seeks.").

the concurrence, who argued that while an individual's conviction may extinguish his liberty interest, a significant life interest remains.[306]

A clear instance of government action violating the protected life interest of an individual occurred in the capital punishment case of *Gardner v. Florida*.[307] The petitioner was convicted of murder and sentenced to death based in part on an undisclosed presentencing report that was not made available to the petitioner or his counsel.[308] The Court noted that the "defendant has a legitimate interest in the character of the procedure [that] leads to the imposition of sentence even if he may have no right to object to a particular result of the sentencing process."[309] The Court concluded that the sentencing process failed to meet the requirements of the Due Process Clause that "no person shall be deprived of life without due process of law."[310]

Alternatively, in *Cruzan v. Missouri Dept. of Health*,[311] the Court found that an incompetent patient has a constitutionally protected due process right to life sustaining treatment. While "it cannot be disputed that the Due Process Clause protects an interest in life as well as an interest in refusing life-sustaining medical treatment,"[312] the State may assert "an unqualified interest in the preservation of human life to be weighed against the constitutionally protected interest of the individual."[313]

Despite this inherent assumption that individuals have a protected life interest simply through being alive,[314] the Court has not extended that interest to the developing fetus. In *Roe v. Wade*[315] and later *Planned Parenthood v. Casey*,[316] the Court rejected the notion that an unborn fetus was a person with a protected life interest within the purview of the Due Process Clause.[317] Based on the nearly universal application of the word "person" within the Constitution in only post-natal contexts, along with freer abortion practices through most of the nineteenth century, the Court was persuaded that "the word 'person,' as used in the Fourteenth Amendment does not include the unborn," and therefore could not have a constitutionally protected life interest.[318] Therefore, "as a matter of federal constitutional law, a developing organism that is not yet a 'person' does not have what is sometimes described as a 'right to life.'"[319]

---

[306] *Id.* at 289 ("When a person has been fairly convicted and sentenced, his liberty interest, in being free from such confinement, has been extinguished. But it is incorrect ... to say that a prisoner has been deprived of all interest in his life before his execution.").

[307] 430 U.S. 349 (1977) as cited by WASSERMAN, *supra* note 2 at 32.

[308] *See Gardner*, 430 U.S. at 353.

[309] *Id.* at 358.

[310] *See id.* at 351, 358.

[311] 497 U.S. 261 (1990).

[312] *Cruzan*, 497 U.S. at 281.

[313] WASSERMAN, *supra* note 2, at 32 (quoting *Cruzan*, 497 U.S. at 282).

[314] Ohio Adult Parole Auth. v. Woodard, 523 U.S. 272, 291 (1998) (Steven, J. dissenting).

[315] 410 U.S. 113 (1973).

[316] 505 U.S. 833 (1992).

[317] *Roe*, 410 U.S. at 157–58.

[318] *Id.*

[319] *Planned Parenthood*, 505 U.S. at 913 (Stevens J., concurring).

Although direct explication of this interest by the Court has been sparse, there appears to be some conception that the life interest exists independent of state law or the nature of government action.[320] And, although the interest apparently endures following conviction, the extent and degree to which that life interest exerts its relevance presently remain unclear.

IV. Conclusion

The 1970s ushered in a procedural due process revolution that greatly expanded the definitions of constitutionally protected due process interests. At the same time, the Court expanded the concept of due process as the home of substantive rights that drew on "liberty" as a textual and conceptual platform. This evolutionary process of recognizing and extending the sphere of constitutionally protected rights forced the Court to grapple with difficult issues in defining the scope and sources of these two strands of due process. Key among them are whether an interest falls within the "life, liberty or property" embrace, and if so, what specific rights follow. What is clear, however, is that procedural due process has undergone substantial changes in the post-bellum period, as courts have confronted new forms of government benefits and sought to apply the traditional due process promise in an altered regulatory environment. The balance between liberty and government discretion has been struck differently across regulatory contexts, as well as across time. Also clear is that procedural rights are entwined with, not separate from, substantive rights. Procedural integrity concerns about notice, transparency, and opportunity to be heard become more acute when the interest being burdened or terminated is regarded as important or fundamental to individual liberty. Finally, procedural due process is designed to police arbitrary government action. It protects individuals from government action that departs from a liberal expectation of government rationality, and that violates reasonable expectations about the proper limits on how government power is exercised.

We turn now to the second step of procedural due process, which requires the Court to assess what process is due once an interest has been identified. We follow this discussion with a survey of the panoply of rights that have been deemed to fall within substantive due process.

---

[320] Phillip John Strach, *Ohio Adult Parole Authority v. Woodard: Breathing New "Life" into an Old Fourteenth Amendment Controversy*, 77 N.C.L. Rev. 891, 919 (1999) (citing *Woodard*, 523 U.S. 272(1998)) (O'Connor, J., concurring in part and concurring in the judgment). Strach notes that while five of the Justices "may have paved the way for groundbreaking due process jurisprudence" through this independently derived life interest, there still exists a number of uncertainties and divisions regarding the nature of clemency and the life interest in the context of procedural due process. *Id.* at 920–92.

{3}

What Process Is Due?

In the two-step framework discussed in chapter 2, the Court first asks whether there has been a deprivation of a protected interest. Only after answering in the affirmative does the Court turn to whether the procedures in place meet the requirements of due process. The Court then balances the interests of the individual against the interests of society in an attempt to approximate a fair and just outcome, one that provides a meaningful check against arbitrary government abuse and one that is consistent with the purposes of the Due Process Clause.

I. Historical Background

The Court's analysis of the procedures required by the Due Process Clauses has evolved over time, as has its analysis of protected interests. The Court first defined the procedures required by due process by reference to settled usages and customs drawn from English common and statutory law, then moved to a more holistic analysis of contemporary and historical laws and customs.[1] Finally, the Court began to consider more abstract notions of fairness and justice for guidance.

In some of the earliest treatments of due process, courts held that the law of the land[2] was simply a guarantee that citizens would be subject to whatever laws had been passed by the legislature, and that they would not be subject to foreign or arbitrary power.[3] This interpretation of due process "stated an uncontroversial

---

[1] Early courts often looked to English statutes for guidance. *See, e.g.*, Murray's Lessee v. Hoboken Land & Improvement Co., 59 U.S. 272, 276–77 (1856) (noting that the Court "look[ed] to those settled usages and modes of proceeding existing in the common and statute law of England ... which are shown not to have been unsuited to their civil and political condition.").

[2] The "law of the land language" originated in the Magna Carta. *See, e.g.*, Frank H. Easterbrook, *Substance and Due Process*, SUP. CT. REV. 85, 95 (1982) ("One of the sources of the due process language is the Magna Carta, in which the King promised to conduct certain matters 'per legem terrae,' or 'by the law of the land.'"). *See* chapter 1 *supra*.

[3] *See* Easterbrook, *supra* note 2, at 95–99 (arguing that the accepted meaning of the due process clause represented Coke's ideas) ("It may be assumed that the Due Process Clause embodies Coke's views at their broadest. This would not affect very many cases. Whatever reading holds, the Due Process Clause places little or no legitimate restraint on the contents of legislation. Judges and Presidents must follow rules laid down in 'law'; judges may not act *ex parte* in important matters; but Congress may establish as law such procedures as it pleases, subject only to the constraint that it not abrogate certain long-recognized judicial procedures when fundamental natural liberties are at stake.") (footnotes omitted).

principle that was expected to be trivial."[4] This may explain why the Due Process Clause of the Fifth Amendment was included with little, if any, debate. It also may explain why the Due Process Clause was not addressed by the United States Supreme Court for sixty-five years after its inclusion, even though the Court was actively interpreting other constitutional provisions.[5] This limited interpretation eventually fell from common use, however, even though it occasionally found support from certain members of the Court[6] and from critics of substantive due process.[7]

In later years, the Due Process Clause became a check on the power of the legislature, and also on the executive and judicial branches. Accordingly, the "law of the land" came to represent principles broader than enacted laws.[8] The Court recognized this broader interpretation in its first decision analyzing the Due Process Clause.[9]

> It is manifest that it was not left to the legislative power to enact any process which might be devised. The article is a restraint on the legislative as well as on the executive and judicial powers of the government, and cannot be so construed as to leave congress free to make any process "due process of law," by its mere will.[10]

This left the question of what criteria should be employed to determine the law of the land. Two different lines of analysis developed. The first is known as

---

[4] *Id.* at 99.

[5] *Id.*

[6] *In re Winship*, 397 U.S. 358, 382 (1970) (Black, J., dissenting) (discussing the Court's broadened understanding of the "law of the land") ("In my view … [the Court] gave 'due process of law' an unjustifiably broad interpretation. For me the only correct meaning of that phrase is that our Government must proceed according to the 'law of the land'—that is, according to written constitutional and statutory provisions as interpreted by court decisions."); *see also* Ryan C. Williams, *The One and Only Substantive Due Process Clause*, 120 Yale L.J. 408, 420 (2010).

[7] Williams, *supra* note 6 (citing to various critics of substantive due process who have pointed to Justice Black's words for support).

[8] Murray's Lessee v. Hoboken Land & Improvement Co., 59 U.S. 272, 276 (1856) ("The constitution contains no description of those processes which it was intended to allow or forbid. It does not even declare what principles are to be applied to ascertain whether it be due process. It is manifest that it was not left to the legislative power to enact any process which might be devised. The article is a restraint on the legislative as well as on the executive and judicial powers of the government, and cannot be so construed as to leave congress free to make any process 'due process of law,' by its mere will.").

[9] The Court's first decision regarding the Due Process Clause of the Fifth Amendment was *Murray's Lessee*. *See, e.g.*, Easterbrook, *supra* note 2, at 100.

[10] *Murray's Lessee*, 59 U.S. at 276; *see also* Easterbrook, *supra* note 2, at 101 ("Justice Curtis's scholarly opinion [in *Murray's Lessee*] traced the origin of the Clause from Magna Carta, explaining that the words due process 'were undoubtedly intended to convey the same meaning as the words' "by the law of the land." He also referred to Coke, and, drawing on Coke's natural law precepts—no longer natural law if they had been embodied in the Fifth Amendment—concluded that 'it was not left to the legislature to enact any process which might be devised,' apparently because free rein for Congress would enable it to destroy every person's natural liberties.") (citing *Murray's Lessee*, 59 U.S. at 276).

the settled usage approach,[11] which argues for a fixed notion of due process that is steeped in tradition. The other argues for the use of a flexible and changing standard for defining due process.[12] Overall, the settled usage approach was prevalent in early due process jurisprudence with continuing support from more traditionalist justices, like Justice Scalia, while the latter, flexible and changing approach, gained support in the mid-twentieth century and became the ubiquitous standard after *Mathews v. Eldridge*.[13]

The Court first articulated its settled usage approach in *Murray's Lessee v. Hoboken Land & Improvement Co.*[14] In *Murray's Lessee*, an action for ejectment in which two parties claimed rights to the same property,[15] the defendants claimed title under a distress warrant that was issued to collect property of a debtor to the government without a prior hearing.[16] The Court ruled that the legislation providing for the distress warrant was subject to due process and subsequently performed a due process analysis to determine constitutionality.[17] In its due process analysis, the Court used a two-part test. The first part of the test "examine[d] the [C]onstitution itself, to see whether this process [was] in conflict with any of its provisions."[18] Then, if there were no conflict, the Court "look[ed] to those settled usages and modes of proceeding existing in the common and statute law of England ... which [were] shown not to have been unsuited to their civil and political condition."[19] Thus, the Court defined due process through a historical analysis.[20]

Subsequent cases expanded on the historical approach, including the recognition of abstract principles of justice. After the adoption of the Fourteenth Amendment, the Court confirmed the applicability of the settled usage approach.[21]

---

[11] The "settled usage" language appears in Justice Curtis's majority opinion in *Murray's Lessee*. 59 U.S. at 277.

[12] *See, e.g.*, Joint Anti-Fascist Refugee Comm. v. McGrath, 341 U.S. 123, 162–63 (1951) (Frankfurter, J., concurring) ("It may fairly be said that, barring only occasional and temporary lapses, this Court has not sought unduly to confine those who have the responsibility of governing by giving the great concept of due process doctrinaire scope. The Court has responded to the infinite variety and perplexity of the tasks of government by recognizing that what is unfair in one situation may be fair in another.").

[13] 424 U.S. 319 (1976).

[14] 59 U.S. 272 (1856).

[15] *Id.* at 274.

[16] *Id.* at 272, 274.

[17] *Id.* at 275–76 ("[W]hether, under the constitution of the United States, a collector of the customs, from whom a balance of account has been found to be due by accounting officers of the treasury, designated for that purpose by law, can be deprived of his liberty, or property, in order to enforce payment of that balance, without the exercise of the judicial power of the United States, and yet by due process of law, within the meaning of those terms in the constitution; and if so, then, secondly, whether the warrant in question was such due process of law?").

[18] *Id.* at 276–77.

[19] *Id.* at 277.

[20] *See, e.g.*, Rhonda Wasserman, Procedural Due process: A Reference Guide to the United States Constitution 7 (Jack Stark ed., 2004) (describing the due process analysis used by the *Murray's Lessee* court as a "historical analysis.").

[21] *See* Pacific Mut. Life Ins. Co. v. Haslip, 499 U.S. 1, 30–31 (1991) (Scalia, J., concurring) ("Subsequent to the decision in *Murray's Lessee*, of course, the Fourteenth Amendment was adopted, adding another

It began expanding this approach in 1884, in *Hurtado v. California*,[22] where the defendant argued that the Due Process Clause of the Fourteenth Amendment requires the government to bring an indictment by a grand jury prior to proceedings in criminal cases.[23] The Court held that the lack of an indictment prior to proceedings in the case did not violate due process.[24] The Court expanded the *Murray's Lessee* analysis by establishing that a common law or traditional usage origin to a statute may be sufficient to satisfy due process, but it is not necessary.[25] According to Justice Scalia, *Hurtado* clarified that "[i]f the government chooses to follow a historically approved procedure, it necessarily provides due process, but if it chooses to depart from historical practice, it does not necessarily deny due process."[26] Thus, the Court in *Hurtado* reaffirmed the role of common law and tradition in establishing the principles of due process, while also introducing the "fundamental justice" concept as an alternative method for weighing due process concerns.[27] Justice Matthews, in addition, briefly stated in his opinion that "[i]t is more consonant to the true philosophy of our historical legal institutions to say that the spirit of personal liberty and individual right ... was preserved and

---

Due Process Clause to the Constitution. The Court soon reaffirmed the teaching of *Murray's Lessee* under the new provision: 'A State cannot deprive a person of his property without due process of law; but this does not necessarily imply that all trials in the State courts affecting the property of persons must be by jury. This requirement of the Constitution is met if the trial is had according to the settled course of judicial proceedings. Due process of law is process due according to the law of the land.'") (quoting Walker v. Sauvinet, 92 U.S. 90, 92-93, (1876)).

[22] 110 U.S. 516 (1884).

[23] *Id.* at 519–20 ("It is claimed on behalf of the prisoner that the conviction and sentence are void, on the ground that they are repugnant to that clause of the fourteenth article of amendment to the constitution of the United States, which is in these words: 'Nor shall any state deprive any person of life, liberty, or property without due process of law.' The proposition of law we are asked to affirm is that an indictment or presentment by a grand jury, as known to the common law of England, is essential to that 'due process of law,' when applied to prosecutions for felonies, which is secured and guarantied by this provision of the constitution of the United States, and which accordingly it is forbidden to the states, respectively, to dispense with in the administration of criminal law.").

[24] *Id.* at 538 ("[W]e are unable to say that the substitution for a presentment or indictment by a grand jury of the proceeding by information after examination and commitment by a magistrate, certifying to the probable guilt of the defendant, with the right on his part to the aid of counsel, and to the cross-examination of the witnesses produced for the prosecution, is not due process of law.") *see also* Wasserman, *supra* note 20, at 11 ("[T]he Court concluded that the Fourteenth Amendment Due Process Clause did not require grand juries in state criminal proceedings.").

[25] *See* Pacific Mut. Life Ins. Co. v. Haslip, 499 U.S. 1, 31–32 (1991) (Scalia, J., concurring) (explaining that "*Hurtado*, then, clarified the proper role of history in a due process analysis: If the government chooses to follow a historically approved procedure, it necessarily provides due process, but if it chooses to depart from historical practice, it does not necessarily deny due process. The remaining business, of course, was to develop a test for determining when a departure from historical practice denies due process.").

[26] *Id.*

[27] *Id.* at 32 (quoting Hurtado v. California, 110 U.S. 516, 535 (1884)) ("The remaining business, of course, was to develop a test for determining when a departure from historical practice denies due process. *Hurtado* provided scant guidance. It merely suggested that due process could be assessed in such cases by reference to 'those fundamental principles of liberty and justice which lie at the base of all our civil and political institutions.'").

developed by a progressive growth and wise adaption to new circumstances."[28] This statement has been cited to demonstrate that due process evolves over time,[29] and represents a departure from strict adherence to tradition in the determination of due process principles.

Despite further refinement of the settled usage approach through *Hurtado*, historical practices remained an important consideration in the Court's analysis. In 1908, in *Twining v. New Jersey*,[30] the Court noted that states were only bound to historical procedure that represented "a fundamental principle of liberty and justice which inheres in the very idea of free government and is the inalienable right of a citizen of such a government."[31] This was, however, to be a limited inquiry.[32] History still played an important role in *Twining*, and the Court described the procedures required by due process as "universally prescribed in all systems of law established by civilized countries. . . ."[33] The Court followed the settled usage approach for fifty years, while slowly changing the applicable standards for determining whether a procedure violates due process and finally shifting its focus from history to a fairness standard.[34]

The Court's progression away from the settled usage approach to a more flexible inquiry occurred incrementally, with each step affording less weight to historical considerations and more to considerations of justice. In 1923,[35] the Court decided the due process issue presented without applying the settled usage approach.[36] Noting that "kangaroo courts[37] are unconstitutional,"[38] the Court rested its conclusion on natural law grounds rather than on statutes or historical procedures.[39] It further receded from the settled usage approach in *Powell v. Alabama*,[40]which treated historical practices as insufficient conditions for establishing due process.[41]

---

[28] *See* Hurtado v. California, 110 U.S. 516, 530 (1884) as quoted by Easterbrook, *supra* note 2, at 103.

[29] *Id.*

[30] 211 U.S. 78 (1908).

[31] Easterbrook, *supra* note 2, at 104 (citing Twining v. New Jersey, 211 U.S. 78, 106 (1908)).

[32] *See id.* (quoting *Twining*, 211 U.S. 106–107) ("[W]e must take care that we do not import into the decision our own personal views of what would be wise, just and fitting rules of government to be adopted by a free people and confound them with constitutional limits."); *see also* Pacific Mut. Life Ins. Co. v. Haslip, 499 U.S. 1, 32 (1991) (Scalia, J., concurring) ("The concept of 'fundamental justice' thus entered the due process lexicon not as a description of what due process entails in general, but as a description of what it entails when traditional procedures are dispensed with.").

[33] Wasserman, *supra* note 20, at 14 (quoting *Twining*, 211 U.S. at 111).

[34] *See, e.g., id.* ("In the years since *Twining*, the Court has emphasized history less and fairness more in defining due process.").

[35] Moore v. Dempsey, 261 U.S. 86 (1923).

[36] *See id.* at 90–92 (explaining its holding that a verdict reached by a court that found itself dominated by a mob cannot be upheld on due process grounds).

[37] According to Merriam Webster's dictionary a kangaroo court is "a mock court in which the principles of law and justice are disregarded or perverted." Webster's Third New International Dictionary 1232 (Philip Babcock Gove et al. eds., 1976).

[38] Easterbrook, *supra* note 2, at 105.

[39] *Id.*

[40] 287 U.S. 45 (1932).

[41] Wasserman, *supra* note 20, at 14.

The Court stated that when an accused is unable to retain his or her own counsel, it is "a necessary requisite of due process of law" that the trial judge appoint counsel.[42] In addition, the Court in *Powell* cited *Murray*, *Hurtado*, and *Twining* without referencing the fact that these cases applied a historical analysis in reaching their decisions.[43]

In *Snyder v. Massachusetts*,[44] fairness was added as a factor to be considered in the due process inquiry. The Court concluded that due process was not violated when a judge presiding over a murder trial took the jury to the scene of the crime without the defendant.[45] The Court stated "the Commonwealth of Massachusetts is free to regulate the procedure of its courts in accordance with its own conception of policy *and fairness*, unless in so doing it offends some principle of justice so rooted in the traditions and conscience of our people as to be ranked as fundamental."[46] In the balance of the opinion, the Court considered whether the questioned behavior violated "fundamental justice," though in light of historical practice.[47]

The next substantial turn away from the settled usage approach came in 1936, when the Court disavowed history in favor of a more nebulous and changing conception of due process. In *Brown v. Mississippi*,[48] the Court could have employed the settled usage approach to rule that confessions gained through torture are a violation of due process because torture is a historically prohibited practice.[49] Instead, the Court justified its decision on the ground that confessions obtained through torture are incompatible with "the [fundamental] sense of justice."[50] In *Adamson v. California*,[51] the Court mirrored *Twining's* holding, but not its historical analysis, by invoking modern notions of just procedures.[52] Four years later, Justice Frankfurter's memorable concurrence in *Joint Anti-Fascist Refugee Committee v. McGrath*[53] described the flexible demands of due process as follows:

> "[D]ue process," unlike some legal rules, is not a technical conception with a fixed content unrelated to time, place and circumstances. Expressing as it does in its ultimate analysis respect enforced by law for that feeling of just treatment which has been evolved through centuries of Anglo-American constitutional history and civilization, "due process" cannot be imprisoned within the

---

[42] Powell v. Alabama, 287 U.S. 45, 71 (1932).

[43] Easterbrook, *supra* note 5, at 106.

[44] 291 U.S. 97 (1934).

[45] *Id.* at 104–105; *see also* Pacific Mut. Life Ins. Co. v. Haslip, 499 U.S. 1, 33 (1991) (Scalia, J., concurring).

[46] *Id.* at 105 (emphasis added); *see also* Pacific Mut. Life Ins. Co., 499 U.S. at 33 (Scalia, J., concurring).

[47] Pacific Mut. Life Ins. Co. v. Haslip, 499 U.S. 1, 34 (1991) (Scalia, J., concurring).

[48] 297 U.S. 278 (1936).

[49] Easterbrook, *supra* note 2, at 106.

[50] Brown v. Mississippi, 297 U.S. 278, 286 (1936).

[51] 332 U.S. 46 (1947).

[52] Easterbrook, *supra* note 2, at 107; *Adamson*, 332 U.S. at 53–59.

[53] 341 U.S. 123 (1951) (Frankfurter, J., concurring).

> treacherous limits of any formula. Representing a profound attitude of fairness between man and man, and more particularly between the individual and government, "due process" is compounded of history, reason, the past course of decisions, and stout confidence in the strength of the democratic faith which we profess. Due process is not a mechanical instrument. It is not a yardstick. It is a process. It is a delicate process of adjustment inescapably involving the exercise of judgment by those whom the Constitution entrusted with the unfolding of the process.[54]

As the historical progression has shown, the Court slowly but surely moved away from the settled usage approach and adopted a more flexible approach—"not a yardstick," but a process. It abandoned the settled usage approach without explicitly overruling the applicability of the approach.[55] This new approach has been regarded as a "'rather freewheeling search for procedures seen as fundamental by modern judges.'"[56] Yet it may prevent the offense to notions of justice that may come from the perpetuation of outdated laws and principles as applied to new circumstances.[57]

The Court's "first unmistakable assertion ... of a general power to establish procedures once legislation specifies substance"[58] came in the watershed modern case, *Goldberg v. Kelly*.[59] As we saw in chapter 2, *Goldberg* held that a welfare benefits pretermination hearing must provide "minimum procedural safeguards, adapted to the particular characteristics of welfare recipients, and to the limited nature of the controversies to be resolved."[60] The Court applied a balancing test to weigh the competing interests of the state and the individual to determine what procedures were required by due process in this particular context.

Consequently, by 1970 the Court had recognized the need to strike a balance between the countervailing interests of the individuals and the state, which required that courts apply a flexible approach to due process. In 1976, the Court further refined this balancing test in *Mathews v. Eldridge*,[61] and set forth the relevant factors for all procedural due process cases.[62] In the Court's words, "[t]he ultimate balance involves a determination as to when, under our constitutional

---

[54] *Id.* at 162–63. Notably Justice Frankfurter's concurrence in *Joint Anti-Fascist* has been identified as support for modern due process analysis. *See, e.g.*, Wasserman, *supra* note 20, at 64 (discussing how the Court has explained that determining which procedures due process requires is a flexible inquiry) (quoting Cafeteria & Rest. Workers Union v. McElroy, 1961, which, in turn, quotes Justice Frankfurter's concurrence in *Joint Anti-Fascist*).

[55] Easterbrook, *supra* note 2, at 108–09.

[56] Wasserman, *supra* note 20, at 14 (quoting Frank H. Easterbrook, *Substance and Due Process*, Sup. Ct. Rev. 85, 107 (1982)).

[57] *Id.* (citing Shaffer v. Heitner, 433 U.S. 186 (1977)).

[58] *See, e.g.*, Easterbrook, *supra* note 2, at 108.

[59] 397 U.S. 254 (1970).

[60] *Id.* at 267.

[61] 424 U.S. 319 (1976).

[62] *See, e.g.*, Gary Lawson, Katharine Ferguson, and Guillermo Montero, *"Oh Lord, Please Don't Let Me be Misunderstood!": Rediscovering the* Mathews v. Eldridge *and* Penn Central *Frameworks*, 81 Notre Dame L. Rev. 7 (2005) ("*Mathews v. Eldridge* dominates modern procedural due process law. There are

system, judicial-type procedures must be imposed upon administrative action to assure fairness."[63]

Despite the changes in the standard for determining what process is due to an individual in a certain context over time, the purpose of these procedures has remained the same: to assure that the government makes fair and accurate adjudicatory decisions.[64] The accuracy of government adjudications, as noted earlier, is a core value of liberal democratic societies that respect the rule of law.[65]

Although the *Eldridge* balancing test aids in determining what procedures due process requires, it merely sets general guideposts. Government actors still must make specific determinations of what procedures are required in particular contexts. In the following sections, we describe the application of the flexible due process test to various settings.

II. Contemporary Rules on the Extent of Process

The Court's procedural due process analysis does not consider procedural rights in a vacuum; instead it is a highly contextualized inquiry that gives deference to the government according to the nature of the regime to which the individual is subject.[66] For example, a probationer who is at risk of having five years of probation revoked has no constitutional right to a state-appointed counsel at a probation revocation hearing except on a case-by-case basis,[67] whereas a minor at risk of being detained for five months *does* have a constitutional right to state-appointed

---

some instances in which due process cases are decided without reference to the *Mathews* framework, but they are self-conscious exceptions to the general rule.") (citations omitted).

[63] *Mathews*, 424 U.S. at 348. *See infra* notes 90–92 and accompanying text.

[64] *See* Edward L. Rubin, *Due Process and the Administrative State*, 72 CAL. L. REV. 1044, 1102 (1984), ("Despite the agonies of the past decade, a consensus exists about the purpose of these procedures: to ensure accurate decisionmaking in government adjudications.").

[65] *Id.* at 1102–03 ("Underlying this concern for accuracy is a notion that inaccurate determinations are unfair to individuals. While accuracy may also be viewed as an ingredient of sound policymaking or efficient operations, our current view of the Constitution is that it is not directed toward matters such as these. Instead, it concerns what Deans Choper and Ely have described as the failures of representational democracy, or what others have described as the set of values that are to be protected from any operation, unsuccessful or otherwise, of the representational process. The concern, therefore, must be that an inaccurate decision impinges on some basic value, the constitutional significance of which is defined either independently, or in terms of other values, or in terms of a democracy's inability to protect it. This basic value is essentially the rule of law—that is, the treatment of individuals in accordance with legal standards. An accuracy requirement imposes standards on the decisionmaker, both as a finder of fact and as an interpreter of law.") *See also* chapter 1, *supra*.

[66] *See* Wolff v. McDonnell, 418 U.S. 539, 556 (1974) ("[T]here must be mutual accommodation between institutional needs and objectives and the provisions of the Constitution that are of general application."); Middendorf v. Henry, 425 U.S. 25, 43 (1976) ("[W]hether this process embodies a right to counsel depends upon an analysis of the interests of the individual and those of the regime to which he is subject.") (citing *McDonnell*, 418 U.S. at 539).

[67] Gagnon v. Scarpelli, 411 U.S. 778, 783–91 (1973).

legal representation during the juvenile justice hearing.[68] The liberty interest of the probationer may be greater in magnitude, but the nature of that interest and the administrative context of the decision differ greatly. As the following cases illustrate, striking a balance between the individual and society using procedural protections as the fulcrum is a microcosm of the larger fairness and contextual issues regarding the Rule of Law discussed in chapter 1.

GENERAL ELEMENTS OF A FAIR HEARING

The Court over time has clarified that the rules and requirements of procedural due process are flexible and contextual, stating that due process is "not a technical conception with a fixed content unrelated to time, place and circumstances" and that, due to the "infinite variety and perplexity of the tasks of government," it is possible that a set of procedural safeguards may be fair in one situation but unfair in another.[69] Part of the complexity in determining the appropriate elements of due process required for a given government "task" is that there are so many different types of procedural protections to choose from, with each type of protection varying in degree. In general, when determining the appropriate procedural protections, the Court looks at whether and to what extent the individual has a right to a timely and adequate notice;[70] an appropriately timed hearing;[71] an impartial decision maker;[72] counsel;[73]

---

[68] *See In re* Gault, 387 U.S. 1, 34–42 (1967).

[69] Joint Anti-Fascist Refugee Comm. v. McGrath, 341 U.S. 123, 162–63 (1951) (Frankfurter, J., concurring).

[70] *See, e.g.,* Mullane v. Cent. Hanover Bank & Trust, Co., 339 U.S. 306, 307 (1950). *Compare* Goss v. Lopez, 419 U.S. 565, 577–83 (1975) (ruling that, due to safety concerns and the supervisory role of schools, notice of temporary school suspension can be given at same time of hearing), *with McDonnell*, 418 U.S. at 563–64 (ruling that in hearings over loss of good time credits for inmates, written notice of charges must be given to inmates at least 24 hours prior to disciplinary hearing).

[71] *Compare* Goldberg v. Kelly, 397 U.S. 254, 260–66 (1970) (ruling that due process demands that recipients of welfare benefits receive an evidentiary hearing prior to termination of benefits), *with* Mathews v. Eldridge, 424 U.S. 319, 347–49 (1976) (determining that a post-deprivation hearing for loss of social security disability benefits is sufficient for due process requirements), *and Lopez*, 419 U.S. at 582–83 (when safety or the preservation of the academic process requires it, schools may immediately give temporary suspensions to students pending a post-deprivation hearing).

[72] *See, e.g., In re* Murchison, 349 U.S. 133, 142 (1955) (holding that it is a violation of the Due Process Clause for a judge to try a litigant for contempt for an offense committed before that same judge in a "judge-grand jury"); Tumey v. State of Ohio, 273 U.S. 510, 532 (1927) ("[T]he requirement of due process of law in judicial procedure is not satisfied by the argument that men of the highest honor and the greatest self-sacrifice could carry it on without danger of injustice. Every procedure which would offer a possible temptation to the average man as a judge to forget the burden of proof required to convict the defendant, or which might lead him not to hold the balance nice, clear, and true between the state and the accused denies the latter due process of law.").

[73] *See, e.g.,* Powell v. Alabama, 287 U.S. 45, 72 (1932) (stating that failure to provide counsel in certain cases would be tantamount to "judicial murder"); *Gault*, 387 U.S. at 34–42 (establishing the right to counsel in juvenile trials). *But see McDonnell*, 418 U.S. at 569–70 (holding that due process does not require that prisoners have the right to appointed or retained council for disciplinary hearings, but illiterate inmates can seek assistance from other inmates or from staff).

disclosure of evidence;[74] the right to call or cross-examine witnesses and to present evidence;[75] a written record of the proceedings and the decision;[76] equal access to appeals;[77] and an appropriate standard used for weighing evidence.[78] These procedural elements are the basis of any fair hearing in an adversarial system. The exact permutation of protections that apply in a given situation produces ample amounts of litigation, giving the Court frequent opportunities to expand, contract, or otherwise redirect the course of the nation's procedural protections.[79]

In addition to determining which of the above *types* of procedural protections are required in a given context, the Court also can determine the *degree* to which that procedural protection is enforced, exponentially increasing the Court's ability to pass judgments on the procedural regimes created by Congress and the states. To extend the example provided above, regardless of how severe or mild the potential deprivation may be, a juvenile is always due state-appointed counsel during a juvenile detention hearing;[80] an individual in a civil contempt hearing can retain a counsel but is not always due state-appointed counsel;[81] a probationer is not always entitled to counsel but the arbiter must provide a written explanation of why counsel was not allowed in that particular situation;[82] and a prisoner is not automatically due an appointed or an individually retained council during a noncriminal

---

[74] *See, e.g.*, Brady v. Maryland, 373 U.S. 83, 87 (1963) (withholding evidence of accomplice's confession violated due process requirements).

[75] *See, e.g.*, Washington v. Texas, 388 U.S. 14, 19 (1967) ("The right to offer the testimony of witnesses, and to compel their attendance, if necessary, is in plain terms the right to present a defense, the right to present the defendant's version of the facts as well as the prosecution's to the jury so it may decide where the truth lies. Just as an accused has the right to confront the prosecution's witnesses for the purpose of challenging their testimony, he has the right to present his own witnesses to establish a defense. This right is a fundamental element of due process of law.").

[76] *See, e.g.*, *McDonnell*, 418 U.S. at 564–66 ("Written records of proceedings will thus protect the inmate against collateral consequences based on a misunderstanding of the nature of the original proceeding. Further, as to the disciplinary action itself, the provision for a written record helps to insure that administrators, faced with possible scrutiny by state officials and the public, and perhaps even the courts, where fundamental constitutional rights may have been abridged, will act fairly."); *Gault*, 387 at 58 ("As the present case illustrates, the consequences of failure to provide an appeal, to record the proceedings, or to make findings or state the grounds for the juvenile court's conclusion may be to throw a burden upon the machinery for habeas corpus, to saddle the reviewing process with the burden of attempting to reconstruct a record, and to impose upon the Juvenile Judge the unseemly duty of testifying under cross-examination as to the events that transpired in the hearings before him.").

[77] *See* Griffin v. Illinois, 351 U.S. 12, 16–19 (1956) (recognizing that, while the states are not constitutionally obligated to provide appellate courts, if they do allow a right to an appeal they must do so in a way that does not discriminate against defendants based on their poverty).

[78] *See, e.g.*, Addington v. Texas, 441 U.S. 418, 426–31 (1979) (ruling that in civil commitment hearings, the standard of proof must be greater than a "preponderance of the evidence" standard, but the "beyond a reasonable doubt" standard is not constitutionally required); *In re* Winship, 397 U.S. 358, 365–68 (1970) (explicitly holding that the Due Process Clause requires that each fact necessary to constitute the crime charged must be proved beyond a reasonable doubt in both criminal and juvenile hearings).

[79] *See supra* notes 70-78 and accompanying text.

[80] *See Gault*, 387 U.S. 1, 34–42 (1967).

[81] *See* Turner v. Rogers, 131 S. Ct. 2507, 2520 (2011).

[82] *See* Gagnon v. Scarpelli, 411 U.S. 778, 783–91 (1973).

disciplinary hearing.[83] The "right to counsel," like other basic procedural protections, exists along a continuum.

A review of the cases demonstrates how procedural protections vary. It also shows the careful balancing act undertaken by the Court as it vacillates between giving deference to the government and jealously preserving its role as a protector of individual's interests. Examining procedural due process protections in a comparative context further establishes that protected interests are not absolute, but subject to various limitations. As is common in most areas of law, in its procedural due process cases, the Court defers to the coordinate branches and the states according to the historical and constitutional role that the judiciary plays in the given context. As such, the Court takes a more deferential approach to determining procedural due process rights for criminal defendants because such determinations are traditionally left to the states.[84] In contrast, the Court takes a very active role in determining procedural rights in civil and administrative cases where the Constitution and historical precedent do not demonstrate a commitment of such power to other branches of government.[85]

The degree to which the Court is proactive or deferential, however, does not necessarily correlate with the degree of procedural protection afforded. In criminal cases, for example, defendants usually receive more procedural protections than in many civil and administrative hearings.[86] A closer analysis of the various contexts in which the Court has considered procedural protections demonstrates how the Court's analysis operates on two dimensions: one that is concerned primarily with balancing the interests of the individual and society, and a second that is concerned primarily with judicial constraints, federalism, and the separation of powers.

DUE PROCESS IN SPECIFIC CONTEXTS

One of the most commonly discussed and basic areas of procedural due process analysis are the civil and administrative contexts. The Court has long recognized "that the right to be heard before being condemned to suffer grievous loss of any kind, even though it may not involve the stigma and hardships of a criminal conviction, is a principle basic to our society"[87] and that "some form of hearing is required before an individual is finally deprived of a property interest."[88] The Court has, moreover, taken an active role in defining the requirements for civil and administrative hearings in comparison to its approach to due process

---

[83] *See* Wolff v. McDonnell, 418 U.S. 539, 569–70 (1974).

[84] *See infra* notes 120–63 and accompanying text.

[85] *See infra* notes 89–118 and accompanying text.

[86] *See* Niki Kuckes, *Civil Due Process, Criminal Due Process*, 25 Yale L. & Pol'y Rev. 1 *passim* (2006).

[87] Joint Anti-Fascist Comm. v. McGrath, 341 U.S. 123, 168 (1951) (Frankfurter, J., concurring).

[88] Mathews v. Eldridge, 424 U.S. 319, 333 (1976).

requirements for criminal hearings.[89] This active role is best demonstrated by the *Mathews v. Eldridge*[90] framework that the Court applies to most civil and administrative procedural questions. The *Eldridge* framework weighs

> [f]irst, the private interest that will be affected by the official action; second, the risk of an erroneous deprivation of such interest through the procedures used, and the probable value, if any, of additional or substitute procedural safeguards; and finally, the Government's interest, including the function involved and the fiscal and administrative burdens that the additional or substitute procedural requirement would entail.[91]

This approach gives the Court substantial leeway in considering practical and equitable arguments, and it is consistent with the Court's claim that legislatures can create interests but it is the Constitution that determines the appropriate procedural protections.[92]

This activist approach to determining adequate procedural safeguards invites the Court to make fine distinctions between competing interests that can create what on the surface often seems like incongruous outcomes. The first "new property" case, *Goldberg v. Kelly*,[93] for example, established that a predeprivation hearing was necessary for the termination of Aid for Families with Dependent Children (AFDC) benefits because the nature of the interest was such that an erroneous deprivation could be especially harmful to the individual.[94] In the very similar case of *Eldridge*,[95] however, the Court distinguished *Goldberg* and ruled that a predeprivation hearing was unnecessary for the termination of social security disability benefits because, while the affected parties were likely to rely on such benefits, the benefits themselves were not means tested.[96] Thus it was neither practically nor logically certain that an erroneous deprivation would result in the

---

[89] *See infra* notes 120–63 and accompanying text. *See also* Kuckes, *supra* note 86.

[90] *Mathews*, 424 U.S. at 334–35.

[91] *Id.* at 335.

[92] *See* Cleveland Bd. of Educ. v. Loudermill, 470 U.S. 532, 541 (1985) (noting that property "cannot be defined by the procedures provided for its deprivation any more than can life or liberty. The right to due process 'is conferred, not by legislative grace, but by constitutional guarantee. While the legislature may elect not to confer a property interest in [public] employment, it may not constitutionally authorize the deprivation of such an interest, once conferred, without appropriate procedural safeguards.'") (quoting Arnette v. Kennedy, 416 U.S. 134, 167 (1974) (Powell, J., concurring)).

[93] 397 U.S. 254 (1970).

[94] *See id.* at 264 ("thus the crucial factor in this context—a factor not present in the case of the blacklisted government contractor, the discharged government employee, the taxpayer denied a tax exemption, or virtually anyone else whose governmental entitlements are ended—is that termination of aid pending resolution of a controversy over eligibility may deprive an eligible recipient of the very means by which to live while he waits. Since he lacks independent resources, his situation becomes immediately desperate.").

[95] *See Mathews*, 424 U.S. at 340.

[96] *See id.* at 340–42.

same substantial harm at issue in *Goldberg*.[97] The difference in outcomes between *Goldberg* and *Eldridge* is due partly to a detailed analysis of the procedures already in place for the deprivation of benefits[98] and partly due to a nuanced distinction between the types of harms likely to be suffered by erroneous deprivation.[99] Hypothetically, the nominal amount of the lost benefit could be the same in both cases and the harm to the individual identical,[100] but the Court's balancing of the equities in *Eldridge* was such that a blanket rule requiring a predeprivation hearing could not be justified using the utilitarian *Eldridge* framework.[101]

That the Court methodically weighs interests through a neutral balancing framework, however, is cold comfort to a recipient of social security benefits. Critics of *Eldridge* thus have focused on the framework's insufficient attention to questions of fairness (the word does not even appear in the Court's articulation of the test)[102] and have objected to attempts to subject universally accepted and essential procedures to its balancing framework.[103] Moreover, the *Eldridge* test only looks at the "individual's interest in the substantive right," and ignores the "'non-instrumental' interest that the individual—or society—may have in procedure for procedure's sake."[104] Because of these limitations on the Court's inquiries, the *Eldridge* test has been criticized for focusing solely on economic efficiency.[105] Critics maintain that this approach is erroneous because

> [a]n efficiency-orientated balancing test ... weighs an inevitable and immediately recognizable administrative cost against a largely prophylactic interest in the use of specific procedural protections. Thus, it is likely that the

---

[97] *Id.* at 340–42 ("In view of the torpidity of this administrative review process, and the typically modest resources of the family unit of the physically disabled worker, the hardship imposed upon the erroneously terminated disability recipient may be significant. Still, the disabled worker's need is likely to be less than that of a welfare recipient. In addition to the possibility of access to private resources, other forms of government assistance will become available where the termination of disability benefits places a worker or his family below the subsistence level.") (citations and footnotes omitted).

[98] *Compare Goldberg*, 397 U.S. at 257–60, 268–71, *with Eldridge*, 424 U.S. at 335–39, 343–47.

[99] *See supra* notes 94 and 97.

[100] Because of discontinuation of his disability benefits, Eldridge had his home foreclosed upon and his furniture reposed, "forcing Eldridge, his wife, and their children to sleep in one bed." *Eldridge*, 424 U.S. at 350 (Brennan, J., dissenting).

[101] *See id.* at 348 ("[T]he Government's interest, and hence that of the public, in conserving scarce fiscal and administrative resources is a factor that must be weighed. At some point the benefit of an additional safeguard to the individual affected by the administrative action and to society in terms of increased assurance that the action is just, may be outweighed by the cost. Significantly, the cost of protecting those whom the preliminary administrative process has identified as likely to be found undeserving may in the end come out of the pockets of the deserving since resources available for any particular program of social welfare are not unlimited.") (citing Henry J. Friendly, *"Some Kind of Hearing,"* 123 U. Pa. L. Rev. 1267, 1276, 1303 (1975)).

[102] Martin H. Redish & Lawrence C. Marshall, *Adjudicatory Independence and the Values of Procedural Due* Process, 95 Yale L.J. 455, 472 (1986).

[103] *Id.* at 468.

[104] *Id.* at 472.

[105] *See, e.g., id.*

> Court's balancing test, lacking any minimum floor of procedural protection, will generally find in favor of the governmental interest.[106]

In addition to discounting the rights and interests of individuals, the *Eldridge* framework may "systematically overestimate the benefits and underestimate the costs of formal decisionmaking," and misallocate resources from program beneficiaries to "the army of lawyers and administrative judges required to implement the new decisionmaking procedures."[107] According to some observers, such utilitarian calculations about the value of procedural protections are better left to the politically accountable branches of government.[108] The *Eldridge* test is thus accused of being inappropriately utilitarian from both ends—some accuse it of being too focused on efficiency, while others claim that it creates procedures that are not efficient enough. Despite these alleged problems with *Eldridge*, the Court nevertheless often invokes the framework to establish varying standards for procedural due process.

Although the *Eldridge* approach to civil cases does give government substantial leeway in decision making, some fundamental rights are given greater value under this approach. These more "rooted" rights include the right to notice and a hearing before the deprivation of a significant interest.[109] The foundational case, *Mullane v. Central Hanover Bank & Trust, Co.*,[110] for example, revolved around the type of notice beneficiaries of a trust were due before the trust company altered their rights regarding the trust account.[111] The Court ruled that providing notice by local publication alone was inadequate, and that the type and form of notice must be such that one who was "desirous of actually informing" the other party of the pending litigation might choose such a method.[112]

The language of the *Mullane* decision was much less centered on balancing practical concerns of procedures than with the protection of the almost inviolable rights to notice and an opportunity to be heard.[113] Similarly, in *Fuentes v. Shevin*,[114] the Court ruled that Florida and Pennsylvania prejudgment replevin statutes[115] were unconstitutional deprivations of property under the Fourteenth Amendment Due Process Clause because they denied the right to be heard prior

---

[106] *Id.* at 473.

[107] *See* Richard J. Pierce, *The Due Process Counterrevolution of the 1990s?*, 96 COLUM. L. REV. 1973, 1999 (1996).

[108] *See id.*

[109] *See* Cleveland Bd. of Educ. v. Loudermill, 470 U.S. 532, 542 (1985).

[110] 339 U.S. 306 (1950).

[111] *Id.* at 307.

[112] *Id.* at 315.

[113] *See Id.* at 313–14 ("Many controversies have raged about the... Due Process Clause but there can be no doubt that at a *minimum* they require that deprivation of life, liberty or property by adjudication be preceded by notice.... This *right* to be heard....") (emphasis added).

[114] 407 U.S. 67 (1972).

[115] *See id.* at 73–78. These statutes allowed people to file a "writ of replevin" to recover property without a hearing prior to seizure if it was alleged that the property was held unlawfully by someone else. *See id.*

to the deprivation.[116] As it did in *Mullane*, the Court in *Fuentes* spoke in terms of rights and minimal fairness requirements for due process,[117] carved out only narrow exceptions to the rule,[118] and generally spoke in more absolutist terms than the freewheeling balancing test *Eldridge* otherwise might allow.

In sum, the Court's modern jurisprudence in civil and administrative due process cases generally allows for flexible determinations of process, yet it does not necessarily demand the same level of procedural protection in all contexts. In criminal cases, for example, defendants enjoy more procedural protections than a litigant does in the civil system despite the Court's deferential treatment of legislatively established criminal procedures.

One reason for this is that the Bill of Rights provides many explicit protections to criminal defendants,[119] including the right against double jeopardy and self incrimination;[120] the right to a speedy trial and to counsel;[121] and the right against excessive bail and cruel and unusual punishment.[122] In addition to these enumerated rights, the Due Process Clauses of the Fifth and Fourteenth Amendments provide "free-standing" rights for criminal defendants.[123] The extra procedural protections are many and varied, including the presumption of innocence[124] the prohibition against the government suppression of certain evidence,[125] and the right against excessive publicity of a criminal trial.[126]

---

[116] *See id.* at 96.

[117] *See, e.g., id.* at 82 ("But no later hearing and no damage award can undo the fact that the arbitrary taking that was subject to the right of procedural due process has already occurred. 'This Court has not ... embraced the general proposition that a wrong may be done if it can be undone.'") (quoting Stanley v. Illinois, 405 U.S. 645, 647 (1972)); *id.* at 83–84 (noting that filing a bond prior to seizing property is not sufficient substitute for a hearing).

[118] *Id.* at 90–92 (citing exceptions like meeting the "needs of a national war effort" or protecting "against economic disaster ... and misbranded drugs and contaminated food.") (footnotes omitted).

[119] *See generally* Kuckes, *supra* note 86, at 18 (outlining the major constitutional protections for defendants at trial).

[120] U.S. Const. amend. V.

[121] U.S. Const. amend. VI.

[122] U.S. Const. amend. VIII.

[123] *See* Kuckes, *supra* note 86, at 18 (citing Jerold H. Israel, *Free-Standing Due Process and Criminal Procedure: The Supreme Court's Search for Interpretive Guidelines*, 45 St. Louis U. L.J. 303, 305 (2001)).

[124] *See* Taylor v. Kentucky, 436 U.S. 478, 484–86 (1978) (refusing to give instruction on the presumption of innocence violates right to fair trial as guaranteed by the Fourteenth Amendment's Due Process Clause); Estelle v. Williams, 425 U.S. 501, 503 (1976) ("To implement the presumption [of innocence], courts must be alert to factors that may undermine the fairness of the fact-finding process. In the administration of criminal justice, courts must carefully guard against dilution of the principle that guilt is to be established by probative evidence and beyond a reasonable doubt.") (forcing defendants to stand trial in prison clothes violates the Due Process protection of presumption of innocence); Kuckes, *supra* note 86, at 18 n.101 (citing Coffin v. United States, 152 U.S. 432, 453 (1894) ("The principle that there is a presumption of innocence in favor of the accused is the undoubted law, axiomatic and elementary, and its enforcement lies at the foundation of the administration of our criminal law.")).

[125] *See* Kuckes, *supra* note 86, at 19 n.103 (citing Brady v. Maryland, 373 U.S. 83, 87 (1963) (defendant in murder trial did not receive a fair hearing per due process requirements because the State withheld a statement in which the defendant's accomplice confessed to the murder)).

[126] *See* Sheppard v. Maxwell, 384 U.S. 333, 362–63 (1966) (ruling the due process requirement of a fair trial by an impartial jury mandates that the trial judge protect defendant from "prejudicial publicity"

Given the myriad procedural protections for criminal trials, it is somewhat incongruous that the Court explicitly rejected the flexible, judicially empowering *Eldridge* balancing framework in criminal cases.[127] In *Patterson v. New York*,[128] the Court ruled that criminal procedures do not violate the Due Process Clause unless they offend "'some principle of justice so rooted in the traditions and conscience of our people as to be ranked as fundamental.'"[129] The New York statute required defendants to prove by a preponderance of evidence the affirmative defense of "extreme emotional distress."[130] In applying its "fundamental principles" test, the Court found New York's statute violated no historical or constitutional standards on affirmative defenses and satisfied the due process requirement that the State prove all the elements of a crime beyond a reasonable doubt.[131]

Fifteen years later, in *Medina v. California*,[132] the Court explicitly rejected the *Eldridge* framework in favor of *Patterson*'s approach.[133] In *Medina*, the defendant contested the constitutionality of a California statute that established a presumption that all criminal defendants are competent to stand trial and placed the burden of proving incompetency on the defendant.[134] Using the *Patterson* framework, the Court analyzed the history and traditions of competency hearings and concluded that there was nothing to suggest that California's statute "transgresses any recognized principle of 'fundamental fairness' in operation."[135] The approach used in both *Patterson* and *Medina* relied heavily on an analysis of historical and contemporary practices to discern which traditions, values, and principles are "fundamental."

The *Patterson* standard is, in part, a recognition that criminal law is prototypically a state enterprise and that principles of federalism dictate substantial deference.[136] The Court also has argued that, structurally, the Fifth Amendment itself should not be interpreted to require expansive procedural protections in the criminal realm given the numerous other provisions in the Bill of Rights that explicitly provide

---

and "control disruptive influences in the courtroom"); Estes v. Texas, 381 U.S. 532, 534–38, 550–52 (1965) (holding that radio and television pretrial publicity violated due process right to a fair hearing).

[127] The Court rejected the *Eldridge* framework in *Medina v. California*, 505 U.S. 437, 443–45 (1992).

[128] 432 U.S. 197 (1977).

[129] *Id.* at 202 (quoting Speiser v. Randall, 357 U.S. 513, 523 (1958)).

[130] *Id.* at 198–200.

[131] *See id.* at 210.

[132] 505 U.S. 437 (1992).

[133] *Id.* at 443–45.

[134] *Id.* at 440–42.

[135] *Id.* at 448 (quoting Dowling v. United States, 493 U.S. 342, 352 (1990)).

[136] *See Patterson*, 432 U.S. at 201–02 ("It goes without saying that preventing and dealing with crime is much more the business of the States than it is of the Federal Government. . . .") (citing Irving v. California, 347 U.S. 128, 134 (1954)); *Medina*, 505 U.S. at 445–46 ("As *Patterson* suggests, because the States have considerable expertise in matters of criminal procedure and the criminal process is grounded in centuries of common-law tradition, it is appropriate to exercise substantial deference to legislative judgments in this area."). *See also* Kuckes *supra* note 86, at 15 n.79.

such protections.[137] Presumably, the Framers would not have included both specific procedural protections and an all-encompassing clause for procedural protections. Consequently, the Court defers to the legislative branch to deal with the "more subtle balancing of society's interests against those of the accused."[138] Despite these arguments, the Court never has applied the *Patterson* test consistently. In *Medina*, the same decision in which the Court rejected *Eldridge* balancing approach, the concurring and dissenting opinions noted that the majority used an analysis that was strikingly similar to the flexible analysis employed in *Eldridge*.[139] The majority discussed equitable concerns such as placing the burden of proof on the defendant in an incompetency hearing given the efficacy of psychiatric diagnosis[140] and distinguished, in detail, the practice from those used in claiming insanity at trial[141] and in waiving a competency hearing prior to trial.[142] Weighing such equitable considerations implies that historically based considerations of "fundamental" fairness are not wholly sufficient for due process purposes.

The Court's unease with a purely deferential and historically grounded approach to due process in criminal cases continued to rear its head post-*Patterson* [143] For example, in *United States v. Raddatz*,[144] the Court employed *Eldridge* to determine that the Due Process Clause does not require a district judge to make a de novo hearing on suppression of evidence.[145] The court can instead accept a magistrate judge's recommendations on the matter.[146] In *Ake v. Oklahoma*,[147] the Court used *Eldridge* to determine that the State must provide indigent defendants with access to psychiatrists to assist in preparing an insanity defense.[148] Moreover, the majority coalitions in *Ake* and *Raddatz* consisted of a wide range of justices, which suggests that the continued invocation of *Eldridge* is not just associated with a distinct subfaction of the Court.[149] Although the Court attempted in *Medina* to explain the use

---

137 *See Medina*, 505 U.S. at 443 ("The Bill of Rights speaks in explicit terms to many aspects of criminal procedure, and the expansion of those constitutional guarantees under the open-ended rubric of the Due Process Clause invites undue interference with both considered legislative judgments and the careful balance that the Constitution strikes between liberty and order.").

138 *Patterson*, 432 U.S. at 210.

139 *See Medina*, 505 U.S. at 454 (O'Connor, J., concurring); *id.* at 461 (Blackmun, J., dissenting). *See also* Kuckes, *supra* note 86, at 16 n.83 (citing the O'Connor concurrence in *Medina*).

140 *Medina*, 505 U.S. at 451.

141 *Id.* at 448–49.

142 *Id.* at 449–51.

143 *See* Kuckes, *supra* note 86, at 15 n.78 (citing criminal cases in which the Court used the *Eldridge* factors post-*Patterson*).

144 447 U.S. 667 (1980).

145 *Id.* at 677–81.

146 *Id.*

147 470 U.S. 68 (1985).

148 *Id.* at 77–83.

149 The majority members in *Ake* were Justices Marshall, Brennan, White, Blackmun, Powell, Stevens, and O'Conner. *See Ake*, 470 U.S. at 77. Eight of the nine justices signed on to opinions in *Raddatz* that used the *Eldridge* framework, including Justices Rehnquist and Burger. *See Raddatz*, 470 U.S. at 677–81; *id.* at 686–87 (Blackmun, J., concurring); *id.* at 679–703 (Marshall, J., dissenting).

of *Eldridge* in those two cases,[150] the existence of such cases demonstrates that the Court has not abandoned completely the *Eldridge* balancing approach, nor has it eschewed considerations of equity, in criminal due process decisions.

The similarities between *Patterson*-in-practice and the *Eldridge* approach can be easily overstated, however. The Court occasionally may invoke the flexible balancing test of *Eldridge* in its criminal process cases, but the *Patterson* framework dominates the analysis, and this framework unquestionably relies more heavily on the history of procedural protections and precedent to determine what counts as "fundamental fairness."[151] Thus in *Montana v. Egelhoff*,[152] the Court looked at contemporary state statutes; it considered cases dating back to the early nineteenth century; and it consulted Coke, Hale, and Blackstone in determining that no fundamental principles are violated by a state's refusal to allow a defense of intoxication for the crime of intentional murder.[153] Similarly, in *Herrera v. Collins*,[154] the Court looked at contemporary practice in the states, but also to English and colonial American common law in cases up to the early twentieth century to determine that the refusal to allow a new trial eight years after conviction in order to weigh newly discovered evidence does not violate fundamental principles of justice.[155] In these cases, the Court adopted a presumption, subject to an analysis of historical practice, that the procedure in question did not violate fundamental principles of fairness.[156]

This deference to historical practices, however, does not mean criminal defendants receive lesser protection than individuals receive in administrative and civil cases. On the contrary, due process protections at criminal *trials* are ample relative to other forms of hearings.[157] But as some scholars point out, this is not necessarily the case in *pretrial* matters.[158] Although the same liberty interests are often at stake in a pretrial hearing,[159] defendants can be charged and detained with

---

[150] *Medina*, 505 U.S. at 444–45.

[151] *See* Kuckes, *supra* note 86, at 16 n.83 (citing cases that use *Medina*'s historical approach).

[152] 518 U.S. 37 (1996).

[153] *Id.* at 43–51.

[154] 506 U.S. 390 (1993).

[155] *Id.* at 407–12.

[156] *See Egelhoff*, 518 U.S. at 47 ("It is not the State which bears the burden of demonstrating that its rule is 'deeply rooted,' but rather respondent who must show that the principle of procedure *violated* by the rule (and allegedly required by due process) is 'so rooted in the traditions and conscience of our people as to be ranked as fundamental.'") (quoting Patterson v. New York, 432 U.S. 197, 202 (1997)); *Herrera*, 506 U.S. at 411 ("[W]e cannot say that Texas' refusal to entertain petitioner's newly discovered evidence eight years after his conviction transgresses a principle of fundamental fairness.").

[157] *Cf.* Kuckes, *supra* note 86, at 3.

[158] *See id.* at 18–34, for an excellent analysis of due process protections during criminal pre- and post-trial.

[159] *See* Gerstein v. Pugh, 420 U.S. 103, 114 (1975) ("The consequences of prolonged detention may be more serious than the interference occasioned by arrest. Pretrial confinement may imperil the suspect's job, interrupt his source of income, and impair his family relationships."). Kuckes, *supra* note 86, at 55 n.287 (citing Bell v. Wolfish, 441 U.S. 520, 569 (1979)) (Marshall, J., dissenting) ("For in terms of the nature of the imposition and the impact on detainees, pretrial incarceration, although necessary to secure defendants' presence at trial, is essentially indistinguishable from punishment. The detainee is

substantially lower procedural protections than they receive at an actual trial.[160] The Court has handled more specific procedural guarantees in the Bill of Rights, specifically the Sixth Amendment right to a speedy trial,[161] as an appropriate floor for pretrial procedural protections in part because they "mirror" the traditional, common law requirements of criminal process per *Patterson* and *Medina*.[162] On its face, however, this line of jurisprudence appears inconsistent with typical due process requirements because meaningful procedural checks occur only after the deprivation when there is a criminal trial.[163]

The juvenile justice system further demonstrates the contextual nuances of the Court's procedural due process calculus, given its similarities to and historical differences from the criminal justice system. If the Court gives deference to the states in the criminal justice system because of their traditional role in handling such matters, then it should be even more deferential in its rulings on a system that mixes both criminal elements and aspects of family law.[164] And indeed, the Court's framework for addressing such cases mirrors its approach in *Patterson* when the Court looks for issues of "fundamental fairness."[165] Despite this, a handful of the Court's decisions have made more drastic changes to the juvenile justice system than perhaps all of the criminal procedural due process cases combined.[166] This is due less to a difference in approach, however, and more to a difference in how the systems operated at the time of the rulings—there were simply more violations of "fundamental fairness" in the juvenile justice system.

As several commentators have noted, the juvenile justice system was created in the nineteenth century as an attempt to divert delinquent youths from

---

involuntarily confined and deprived of the freedom 'to be with his family and friends and to form the other enduring attachments of normal life....'" (footnote and citation omitted)); Kuckes, *supra* note 86, at 20–21.

[160] *See* Kuckes, *supra* note 86, at 20–34. Professor Kuckes cites several cases in support of this assertion, including *Baker v. McCollan*, 443 U.S. 137 (1979) (making an arrest based on probable cause is sufficient process for Fourteenth Amendment purposes to justify deprivation of liberty via pretrial detention) and *Lem Woon v. Oregon*, 229 U.S. 586, 590 (1913) ("But since, as this court has so often held, the 'due process of law' clause does not require the state to adopt the institution and procedure of a grand jury, we are unable to see upon what theory it can be held that an examination, or the opportunity for one, prior to the formal accusation by the district attorney is obligatory upon the States.") (holding that the Due Process Clause of the Fourteenth Amendment does not require States to provide a grand jury or other formal preliminary hearings prior to filing criminal charges against a defendant).

[161] U.S. Const. Amend. VI.

[162] *See* Albright v. Oliver, 510 U.S. 266, 282 (1994) (Kennedy, J., concurring).

[163] This is especially true given that, in 2000, defendants who were not released from pretrial detention on an unsecured bond, with conditions, or by some other means were detained on average 106 days. Bureau of Justice Statistics, U.S. Dept. of Justice Statistics, Pub. No. NCJ 194067, Compendium of Federal Justice Statistics, 2000, at 49 (2002), http://bjs.ojp.usdoj.gov/content/pub/pdf/cfjs0003.pdf (accessed 8/19/2011).

[164] *See* Sandra Day O'Connor, *The Supreme Court and the Family*, 3. U. Pa. J. Const. L. 573, 574 (2001).

[165] *See infra* note 195 and accompanying text.

[166] *See infra* notes 173–94 and accompanying text.

developing into adult criminals.[167] It attempted to accomplish this rehabilitative goal by employing a nonadversarial, social agency style of proceedings that focused less on factual determinations of guilt or levying proportional punishment than on determining and treating the therapeutic needs of the juvenile.[168] The judge was likened to a "father" figure and regular procedural protections like the right to counsel or evidentiary rules were eschewed in favor of a cooperative approach to proceedings.[169] Unfortunately, during the mid-twentieth century a lack of resources and the perceived increase of serious juvenile crime combined to create a juvenile court that had either abandoned or was incapable of pursuing the rehabilitative ideal.[170] Juveniles thus were subject to a court system that was punitive in nature similar to the adult criminal justice system but one that lacked the procedural protections afforded adults.[171] Consequently, juvenile sentences consequently were often arbitrary and harsh, something that was compounded by the fact that the sentences were not necessarily tied to any particular crime but instead were largely dependent upon the judge's discretion.[172]

In a series of cases in the mid-twentieth century, the Court confronted the problems that had become endemic in the juvenile justice system. In these cases,[173] the court vastly expanded and qualified the procedural protections due juveniles, and in effect required that the juvenile courts operate in a manner more similar to the adult criminal justice system. In *In re Gault*, a fifteen-year-old was sentenced to six years of detention for allegedly having made or participated in a lewd phone call.[174] The juvenile hearing lacked basic procedural protections or a record of the proceedings.[175] On appeal the trial judge was required to give testimony as to what occurred.[176] The Court reasoned that a juvenile's liberty is no less valuable than an adult's[177] and that juvenile courts consequently should be required to employ

---

[167] *See* Marygold S. Melli, *Symposium: Juvenile Justice Reform: Introduction: Juvenile Justice Reform in Context*, 1996 WIS. L. REV. 375, 376–78. *See also* Barry C. Feld, *Violent Youth and Public Policy: A Case Study of Juvenile Justice Law Reform*, 79 MINN. L. REV. 965, 970–73 (1995).

[168] Melli, *supra* note 167, at 378–80.

[169] *Id.*

[170] *See id.* at 383–84. It should be noted that the juvenile courts may not have been intended to treat serious crimes at all and instead focused only on delinquent behavior which, if committed by an adult, would not be considered a crime at all. *Id.* at 380–82.

[171] *See id.* at 384.

[172] *See id. See also In re* Gault, 387 U.S. 1, 29 (1967) (fifteen-year-old defendant sentenced to detention for up to six years for an offense that, were the defendant an adult, would carry a fine of up to fifty dollars or imprisonment in jail for no more than two months).

[173] Kent v. United States 383 U.S. 541 (1966); *In re* Gault, 387 U.S. 1 (1967); *In re* Winship, 397 U.S. 358 (1970); McKeiver v. Pennsylvania, 403 U.S. 528 (1971).

[174] *See Gault*, 387 U.S. at 4–5.

[175] *See id.* at 5–11.

[176] *See id.*

[177] *Id.* at 27 ("A boy is charged with misconduct. The boy is committed to an institution where he may be restrained of liberty for years. It is of no constitutional consequence—and of limited practical meaning—that the institution to which he is committed is called an Industrial School. The fact of the matter is that, however euphemistic the title, a 'receiving home' or an 'industrial school' for juveniles is

similar procedural protections as exist in the adult system, including the right to notice,[178] an explanation of the charges,[179] the right to confront witnesses,[180] the privilege against self-incrimination,[181] and the right to counsel.[182] The Court also counseled that policies to institute recordings of the proceeding and allow the right of an appeal would be advisable given the administrative burden of doing otherwise.[183]

In *In re Winship*,[184] a twelve-year-old was convicted in a juvenile proceeding of stealing $112 from a woman's wallet on a "preponderance of the evidence" standard and was sentenced to six years at a training school.[185] The Court ruled that juveniles' interests in liberty are not diminished due to age and, as such, that the criminal justice system's "beyond a reasonable doubt" standard was required.[186] In *Kent v. United States*,[187] a sixteen-year-old was waived from juvenile court into the district court without first having a hearing or receiving any procedural safeguards.[188] The Court ruled that a predeprivation hearing and the presence of counsel are required prior to waiving a juvenile into criminal proceedings.[189] Finally, in *McKeiver v. Pennsylvania*,[190] the Court consolidated a number of appeals from cases in which juveniles were convicted for a variety of acts ranging from the theft of 25 cents[191] to taking part in a protest,[192] but all were appealed on the grounds that the lack of a jury trial in the juvenile courts violated the Due Process Clause.[193] The Court ruled that jury trials, while important, are not always necessary in every proceeding and that a constitutional mandate for jury trials in the juvenile system would be unwise.[194]

Throughout these decisions, the Court showed particular concern for the rights and interests of juvenile defendants but did not establish any explicit standard for weighing those interests against the needs of the public or against the

---

an institution of confinement in which the child is incarcerated for a greater or lesser time. His world becomes 'a building with whitewashed walls, regimented routine and institutional hours . . . .' Instead of mother and father and sisters and brothers and friends and classmates, his world is peopled by guards, custodians, state employees, and 'delinquents' confined with him for anything from waywardness to rape and homicide.") (citations omitted).

[178] *See id.* at 31–34.

[179] *See id.*

[180] *See id.* at 42–57.

[181] *See id.*

[182] *See id.* at 34–42.

[183] *See id.* at 57–58.

[184] 397 U.S. 358 (1970).

[185] *See id.* at 359–60.

[186] *See id.* at 368.

[187] 383 U.S. 541 (1996).

[188] *Id.* at 543–46.

[189] *See id.* at 561–62.

[190] 403 U.S. 528 (1971).

[191] *Id.* at 536.

[192] *Id.*

[193] *Id.* at 530.

[194] *See id.* at 540–51. The Court also noted that jury trials are not required in all proceedings, including proceedings in equity, deportation, or military trials. *See id.* at 543.

administrative costs and burdens of the added procedural guarantees. Instead, it adopted a "fundamental fairness" standard.[195] The Court's analysis focused on the likely burdens or benefits that a given procedural protection would pose for juvenile defendants, given that they are being tried in a system that attempts to but often falls short of acting in the juvenile's best interests. The Court found that the right to notice and counsel are necessary to protect against the potential for capricious acts of judges,[196] but cautioned against jury trials because they may lead to unnecessarily adversarial proceedings.[197] Juvenile defendants receive many of the same procedural protections of adult criminal defendants because the juvenile system operates very similarly to the criminal justice system and because the same liberty interests are at stake. At the same time, the Court acknowledged the different goals of the system and diminished the procedural safeguards as a result.[198]

That the goals of a given administrative regime influence the required procedural protections is aptly demonstrated by the Court's procedural due process decisions in civil commitment cases, where the therapeutic purpose of commitment produces lower procedural protections than is warranted in the criminal or juvenile justice systems, while still maintaining an adequate check against erroneous deprivations.[199] Like criminal and juvenile justice cases, civil commitment cases implicate fundamental liberty interests because they can result in long-term confinement.[200] The Court also has recognized that being committed involuntarily for a mental disorder carries with it a risk of stigmatization and reputational harm.[201] This latter harm can be important enough to warrant the full array of procedural protections on its own, as demonstrated by *Vitek v. Jones*,[202] in which the appellee, already an inmate confined by the state, was at risk of being committed to a mental institution.[203] The Court ruled that, while the prisoner's right to be

---

[195] McKeiver v. Pennsylvania, 403 U.S. 528, 543 (1971) ("All the litigants here agree that the applicable due process standard in juvenile proceedings, as developed by *Gault* and *Winship*, is fundamental fairness.").

[196] *See, e.g., In re* Gault, 387 U.S. 1, 18–19 (1967) ("The absence of procedural rules based upon constitutional principle has not always produced fair, efficient, and effective procedures. Departures from established principles of due process have frequently resulted not in enlightened procedure, but in arbitrariness.").

[197] *See McKeiver*, 403 U.S. at 545.

[198] For more on the juvenile justice system, *see generally* Barry C. Feld, *The Transformation of the Juvenile Court*, 75 Minn. L. Rev. 691 (1991).

[199] *See infra* notes 205–23 and accompanying text.

[200] *See* Addington v. Texas, 441 U.S. 418, 425 (1979) ("[C]ivil commitment for any purpose constitutes a significant deprivation of liberty that requires due process protection."); Foucha v. Louisiana, 504 U.S. 71, 80 (1992) ("Freedom from bodily restraint has always been at the core of the liberty protected by the Due Process Clause from arbitrary governmental action.")

[201] *See Addington*, 441 U.S. at 425–26 ("[I]nvoluntary commitment to a mental hospital ... can engender adverse social consequences to the individual. Whether we label this phenomenon 'stigma' or choose to call it something else is less important than that we recognize that it can occur and that it can have a very significant impact on the individual."). *See also* Vitek v. Jones, 445 U.S. 480, 491–92 (1980).

[202] 445 U.S. 480 (1980).

[203] *Id.* at 484–85.

free from confinement was "extinguished" by his criminal conviction, his right to be free from psychiatric treatment and its stigma was undiminished.[204] Despite its recognition of the individual's strong interests in being free of confinement and stigmatization, however, the Court recognizes that such interests are tempered by the potential that civil commitment can benefit those individuals who are truly in need of protection by the state.[205] In using the *Eldridge* balancing framework, it is this more limited liberty interest that produces the marginally less protective procedures for civil commitment cases.

As stated in *Vitek v. Jones,*[206] a civil commitment proceeding requires notice, a hearing, the right to present evidence and confront witnesses, the right to counsel, an independent decision maker, a written statement of the reason for the decision, and timely notice "of the foregoing rights."[207] In addition, if a person is committed, the length of the commitment must bear some "reasonable relation to the purpose for which the individual is committed."[208] Accordingly, it is a violation of due process to indefinitely detain a deaf, mute, and severely mentally handicapped criminal defendant until the defendant is deemed competent to stand trial if there is no hope that he or she will achieve that status.[209] Instead, the state must either institute a normal civil commitment proceeding or release the person.[210] Similarly, the state can only commit people if they are a danger to themselves or others *and* are mentally ill.[211]

Yet the same therapeutic goals that provide important protections during civil commitment proceedings make it easier to be committed for longer periods of time than would be the case under the punitive regime of the criminal justice system. The length of civil commitment is limited by its purpose,[212] but because civil commitment's purpose is tied to the individual's mental illness, the length of commitment also can be unlimited. In *Jones v. United States,*[213] for example, the petitioner was found not guilty by reason of insanity and was committed to an institution for longer than he would have been detained had he received the maximum criminal sentence for his offense.[214] The Court reasoned that, regardless of how serious the criminal act, a person committed by reason of insanity can be released as soon

---

[204] *Id.* at 492–94.

[205] *See Addington*, 441 U.S. at 428–29 (explaining that the "heavy standard" of criminal cases are not applied to civil commitment cases because it is not necessarily true that "it is much better for a mentally ill person to 'go free' than for a mentally normal person to be committed").

[206] 445 U.S. 480 (1980).

[207] *See Vitek*, 445 U.S. at 494–95.

[208] Jackson v. Indiana, 406 U.S. 715, 738 (1972).

[209] *See id.* at 715–16, 738–39.

[210] *Id.* at 738.

[211] *See* Foucha v. Louisiana, 504 U.S. 71, 78–83 (1992) (ruling that having an "anti-social personality" and being potentially dangerous were insufficient grounds for a state to refuse to release a petitioner who had been committed after being found not guilty by reason of insanity).

[212] *See Jackson*, 406 U.S. at 738.

[213] 463 U.S. 354 (1983).

[214] *Id.* at 359–61.

as he has recovered from his mental illness and also may be detained as long as necessary for recovery.[215] In either event, there is no necessary correlation between the gravity of the offense and the length of commitment.[216] Further, the Court in *Jones* ruled that if someone is not guilty by reason of insanity, something that can often be proved by preponderance of evidence, he can be committed automatically to a mental institution and indefinitely detained even if normal civil commitment hearings have a higher standard for proving insanity.[217]

Even in a normal civil commitment proceeding, though, the constitutionally required evidentiary standing is no higher than a "clear and convincing" standard of evidence.[218] This is partly because a "beyond a reasonable doubt" standard would be practically impossible to establish given the inherent ambiguities of psychological diagnosis[219] but also because, as mentioned above, the harms that come with erroneous deprivation do not always outweigh the harms associated with failing to provide treatment to someone with a truly debilitating mental illness.[220] This approach was reaffirmed in *Heller v. Doe*,[221] where the Court ruled that allowing family members to present testimony in a civil commitment hearing for mentally disabled people does not violate principles of due process even if it does decrease the likelihood of a favorable outcome for the defendant,[222] as the chief aim of the proceeding is to produce an accurate determination.[223] Although there are significant procedural safeguards for civil commitment, as in the criminal or juvenile justice context where important liberty interests are also at stake, the safeguards are nonetheless diminished because of the tempered interests for liberty in this context and because the practical necessities of ruling on matters of mental instability make exacting standards impracticable. These rulings make clear that, when balancing the interests of individuals and society, the Court will calibrate the scale according to the purposes of the governmental regime in question. Civil commitment proceedings exist to protect society from the mentally ill but also to protect the mentally ill from themselves. The procedural protections are adjusted accordingly.

This balancing act of individual and social interests in civil commitment proceedings has an analogue in the prison, parole, and probation contexts. Prisoners,

---

[215] *See id.* at 369.

[216] *See id.*

[217] *See id.* at 366–68. The Court noted that the higher evidentiary standard in a civil commitment proceeding is necessary to protect against erroneous deprivations of liberty for people who exhibit merely abnormal or eccentric behavior. In the case at hand, in contrast, the defendant himself offered the defense of insanity and the fact that he explained his criminal act as being a product of insanity protects against the risk of being committed for merely idiosyncratic behavior. *Id.*

[218] *See* Addington v. Texas, 441 U.S. 418, 432–33 (1979).

[219] *Id.* at 429–30.

[220] *Id.* at 428–29.

[221] 509 U.S. 312 (1993).

[222] *Id.* at 330–33 ("'The Due Process Clause does not … require a State to adopt one procedure over another on the basis that it may produce results more favorable to' the party challenging the existing procedures.") (quoting Medina v. California, 505 U.S. 437, 451 (1992)).

[223] *Id.* at 332–33.

probationers, and parolees present a thematically similar context to civil commitment hearings because the liberty deprivation is very real but the administrative context and institutional purposes are different from the trial context of a criminal or juvenile hearing. As stated in chapter 2, the Supreme Court has established that people convicted of crimes still possess a limited liberty interest in addition to their life and property interests.[224] The procedures used for protecting these interests, however, represent a balance struck against the often pressing needs of the government, given the goals of the penological system and the supervisory context generally. An in-depth look at the different types of deprivations and their corollary procedural protections demonstrates the importance of this balancing approach.

The parole and probation systems are compliments to imprisonment within the broader penological system in that they supervise individuals but also attempt to positively reintegrate them into society through the restriction of certain negative behaviors and through rehabilitative efforts.[225] Because parole and probation are designed to aid in reintegration into society and to reduce the costs to the prison system, violation of parole or prohibition conditions typically only result in revocation if the violation is "serious and continuing so as to indicate that the parolee is not adjusting properly and cannot be counted on to avoid antisocial activity."[226] There is, as in the juvenile context, some need for discretion and flexibility in revocation hearings both to accurately determine whether a violation of parole or probation conditions occurred and to determine whether such a violation is sufficient to warrant revocation.[227] In consideration of these countervailing interests, the Court emphasized that the process should be focused narrowly and be flexible, but that the minimal procedural requirements prior to revocation include the following:

> (a) written notice of the claimed violations of parole; (b) disclosure to the parolee of evidence against him; (c) opportunity to be heard in person and to present witnesses and documentary evidence; (d) the right to confront and cross-examine adverse witnesses (unless the hearing officer specifically finds good cause for not allowing confrontation); (e) a "neutral and detached" hearing body such as a traditional parole board, members of which need not be judicial officers or lawyers; and (f) a written statement by the factfinders as to the evidence relied on and reasons for revoking parole.[228]

---

[224] *See* Wolff v. McDonnell, 418 U.S. 539, 555–56 (1974) ("But though his rights may be diminished by the needs and exigencies of the institutional environment, a prisoner is not wholly stripped of constitutional protections when he is imprisoned for crime. There is no iron curtain drawn between the Constitution and the prisons of this country.").

[225] *See* Gagnon v. Scarpelli, 411 U.S. 778, 785 (1973); Morrissey v. Brewer, 408 U.S. 471, 477–78 (1972).

[226] *Morrissey*, 408 U.S. at 479 (footnote omitted).

[227] *Cf. id.* at 479–80 (noting that parole revocation hearings are not purely factual and require discretion); *Gagnon*, 411 U.S. at 784 (stating that probation and parole officers are traditionally afforded wide latitude because they are tasked with supervising "a course or rehabilitation").

[228] *Morrissey*, 408 U.S. at 489. The *Morrissey* requirements were applied to probation revocation hearings in *Gagnon*. *See Gagnon*, 411 U.S. at 782.

The Court avoided a rigid rule on the right to counsel during a revocation hearing and instead ruled that counsel should be provided if the probationer or parolee requests one, when he or she has a colorable defense, and especially if he or she is unable to effectively represent himself.[229]

Within prisons themselves, however, the balance of interests shifts to accommodate the drastically different administrative and supervisory functions. The need to ensure order and safety for prisoners and administrators adds to the state's interests and makes procedural protections like those afforded to parolees and probationers more burdensome and even unsafe.[230] The procedural protections due inmates prior to the loss of good time credits or the imposition of solitary confinement demonstrate this altered balance. A "good time credit" is awarded to inmates for demonstrating good behavior and is used to take time off of the inmate's prison sentence.[231] But just as credits can be given for good behavior, they can be revoked for violating prison regulations.[232] Another punishment for violating prison regulations is the imposition of confinement in a disciplinary cell.[233] The Court has recognized that prisoners have a liberty interest in good time credits in addition to a limited interest in avoiding solitary confinement[234] and thus deserve procedural guarantees to protect against erroneous or unfair deprivation of those interests.[235] At the same time, the realities of the prison context make a requirement of those protections required in *Morrissey* and *Gagnon*, much less the full penumbra of procedural protections available in criminal trials, inadvisable.[236] So prisoners are, like probationers and parolees, due advanced written notice of the claimed violation and a "written statement of the factfinders as to the evidence relied upon and the reasons for the disciplinary action taken."[237] In contrast to parolees and probationers, prisoners have the right to call witnesses and present evidence only if doing so "will not be unduly hazardous to institutional safety and correction goals"[238] and they do not have the right to confront and cross-examine witnesses.[239] Even though the liberty interests might be the same between a prisoner who stands to lose a

---

[229] *Gagnon*, 411 U.S. at 790–91.

[230] *See, e.g.*, Wolff v. McDonnell, 418 U.S. 539, 560–63 (1974) ("[T]here would be great unwisdom in encasing the disciplinary procedures in an inflexible constitutional straitjacket that would necessarily call for adversary proceedings typical of the criminal trial....") (describing the practical difference between disciplinary proceedings in prison and parole revocation hearings and criminal trials).

[231] *See id.* at 546 n.6.

[232] *See id.* at 546–47.

[233] *See id.*

[234] *But see* Sandin v. Conner, 515 U.S. 472, 485–87 (1995) (ruling that, in comparison to normal prison conditions, thirty days of disciplinary segregation was not a significant deprivation of liberty that implicates due process protections).

[235] *See Wolff*, 418 U.S. at 556–58.

[236] *See id.* at 571–72.

[237] *Id.* at 563.

[238] *Id.* at 566.

[239] *Id.* at 567–68. Further, while prisoners also have no right to counsel they can be assisted by other inmates if they are illiterate or otherwise incapable of mounting an effective defense. *Id.* at 569–70.

year's worth of good time credits and a parolee who stands to return to prison for one year, the procedural protections are vastly different, mainly because of the institutional interests at stake.

As in the criminal context, the Court takes a deferential stance toward the procedures established by Congress when reviewing military justice cases. Finding that the Framers intended Congress to determine the appropriate procedures for ensuring discipline and duty within the military,[240] the Court has reduced its role to enforce only those violations of due process that "are so extraordinarily weighty" that they "overcome the balance struck by Congress."[241] This analysis gives heavy deference to the judicial procedures prescribed by Congress, especially if they align with historical practice.[242] Two cases in particular demonstrate this approach and its consequences for soldiers who are tried in military courts.

In *Middendorf v. Henry*,[243] the Court addressed whether enlisted members of the United States Marine Corps were due counsel at summary court-martial proceedings.[244] In describing why the Sixth Amendment does not establish a right to counsel in summary court-martial proceedings, the Court implied that the slippery slope of requiring counsel for every proceeding that could result in a loss of liberty in the military would have damaging effects on military discipline and preparedness.[245] The Court used a similarly deferential approach to determining whether the right to counsel is protected under the Due Process Clause.[246] Despite recognizing that military personnel had protected interests under the Due Process Clause, the Court gave substantial deference to the procedural balances determined to be appropriate by Congress, stating that the civilian courts were the wrong place to weigh the relevant military discipline and duty interests.[247]

The Court cemented this deferential standard in *Weiss v. United States*,[248] when it officially stated that neither the criminal law's *Medina* nor civil law's *Eldridge*

---

[240] *See* Burns v. Wilson, 346 U.S. 137, 140 (1953) ("Military law, like state law, is a jurisprudence which exists separate and apart from the law which governs in our federal judicial establishment. This Court has played no role in its development; we have exerted no supervisory power over the courts which enforce it; the rights of men in the armed forces must perforce be conditioned to meet certain overriding demands of discipline and duty, and the civil courts are not the agencies which must determine the precise balance to be struck in this adjustment. *The Framers expressly entrusted that task to Congress*.") (emphasis added) (footnotes omitted).

[241] Weiss v. United States, 510 U.S. 163, 179 (1994).

[242] *See, e.g.*, Middendorf v. Henry, 425 U.S. 25, 43 (1976) (noting that analysis of whether service members are due counsel at a court martial hearing must give "particular deference" to Congress's authority in regulating "the land and naval forces").

[243] 425 U.S. 25 (1976).

[244] *Id.* at 28.

[245] *See id.* at 34–36 ("If we were to ... require counsel before a summary court-martial proceeding simply because loss of liberty may result from such a proceeding, it would seem all but inescapable that counsel would likewise be required for the lowest level of military proceeding for dealing with the most minor offenses.") (establishing that summary court-martial proceedings are not criminal proceedings for Sixth Amendment purposes).

[246] *See id.* at 42 (citing Gagnon v. Scarpelli, 411 U.S. 778 (1973)).

[247] *See id.* at 42–48.

[248] 510 U.S. 163 (1994).

framework was appropriate for analyzing procedural due process questions in the military context.[249] Instead, the Court held that *Middendorf*'s approach should be adopted.[250] In determining whether the Fifth Amendment's Due Process Clause requires military judges to have a fixed term of office, the Court asked whether "the 'factors militating in favor [of the procedure] are so extraordinarily weighty as to overcome the balance struck by Congress.'"[251] The Court noted that the long history of conducting court-martials in the presence of nontenured judges suggested "the 'absence of a fundamental fairness problem,'"[252] a suggestion that was confirmed by other procedures within the Uniform Code of Military Justice that preserve the independence and hence impartiality of a military judge.[253] *Middendorf* and *Weiss* establish the lengths to which the Court will defer to Congressional procedures in the military context given that they establish that military personnel are due neither counsel nor tenured judges in court-martial proceedings even though such proceedings can result in substantial deprivations of liberty.

The deferential approach that the Court takes to areas traditionally handled by the political branches seems to stretch the purpose of the Due Process Clause, but not nearly so much as its treatment of preventive detention cases.[254] The most well-known, if relatively uncommon, form of preventive detention is the government's detention of enemy combatants in places like the Guantanamo prison. It may surprise some to learn that the Constitution does not explicitly prohibit preventive detention; the practice has a long history in the United States.[255] More common examples of preventive detention are holding criminal defendants on bail, detaining immigrants and material witnesses, and committing the mentally ill to civil commitment centers.[256] To give a sense of how ubiquitous the practice is, one could argue that almost all criminal prison sentences are partially preventive. Technically speaking, if part of a criminal sentence is intended to increase safety by incarcerating a criminal who the court believes is dangerous and likely to commit more crimes in the future, that criminal sentence is based in part on "preventive considerations."[257]

Preventive detention cases strike at the heart of the Due Process Clause because the government is depriving someone of his or her physical liberty not because the person has been formally accused of already having committed some harm but

---

[249] *See id.* at 177–78.

[250] *See id.*

[251] *Id.* at 177 (quoting Middendorf v. Henry, 425 U.S. 25, 44 (1976)).

[252] *See id.* at 179 (quoting United States v. Graf, 35 M.J. 450, 462 (1992))

[253] *See id.* at 179–80.

[254] Here we use preventive detention to mean detaining someone in order to prevent some sort of harm from occurring.

[255] *See* David Cole, *Out of the Shadows: Preventive Detention, Suspected Terrorists, and War*, 97 CAL. L. REV. 693, 700–04 (2009).

[256] *See* Cole, *supra* note 255, at 700–04.

[257] *See* Cole, *supra* note 255, at 695 (citing Paul H. Robinson, Commentary, *Punishing Dangerousness: Cloaking Preventive Detention as Criminal Justice*, 114 HARV. L. REV. 1429 (2001)).

because, arguably, doing so prevents a future harm from occurring.[258] Even though the detainee is being imprisoned, this is not supposed to be a punishment. Indeed, the detained person may not have done anything to "deserve" detention. Such a power elicits in many people the fear of returning to the "Star Chamber" practices of an older era when the rule of law struggled with the rules of men.[259] Moreover, the procedures for determining whether preventive detention is warranted can be lax in comparison to a criminal hearing.[260]

Given this concern over its abuse, preventive detention is rarely constitutional.[261] Scholars have argued that preventive detention is constitutionally justified only when it meets several criteria: first, the preventive detention must be nonpunitive and, if not, traditional criminal procedures must be applied; second, the detention must be related to a legitimate government interest and as such cannot be indefinite absent a compelling reason; and finally, the reasons for preventive detention must be specific to the individual detainee.[262] These factors mimic those present in *Eldridge* because they focus on the costs of added procedures and the government interests in avoiding those costs.[263] Two high-profile areas demonstrate this approach well: immigration and enemy combatant detention cases.

The United States government is typically treated as having plenary power to create immigration law within certain constitutional limitations.[264] One limitation is a strict bar on the punitive use of preventive detention for immigrants.[265] Additionally, preventive detention must serve a legitimate government interest like assuring the immigrant's presence at a hearing or preventing danger to the community.[266] But the period of detention must actually serve the stated goal.[267] Indefinite detention cannot be justified absent such special showing of "dangerousness."[268] In *Zadvydas v. Davis*,[269] for example, the government had been unable to find a

---

[258] Although definitions of "preventive detention" vary across countries, an underlying premise is that the detained person has not yet been charged with an offense and that detention is sought in order to prevent the detainee from evading future efforts to charge and try the detainee or to prevent the detainee from committing harm upon release. *See* Stella Burch Elias, *Rethinking "Preventive Detention" from a Comparative Perspective: Three Frameworks for Detaining Terrorists Suspects*, 41 COLUM. HUM. RTS. L. REV. 99, 110–13 (2009).

[259] *See* John J. Farmer, Jr., Lecture, *The 2004 Paul Miller Distinguished Lecture: The Rule of Law in an Age of Terror*, 57 RUTGERS L. REV. 747, 765 (2005) (quoting Rumsfeld v. Padilla, 542 U.S. 426, 465 (2004) (Stevens, J., dissenting)).

[260] *See, e.g.*, Hamdi v. Rumsfeld, 542 U.S. 507, 533–34 (2004) (describing the due process clause mandated procedures required in an enemy combatant hearing).

[261] *See* Zadvydas v. Davis, 533 U.S. 678, 690 (2001); David Cole, *In Aid of Removal: Due Process Limits on Immigration Detention*, 51 Emory L.J. 1003, 1010 (2002).

[262] *See* Cole, *supra* note 255, at 708.

[263] *Compare Zadvydas*, 533 U.S. at 690–92, *with* Mathews v. Eldridge, 424 U.S. 319, 335–47 (1976).

[264] *See Zadvydas*, 533 U.S. at 695; Cole, *supra* note 261, at 1014–17.

[265] *See Zadvydas*, 533 U.S. at 690; Cole, *supra* note 261, at 1014–17.

[266] *See Zadvydas*, 533 U.S. at 690–91.

[267] *See id.* at 690.

[268] *See id.* at 690–92.

[269] 533 U.S. 678 (2001).

country that would accept Zadvydas and had held him in detention for over a year in the process.[270] The government argued that there was no limit to the amount of time it could detain Zadvydas while attempting to permanently remove him, a proposition the Court rejected.[271] While conceding that detention is presumptively reasonable within a six-month period, the Court held that longer periods required some showing that the detention would not be indefinite.[272] Absent sufficient showing that removal is significantly likely in the "reasonably foreseeable future," the detainee (presumably) would have to be released.[273]

Assuming the limits are satisfied, however, immigrants may be detained with fewer procedural protections than would be necessary in a criminal matter.[274] For instance, *Demore v. Kim*[275] demonstrates the extent to which the Court is willing to defer to Congress's determination that detention is necessary. Kim was an immigrant convicted of first-degree burglary.[276] According to an amendment to the Immigration and Nationality Act (INA),[277] the Attorney General is required to detain any immigrant pending a deportation hearing if the immigrant is "deportable" due to having committed one of a legislatively determined list of crimes.[278] Kim's crimes amounted to "crimes of moral turpitude," qualifying him for deportation and the mandatory detention provision.[279] Kim challenged the INA provision on due process grounds, claiming that his detention violated his procedural due process rights because the government did not make any findings that he posed a flight risk or was a danger to society.[280] Even though Kim had already been detained six months prior to the order of habeas corpus relief, the Court ruled that it was not indefinite because it would last only until he was deported and that such a detention period fits the valid government goals of preventing flight and protecting society.[281] In doing so, the Court determined that Congress can, as a matter of law—and not through individual hearings—determine categories of immigrants who are dangerous or are flight risks based on legislative findings alone.[282] In doing so, the Court recognized that "'[i]n the exercise of its broad power

[270] *See id.* at 684.

[271] *See id.* at 688–89.

[272] *See id.* at 701.

[273] *See id.* The Court never explicitly stated that if the government failed to carry its burden the remedy would be the immediate release of the immigrant.

[274] *See* Demore v. Kim, 538 U.S. 510 (2003) (ruling that a statute mandating detention pending a hearing to remove an immigrant from the country is not a violation of the Due Process Clause); *see also* Faiza W. Sayed, Note, *Challenging Detention: Why Immigration Detainees Receive Less Process Than "Enemy Combatants" and Why They Deserve More*, 111 Colum. L. Rev. 1833 (2011).

[275] 538 U.S. 510 (2003).

[276] *See id.* at 513.

[277] 8 U.S.C. § 1226(c).

[278] *Kim*, 538 U.S. at 513.

[279] *See id.* at 513 n.1 (citing 8 U.S.C. § 1227(a)(2)(A)(ii)).

[280] *See id.* at 513–14.

[281] *See id.* at 527–31.

[282] *See id.*

over naturalization and immigration, Congress regularly makes rules that would be unacceptable if applied to citizens.'"[283] As is the case in other contexts, then, the Court is willing to defer to the government over important procedural protections given the unique nature of the context.

Immigration detention cases overlap with the enemy combatant detention cases both thematically and practically. The thematic link is that both types of detention are justified, in part, on the government's inherent powers to secure our nation against external threats.[284] The practical link is that the government will often use immigration detention and deportation rules as a complement or replacement for using enemy combatant detention procedures.[285] Proving terrorism charges can be difficult and using the immigration detention and deportation process as a pretext for detaining and removing a suspected terrorist from the nation is often a more straightforward approach.[286] Although the government may occasionally choose to use the immigration system, preventive detention of enemy combatants can be accomplished directly and constitutionally.[287] As in the immigration context, a closer analysis of cases in which the Court deals with the preventive detention of enemy combatants demonstrates the balance the Court attempts to strike between safety and the rule of law.

One of the foundational cases in enemy combatant law was *Ex Parte Milligan*,[288] a post-Civil War case. To fully understand *Milligan*, one must appreciate its historical context. In addition to challenging the very core of our nation, the Civil War presented unique legal challenges. First and foremost was whether and to what extent civilian courts could operate during times of unrest.[289] The writ of habeas corpus, which gives prisoners the right to challenge their detention in court, cannot be suspended except to preserve public safety in times of rebellion or invasion.[290] President Lincoln was reluctant to suspend the writ prior to official hostilities with the South. When Virginia and Maryland threatened to secede, however, this put

---

[283] *See id.* at 521 (quoting Mathews v. Diaz, 426 U.S. 67, 79–80 (1976)).

[284] *See* Harisiades v. Shaughnessy, 342 U.S. 580, 588–89 (1952) ("It is pertinent to observe that any policy toward aliens is vitally and intricately interwoven with contemporaneous policies in regard to the conduct of foreign relations, the war power, and the maintenance of a republican form of government. Such matters are so exclusively entrusted to the political branches of government as to be largely immune from judicial inquiry or interference."); Ex Parte Quirin, 317 U.S. 1, 26 (1942) ("The Constitution thus invests the President as Commander in Chief with the power to wage war which Congress has declared, and to carry into effect all laws passed by Congress for the conduct of war and for the government and regulation of the Armed Forces, and all laws defining and punishing offences against the law of nations, including those which pertain to the conduct of war.").

[285] *See* David A. Martin, National Security Discussion, *Preventive Detention: Immigration Law Lessons for the Enemy Combatant Debate: Testimony before the National Commission on Terrorist Attacks Upon the United State*, 18 GEO. IMMIGR. L.J. 305, 309–10 (2004).

[286] *See id.*

[287] *See infra* notes 288–329 and accompanying text.

[288] 71 U.S. 2 (1886).

[289] *See generally* Sherrill Halbert, *The Suspension of the Writ of Habeas Corpus by President Lincoln*, 2 AM. J. LEGAL HISTORY 95 (1958).

[290] U.S. CONST. art. 1, §9, cl. 2.

the "pincers" on the nation's capital and Lincoln was forced to authorize the limited suspension of habeas corpus in Maryland shortly after the fall of Fort Sumter.[291] There was, initially, a question over the legality of the president's actions given that the pertinent constitutional clause originates in Article I, which implies that the power to suspend the writ belongs primarily or entirely to Congress.[292] Congress made the issue moot in 1863, however, by statutorily authorizing the President to suspend the writ during the duration of the rebellion, but not before Lincoln unilaterally suspended the writ seven more times.[293] A constitutional crisis thus was avoided by first ignoring and later ratifying the extreme but possibly necessary steps that Lincoln took to preserve order.

The aftermath of the war did not lessen the frequency or seriousness of challenges to the constitutional order and the rule of law. The Court and Congress were divided on the legality of the reconstruction of the South, and disputes over habeas corpus and *Ex Parte Milligan* "can be understood in the broader context" of that struggle.[294] Milligan was a citizen and resident of Indiana who was arrested and tried by a military commission and sentenced to be hanged.[295] The questions presented to the Court were whether Milligan could file a writ of habeas corpus to have his case heard in the first place and whether, on the merits, the manner of his arrest and conviction were legal.[296] The Court framed the case as raising fundamental and "grave" questions, stating that it was "the birthright of every American citizen when charged with crime to be tried and punished according to law."[297] In effect, the question was whether, in times of emergency, the government could suspend or abridge certain constitutional rights in order to secure peace.[298] At the outset, the Court had lamented that during the "wicked rebellion" it was difficult to consider judicial questions with "calmness and discussion," but that once safety had been assured questions such as the one posed by Milligan could be considered dispassionately and without "the admixture of any element not required to form a legal judgment."[299] Taking seriously its implicit critique of the government's legal

---

[291] *See* Halbert, *supra* note 289, at 97–99 (noting that President Lincoln was more comfortable bombarding cities in Maryland than suspending the writ of habeas corpus there); *see also* Daniel Farber, Lincoln's Constitution 157–59 (2003).

[292] *See* Farber, *supra* note 291; Halbert, *supra* note 289, at 99–100; *see also* Ex Parte Merryman, 246 F. Cas. 144, 148–49 (1861). In *Merryman*, Justice Taney ruled that Lincoln lacked authority to suspend the writ and actually tried to have Merryman released from military prison but prison officials refused to let "Taney's marshal serve a document at the prison to release Merryman." Louis Fisher, *National Security Law: The Judicial Role*, *in* Freedom and the Rule of Law 203, 210 (Anthony A. Peacock ed., 2010).

[293] *See* Farber, *supra* note 291; Halbert, *supra* note 289, at 103–104; *see also* Alan Clarke, *Habeas Corpus: The Historical Debate*, 14 N.Y.L. Sch. J. Hum. Rts 375, 402 (1998).

[294] *See* Clarke, *supra* note 293, at 402–403.

[295] *Milligan*, 71 U.S. at 118.

[296] *Milligan*, 71 U.S. at 108–09, 119.

[297] *Milligan*, 71 U.S. at 118–19.

[298] *Cf. Milligan*, 71 U.S. at 119–20 (explaining the constitutional rights in question and that part of the basis for their inclusion in the Constitution was to protect civilians from military trials).

[299] *Milligan*, 71 U.S. at 109.

infractions during the war, the Court concluded that constitutional rights were designed by people familiar with conflict and were intended to apply equally in times of war and peace.[300] If Milligan was a civilian in Indiana, a state with open, working civilian courts, then it was a violation of his constitutional rights for the government to detain him and treat him as a prisoner of war.[301]

Ex Parte Milligan attempted to establish a firm rule about the durability of constitutional rights. In a nation reeling from a civil war and with fears of domestic insurrection, the Court still insisted that civilians be tried in civilian courts. This principled stand would be tested, thoroughly, during future conflicts. *Ex Parte Quirin*,[302] for example, dealt with a military trial of would-be Nazi saboteurs during World War II. The Court ruled that, according to the laws of war, enemy belligerents can be tried by military tribunals even if civilian courts are open and even if the belligerent is a citizen of the United States.[303] The Court squared this conclusion with the holding of *Milligan* by claiming that *Milligan* dealt with a "non-belligerent," someone not "associated with the armed forces of the enemy," whereas the litigants in question were clearly belligerents aligned with a foreign enemy.[304] *Quirin*, thus, not only expanded the government's war time powers but established the principle that the extent to which someone may enjoy their constitutional rights depends upon their status as defined by the government.[305] *Milligan's* protections were beginning to slowly wear away, and battles were waged over definitions rather than principles.[306]

The government's current response to a major security threat further eroded *Milligan*. The Court in *Milligan* lamented that the machinery of justice cannot operate dispassionately in times of conflict. This concern is just as relevant in the twenty-first century as it was in the nineteenth century.[307] Whether the modern Court properly heeded this warning in its recent rulings on enemy combatants and due process is debatable. Nevertheless, these cases clearly represent a new chapter in the Court's catalog of context-based procedural due process rights.

---

[300] *Milligan*, 71 U.S. at 120–21 ("The Constitution of the United States is a law for rulers and people, equally in war and in peace, and covers with the shield of its protection all classes of men, at all times, and under all circumstances. No doctrine, involving more pernicious consequences, was ever invented by the wit of man than that any of its provisions can be suspended during any of the great exigencies of government. Such a doctrine leads directly to anarchy or despotism. . . .").

[301] *See Milligan*, 71 U.S. at 131; *see also* Jesselyn A. Radack, *You Say Defendant, I Say Combatant: Opportunistic Treatment of Terrorism Suspects Held in the United States and the Need for Due Process*, 29 NYU Rev. L. & Soc. Change 525, 259–30.

[302] 317 U.S. 1 (1942).

[303] *See Quirin*, 317 U.S. at 44–45.

[304] *See id.* at 45.

[305] *Cf. id.* (comparing unlawful belligerents in the case at hand to the non-belligerent in *Milligan*).

[306] *See generally* Radack, *supra* note 301 (arguing that the term "enemy combatant" is a key tool in the government's attempt to bypass the legal system's procedural requirements for civilian and military justice); *see also* Harold Hongju Koh, *The Case Against Military Commissions*, 337 Am. J. Int'l L. 337, 340 n.17 (2002) (noting that the *Quirin* justices themselves were disappointed with the manner in which the Court's result was obtained and disturbed over its precedent).

[307] *See supra* note 299 and accompanying text.

The terrorist attacks on September 11, 2001, challenged the fabric of the nation while also impacting our legal landscape regarding the rule of law. Anecdotal evidence exists of situations in which legal rules were relaxed to accommodate the needs of law enforcement in the direct aftermath of the attacks.[308] The government began to engage in broad, systematic, and long-term efforts to combat terrorism and did so by taking an expansive view of existing laws and doctrine on executive power in times of war.[309] The justification for the lowering of process barriers was that national security interests so required.[310] Although the current legal battles have been fought more specifically on the constitutional terrains of the proper scope of executive power and the application of the writ of habeas corpus, due process concerns have surfaced as well.[311]

The principal case dealing with due process and enemy combatants in the war on terror is *Hamdi v. Rumsfeld*.[312] In *Hamdi*, a plurality of a deeply divided Court confirmed that *Quirin* authorizes the military to detain or try a United States citizen accused of being an enemy combatant. It gave the same significance to Milligan's "non-belligerent" status as did the Court in *Quirin*.[313] Hamdi was a U.S. citizen, born in Louisiana, who was captured in Afghanistan by coalition troops.[314] He was interrogated by the United States military and subsequently transferred to and detained in the United States when it became clear that he was a U.S. citizen.[315] The majority of the Court ruled that the government was statutorily and constitutionally justified in detaining Hamdi because of its initial determination that Hamdi was an enemy combatant.[316] The only real question was what procedures, if any, were required when Hamdi contested his status.[317]

The Court rejected the assertion that the habeas determination could be made as a matter of law on the ground that Hamdi's seizure took place in a combat zone.

---

[308] *See* Farmer, *supra* note 259, at 752 (recounting the decision to allow warrantless searches of garbage cans in contravention of a recent state Supreme Court case prohibiting that practice).

[309] *See* Roberto Iraola, *Enemy Combatants, the Courts, and the Constitution*, 56 OKLA. L. REV. 565, 571–73 (2003) (describing the domestic policies enacted in response to the 9/11 attacks).

[310] *See, e.g.*, Koh, *supra* note 306 (describing the practices but arguing against the use of military commissions).

[311] *See generally* Iraola, *supra* note 309.

[312] 542 U.S. 507 (2004). Other important cases include Boumediene v. Bush, 553 U.S. 723 (2008) (holding that the government cannot suspend the writ of habeas corpus to enemy combatants detained in Guantanamo Bay); Hamdan v. Rumsfeld, 548 U.S. 557 (2006) (ruling that the President lacks authority to try enemy combatants in military commissions); Rumsfeld v. Padilla, 542 U.S. 426 (2004) (avoiding the merits of a habeas petition by ruling on jurisdictional grounds); Rasul v. Bush, 542 U.S. 466 (2004) (ruling that federal courts have jurisdiction to hear habeas petitions from prisoners indefinitely detained as enemy combatants).

[313] *Hamdi*, 542 U.S. at 519, 521–22 (citing Ex Parte Quirin, 317 U.S. 1, 30–31 (1941)).

[314] *Hamdi*, 542 U.S. at 510.

[315] *Id.* at 510–11.

[316] *See id.* at 517–24 (ruling that the Authorization for Use of Military Force Act (AUMF) justified detention of enemy combatants in Afghanistan and that that statutory power as granted by the AUMF is itself justified as a fundamental incident of war).

[317] *See id.* at 523–25.

Whether Hamdi was actually in a zone of combat, much less an active participant in an armed conflict, was disputed.[318] The question thus was whether, as the government argued, the Court should give broad deference to the government's factual determination given the nature of the case and the national security interests involved or, as the district court had ruled, whether the Court should require procedures similar to a criminal hearing.[319] Both sides emphasized the "tension that often exists between the autonomy that the Government asserts is necessary in order to pursue effectively a particular goal and the process that a citizen contends he is due before he is deprived of a constitutional right."[320] Finding the right balance in such situations, the Court claimed, is typically accomplished by the *Eldridge* factors.[321]

In applying the *Eldridge* framework to the case at hand, the Court was careful not to minimize Hamdi's liberty interest, calling it "the most elemental of liberty interests" and noting that deprivations of liberty without trial is a "carefully limited exception."[322] Moreover, the Court explicitly stated that Hamdi's liberty interests were not diminished by the fact that the nation was at war nor were they tarnished due to the allegations levied against him. The government's interests, in order to carry the argument, must offset the full and "fundamental nature of a citizen's right to be free."[323] The government's offsetting interests, however, were also considerable. In addition to concerns over releasing enemy combatants to resume their war against America, the government argued that enhanced procedural protections for enemy combatant detainees—protections like producing evidence that may be classified or "buried under the rubble of war"—would create practical barriers that could damage the war effort.[324]

The Court ruled that the appropriate balance between the individual's and government's interests was somewhere in between what each party had urged. Detainees must be given notice of the factual basis for their classification as enemy combatants and must have a "fair opportunity to rebut the Government's factual assertions before a neutral decisionmaker."[325] But hearsay evidence can be admitted, and if the government produces credible evidence in support of its position, detainees must rebut a presumption that they are enemy combatants.[326] The Court was silent on the specific procedures that must be employed on remand, such as the extent to which Hamdi could engage in discovery.[327] The government later avoided resolving those questions by simply releasing Hamdi.[328]

---

[318] *See id at* 526–27.

[319] *See id.* at 527–28.

[320] *Id.* at 528.

[321] *See id.* at 528–29.

[322] *Id.* at 529.

[323] *Hamdi*, 542 U.S. at 530–31.

[324] *See id.* at 531–32.

[325] *See id.* at 533.

[326] *See id.* at 533–34.

[327] *See* Jenny S. Martinez, *Process and Substance in the "War on Terror*," 108 COLUM. L. REV. 1013, 1048 (2008).

[328] *See id.*

This trilogy of cases makes a notable addition to our understanding of the Court's approach to procedural due process questions. *Milligan* attempted to set clear constitutional boundaries even in times of war. *Quirin* sidestepped those protections through a definitional qualification. And *Hamdi* concluded by cementing the distinction between nonbelligerents and enemy combatants and establishing new, if minimal, procedures to ensure that the former is not mistaken for the latter. The Due Process Clause's purpose is to protect against erroneous and arbitrary government deprivations. Constitutional rights should apply equally in times of peace and war, but the progression of these cases show that the Court's due process analysis does not blink at the realities of war and accommodates the special government interests at stake.[329]

The Court's enemy combatant jurisprudence is, in some ways, a recognition that our traditional systems for handling government deprivations are inadequate to handle the new tensions created by the war on terror.[330] The evidentiary rules and publicity of our civil and criminal justice system make them impractical and perhaps even dangerous for trying certain enemy combatants.[331] For example, the government may strongly suspect that someone is a terrorist but still lack enough evidence to prosecute them in a criminal court, creating a disincentive to take actions to prevent potential attacks.[332] The military model of approaching enemy combatants is similarly limited by rules of international law and the conventions of war, making a purely military approach ill equipped to deal with an asymmetrical conflict of a nation-state against an ideological movement.[333] For example, the laws of war limit interrogations to determining the captured soldier's name, rank, and serial number, a limitation that is obviously less relevant in the war on terror than it would have been in World War II.[334] Some argue that the unique conflict facing our nation requires a hybrid model—one that creates an "enemy combatant" category—which would allow for near-indefinite detention, interrogation of detainees (that would otherwise be prohibited by the Geneva Convention), and would not require a full-scale investigations and hearings for each detainee.[335]

The Court's application of the *Eldridge* factors to the detention of enemy combatants implies a general willingness to be flexible on due process concerns where national security and military actions are implicated. In some respects, the *Eldridge* factors are an ideal vehicle for handling enemy combatant detention cases because such government action exists in a legal gray area in that it deals partially with

---

[329] *See Hamdi*, 542 U.S. at 531.

[330] *See* Farmer, *supra* note 259, at 759–61.

[331] *See* Farmer, *supra* note 259, at 759–60.

[332] *See* Farmer, *supra* note 259, at 756–58 (giving the example of Mohdar Abdullah who was eventually detained and deported under immigration charges).

[333] *See* Farmer, *supra* note 259, at 760–61.

[334] *See* Farmer, *supra* note 259, at 760–61.

[335] *Cf.* Farmer, *supra* note 259, at 760–61.

criminal and military matters and with domestic and international laws.[336] A flexible framework is more capable of adapting to novel legal conflicts than bright line rules, the latter being prone to principled but potentially impractical outcomes.[337]

The same conflict that created the ambiguous legal compromises over detention of enemy combatants has produced another similar if more troubling legal conflict: whether and to what extent the Due Process Clause limits the government's ability to conduct targeted killings as part of the war on terror. Targeted killings—which are defined as the intentional and deliberate use of lethal force against a specific individual, usually in the context of an issue of international law or security—[338] exist at the far end of the context-based continuum of due process jurisprudence. They implicate the most essential protected interest—life—and yet receive the weakest procedural safeguards.

Targeted killings can be differentiated from assassinations in that the latter are, by definition, illegal killings whereas the former are permissible under certain legal frameworks.[339] The primary methods of executing targeted killings by the United States are drone strikes[340] and kill/capture missions.[341] The frequency with which the government resorts to such tactics raises a very real and pressing question about what, if any, constitutional protections apply to the "targets" of these missions, especially if the target happens to be an American citizen. As of the time of this writing, the Court has not applied the *Eldridge* factors to a targeted killing, but the government's official position, one that has received at least some support,[342] is that *Eldridge* applies to the decision to use lethal force against enemy combatants and that the government's process for determining whether to use such is constitutionally sufficient.[343]

The government currently claims that it can use lethal force against enemy combatants, even American civilians, if the combatant poses an imminent threat

---

[336] *See* Richard Murphy & Afsheen John Radsan, *Due Process and Targeted Killings*, 31 CARDOZO L. REV. 405, 434–37 (2009) (providing reasons for why a functionalist approach to anti-terrorist actions is necessary).

[337] *See, e.g.*, Hamdi v. Rumsfeld, 542 U.S. 507, 554–79 (2004) (Scalia, J., dissenting) (arguing that Hamdi must be granted a habeas decree or that criminal charges must be filed or that Congress must suspend habeas corpus). Justice Scalia's bright line approach to enemy combatant detention would likely cause a constitutional showdown wherein Congress and the executive branch are forced to respond to the Court's decrees.

[338] *See* Philip Alston, *The CIA and Targeted Killings Beyond Borders*, 2 HARV. NAT'L SEC. J. 283, 297–98 (2011);

[339] *See* Mark V. Vlasic, *Assassination & Targeted Killing—A Historical and Post-Bin Laden Legal Analysis*, 43 GEO. J. INT'L L. 259, 268 (2012) (emphasizing that a targeted killing is different from an assassination in that the latter is an illegal form of the former); *see also id.* at 281–96 (discussing U.S. domestic law and whether targeted killings are legal under domestic rules that bar political assassinations).

[340] *See* Alston, *supra* note 338, at 324–33(estimating that several hundred strikes have taken place since 2004, killing more than a thousand people in total).

[341] *See id.* at 333–41 (estimating that hundreds of such raids are executed each month in Afghanistan and about 80 percent result in captures).

[342] *See, e.g.*, John Yoo, *Assassination or Targeted Killings After 9/11*, 56 N.Y.L. SCH. L. REV. 57 (2011).

[343] *See* Attorney Gen. Eric Holder, Speech at Northwestern University School of Law (March 5, 2012), http://www.justice.gov/iso/opa/ag/speeches/2012/ag-speech-1203051.html.

to American security, if capture is not feasible, and if the use of force would be compatible with of the law of war.[344] Whether a threat is imminent depends upon a balanced consideration of whether missing the window of opportunity to act will likely lead to a future attack that cannot be prevented through other means.[345] Similarly, whether capture is a feasible option depends upon a "fact specific" and "time sensitive" consideration that takes into account risk to U.S. civilians and troops if a capture is attempted.[346] And finally, the principles of the law of war require, among other things, that lethal force is only used against targets who have military value and who are combatants or are directly participating in hostilities. Also, the expected collateral damage must be proportional to the military advantages gained.[347] According to the government, despite the magnitude of the individual interests involved, the societal costs of additional procedural protections do not compensate for the reduced risk of an erroneous deprivation.[348] Provided the government adheres to the principles described above, the Due Process Clause does not provide additional procedural protections to individuals who are targeted with lethal force pursuant to the war on terror.[349] The government need not even submit its decision to an impartial party prior to the use of force.[350] This minimalist stance on due process requirements has at least some implicit support from Justice Thomas, who pointed out in *Hamdi* that it would be untenable to require notice and a fair hearing prior to executing a targeted strike of a known terrorist on foreign soil.[351]

The government's position on the constitutionality of targeted killing is problematic for at least two reasons. First, it does not enunciate any procedural methods by which arbitrary or erroneous deprivations can be prevented. The principles the government outlines describing the conditions under which targeted killings can be justified are just that: principles. They may inform us of how the government would define the principled and legal use of lethal force, but we still know very little about the procedures it uses to ensure its actions meet that definition.[352]

There are some indications that President George W. Bush delegated the authority to authorize targeted killings to the Director of the CIA who, in turn, delegated the authority to the head of Counterterrorism, neither of whom is an elected official nor are they confirmed by the Senate.[353] There have been few public declarations from those individuals or the government that informs the public about

---

[344] *See id.*

[345] *See id.*

[346] *See id.*

[347] *See id.*

[348] *See id.*

[349] *See id.*

[350] *Cf. id.*

[351] *See* Hamdi v. Rumsfeld, 542 U.S. 507, 597 (2005) (Thomas, J., dissenting). *But see* Murphy & Radsan, *supra* note 336 (arguing that the courts have a role to play in targeted military strikes).

[352] *See* Alston, *supra* note 338, at 374–406.

[353] *See id.* at 357; Murphy & Radsan, *supra* note 336, at 413.

the procedures in place to ensure that the targets posed imminent threats or that capture was not possible. Similarly, there is a lack of clear understanding of how the Obama administration handles those same decisions,[354] except that appropriate members of Congress are periodically informed of the administration's antiterrorism efforts.[355] The government's stance, then, seems to rest on the assertion that, under the *Eldridge* framework, the societal interests of an efficient antiterrorism operation are so paramount that they preclude the requirement of *any* external procedural protections prior to the use of lethal force. The Due Process Clauses are designed to protect against arbitrary and unprincipled government behavior by requiring the government to provide clear, certain procedural steps prior to depriving a citizen of a protected interest.[356]

The second problem with the government's stance is related to the first: it is difficult, if not impossible, to provide a post-deprivation check against the arbitrary or erroneous deprivation when the deprivation involves the targeted killing. Survivors are likely rare and would be understandably reticent to seek redress in an American court.[357] Further, *Bivens*-style actions or suits filed on behalf of a target face substantial procedural hurdles, including traditional standing problems, qualified immunity provisions, and separation of powers issues.[358] Arguably, in times of crisis, power tends to flow toward the executive.[359] Like President Lincoln—who detained enemy combatants during the Civil War—the modern executive has asked for and implicitly been granted the authority to deprive citizens of constitutionally protected rights without oversight in the name of national security.[360]

The Court's ruling in *Hamdi* and its silence over the use of lethal force can be seen as an attempt to square its procedural due process jurisprudence with modern "war" realities. An optimistic view of the Court's behavior is that it is attempting to stay relevant so that it can restrain government abuse without unnecessarily interfering with the government's mission of keeping the nation safe. Those who take a more pessimistic view of the Court's preventive detention case may need to consider that context-based exceptions to procedural due process cases are, in fact, the rule.[361] The practical question is whether the federal courts are able to properly balance the security interests of the nation with the liberty and autonomy interests of the individual.

---

[354] *See* Alston, *supra* note 338, at 341–60.

[355] *See* Holder speech, *supra* note 343.

[356] *See supra* notes 8–10 and accompanying text.

[357] *See* Murphy & Radsan, *supra* note 336, at 442.

[358] *See id.* at 441–44; *see also* Al-Aulaqi v. Obama, 727 F. Supp. 2d 1, 15–54 (D.D.C. 2010) (outlining the various legal barriers to filing a suit against the government for placing someone on a targeted killing list). *See generally Martinez, supra* note 327, at 1033–41 (2008) (discussing the ways in which procedural questions can be used to avoid substantive issues).

[359] *See* Murphy & Radsan, *supra* note 336, at 428.

[360] *See supra* notes 289–293 and accompanying text.

[361] *See* Martinez, *supra* note 327, at 1047–48; *supra* notes 87–351 and accompanying text.

III. Conclusion

A review of the Court's due process cases in different contexts demonstrates the extent to which procedural guarantees are flexible, fluid, and determined by the interests of the individual and the needs of government. The Court takes into consideration the nature of the interest, not just its magnitude, which helps explain why it gives marginally less procedural protections in the juvenile and civil commitment context, where the individual may actually benefit from confinement. On the other hand, the Court is very mindful of the administrative costs of added procedural protections, especially when those costs include risks to safety. The procedural requirements are, unsurprisingly, at their minimum in the prison, military, and enemy combatant context.

In addition to weighing the interests of the individual and the costs to society, the Court includes another factor—deference to Congress—in its due process decisions. The Court is perhaps most active in the areas of law where Congress itself has created the very interests that are being deprived. At the same time, taking an active approach to determining procedural requirements does not mean that the Court insists on the highest level of due process rights as demonstrated by *Eldridge*. In contrast, the Court takes a very deferential stance when analyzing due process rights in the criminal context where the interests in play—the defendants' liberty and sometimes life—are protected interests that exist above and beyond Congress's purview through the Bill of Rights protections. All things being equal, then, one should expect to see more procedural protections when the Court is ruling on matters involving more important interests—such as rooted, fundamental rights—and in areas that require less judicial deference to Congress or the States. As the preceding analysis shows, however, that relationship is not entirely linear.

Taken together, these procedural due process cases display the tensions inherent in a legal order that strives to advance the rule of law but also to respect the practical demands of governance. The Court seeks to extend the protection of substantive rights and spread robust procedural guarantees without exceeding its institutional powers or invading lawmaking or executive autonomy. Unfortunately, these pursuits are often countervailing, which demonstrates how difficult and necessary it is to achieve a "thick" rule of law in all its forms.[362]

Nevertheless, the doctrine on procedural due process rights establishes fundamental principles of justice within a liberal democratic order. Respect for nonarbitrary, accurate, and predictable rules that constrain government is a pervasive concern. Closely related concerns are the due process attention to settled expectations and traditions, the preference for prospective versus post-hoc regulations, and the interest in transparency. Procedural fairness also requires, especially in "thick" due process scenarios, impartial decisionmakers who follow the applicable process

[362] *See* Brian Tamanaha, On The Rule of Law: History, Politics, Theory 91 (2004).

and substance requirements, and do so in an even-handed manner. Flexibility—in the sense of shaping process to contexts and accommodating competing collective and individual interests— likewise matters. These restraints on government, in turn, reflect the historical interest in assuring that government actors observe structural limits on their authority. Finally, procedurally sound government regulations provide individuals with fair notice and the opportunity to challenge the applicable government policy, though the process due may be calibrated to the gravity of the potential harm that government may inflict. In other words, the government action and the procedures themselves should be mindful of a principle that may best be captured by the word "proportional." The "rationality" of government action, in *all* of these senses, therefore, is a core concern that transcends the many contextual nuances of the vast due process terrain.

{4}

What Liberties Are Protected?

As we have seen, post-bellum constitutional due process has both a procedural and a substantive dimension. The latter has been derived from the liberty component of due process, which has been construed to protect a range of fundamental rights that include reproductive liberties, family rights, sexual autonomy, informational privacy, the right to refuse medical treatment, and nearly all of the specific rights included in the original Bill of Rights. Substantive due process also protects nonfundamental rights, such as socioeconomic liberty, but the constitutional protection of these rights is extremely deferential to government: only irrational or truly outrageous government action violates the current test for such rights.

Few aspects of due process are more complicated, capacious, or contested than this substantive liberty component. The constitutional interpretation and normative issues raised by the right not to be deprived of liberty without due process of law have divided the Court and commentators in ways that defy compromise or even easy summarization of the conflicting viewpoints. We offer here an overview of the major principles and debates, and focus primarily on the post-bellum Fifth and Fourteenth Amendment case law that develops substantive due process. The emphasis thus is on the *judicial construction of liberty* and an evolving doctrine that is ever "headed for parts unknown."[1]

A further clarification of substantive liberty bears repeating. The cases set forth two primary categories of liberty interests. The first category includes liberty interests defined by government, as to which "the Due Process Clause requires fair procedures for [their] vindication."[2] As chapter 2 explained, even when federal constitutional law itself does not create a liberty interest, federal due process requires that there be constitutionally adequate procedures to protect the government-created liberty interest. If, for example, the state provides a right to seek parole before the completion of a valid sentence—which is not a liberty interest under federal constitutional law—then due process requires a constitutionally adequate state procedure for evaluating eligibility for parole.[3]

---

[1] *See* Walton H. Hamilton, *The Path of Due Process of Law*, XLVIII Ethics 269, 270 (1938).

[2] *See* Swarthout v. Cooke, 131 S. Ct. 859, 862 (2011) (per curiam). *See* chapter 2 *supra* for a fuller description of this aspect of due process liberty.

[3] *Id.* (noting that a writ of federal habeas corpus would only lie for possible error in process; it would not lie for error of state law with respect to any state-created liberty interest in parole).

The second category of liberty interests are ones derived directly from due process. These liberties have been the source of the greatest critical consternation. As explained in chapter 2, such federal liberty interests not only trigger federal *procedural* due process protection; they also impose substantive restraints on the *content* of federal, state, and local laws.

Some justices, joined by several influential commentators, believe that this substantive strand of due process interests is ungrounded in text, history, or common sense. To them, the constitutional provision for "due *process*" means only that where "life, liberty, or property" is at stake there must be constitutionally adequate *procedures*.[4] There is no independent substantive content to this provision. To claim otherwise, they argue, is "oxymoronic."[5]

Others agree with this limited account of the Due Process Clause, but insist that important substantive rights were conferred by the Privileges or Immunities and Equal Protection Clauses of the Fourteenth Amendment, not by the Due Process Clause per se.[6] In their view, the historical record supports the view that privileges or immunities in particular were meant to embrace certain natural rights, which include at least some of the rights enshrined in the Bill of Rights but may extend beyond those as well.[7] Their doctrinal focus is on the *Slaughter-House Cases*, decided in 1872, in which the Court wrongly—by their lights—read the Privileges or Immunities Clause very narrowly to embrace only a short list of rights enjoyed by United States citizens, as such, instead of defining these rights more expansively to include fundamental rights that parallel the rights identified as fundamental under the Privileges and Immunities Clause of Article IV.[8]

Still others would use the Due Process Clause as the textual anchor for substantive rights, but disagree about how to define the rights that merit this status.

---

[4] *See, e.g.*, Albright v. Oliver, 510 U.S. 266, 275 (1994) (Scalia, J., concurring) ("I reject the proposition that the Due Process Clause guarantees certain (unspecified) liberties, rather than merely guarantees certain procedures as a prerequisite to deprivation of liberty.").

[5] *See, e.g.*, United States v. Carlton, 512 U.S. 26, 39 (1994) (Scalia, J., concurring) ("If I thought that 'substantive due process' were a constitutional right, rather than an oxymoron ... "). *See also* CHARLES L. BLACK, JR., A NEW BIRTH OF FREEDOM: HUMAN RIGHTS, NAMED AND UNNAMED 3 (1997) (describing substantive due process as a "paradoxical, even oxymoronic phrase").

[6] *See, e.g.*, AKHIL REED AMAR, THE BILL OF RIGHTS, 165–80 (discussing history of "privileges or immunities" and why this clause properly should be read as a source of wider range of substantive rights). *See also* chapter 3, *supra*.

[7] *See id. See also* WILLIAM E. NELSON, THE FOURTEENTH AMENDMENT: FROM POLITICAL PRINCIPLE TO JUDICIAL DOCTRINE 7–8(2d ed. 1997); Kurt T. Lash, *The Origins of the Privileges or Immunities Clause, Part II: John Bingham and the Second Draft of the Fourteenth Amendment*, 99 GEO. L.J. 329 (2011); Alan Gura et al., *The Tell-Tale Privileges or Immunities Clause*, 2010 CATO SUP. CT. REV. 163, 183 (2010).

[8] Slaughter-House Cases, 83 U.S. 36 (1873). *See* Hamilton, *supra* note 1, at 277–83 (1938) (describing the opinions in the Slaughter-House Cases in especially eloquent and entertaining fashion). *See also* our discussion of *Slaughter-House Cases* in chapter 2, *supra*. *See also* Kermit Roosevelt III, *What If* Slaughter-House *Had Been Decided Differently*? 45 IND. L. REV. 61 (2011) (discussing critiques of *Slaughter-House* and analyzing what the consequences for due process and equal protection might have been had the case not eviscerated the Privileges or Immunities Clause).

The United States Supreme Court itself has embraced this understanding of due process, but has struggled to explain and justify this view.

Justice Black famously argued that due process substantive rights should be derived from the first eight amendments of the Constitution, which should be incorporated into the Fourteenth Amendment "jot for jot."[9] This would, he believed, root the open-ended due process clause in something more fixed than penumbras, and give symmetrical and national voice to the Bill of Rights promises. From this perspective, the Bill of Rights in total, not in parts or as an incomplete articulation of the rights territory, should govern.

A majority of the Court never embraced Justice Black's position, though as a practical matter the Court has evolved toward it. Instead, the Court has followed a process of so-called "selective incorporation," under which it evaluates each amendment independently to determine whether it is "fundamental to ordered liberty" and thus applies to the states through the Due Process Clause of the Fourteenth Amendment.[10] Once the Court determines that an amendment should be selectively incorporated, it then analyzes whether the right in question should be read to mean the same thing when applied to the states as it does when applied to the federal government. In other words, are the two applications "symmetrical,"[11] as Black insisted?

For some of the justices, selective incorporation of the Bill of Rights misses the textual and historical marks: the Due Process Clause of the Fourteenth Amendment "stands on its own bottom" and has *independent* meaning.[12] Although the rights named in the Bill of Rights may be—indeed now are, by all of the justices' lights—*illustrative* of those that the Framers deemed to be fundamental, this list is neither dispositive nor exhaustive of what due process vis-à-vis *the states* requires as a matter of the Reconstruction Framers' intent.

In all of these discussions, the term "liberty" within the Due Process Clause of the Fourteenth Amendment assumes great significance: it *creates* federal constitutional rights. Moreover, even the list of enumerated or unenumerated "fundamental" rights is not necessarily exhaustive. Rather, due process may require substantive rationality even in cases that do not trigger fundamental rights per se.[13] In other words, due process arguably imposes a baseline constitutional requirement of non-arbitrary, non-capricious lawmaking *and* law enforcement. Often traced to the famous *Calder v. Bull* passage by Justice Samuel Chase that one

---

[9] This is how Justice Harlan described Justice Black's theory of incorporation of the Bill of Rights into the Fourteenth Amendment. *See* Duncan v. Louisiana, 391 U.S. 145, 181 (1968) (Harlan, J., dissenting). Justice Black's view can be found in Adamson v. California, 332 U.S. 46, 74–75 (1947) (Black, J., dissenting).

[10] For a summary of the Court's approach and applying it to the Second Amendment, *see* McDonald v. City of Chicago, 130 S. Ct. 3020, 3036–42 (2010).

[11] *See id.* (discussing presumption in favor of symmetrical readings).

[12] Griswold v. Connecticut, 381 U.S. 479, 500 (Harlan, J., concurring).

[13] *See McDonald,* 130 S. Ct. at 3101 (Stevens, J., dissenting).

cannot "take from A to give to B"[14]-at least not without good cause—due process is thought to capture both a substantive sense of rationality (the law itself must be sound), as well as a procedural sense of rationality (the law must be enforced in a sensible and fair manner). This rationality baseline applies in all contexts, not only in cases that involve specific fundamental rights, though the anxiety over irrational or capricious government conduct is at its peak in such cases and thus more likely to trigger judicial intervention.

Another complexity deals with the relationship between the Due Process Clause of the Fifth Amendment and the Fourteenth Amendment. The former does not have an equal protection clause, but the latter does. As the post-bellum Court began to interpret the Equal Protection Clause of the Fourteenth Amendment, the issue arose whether these principles bound the federal government as well as the states.[15] Are racially segregated public schools "unlawful" in the District of Columbia—a federal enclave—no less than in the states? The Court's response was in the affirmative: due process embraces notions of equality.[16] This approach—applying rights that were first defined in cases involving the Fourteenth Amendment to limit the federal government—has been called "reverse incorporation."

A related issue is how to pinpoint the relevant historical moment to consider in determining what a substantive due process right means, as a matter of "original intent" or in an effort to identify the "public meaning" of the right at the time it was adopted. Freedom of expression is both an enumerated right under the First Amendment, and also was interpreted by the Court in 1925 to be included in the Fourteenth Amendment.[17] Should the Court examine the meaning of freedom of expression in 1798, in 1868, or in 1925 when it determines the original or public meaning of freedom of speech restraints on the states? Does freedom of speech mean something different when it is abridged by the federal government versus the states, or is there a kind of "feedback effect"[18] that brings First Amendment principles into harmony regardless of whether the government action is federal or state? If it is the latter, then what are we to make of strong claims that the modern meaning of due process should be determined by reference to public meaning of the language in historical context, or of the idea that due process must be determined by reference to traditions? Whose public meaning or traditions should be considered, and as of when?

Once one determines that there is a substantive component to due process under *any* of these theories, however, the key question becomes how to limit the doctrine in a principled manner. This is particularly problematic in cases in

---

[14] *See* Calder v. Bull, 3 U.S. (3 Dall.) 386, 388 (1798). *See* chapter 1, *supra*.

[15] See discussion of "reverse incorporation" at notes 167–211*infra*.

[16] *See* Bolling v. Sharpe, 347 U.S. 497 (1954).

[17] Gitlow v. New York, 268 U.S. 652 (1925).

[18] The phrase is Akhil Amar's. *See* Akhil Reed Amar, *The Bill of Rights and the Fourteenth Amendment*, 101 YALE L.J. 1193, 1281 (1992).

which the Court identifies an "unenumerated" right, such as privacy or the right of intimate association. As the Court has warned:

> Substantive due process has at times been a treacherous field for this Court. There *are* risks when the judicial branch gives enhanced protection to certain substantive liberties without the guidance of the more specific provisions of the Bill of Rights. As the history of the *Lochner* era demonstrates, there is a reason for concern lest the only limits to such judicial intervention become the predilections of those who happen to be Members of this Court. That history counsels caution and restraint. But it does not counsel abandonment.[19]

Justice Black's approach had to commend it, at the least, the textual anchors of the Bill of Rights and the case law thereunder. But as many commentators have noted, that text too is ambiguous. Most notably, it includes the Ninth Amendment, which lends considerable force to claims that the Framers did not intend that the enumerated rights were exhaustive. And in any event, the intent of these first Framers must be modified if not supplanted by the intent of the Reconstruction Framers, who had experienced a shattering of many of the assumptions about rights and especially about the relationship between the states and the federal government that likely drove the first Framers. The original Bill of Rights had federalism implications and intentions that cannot reasonably be mapped neatly onto the Fourteenth Amendment. On the contrary, the Fourteenth Amendment must be read as a renunciation of stricter federalism-driven notions of constitutional rights because it expressly applies such rights to the states and gives Congress the power to enforce them.[20]

Nevertheless, federalism concerns about due process and other matters of constitutional interpretation have hardly disappeared. For one thing, they drove early restrictive interpretations of the scope of the Fourteenth Amendment. They also spiked in later eras as some justices and commentators argued for less federal—including, but not limited to federal judicial—interference with local political and legislative autonomy. Finding a new or expanded right under the Fourteenth Amendment means checking state and local governments' ability to determine policy though political processes. When one favors these policies, one resents any judicial doctrine that blocks them. At times, objections to due process limits on government power have been cast as calls for more robust state or local "rights," and have focused on the federal level of the restriction rather than on the restriction itself.

Isolating the federalism-based arguments against due process limitations on government, however, is its own puzzle. In the high-pitched national debates

---

[19] Moore v. City of East Cleveland, 431 U.S. 494, 502 (1977) (Powell, J.) (emphasis in original) (footnote reference omitted).

[20] *See, e.g.*, Randy E. Barnett, *The Proper Scope of the Police Power*, 79 Notre Dame L. Rev. 429, 462 (2004).

about federal health care reform during 2010–2012, for example, the primary lawsuit[21] and much of the partisan rhetoric against the reforms centered on whether the federal government had legislative power under the Commerce Clause, Tax and Spend Clause, or Necessary and Proper Clause to require individuals to buy health insurance. These arguments focused on the limited nature of the federal government and the invasion of state and local autonomy, as well as the invasion of individual rights, when the federal government exceeds its constitutional authority. But the arguments against the individual mandate provision also had a pure individual liberty cast as well. In fact, the root of much popular anger about being required to purchase health insurance likely had less to do with *Congress* requiring this, than with "nanny-state" government—at any level—requiring that people purchase health insurance, prompting some to scoff that government next may require us to "buy broccoli."[22] The latter arguments are quintessentially libertarian-based objections that presumably would support judicial intervention under substantive due process to overturn a *federal or state* mandate to purchase insurance. The thin protection that current substantive due process doctrine offers against such government demands made a pure due process argument against the federal measure almost certainly a loser. But this was the heart of many lay peoples' objections to the measure. Had the argument been cast as a liberty-based due process argument, however, this would have had profound federalism and separation of powers implications, given the Court's tendency to read the Fifth and Fourteenth Amendment mandates symmetrically. It also would have required the Court to reconsider the substantial body of post-1937 due process case law that grants extremely broad discretion to government over socioeconomic matters.

Concerns about "judicial predilections" alone determining the content of due process rights and disrupting the will of the people come from multiple political camps and span multiple doctrinal terrains, though again the substantive due process cases loom particularly large in these debates. Some social conservatives regard cases like *Lawrence v. Texas*—which struck down a Texas sodomy law—as unprincipled judicial incursions into the ability of political majorities to regulate moral and cultural matters.[23] Some also decry the Court's retreat from more rigorous or even light oversight of government regulation in the realm of socioeconomic legislation on the grounds that property rights and freedom of contract deserve greater protection from governmental overreaching.

Progressives, in contrast, lament the ways in which the Court has tended over time to block or tame legislative innovations that further their agendas, including

---

[21] *See* National Federation of Independent Business v. Sibelius, 132 S. Ct. 2566 (2012) (upholding the individual mandate of the Patient Protection and Affordable Care Act, Pub. L. No. 111-148, 124 Stat. 119 (2010)).

[22] *See* David Orentlicher, *Can Congress Make You Buy Broccoli? And Why It Really Doesn't Matter*, 84 S. Cal. L. Rev. 9 (2011) (discussing controversy over federal mandate to buy health insurance and argument it could mean Congress could make individuals purchase other products, including broccoli.).

[23] Lawrence v. Texas, 539 U.S. 558 (2003).

workplace safety, employment, or civil rights laws.[24] Both conservatives and progressives thus often take a dim view of broad judicial authority, and many within both camps prefer to leave liberty rights and their evolving meanings in the hands of elected officials.

Finally, even those who regard judicially imposed substantive due process brakes on government as a mostly worthy means of promoting libertarian objectives—in moral, social, economic and other contexts—realize that liberties can intersect and conflict: judicial choices between them can be condemned as little more than "judicial predilections." Such issues are particularly visible where notions of freedom of private association or religious freedom conflict with others' rights to expression or conduct. How, for example, should courts balance religious objections to employee speech or conduct that may be protected by federal or state employment discrimination laws, or by constitutional law?

In short, no matter where the Court turns in this wide corner of constitutional law, it encounters thoughtful objections and occasionally withering and often ideologically inflected critiques. Moreover, some of the most sharp-edged critiques have come from within the Court itself. Justice Scalia, whom the Wall Street Journal once described as "delightfully brutal,"[25] heads up the substantive due-process-skeptic wing of the current Court and has used some of his most florid prose in these cases. Such friendly fire surely fuels others' willingness to accuse the Court of "making law" in this area, and exceeding judicial authority.

Our goal in this section is not to exhaust these theoretical and political arguments, but to highlight the many background complexities that have a bearing on the liberty principle within due process doctrine. A guideline to the currently controlling responses to the foregoing theoretical issues is as follows, and should help in thinking about the sprawling case law and its nuances:

- Due process does include a "substantive" component
- Most, but not all, of the rights identified in the Bill of Rights have been "selectively incorporated" into the Fourteenth Amendment
- Where the right has been selectively incorporated, there is a presumption of symmetry, which can include a form of "reverse incorporation" or "feedback effect"
- One of the most important such examples of "reverse incorporation" from the Fourteenth Amendment back to the Bill of Rights is the notion that the Fifth Amendment Due Process Clause has an "equality" component

[24] For critiques of judicial activism from progressive scholars, *see* Larry D. Kramer, The People Themselves: Popular Constitutionalism and Judicial Review, 152, 229 (2004); Mark Tushnet, Taking the Constitution Away From the Courts, (1999). For an argument that the Court has, over time, blocked progressive causes and undermined state autonomy over common law, *see* Jack Beerman, *The Supreme Common Law Court of the United States*, 18 B.U. Pub. Int'l L. J. 119, 119 (2008).

[25] Five Gun Salute, *WSJ Review and Outlook*, June 29, 2010, http://online.wsj.com/article/SB10001424052748703964104575334721392301704.html

- The Privileges or Immunities Clause has been interpreted to include only a very narrow band of rights enjoyed by United States citizens, as such
- Substantive due process includes certain "unenumerated" and fundamental rights—whether derived from the Ninth Amendment, from "penumbras" of the Constitution that protect rights such as "privacy," or from the liberty language of the Fourteenth Amendment itself
- Substantive due process includes a baseline expectation of rational, nonarbitrary government conduct
- Fundamental rights trigger elevated judicial scrutiny that varies from right to right
- Nonfundamental rights trigger very low-level, "rational basis" scrutiny that typically, though not inevitably, means that a court will not overturn the government act
- In determining what is "fundamental," the Court relies on traditional and American notions of ordered liberty, rather than more open-ended or nondomestic concepts of liberty
- The Court continues to disagree internally about whether substantive due process is a legitimate constitutional concept at all, which leads some of the justices to favor the most restrictive and narrow accounts of rights that already have been identified, and to refuse to expand the list to include any "new" rights
- Despite doubts about whether the Privileges or Immunities Clause should have been the proper starting point for analyzing substantive rights that are now labeled "substantive due process rights," on the current Court, only Justice Thomas favors relocating these rights and beginning the interpretation process anew.

This summary demonstrates why there is far less controversy over the Court's application of liberty in the first sense—i.e., requiring that liberty interests defined by the states be deprived only through adequate procedures—than in the second sense of limiting state regulatory powers per se. Determining what process is due presents its own difficulties, as we saw in chapter 3; but fewer people doubt that this is a proper matter of constitutional concern and thus a proper matter for judicial review. Determining whether fundamental principles of ordered liberty deny states the right to define marriage, to regulate or prohibit access to abortions, or to compel disclosure of private information, is another matter altogether. We turn now to the landscape of these challenging liberty cases.

I. Liberty as Substantive Right

The Bill of Rights specifically restricts the federal government from violating a host of enumerated rights, which include due process. The Fourteenth Amendment, in contrast, more simply prevents the states from depriving a person of "life, liberty or property" without due process of law. It also prohibits the states from making or enforcing any law that abridges the privileges or immunities of citizens of the United States. Finally, it prevents the states from depriving any person of the equal protection of the laws.

As noted in chapter 2, the Court in 1872 read the Privileges or Immunities Clause—which only protects United States citizens, and does not apply to corporations—very narrowly. Despite historical and scholarly support for a broader reading, the Court in 2010 reconfirmed the *Slaughter-House Cases* and declined to substitute this clause for the Due Process Clause as the anchor for so-called substantive or "incorporated" rights.[26] It applied this due process case law to conclude that the Second Amendment right to bear arms properly should be included in the rights selectively incorporated into the Fourteenth Amendment, and likewise noted that where a right is incorporated into the Fourteenth Amendment it presumptively should be read symmetrically—that is, the right means the same thing whether it applies to the federal government or to state and local governments.[27]

Within the category of liberty-based due process rights, there are three subcategories of rights. The first subcategory covers "nonfundamental" rights, which trigger a very lax—some would say toothless—level of judicial review that requires the party challenging government action to establish that the government lacked a rational basis for the action. The second subcategory covers unenumerated substantive rights that the Court has identified as fundamental to ordered liberty despite the absence of specific constitutional text that enumerates the right as such. The most notable examples of this last type of liberty interest are those based on a notion of individual privacy. The final subcategory includes enumerated fundamental rights that have been selectively incorporated from the Bill of Rights.

NONFUNDAMENTAL RIGHTS

The history of the nonfundamental or "rational basis" strand of due process has been an undulating rise and fall of judicial aggressiveness in reviewing government action. Although the heart of due process throughout its history has been a concern about arbitrary and capricious government action, one person's irrational government action may be another person's sound government policy. And judicial intervention into democratic policy-making—even on the messy edges of rationality—triggers anxiety about judicial encroachment into the legislative and executive domains. Consequently, even deep cynicism about the "rationality" of political processes may not mean one will endorse close or even modest judicial second guessing of political compromises. Nor does history provide mono-vocal or unambiguous guidance. To say that due process requires respect for the "law

---

[26] *See* McDonald v. City of Chicago, 130 S. Ct. 3020 (2010). *See also* chapter 2, text accompanying notes 55–58, *supra*.

[27] *Id.*

of the land" may mean only that a law that is properly passed can and should be enforced, rather than requiring that only laws that are worthy of respect should be judicially sanctioned. Finally, even if due process does impose a baseline rationality requirement, one must anchor and define this concept.

The late nineteenth century presented the Court with its first serious tests of these principles. As new social and economic interests began to transform America, private industry and expanded public regulatory efforts began to collide. Eighteenth century, individual-centered notions of property and liberty were challenged by nineteenth-century innovations and the rise of corporations.

Because the Privileges or Immunities Clause of the Fourteenth Amendment was thought to apply solely to nonaliens and natural persons, the Due Process Clause offered a more hospitable home for corporate entities to advance claims that they were "persons" for purposes of its protection,[28] and that they likewise were entitled to a kind of natural law protection of their due process-based "liberty" to engage in business without undue governmental interference. They began with arguments based on the liberty of contract, which assumed that a corporation had the freedom to bargain with an individual worker for his or her labor, or with a seller or buyer of goods. The police powers of the states, although vast, did not allow them to infringe on workers' right to freely negotiate the terms of their engagement with their employers, or to interfere with other contractual liberties. That is, liberty extended beyond a more literal freedom to move or freedom from physical restraint, as it might arise in a criminal procedure context.

A particularly significant case of the era was *Allgeyer v. Louisiana*,[29] in which a unanimous Court struck down a Louisiana insurance law on the ground that it deprived a local firm of the due process right to purchase insurance from an out-of-state seller. Justice Peckham famously described the right at stake as follows:

> The liberty mentioned ... means not only the right of the citizen to be free from the mere physical restraint of his person, as by incarceration, but the term is deemed to embrace the right of the citizen to be free in the enjoyment of all his faculties: ... to pursue any livelihood or avocation, and for that purpose to enter into all contracts which may be proper, necessary and essential.[30]

Not only did this new right extend beyond freedom from physical restraint; it was a restraint on the alleged right of contract itself, rather than merely a guarantee of procedural protection. The potential limit on state police powers implied by such a right was significant indeed.

The Court elaborated on this "right to contract" in *Lochner v. New York*,[31] decided eight years after *Allgeyer*. The case involved a New York law that regulated the

---

[28] *See, e.g.*, Minneapolis & St. L. Ry. Co. v. Beckwith, 129 U.S. 26, 28 (1886) (applying due process to corporation).

[29] 165 U.S. 578 (1897). *See also* chapter 1, *supra*.

[30] *Id.* at 589.

[31] 198 U.S. 45 (1905).

hours of bakers. The Court concluded that the New York law was unconstitutional because the state failed to adequately demonstrate a "direct relation, as a means to an end"[32] between its regulations and the concededly legitimate state interest in food and worker safety. The Court noted that some restrictions on worker hours may pass this test—such as limitations on the hours of miners who work beneath ground in especially dangerous contexts—but bakers did not operate under similarly perilous working conditions.[33]

Lochner was written over two important dissents. Justice Harlan disagreed with the Court's application of the end-means test.[34] Justice Holmes launched a more fundamental objection, in which he argued that due process requires only that "a rational and fair man necessarily would admit that the statute proposed would infringe fundamental principles as they have been understood by the traditions of our people and our law."[35] His due process test was a low hurdle for states to surmount, and offered greater room for state and federal government experimentation in addressing the perceived social and economic problems occasioned by industrialization, a changing labor force, and other early twentieth-century developments.

The Holmes view ultimately prevailed, and the Court eventually retreated from the *Lochner* high-water mark of judicial close scrutiny of socioeconomic legislation. In 1937, in *West Coast Hotel v. Parrish*,[36] Chief Justice Hughes situated the individual liberty of due process in a larger, social context: liberty must be construed "in a social organization which requires the protection of laws against the evils which menace the health, safety, morals and welfare of the people."[37] In short, regulation that is "reasonable in relation to its subject and is adapted to the interest of the community is due process of the law."[38] This officially ended the so-called *Lochner* era and ushered in a new approach to judicial review of socioeconomic legislation. Under this approach, due process required only minimal rationality, an exceedingly easy test to satisfy.

Yet it is important to note the historical context of the Court's due process retreat. As Chief Justice Hughes observed, "[l]iberty in each of its phases has its history and its connotation."[39] The underlying principle thus was less a matter of judicial conservatism than judicial realism and recognition that external socioeconomic conditions may inspire new forms of regulation designed to cope with new forms of socioeconomic problems and their impact on individual liberty.

---

[32] *Id.* at 57.

[33] *Cf.* Holden v. Hardy, 169 U.S. 366 (1898) (upholding regulations regarding miners' working conditions).

[34] 198 U.S. at 69 (Harlan, J., dissenting).

[35] *Id.* at 76 (Holmes, J., dissenting).

[36] 300 U.S. 379 (1937). *See also* Nebbia v. New York, 291 U.S. 502 (1934) (foreshadowing *West Coast Hotel*). *See* chapter 1, *supra*.

[37] 300 U.S. at 391.

[38] *Id.*

[39] *Id.*

A judiciary that thwarts such reforms may not only be vulnerable to strategies such as "Court-packing" but may fossilize law and hobble legal innovation.

If anything, this mid-twentieth century concern about allowing room for innovation in the realm of socioeconomic regulation while protecting human rights has intensified in the early twenty-first century, given the pace of new technologies and other developments that raise liberty-based concerns. Forms of communication, surveillance, industry, employment, education, public safety, transportation, commerce, medicine and public health, economics, social relations, politics, law enforcement, and much else that shapes human life and personal identity evolve; it thus should be little surprise that a constitutional right that protects "persons" from government overreaching and arbitrariness in these domains also would evolve.[40] Again, however, this does not point inexorably in the direction of deep judicial deference to legislative or executive policy, or to more aggressive constitutional protection from that policy. The basic due process inquiry still focuses on the whether the laws in question are in fact "reasonable in relation to [their] subject and ... adapted to the interest of the community."[41] The "interest of the community" condition within that basic equation implies that substantive rationality means that the ends in question must in fact be public ends, and must promote a legitimate community good, but these are confoundingly vague limits.

The Court virtually abandoned work of policing the latter kind of irrationality, post-*Lochner.* It moved from liberty of contract and meaningful judicial review of socioeconomic legislation, to a very powerful presumption of rationality absent a judicially-recognized "fundamental right."[42] Some justices believed these fundamental rights could only be found—if at all—by reference to the enumerated rights in the Bill of Rights.[43] Yet the *Lochner*-era notion that there are unenumerated due process rights that likewise deserve elevated scrutiny did not perish.

Indeed, even the general principle that due process review of socioeconomic matters today receives only rational basis scrutiny must be bracketed. In cases that some argue entail *Lochner*-type protection of property or economic interests, the Court has set aside punitive damage awards as "excessive" under the Fourteenth Amendment.[44] The Court has insisted that these awards must fall within a rational range, in light of the reprehensibility of the defendant's conduct, the disparity between the harm to the plaintiff and the punitive damages award, and the

---

[40] We discuss this evolutionary imperative in chapter 6, *infra*

[41] *West Coast Hotel*, 300 U.S. at 391.

[42] The shift away from elevated judicial review also corresponds with the rise of the administrative branch of the federal government, where due process constrains administrative processes but courts give substantial deference to agency substantive decisions, especially when they involve technical matters within their statutory authority. *See* Chevron USA, Inc v. NRDC, 467 U.S. 837, 842–43 (1984).

[43] United States v. Carolene Products, 304 U.S. 144, 152–53 n.4 (1938).

[44] *See* BMW v. Gore, 517 U.S. 559 (1996); TXO Production Corp. v. Alliance Resources Corp., 509 U.S. 443 (1993). See discussion of punitive damages in chapter 5, *infra*.

difference between the size of the award in the given case and civil penalties authorized or imposed in similar cases.[45] *Lochner* may therefore be better described as dormant than as dead.

FUNDAMENTAL RIGHTS—UNENUMERATED

The primary judicial focus since the Court's post-*Lochner* retreat from liberty of contract has been on whether there are other, higher-value rights under due process, and if so how to identify and interpret them. To say that a right is "fundamental," according to all accounts, means that the right will receive elevated judicial scrutiny; but this does not answer the thornier question of what elevated scrutiny means, or how to balance the fundamental right against competing important or compelling government interests in burdening the right. And again, it does not answer the question of how to determine which rights qualify for this higher level of judicial respect.

One of the *Lochner* era due process cases that survived—at least in part—the Court's retreat from liberty of contract is instructive in this regard. In *Meyer v. Nebraska*, the Court struck down a state ban on the teaching of foreign languages to schoolchildren.[46] The Court observed that due process included "not merely freedom from bodily restraint but also the right of the individual to contract, to engage in any of the common occupations of life, to acquire useful knowledge, to marry, to establish a home and bring up children, to worship God according to the dictates of his own conscience, and generally to enjoy those privileges long recognized at common law as essential to the orderly pursuit of happiness by free men."[47]

The *Meyer* list of liberties was notable for its inclusion of rights that are nowhere specifically enumerated in the Bill of Rights, let alone in the Due Process Clauses themselves. That is, due process liberty means more than procedure, and more than specific liberties like freedom of expression or religion. Put another way, we do have "an unwritten Constitution."[48] But what else might this unspecified form of liberty include?

In the modern era, unenumerated liberty rights have been limited to the sphere of personal liberties, rather than economic or property rights. Perhaps the most important of the cases that define these liberties is the Court's watershed 1965 decision in *Griswold v. Connecticut*, in which the Court struck down a Connecticut law that made it illegal to use or to counsel others regarding the use of contraceptives.[49]

---

[45] Cooper Industries, Inc. v. Leatherman Tool Group, Inc., 532 U.S. 424, 440 (2001). *See also* State Farm Mutual Automobile Ins. Co. v. Campbell, 538 U.S. 408, 419 (2003) (discussing definition of "reprehensibility"); Philip Morris USA v. Williams, 549 U.S. 346, 353–55 (2007) (discussing evidence that properly maybe replied upon to establish reprehensibility). *See* our discussion of punitive damages in chapter 5.

[46] 262 U.S. 390 (1923).

[47] *Id.* at 399.

[48] *See* Thomas C. Grey, *Do We Have an Unwritten Constitution*?, 27 STAN. L. REV. 703 (1975).

[49] 381 U.S. 479 (1965). *See also* chapter 2, text accompanying notes 87–97, *supra*.

As we saw in chapter 2, the Court in *Griswold* concluded that the law interfered with married couples' right to marital "privacy," which it traced to "several fundamental constitutional guarantees."[50] At the same time, however, the Court expressly denied that it was reviving *Lochner*-type review of government action that burdens other, nonpersonal liberties.[51] Negotiating between these two impulses—protecting liberty but not exceeding judicial authority and invading the law-making powers of the representative branches of government—has been a very difficult and often politically charged process.

In particular, the Court's efforts to provide textual or other support for treating "privacy" as a liberty right beyond state police powers met with powerful scholarly and public resistance. Despite this resistance, the concept of substantive due process liberties that exceed specific, enumerated rights has endured, especially in the realm of so-called family rights. In fact, some modern due process defenders not only regard substantive due process as a legitimate home for unenumerated individual rights that constrain government power, but also believe that *Lochner* itself was based on a historically defensible assumption that due process includes such rights. As such, they argue, the intellectual moorings of *Lochner*—if not its specific holding—deserve reconsideration.[52] The abolitionist roots of the Fourteenth Amendment also have received renewed scholarly attention in ways that support a substantive liberty component to due process.[53]

The concept of a rational basis floor for any legitimate legislative and executive action likewise has endured, though this remains an exceedingly easy test to satisfy, as we already have seen in the earlier introduction to post-*Lochner* decisions on socioeconomic legislation. That is, substantive due process constraints today are not limited to enumerated rights; and they also are not limited to fundamental rights, even if courts rarely overturn government action on this basis.

Nevertheless, the Court and commentators have continued to disagree about all of these issues. In his dissenting opinion in *McDonald v. City of Chicago*, decided in 2010, Justice Stevens summarized modern due process as follows:

> Government action that shocks the conscience, pointlessly infringes settled expectations, trespasses into sensitive private realms or life choices without adequate justification, perpetuates gross injustice, or simply lacks a rational basis will always be vulnerable to judicial invalidation. Nor does the fact that an asserted right falls within one of these categories end the inquiry. More fundamental rights may receive more robust judicial protection, but

---

50 381 U.S. at 485.

51 *Id.* at 482.

52 *See, e.g.*, David E. Bernstein, Rehabilitating Lochner: Defending Individual Rights Against Progressive Reform (2011) (arguing that a substantive interpretation of due process predates the adoption of the Fourteenth Amendment and was relied upon by some abolitionists arguing against slavery in the federal territories on Fifth Amendment grounds).

53 *See, e.g.*, Randy E. Barnett, *Whence Comes Section One?: The Abolitionist Origins of the Fourteenth Amendment*, 3:1 Journal of Legal Analysis 165 (Spring 2011).

> the strength of the individual's liberty interests and the State's regulatory interests must always be assessed and compared. No right is absolute.[54]

Yet Justice Alito, writing for the plurality in the same case, summarized the task of defining due process rights quite differently and did not clarify whether he agrees that nonfundamental rights remain constitutionally protected. In his view, the Court must "decide whether the right ... is fundamental to our scheme of ordered liberty ... or ... whether this right is 'deeply rooted in this Nation's history and tradition.'"[55]

Much hinges on which of these passages one embraces. If Justice Alito's account was meant as a general statement of due process principles, and if a majority of the Court were to agree with this account, then due process only protects individuals from arbitrary government conduct when the conduct invades a fundamental right, identified as such by the Court. Tradition—and only American, deeply-rooted tradition—is the touchstone for these fundamental rights. Under this construction of due process, courts play a modest role in policing arbitrary government action apart from the few areas in which tradition speaks consistently and unambiguously, and efforts to expand or add to these traditional rights are greeted with substantial judicial skepticism.

Limiting substantive due process in this and other ways has doctrinal support. For example, the Court has held that general due process principles cannot be invoked where more specific constitutional text arguably applies to the same scenario. In *Graham v. Connor*, the Court held that the Fourth Amendment effectively preempts any substantive due process claim that law enforcement officers used excessive force in the course of an arrest.[56] The Court also has tended to interpret the nonenumerated fundamental rights that it already has recognized very narrowly.[57]

The wider view of precedent presented here, however, suggests that Justice Stevens's account of due process is more complete: due process protection does go beyond enumerated, fundamental rights. For example, the Court has noted that law enforcement may violate "'fundamental fairness, shocking to the universal sense of justice' mandated by the Due Process Clause of the Fifth Amendment."[58] More generally, although the test is almost impossible to flunk, the general principle still

---

[54] 130 S. Ct. 3020, 3101 (Stevens, J. dissenting).

[55] *Id.* at 3036 (internal quotations omitted).

[56] 490 U.S. 386, 395 (1989). *See* Albright v. Oliver, 510 U.S. 266 (1994) (plurality opinion) (applying *Graham* in a malicious prosecution scenario to preclude the plaintiff from raising a substantive due process claim where the Fourth Amendment arguably covered the terrain). For a critique of *Graham*, see Toni M. Massaro, *Reviving Hugo Black? The Court's "Jot for Jot" Account of Substantive Due Process*, 73 N.Y.U. L. Rev. 1086 (1998).

[57] Justice Scalia in particular favors this strategy for limiting the reach of these rights. *See, e.g.*, Michael H. v. Gerald D. 491 U.S. 110, 128 n.6 (1989) (plurality opinion). *But see id.* at 132 (O'Connor, J., and Kennedy, J., concurring in part) (rejecting Scalia's more restrictive approach).

[58] Kinsella v. United States ex rel. Singleton, 361 U.S. 234, 246 (1960) (*quoting* Betts v. Brady, 316 U.S. 455, 462 (1942)). *See also* Rochin v. California, 342 U.S. 65, 172 (1952).

holds that socioeconomic legislation triggers low-level rational basis review, under which the burden is on the party opposing the legislation to show that no set of facts that were known or reasonably could have been assumed lend support to the legislation.[59] The idea harkens back to earlier notions that due process is a protection against arbitrary government in general, and may even track back to the colonial period when due process was "a catch-all phrase for human rights rather than a phrase with a well-defined content."[60] The elusiveness of this vague term, observed one early twentieth-century commentator, "is perhaps the strongest evidence that the protection secured is general rather than specific."[61] In any event, both history and a considerable body of cases lend support to Justice Stevens's description of the due process landscape.

Moreover, even the recent doctrinal record includes cases that depart from the pattern of strictly cabining substantive due process. The most notable—and controversial—of these decisions is *Lawrence v. Texas*.[62] Justice Kennedy's opinion in *Lawrence* cited the Court's earlier privacy decisions, and pointed to evolving socio-legal principles in holding that adults have a protected liberty interest in intimate sexual conduct that includes same-sex conduct between consenting adults in the privacy of their own home.[63] Kennedy did not name this as a fundamental right per se, but concluded that the state sodomy statute "furthers no legitimate state interest which can justify its intrusion into the personal and private life of the individual."[64] He also stated that "[h]istory and tradition are the starting point but not in all cases the ending point of the substantive due process inquiry."[65] Although this opinion was worded cautiously, and expressly denied that it necessarily lent support to claims for "formal recognition to any relationship that homosexual persons seek to enter,"[66] it preserved breathing room within substantive due process that advocates seeking to expand due process liberty have since sought to exploit.

For all of these reasons, constitutional due process continues to morph, and continues to inspire hope and anxiety as courts wrestle with its enigmatic commands about the "balance of convenience between private rights and public welfare."[67] The present terrain of fundamental, unenumerated due process rights falls into the following categories: family rights, reproductive rights, intimate association

---

[59] United States v. Carolene Products Co., 304 U.S. 144, 154 (1938). *See also* Williamson v. Lee Optical, Inc., 348 U.S. 483, 488 (1955).

[60] *See* Rodney L. Mott, Due Process of Law 142 (1926) (discussing colonial history of due process).

[61] *Id.* at 592.

[62] 539 U.S. 558 (2003).

[63] *Id.* at 568.

[64] *Id.* at 578.

[65] *Id.* at 572 (internal quotation marks omitted).

[66] *Id.* at 578.

[67] Mott, *supra* note 60, at 597.

and sexual autonomy rights, medical self-determination rights, freedom of movement, the right to special care when government constrains that movement (e.g., through incarceration or institutionalization), access to courts, and informational privacy. It also includes hybrid due process rights that fall in the nether world between "substance" and "process"—such as the law of personal jurisdiction, which we canvas in chapter 5.

We now turn to more specific elaboration of the current categories of fundamental, unenumerated rights.

Family Rights

As noted above, the Court in *Meyer* anticipated subsequent case law that provided substantive due process protection for family matters. Two years later, the Court struck down a state law that required parents to send their children to public, rather than private school, on due process grounds.[68] The Court regarded the law as an unreasonable interference with parents' and guardians' rights to "direct the upbringing and education of children under their control."[69]

The right to marry lies at the core of the family rights protected under substantive due process. But the scope of the right itself—whether, for example, it may be restricted on the basis of the race of the couple—has been a source of significant judicial and public controversy. In *Loving v. Virginia*, the Court struck down a Virginia anti-miscegenation law on due process and equal protection grounds, despite the long lineage of such race-based prohibitions.[70] Eleven years thereafter, the Court specifically declared that "the right to marry is part of the fundamental 'right of privacy' implicit in the ... Due Process Clause."[71] The cases nevertheless allow states to burden access to the right, provided they are not so substantial that they "significantly interfere with decisions to enter into the marital relationship."[72] The latter form of restrictions trigger strict scrutiny, whereas other, less significant restrictions such as minimum age requirements or waiting periods for divorce trigger more relaxed judicial scrutiny.

In the modern era, states' rights to prohibit same-sex, or even plural, marriages are a matter of particularly intense public debate. In 1879 the Court held that a state properly could criminalize polygamy,[73] which supports a traditional, Western conception of state power to define marriage. Plural marriages, however, are more common within some non-Western and some fundamentalist Mormon religious cultures, which has prompted some to question whether marital privacy

---

[68] Pierce v. Society of Sisters, 268 U.S. 510 (1925).

[69] *Id.* at 534–35. *Cf.* Brown v. Entertainment Merchants Association, 131 S. Ct. 2729, 2752 (2011) (Thomas, J., dissenting) (arguing that minors lack a historically grounded first amendment right to receive information without parental, intermediating approval).

[70] 389 U.S. 1, 12 (1967).

[71] Zablocki v. Redhail, 434 U.S. 374, 384 (1978).

[72] *Id.* at 386.

[73] Reynolds v. United States, 98 U.S. 45 (1879).

should be interpreted more broadly to embrace these unions and, if not, why not.[74] Likewise, the issue of whether there is a constitutional right to same-sex marriage has focused on the role of tradition in defining the fundamental right to marry, and on whether prohibitions of such state-sanctioned unions violate baseline rational basis requirements under federal or state constitutional law, even if they do not interfere with a traditional right to marry.[75] In some of the cases, the stress is on equal protection principles rather than on substantive due process per se, and hinge on whether the refusal to grant same-sex couples the status of marriage is rational given other protections already afforded them in some states.[76] Arguments for same-sex marriage also often rely on *Lawrence v. Texas*, which invoked liberty as a basis for striking down a criminal law that prohibited same-sex sodomy between consenting adults, even in the privacy of their own homes.[77] A decision that private, consensual sexual intimacy between same-sex partners is constitutionally *protected* does not, of course, lead inexorably to the conclusion that marriage status must be conferred on such couples who seek it. But it removes a very serious obstacle to the argument. As some who object to *Lawrence* have argued, it hardly makes sense to claim a substantive due process right to same-sex unions if certain intimate conduct can be criminalized, even though the conduct may be an important if not defining part of some, though obviously not all, same-sex relationships.[78]

Beyond the core right to marry lie related family rights that often flow from this relationship. The Court has stated that marriage initiates the "relationship that is at the foundation of the family in our society,"[79] which in turn lies within the

---

[74] A recent challenge to state prohibitions on plural marriages demonstrates that the issue has not disappeared. See Brown v. Herbert, Case No. 2:2011cv00652 (C.D. Utah 2011) (challenging Utah criminal bigamy law on due process, equal protection, free exercise, freedom of speech, freedom of association, and establishment clause grounds).

[75] *See* Varnum v. Brien, 763 N.W.2d 862 (Iowa 2009); Goodridge v. Department of Public Health, 440 Mass. 309, 329, 331, 798 N.E.2d 941, 959, 961 (Mass. 2003); Hernandez v. Robles, 7 N.Y.3d 338 (Court of Appeals NY 2006); Anderson v. King County, 158 Wash. 2d 1, 10, 138 P.3d 963, 969 (Wash. 2006); Baehr v. Lewin, 852 P.2d 44 (Haw. 1993).

[76] *See*, e.g. Perry v. Brown, 671 F.3d 1052 (9th Cir. 2012) (striking down California Proposition 8 on equal protection grounds narrowly tailored to California laws that grant same-sex couples a host of other rights short of marriage). *Cf.* Gill v. Office of Personnel Management, 682 F.3d 1 (1st Cir. 2012) (striking down section 3 of the Defense of Marriage Act, 1 U.S.C. sec. 7, which denies federal economic and other benefits to same-sex couples lawfully married and to surviving spouses thus married).

[77] 539 U.S. 558, 567 (2003). The argument for judicial intervention, of course, encounters strong resistance from those who believe this is a matter for legislatures, not courts, to decide. One response to the argument is the familiar one advanced in favor of judicial intervention when necessary to correct for political process defects in democratic processes. *See* Jane S. Schacter, *Ely at the Altar: Political Process Theory Through the Lens of the Marriage Debate*, 109 Mich. L. Rev. 1363 (2011) (analyzing the famous Ely "political process theory" under which courts are justified in second-guessing majoritarian decisions when the democratic process in question disadvantages a particular social group, and applying that theory to the same-sex marriage debate).

[78] *See* 539 U.S at 587 (Scalia, J., dissenting).

[79] Zablocki v. Redhail, 434 U.S. at 386.

fundamental right of privacy. Here again, however, the Court has had to distinguish between substantial and nonsubstantial interferences with these so-called family rights, and also has had to define the boundaries of "family" that trigger this constitutional protection. More peripherally or distantly related persons, as well as unrelated persons, may in some cases have important bonds that are as close as those between parents and their biological offspring. Recognizing this, the Court has invalidated an ordinance that prevented a grandmother from living with her son and two grandsons in the same home,[80] but did not extend this protection to unrelated college students.[81]

Even a biological bond, however, may not always suffice. For example, a state may define child visitation rights in a manner that allows nonparents to obtain a court order allowing them to visit the child. They may not, however, order visitation even by the child's paternal grandparents over the opposition of the parent or parents where other conditions—such as that the custodial parent is unfit—are not met. Yet the lines between and among the interests of the respective parties in such cases are hardly clear. The Court in *Troxel v. Granville*[82] confronted such a case and split badly in striking down the nonparental visitation statute in question. A plurality of the Court did not deny that a properly narrow statute might grant such rights without violating the parental due process right. But it determined the statute was unconstitutional as applied.[83] Two dissenting justices—Stevens and Kennedy—specifically recognized that the children themselves may have a fundamental liberty interest in preserving relationships with nonparents.[84]

Biological bonds likewise did not suffice in *Michael H. v. Gerald D.*, which involved a request for visitation rights by the biological father of a child born to a woman who was then in a legal marriage to another man.[85] The biological father claimed that he had a fundamental due process interest in preserving his relationship with his biological daughter. Justice Scalia, in a plurality opinion, rejected this claim and read the family right embraced by due process very narrowly to exclude this relationship, noting the long legal history of presuming that a child born during the course of lawful marriage is the offspring of the mother's legal husband. Adulterous natural fathers, according to Justice Scalia, cannot invoke a tradition-based liberty interest under due process to protect their parental interests.[86] The case prompted a concurring opinion joined by Justices O'Connor and Kennedy in which they agreed that history and tradition matter to the due process analysis, but did not

---

[80] *See* Moore v. City of East Cleveland, 431 U.S. 494 (1977).

[81] Village of Belle Terre v. Boraas, 416 U.S. 1 (1974).

[82] 530 U.S. 57 (2000).

[83] *Id.* at 73.

[84] *Id.* at 86 (Stevens., J., dissenting); *Id.* at 98–99 (Kennedy, J., dissenting).

[85] 491 U.S. 110 (1989).

[86] *Id.* at 123–27. As Justice Scalia noted, "This is not the stuff of which fundamental rights qualifying as liberty interests are made." *Id.* at 127.

agree with Justice Scalia's strict approach to the level of generality in determining the scope of a right.[87]

Few cases better illustrate the Court's internal divisions about how to think about unenumerated substantive due process rights than *Michael H.* As we have seen, Justice Scalia is on record as believing that substantive due process is textually and historically ungrounded and oxymoronic; were he writing on a clean slate, he would not find them anew under due process. His alternative strategy is to construe the rights that the Court has identified as narrowly as possible, which makes his "specific trumps general" approach to defining these rights a logical part of that general strategy. That he would do so even in the context of family rights lends particular force to his claim that he will give them only the force that history, strictly construed, allows. If there is one category of unenumerated rights that tends to attracts significant crosscutting favor, it is family rights. Religious and cultural conservatives, no less than many religious and cultural liberals, often find the notion of family and marital privacy attractive—though powerful reasons remain for government to preserve authority over these domains.

There is no doubt, of course, that Justice Scalia would not extend the right of marital privacy to same-sex couples or to partners in a plural marriage. Justice Thomas likewise has staked out a position denying the legitimacy of substantive due process and thus would join Justice Scalia in refusing to extend marital privacy to embrace same-sex or plural unions. Justice Alito, who joined the Court after Justice O'Connor stepped down, already has emerged as a more conservative voice than Justice O'Connor in many contexts that suggest he also is disinclined to give an expansive reading to family rights. In forecasting the current Court's future rulings on marital and family privacy, all eyes therefore are on Justice Kennedy, who has been willing in key cases such as *Lawrence* to downplay history and to give a broader reading to liberty than the strict construction that his fellow conservative colleagues favor.

REPRODUCTIVE RIGHTS

Reproductive rights originally were rooted less in sexual autonomy per se than as an extension of marital privacy. *Griswold v. Connecticut,* one of the fonts of modern privacy law, focused on the right of marital couples to use and receive information about contraceptives. As it was in the much later cases of *Troxel* and *Michael H.*, however, the Court in *Griswold* was badly divided. Justice Douglas, writing for the Court, did not link the right to contraceptives to the liberty of due process. Instead, he followed a form of incorporation of rights from the Bill of Rights in which he identified specific amendments—the First, Third, Fourth, and Fifth—and argued that they had "penumbras" that "help give them life and substance."[88] Within these emanations was the right to marital privacy. *Meyer* and *Pierce*, Justice Douglas

---

[87] *Id.* at 132 (O'Connor, J., and Kennedy, J., concurring in part).

[88] *Griswold,* 381 U.S. at 484.

asserted, are better understood as identifying this sort of Bill of Rights-based right, rather than a liberty interest unmoored from any specific constitutional text.

Justice Harlan disagreed, and relied directly on the liberty language of the Fourteenth Amendment. This comported with his more general view that the Due Process Clause of the Fourteenth Amendment stands on its own bottom, such that the rights must be found there or as "implicit in the concept of ordered liberty."[89]

A third approach, followed by three other justices, was based on the Ninth Amendment, which provides that "[t]he enumeration in the Constitution of certain rights shall not be construed to deny or disparage others retained by the people."[90] In their view, this amendment supports the conclusion that the Fourteenth Amendment properly can be construed to extend beyond rights specifically enumerated in the Constitution.

As noted above, the Court gravitated to the Harlan approach, rather than relying either on penumbras or the Ninth Amendment. It also extended reproductive rights beyond the marital privacy zone. Nonmarital partners too have a fundamental right to choose "whether to bear or beget a child,"[91] and a woman's fundamental liberty rights include a bounded right to terminate a pregnancy in the early stages.[92]

The latter interpretation of due process liberty arguably has been the most controversial decision to date under the Fourteenth Amendment, apart (perhaps) from the *Slaughter-House Cases*. The Court first attempted to demarcate the lines between the woman's liberty interest and the government's competing interests in protecting maternal health and in protecting potential life by setting forth a trimester approach. The state interest in protecting maternal health became compelling after the first trimester; its interest in protecting potential life became compelling after viability (i.e., the fetus is capable of living outside the womb), which roughly coincides with the end of the second trimester. That is, states could regulate but not prohibit abortions after the first trimester in ways designed to promote maternal health. After viability, they could regulate and prohibit abortion except where it is necessary, in appropriate medical judgment, for the preservation of the life or health of the mother.

The framework was completely unacceptable to those who believed that life begins at conception, such that the due process rights of the fetus to "life, liberty, and property" began at that moment. It also was unacceptable to all who believed that

[89] *Id.* at 500 (Harlan, J., concurring).

[90] *Id.* at 488 (Goldberg, J, concurring). Justices Stewart and Black disagreed with Justice Harlan's construction of the Ninth Amendment and read it instead to be a provision based on preserving the federalism balance and assuring that the federal government would not exceed its limited powers. *Id.* at 529–30 (Justices Stewart and Black, dissenting). This reading, however, arguably renders the Ninth Amendment redundant insofar as the Tenth Amendment more explicitly preserves this federalism balance.

[91] Eisenstadt v. Baird, 405 U.S. 438 (1972).

[92] Roe v. Wade, 410 U.S. 113, 153 (1973).

substantive due process itself was nonsense, or that it could only be read to include enumerated or—at the farther edges—traditional unenumerated rights. In many states, the objections to the right manifested itself in aggressive regulation of the right, pushing the boundaries of state regulatory authority as far as possible within the trimester framework. The legislation ranged from requiring waiting periods, to mandatory counseling, to parental notification, to denial of funding for nontherapeutic abortions, to other restrictions on the types of abortion procedures available to pregnant women. The Court's own internal struggle over *Roe* led to fractured opinions and often to less-than-strict review of these burdens on the right.

The confirmation process of new Supreme Court justices often zeroed in on the nominees perceived position on *Roe* and its progeny. Closely related concerns were the nominee's views about *stare decisis*, originalism as a method of constitutional interpretation, and more general anxieties about "judicial activism." The Court's right to privacy case law thus became a lightning rod in judicial selections and also, by extension, in presidential elections.

Tensions mounted within and beyond the Court, and eventually the Court retreated from the *Roe* trimester approach in favor of a significantly modified approach outlined in 1992 in *Planned Parenthood v. Casey*.[93] Once again, the Court was internally divided, and sharply so. Claiming to preserve the "essential holding of *Roe*," the Court jettisoned the trimester framework in favor of an expanded state interest in potential life throughout the entire pregnancy.[94] Viability remained an important line, however, insofar as it constituted the point at which the state interest in potential life became constitutionally sufficient to ban a nontherapeutic abortion, i.e., abortion was not necessary to preserve the health or life of the mother.[95] Moreover, the right no longer triggered strict scrutiny. Rather, a law could be struck down if it imposed an *undue burden* on the right to abortion, which in turn meant its "purpose or effect was to place a substantial obstacle in the path of a woman seeking an abortion before the fetus attains viability."[96] A law designed to persuade the woman to favor childbirth over abortion did not, according to the joint opinion, constitute such an undue burden. A law that has the incidental effect of making abortion more expensive or difficult was not necessarily one designed to prohibit abortion before viability. Although only three justices joined in this joint opinion—O'Connor, Souter, and Kennedy—it constituted the holding of the case given that it was the position taken by the justices who concurred in the judgments on the narrowest grounds.[97]

Consequently, though it remains part of popular parlance to condemn the abortion cases as though the rule were still "*Roe v. Wade*," with its trimester approach,

---

[93] 505 U.S. 833 (1992).

[94] *Id.* at 876.

[95] *Id.* at 860.

[96] *Id.* at 877.

[97] *See* Marks v. United States, 430 U.S. 188, 193 (1977).

a more accurate banner would be "*Planned Parenthood v. Casey*" and its undue burden approach. Indeed, it should also include *Gonzales v. Carhart*,[98] in which Justice Kennedy again vacillated. He had joined the joint opinion upholding the "essential holding of *Roe*," but in *Gonzales* wrote an opinion that stressed the emotional toll of abortion on the mother, and that further expanded the state's right to regulate abortion despite the argument that the health of the mother might better be protected by the method prohibited by Congress: partial birth abortion. More specifically, the federal act, passed under the Commerce Clause powers of Congress, bans intact dilation and extraction procedures but allows the standard dilation and extraction procedure. The prohibition on intact D & E abortions does not apply when it is necessary to save the life of the mother, but makes no similar exception based on the health versus life of the mother.

In a facial challenge to the Act based on substantive due process, the Court in *Gonzales* held that the undue burden test was not violated. Congress had a legitimate interest in barring an inhumane procedure that would undermine respect for human life and for the medical profession. Congress did not prohibit the standard D & E, and it concluded—against significant, but not uncontested, evidence from the medical community—that the intact D & E procedure was not medically necessary. Although the Court noted that it was not bound by the congressional findings regarding medical necessity, it found no persuasive evidence that the congressional purpose or effect was to place an undue burden on the right to seek a previability abortion. The Court upheld the federal act on a facial challenge, though it left open the possibility of an "as applied" challenge.[99]

The opinion is a notable one in the abortion rights arena, because the challenged restriction on a previability abortion did not provide expressly for an exception where the health of the mother was implicated. That is, Congress not only prohibited a *previability* procedure, it prohibited one that may be deemed *therapeutic*. Nevertheless, it did not prohibit the previability abortion altogether, just one method of obtaining it. Although the Court noted that the medical community is divided on the issue of whether partial-birth abortions are less risky than the standard D & E procedure, and noted that it would not simply defer to congressional findings on this contested factual matter, it also emphasized the psychological impact of abortion on the woman—especially her remorse. In this last respect, some observers argued the opinion was paternalistic and out of step with the nature of protection of individual autonomy in other areas of individual liberties. The Court has not listed post-decisional remorse as a relevant factor in defining the scope of other individual liberties—such as the right to control the upbringing of a child, or the right to marriage. The liberty-based right to abortion therefore remains a highly complex and bounded right that is riddled with internal, contradictory impulses.

---

[98] 550 U.S. 124 (2007).

[99] *Id.* at 167.

INTIMATE ASSOCIATION AND SEXUAL AUTONOMY RIGHTS

As we have seen, the notion of unenumerated substantive due process rights began with the right to contract and related objections to government power that interfered with individual economic liberty. The rise and fall of *Lochner*-ism thus remains an important backdrop to the revival of substantive due process in the realm of personal liberties. The key case in the revival was *Griswold*, which first associated the privacy interest with marital privacy. The right later was expanded more generally to embrace the decision to beget (or not to beget) a child.

From this platform of reproductive autonomy, it was nearly inevitable that the Court eventually would be confronted with privacy claims that sought to protect the underlying sexual intimacy that may give rise to conception, as well as to sexual intimacy between adult partners regardless of whether conception is possible. Yet the notion that constitutional liberty extends to sexual autonomy is vigorously denied by some critics of substantive due process. They most definitely deny that this intimacy right should be read expansively.

The Court in *Lawrence v. Texas*[100] struggled with a particularly challenging application of sexual intimacy privacy: same-sex sodomy. Standing in the clear path of a holding that same-sex sexual intimacy was constitutionally protected was the Court's decision in *Bowers v. Hardwick*, which held that proscriptions against homosexual sodomy have "ancient roots" and thus do not violate traditional notions of ordered liberty.[101] Indeed, the behavior had been criminalized and thus could not—according to the Court in *Bowers*—reasonably be regarded as a fundamental right.

Yet an intervening opinion—*Romer v. Evans*[102]—cast at least some doubt on the status of *Bowers*. In that case the Court struck down on equal protection grounds Colorado's Amendment 2, a state constitutional provision that rescinded state and local laws that prohibited discrimination based on sexual orientation and barred future legislative, executive, or judicial action to prohibit such discrimination. The Court concluded that the measure lacked a rational relationship to any legitimate governmental interest.[103] Under equal protection law, as is true under due process law, the rational basis test is a very difficult test to fail. Thus it was remarkable that the Court found the Colorado law unconstitutional on this basis. The opinion sparked the now-famous dissent by Justice Scalia, which began with his provocative (and to many, intellectually inaccessible) statement that the Court had "mistaken a *Kulturkampf* for a fit of spite."[104] He later took a step further, and condemned the Court for signing on to the "so-called homosexual agenda."[105] In *Romer*, he

---

[100] 539 U.S. 558 (2003).
[101] 478 U.S. 186 (1986).
[102] 517 U.S. 620 (1996).
[103] *Id.* at 632.
[104] *Id.* at 636 (Scalia, J., dissenting).
[105] Lawrence v. Texas, 539 U.S. 558, 602–603 (2003) (Scalia, J., dissenting).

excoriated the Court for its analytical incoherence. In his view, the logic of *Bowers* and the logic of *Romer* could not be reconciled.

In this last respect, Justice Scalia proved to be correct. *Romer* and *Bowers* were not easily reconciled, and one of them had to fall. Seven years later, the Court in *Lawrence* recognized this and overruled *Bowers*. A majority of the Court concluded that adults have a constitutionally protected liberty interest in private, consensual sexual intimacy. According to the majority, the issue was not properly framed as the narrow "right to engage in sodomy," but the more general right to engage in sexual intimacy. Writing for the Court, Justice Kennedy focused both on sexual privacy as such, and on the more doctrinally pervasive notion that the home is "the most private of places."[106]

Yet Justice Kennedy was cautious in mapping out this liberty. He did not state that the applicable right was fundamental per se; rather, he concluded that the state law in question "furthers no legitimate state interest which can justify its intrusion into the personal and private life of the individual."[107] In other words, the state law lacked even a rational basis.

In a concurring opinion, Justice O'Connor instead focused on equal protection. In her view, the Texas statute was constitutionally flawed because it only regulated oral or anal sex between same-sex, not heterosexual, couples.[108]

The absence of clear language in the Kennedy opinion to elevate the right in question to fundamental status was doctrinally significant in ways that continue to be explored. For one thing, it suggests that rational basis review remains alive and well, and hardly "toothless." It also casts doubt on whether the right to same-sex intimacy plausibly may be extended to cover same-sex marriage. Justice Kennedy clearly anticipated the concern about the potential reach of his opinion and expressly noted that the case was being narrowly decided: it did not involve minors, non-consensual relations, public conduct, or prostitution and did not involve "whether the government must give formal recognition to any relationship that homosexual persons seek to enter."[109] Nevertheless, it was difficult not to see the relevance of the opinion to same-sex marriage disputes, and the current efforts to extend *Lawrence* to same-sex unions surely were inevitable. Just as reproductive rights began in the zone of marital privacy but then migrated out to embrace nonmarital privacy, and to encompass a broader notion of relationship autonomy, so the *Lawrence*-based notion of same-sex sexual intimacy privacy may migrate out to limit the state's right to deny a same-sex partner the full status of a relationship that may be informed by, but not defined by, sexual intimacy. States thus eventually must answer the following question: what is the *rational basis* for denying this status, if no rational basis supports prohibiting the underlying, consensual adult sexual relationship?[110]

---

[106] 539 U.S. at 567.

[107] *Id.* at 578.

[108] *Id.* at 579–85 (O'Connor, J., concurring).

[109] 539 U.S. at 578.

[110] Due process may figure in the same-sex marriage debate in still another way. Professor Steve Sanders argues that couples who marry lawfully in one state may have a liberty interest in respect for

The opinion in *Lawrence* clearly has significant potential ramifications beyond the narrow zone of consensual sexual intimacy. It thus was not surprising that it prompted another, deeply caustic dissent by Justice Scalia, in which he lambasted the Court for offering an ungrounded new liberty right. In his view, the failure to identify the right at stake as "fundamental" meant that the rational basis test applied. This in turn required the Court to defer to the state's judgment, particularly in light of *Bowers* and the history of criminalizing same-sex intimacy.[111] That the Court did not defer to the state judgment boded ill for its ability to deny in future cases that substantive due process likewise limited state power to restrict marriage to opposite sex partners, or even to prohibit plural marriages. More generally, of course, Scalia has repeatedly indicated that he does not believe in substantive due process per se, as a matter of constitutional principle. But he was particularly incensed by what he viewed as a judge-made riff on fundamental rights that was the product of "law-trained elites" influencing decisions, and a lack of respect for traditional values and practices vis-à-vis morality.

Justice Scalia's undisguised outrage at the Court for "inventing" this allegedly new, privacy-based right endured. He later delivered a public address in which he sarcastically denounced the Court for finding the right to same-sex intimacy in the "I don't know, the Homosexuality Clause of the Bill of Rights."[112] His denunciations of the doctrine and any evolutionary approach to due process resonated with many socially conservative Americans, and likely had a greater impact than any academic or other indictments of Court doctrine because they came from within the Court. Cries of judicial activism from other critics often invoked Justice Scalia's specific claims and shrill tone, and concerns about the future of evolutionary due process more generally, not just the law regarding same-sex intimacy, escalated.

Most significantly, opposition to substantive due process and judicial activism—once dominated by Progressives seeking to promote socioeconomic reform—often came from conservative camps seeking to protect traditional values, by their lights, as expressed in government regulations designed to promote these values. As the ideological balance of the Court has shifted anew, especially with the replacement of Justice Sandra Day O'Connor by Justice Samuel Alito, there is some reason to expect that this more ideologically conservative Court might move even further away from a dynamic construction of substantive due process, and might cabin, if not overrule completely, some of the more liberal constructions of due process liberty.

---

the marriage when they migrate to another state. This is not, he says, a fundamental right to same-sex marriage, but an aspect of reasonable expectations and marital and family privacy. A state's interest in refusing to recognize a marriage performed in another state figures in his analysis, but it is not sufficient to justify nonrecognition under the intermediate level of scrutiny that arguably would apply. *See* Steve Sanders, *The Constitutional Right to (Keep Your) Same-Sex Marriage*, 110 MICH. L. REV. 1421 (2012).

[111] *Lawrence*, 539 U.S. 558, 602–03 (2003) (Scalia, J., dissenting).

[112] JOAN BISKUPIC, AN AMERICAN ORIGINAL 221 (2009) (describing Justice Scalia's address to the Manhattan Institute).

Whether this shift occurs, though, will depend in large part on how the current Court treats *stare decisis*. Some of the more controversial rulings, including *Lawrence*, now have become part of national expectations about baseline liberties. A Court ruling overturning the nearly decade-old ruling in *Lawrence* would seem shocking today to many people, not merely to those who believed the 1986 ruling in *Bowers* was an abomination.

It also will depend upon the nature of the liberties asserted. The antilibertarian ramifications of Justice Scalia or Thomas-style strict construction of substantive due process make the future course of the doctrine much harder to chart than any simple "conservative versus progressive" dichotomy suggests. This may become particularly evident when the Court confronts future cases involving informational disclosure of personal matters that can be compromised in dramatically more intrusive ways due to technological advances. The now dominant conservative wing of the Court may not agree internally about the ongoing meanings of constitutional liberty and privacy, including sexual liberty and privacy.

Whatever the Court does when it confronts emerging issues, it will not only excavate the traditional meaning of liberty, but also influence if not construct its modern meaning. If this is judicial activism, then it is as much a part of our traditional notions of liberty and of judicial decisionmaking as the constitutional text itself. We will say much more on this aspect of judge-made law later in our examination of the arc of American notions of due process.

MEDICAL SELF-DETERMINATION RIGHTS

Scientific developments not only have affected modern notions of liberty in the realm of conception and other "beginning of life" arena, but also Americans' ideas about end-of-life decisions. Medical advances and the multiple ways in which government is involved in regulating access to medical care have made end-of-life an inherently medicalized and often governmentalized chapter of human existence for many people. Medical advancements can mean extended life for people in a greatly reduced or even persistently vegetative state, often with elaborate medical support, when in earlier eras they would have stood virtually no chance of survival. Determining the right of a patient to refuse life-saving treatment thus has become enormously complex, as has the right to refuse other medical interventions that might improve one's quality of life.

Of course, the right to refuse medical treatment has a corollary: the right to choose among available medical procedures. As we have seen, a woman has a bounded right to elect to abort a fetus, which is strongest when the abortion is necessary to preserve her health or life.[113] The right to opt to receive or refuse medical

---

[113] *See* Stenberg v. Carhart, 530 U.S. 914 (2000).

treatment thus is best viewed as components of a more general, admittedly fuzzy, right to make important life decisions.[114]

The right to control one's medical treatment is, like other liberty rights, a bracketed one. It does not give rise to a general constitutional right to treatment or drugs that are outlawed by the government. In the context of medical marijuana and other unorthodox pain or cancer therapies, the tension between individual autonomy and the government's interest in public health has prompted litigation testing the limits of government authority.

The cases begin with the assumption that one does not have a constitutionally protected right to commit suicide—as problematic as that baseline assumption may be from a libertarian perspective. Yet one has a constitutionally protected, though not unlimited, right to refuse medical treatment. That is, one arguably has a right to refuse treatment that would save one's life, even if one does not have a right to commit suicide. A sane, adult, Type-I diabetic who refused to undergo the grueling regimen of insulin shots conceivably could simply refuse to undergo the treatment that is necessary to sustain her life. In such a case, the government's right to prevent suicide would conflict with the individual's right of self-determination, but as a practical matter the state is unlikely to intervene unless a physician or family member or other person first seeks government assistance. Less dramatically, a Stage II breast cancer patient might refuse chemotherapy despite abundant medical evidence that the harms of the treatment are outweighed by the potential life-saving or life-extending benefits. For the state to intervene in any of these scenarios, it likely must demonstrate that it has a compelling reason to burden the individual's fundamental right to control his or her medical treatment, and that its intervention is the least restrictive means of furthering that purpose. Again, however, as a practical matter these thorny issues are underlitigated because they often are managed within the doctor–patient relationship according to general principles of patient control over his or her medical care, and dealt with privately; the government typically is not directly involved in the decision process.

Even a prisoner, who has more limited liberty rights while incarcerated, has a right to refuse antipsychotic drugs, though the interest is not absolute.[115] Where a prisoner may be harmful to himself or others, the state may be permitted to forcibly administer antipsychotic drugs.

The involvement of medical personnel and family members in personal medical decisions for patients who are physically and sometimes mentally compromised, however, complicates greatly the issue of control over medical treatment. It is one thing to refuse life-sustaining medical measures when one is sane, terminally ill, conscious, and the measure itself is painful or has other side effects. It is quite another to ask independent medical personnel or designated representatives to

---

[114] *See* Whalen v. Roe, 429 U.S. 589, 599–600 (1977).

[115] *See* Washington v. Harper, 494 U.S. 210 (1990).

actively assist in precipitating death by removing life-sustaining hydration and nutrition or other support. Can individuals make the decision to refuse life-sustaining treatment in advance of a life-threatening illness or accident, and expect that their intentions will be honored by others when they are unable to express them themselves?

There are relatively few cases that address these complicated questions. The leading ones do not establish any fundamental "right to die," but acknowledge the gray line between the bounded liberty interest in controlling one's medical care and refusing essential medical treatment. In *Cruzan v. Missouri Department of Health*, the Court acknowledged that prior case law implied a right to refuse unwanted medical treatment that extended to "the forced administration of life-sustaining medical treatment, and even of artificially-delivered food and water essential to life."[116] Yet it refused to find any "right to die" and instead said that it would assume for purposes of the case before it that a competent person had such a right.[117] The Court later noted that *Cruzan* "assumed, and strongly suggested" that due process includes a fundamental right to refuse life-saving treatment, but emphasized again that *Cruzan* did not so *hold*.[118]

In this arena, as in other due process realms, the recent changes in Court composition may prove to be determinative. Chief Justice Rehnquist and Justice O'Connor—both of whom expressed support for the notion that there is a constitutionally protected right to refuse life-saving medical treatment—have since been replaced by Chief Justice Roberts and Justice Alito, whose views on this issue are unknown. At present, the case law provides logical support for such a right, but no clear holding. States may demand clear and convincing evidence of the patient's interests, in furtherance of the states' interest in public health and safety. Moreover, the right at stake belongs solely to the patient; the state may choose to adopt procedures that defer solely to the patient's wishes rather than family members.[119] As such, those seeking to assure maximum autonomy over such decisions may need to anticipate this by executing living wills, according to state regulations, and naming surrogates who can act for them should they become incompetent.

The Court also has been quite clear that there is no constitutionally protected interest in demanding life-ending medication. In other words, there is no right to physician-assisted suicide even for terminally ill patients seeking to determine the time and manner of their deaths. In *Washington v. Glucksberg*, the Court confronted this issue and flatly (and unanimously) rejected the notion that the due process right to liberty embraces such an interest.[120] In a concurring opinion, several justices qualified this by noting that they might rule differently in a case where

---

[116] 497 U.S. 261, 279 (1990).

[117] *Id.*

[118] Washington v. Glucksberg, 521 U.S. 702, 720 (1997).

[119] Cruzan, 497 U.S. at 286–87.

[120] 521 U.S. 702, 727.

a mentally competent person was experiencing "great suffering" and sought to control the circumstances of his or her imminent death.[121]

An important feature of *Glucksberg* was the method by which the Court reached its conclusion, and the contrast between this method and the one used in *Lawrence*. In *Glucksberg*, Chief Justice Rehnquist emphasized that the due process inquiry hinges on history and tradition, and required that a right be "deeply rooted" in American history or tradition to merit constitutional protection.[122] In *Lawrence*, Justice Kennedy examined history of anti-sodomy laws, but found the evidence against the right to sexual intimacy for same-sex partners to be less powerful than *Bowers* had claimed, and also indicated a willingness to read history and tradition more expansively than the narrowest possible construction of recognized liberties. As we saw in *Michael H.*, the Court is internally conflicted about the level of specificity used to determine whether a right enjoys traditional respect, as well as on whether history should be dispositive versus instructive. Thus *Glucksberg* is an important example of a basic approach to substantive due process problems, but cannot be read in isolation or as the Court's solely anthontative statement about how to analyze unenumerated rights.

FREEDOM OF MOVEMENT

A fairly obvious aspect of liberty involves freedom from arbitrary physical constraint. This right imposes on government significant procedural requirements before institutionalizing or incarcerating individuals, as well as compelling substantive justifications at the threshold for placing them under government control. Once they are properly incarcerated or institutionalized, however, the government may limit their movement and other liberties. For example, the state may place a prisoner in solitary confinement[123] and can constrain the movement of a mental patient in ways that would violate due process rights beyond these settings. Prisoners may object to conditions within government-run institutions on other liberty grounds, but a criminal conviction with a sentence of imprisonment terminates any liberty interest in freedom of movement. Patients have greater rights than prisoners,[124] yet the test is significantly more forgiving than the strict scrutiny test that applies in nonbounded settings.

A corollary of the state's greater control over incarcerated and institutionalized persons is its duty of care toward prisoners and patients. As is true of public school students during school hours and while under school authority, these persons have the right to an affirmative duty of care. This is a departure from the

[121] *Id.* at 736 (O'Connor, J., Ginsburg, J., and Breyer, J., concurring). Justice Stevens also indicated that he would regard such circumstances as presenting stronger arguments for a right to assisted suicide. *Id.* at 741–42 (Stevens, J., concurring).

[122] *Id.* at 727.

[123] Hewitt v. Helms, 459 U.S. 460 (1983)

[124] *See* Youngberg v. Romero, 457 U.S. 307, 324 (1982).

normal structure of constitutional liberties, which is to protect the individual from government action rather than to impose any positive duty on the government. Absent such a special relationship or other restraint of liberty that prevents individuals from caring for their own basic needs, the government has no affirmative duty to provide for these needs or to protect individuals from harm from others.[125] Even where government has deprived them of liberty, as in the prison setting, the duty of care owed is to prevent harmful actions by government that are deliberate, rather than merely negligent.

In nonbounded realms, the right to move freely often is referred to as the "right to travel," which has been located within several constitutional provisions as well as the Due Process Clause.[126] The due process right to freedom of movement may be implicated in cases involving anti-loitering laws[127] and in cases involving restrictions on foreign travel.

INFORMATIONAL PRIVACY

Finally, the Court has "referred broadly to a constitutional privacy 'interest in avoiding disclosure of personal matters.'"[128] The case law, however, is quite scanty and over thirty years old,[129] and at least two current justices—Scalia and Thomas—recently made clear that they do not believe due process includes such a right. Indeed, Justice Scalia described the notion that there is a historical and tradition-based right to informational privacy as "farcical."[130]

Yet few things may matter more to evolving notions of privacy than whether individuals must rely on legislatures rather than on the Constitution to protect them from ever more intrusive means of uncovering personal information. Security screening devices, government background investigations incident to employment or as conditions to benefits, credit, loans, insurance, or other government-run programs, and a range of other ways in which government can, and does, intrude into personal realms all raise concerns about liberty-based limits on the government's "need to know."

Similar issues arise in Fourth Amendment cases, where government surveillance technology has advanced to the point that government is able to monitor

---

[125] *See* DeShaney v. Winnebago County Dep't of Social Services, 489 U.S. 189, 200–201 (1989).

[126] *See, e.g.*, Shapiro v. Thompson, 394 U.S. 618 (1969) (relying on the Equal Protection Clause to strike down durational residency requirements for welfare benefits); Saenz v. Roe, 526 U.S. 489 (1999) (relying on the Privileges or Immunities Clause to strike down a durational residency requirement for welfare benefits).

[127] *See* City of Chicago v. Morales, 527 U.S. 41 (1999); Papachristou v. City of Jacksonville, 405 U.S. 156 (1972).

[128] NASA v. Nelson, 131 S. Ct. 746 (2011).

[129] *See* Whalen v. Roe, 429 U.S. 589, 599–600 (1977); Nixon v. Administrator of General Services, 433 U.S. 425, 457 (1977).

[130] NASA v. Nelson, 131 S. Ct. 746, 764 (Scalia, J., concurring in the judgment).

individuals' whereabouts[131] and personal information to an unmatched degree. The difference, of course, is that the Fourth Amendment is an enumerated right that has long been held to include protection against unreasonable searches and seizures based on reasonable expectations of privacy.[132] It has not been thought to extend to things in plain view, which ordinarily would include one's physical location. But the government only recently has developed the ability to monitor location so precisely and continuously, without massive deployment of government resources and personnel. Technology also enables government to pinpoint and track cell phone use without listening to the conversations themselves in ways that only now are becoming widely understood. Wiretapping laws currently do not extend to these types of tracking devices, and courts only recently have been confronted with claims that they may constitute violations of reasonable expectations of privacy.[133] For reasons already discussed, the Court in a Fourth Amendment case is likely to refuse to apply substantive due process at all, on the ground that the more specific constitutional provision trumps the murkier, substantive due-process-based claim.[134] Whether this approach makes sense, and whether due process properly should be construed to add *anything* to this Fourth Amendment analysis, may become a more serious question as governmental surveillance methods develop. Whether due process in any other context embraces an independent substantive right to informational privacy almost certainly will be an issue the Court must resolve. A majority of the current Court may vote to avoid reaching the due process question in a Fourth Amendment case. But the fate of the second claim—i.e., that there is a constitutionally protected due process right to informational privacy—is far less clear. It will depend on whether three colleagues agree with Justices Scalia and Thomas, who have already flatly insisted there is no such right.

Here again, resistance to a more generous approach to substantive due process may not be a matter of "conservative versus liberal" inclinations. Conservative libertarians, as well as many liberal progressives, likely regard informational privacy as worthy of constitutional, not merely statutory, protection and thus may favor a more elastic view of due process than a narrow, "history and tradition"-based approach might allow. Thus it is not enough to observe that a majority of the current Court is decidedly "conservative," particularly since the departure of Justice O'Connor. Moreover, as we have seen in examining the ways in which Justice

---

[131] The Court held in a recent Fourth Amendment case that a hidden GPS device used to monitor a criminal suspect's whereabouts constituted a "search." Although the case was very narrowly decided, it is significant that Justice Alito criticized the plurality opinion by Justice Scalia for using outdated eighteenth-century property notions to resolve the modern case. *See* United States v. Jones, 132 S. Ct. 945, 962–65 (2012). (Alito, J. concurring in the judgment).

[132] Katz v. United States, 389 U.S. 347 (1967).

[133] Jennifer Valentino-Devries, *Keeping "Stingrays" Secret Makes Case Tougher for Prosecutors*, WSJ, Sept. 23, 2011, p. 1 (discussing United States v. Rigmaiden, Case No. CR08-0814-01-PHX-DGC (D. Az. 2011) Arizona federal district court case involving cell phone tracking devices used by government).

[134] *See* text accompanying notes 56–57, *supra*.

Kennedy has shifted in the some of these cases, context matters in how much weight a particular justice may give to history and tradition.

Whatever basic principles and methodology the modern Court deploys to determine the scope of due process in this area, of course, will affect how that scope is determined in other realms. Lawyers and the justices themselves will rely on the principles and methodologies across the substantive due process spectrum when analyzing a particular controversy. The current options range from a fairly strict interpretation of history and tradition on display in cases like *Glucksberg*, to the more forgiving and dynamic approach, both on display in cases like *Lawrence*.

SUBSTANTIVE DUE PROCESS AND EXECUTIVE ACTION: DOES IT "SHOCK THE CONSCIENCE?"

The foregoing unenumerated liberty-based rights arise primarily, though not exclusively, in the context of legislative action. Yet substantive due process also constrains executive power, and arguably imposes a rationality limitation on the exercise of that power. Again, however, the modern viability of the doctrine remains unclear, and its constitutional existence is strongly denied by the same justices who condemn substantive due process more generally.

The lead case is *Rochin v. California*,[135] decided in 1952. The Court in that now-dated opinion stated that the judge's role includes the enforcement of "those canons of decency and fairness which express the notions of justice of the English-speaking peoples even toward those charged with the most heinous offenses."[136] In terms that Justice Scalia, for one, regards as hopelessly open-textured, Justice Frankfurter acknowledged the ambiguity of a "decency" restraint, noting that "[i]n dealing not with the machinery of government but with human rights, the absence of formal exactitude, or want of fixity of meaning, is not an unused or even regrettable attribute of constitutional provisions."[137] This is inevitably a matter of "judgment,"[138] which is not free-floating but based upon "considerations deeply rooted in reason and in the compelling traditions of the legal profession."[139] In his view, a "shocks the conscience" due process boundary was "historic and generative."[140]

Whether this test survives, however, is much disputed. The Court invoked the test in *Breithaupt v. Abram*,[141] but concluded it was not violated under facts quite similar to involuntary stomach-pumping at issue in *Rochin*: police had directed an emergency room doctor to draw blood from an unconscious driver, who under

---

[135] 342 U.S. 165 (1952).
[136] *Id.* at 169.
[137] *Id.*
[138] *Id.*
[139] *Id.*
[140] Irvine v. California, 347 U.S. 128, 146 (1954).
[141] 352 U.S. 432 (1957).

the influence of alcohol, had caused an accident that killed several people. The Court denied that the nonconsensual blood test violated the due process rights.[142]

Several decades later, the Court again referred to "conscience-shocking" conduct as unconstitutional, but concluded the standard was not met when a city failed to train or warn city workers about asphyxiation dangers and a sewer worker died while attempting to clear a sewer line underground.[143] Then, in 1998, the Court in *County of Sacramento v. Lewis* addressed whether the constitutional due process rights of a teenager were violated when the sheriff's deputy pursued a motorcycle at 100 miles an hour through a residential neighborhood, at a distance of 100 feet.[144] In analyzing the applicable standard of review, the Court stated that "we have spoken of the cognizable level of executive abuse of power as that which shocks the conscience."[145] Again, however, the Court concluded that the standard was not met.

The notion that executive power is constrained by such a vague standard evoked a characteristically acid response from Justice Scalia, who described the shocks-the-conscience test as "the *ne plus ultra*, the Napoleon Brandy, the Mahatma Gandhi, the Cellophane of subjectivity."[146] There is no doubt that Justice Scalia, along with Justice Thomas, still adheres to the view that the test is an ahistorical and groundless one that should be jettisoned.

Nevertheless, as Justice Stevens's 2010 opinion in *McDonald* indicates,[147] the idea lives on that government, including executive officials, must observe baseline due process expectations about decency and reason that the judiciary can enforce in extreme cases.[148] Although courts rarely apply the standard, and even more rarely find it to be violated, they continue to invoke it. Like the rational basis test more generally, the shocks-the-conscience test therefore may be described as a background principle that expresses an abiding, however murky, due process concern. Whenever it surfaces, it encounters fierce opposition by judges who regard such an open-ended test as hopelessly subjective.[149] But these protests typically are met with the sensible and pragmatic defense that "although … neither life nor law can always be made convenient and easy … [o]utrageousness is a concept, not a constant."[150]

Indeed, the exceptional hostility to substantive due process on the ground that it demands judicial judgment calls is quite puzzling. The Court in other areas has

---

[142] *Id.* at 436.

[143] Collins v. Harker Heights, 503 U.S. 115 (1992).

[144] 523 U.S. 833, 836–37 (1998).

[145] *Id.* at 846.

[146] *Id.* at 861 (Scalia, J., concurring in the judgment).

[147] 130 S. Ct. 3020, 3101 (Stevens, J., dissenting).

[148] *See, e.g.*, Hampton v. United States, 424 U.S. 484, 492 (Powell, J., concurring in the judgment).

[149] *See, e.g.*, United States v. Miller, 891 F.2d 1265, 1271, 1273 (Easterbrook, J., concurring) (describing the due process shocks-the-conscience test as "not a rule of any kind, let alone a command of the Due Process Clause").

[150] United States v. Santana, 6 F.3d 1, 4 (1st Cir. 1993).

deployed equally fluid benchmarks without evoking comparably heated resistance. For example, in its "regulatory takings" cases the Court requires that government restrictions on property rights not "go too far" lest they become a taking.[151] Nor is it a compelling explanation that substantive due process has no historical support, as the foregoing discussion of the history of due process and the rule of law makes clear.

Finally, the Court has evinced renewed willingness to check legislative and executive power in other areas of constitutional law in ways that draw on the implicit "structure" of the Constitution, rather than on express commands interpreted at the most specific level of generality.[152] And, even where textual powers are expressly enumerated—such as the Commerce Clause authority of Congress—the Court has developed "a rational basis with bite" version of judicial review to constrain that power.[153] There is little reason to think the courts are demonstrably better at articulating judicially manageable "rationality" limits to government authority in the commerce clause arena than they are in the due process realm. Even more remarkably, the Court has relied on the federal Commerce Clause as the basis for checking *state* legislative power under the judicially-constructed dormant commerce clause doctrine, even when the state legislation is not facially or otherwise discriminatory.[154] This last example is particularly striking because the dormant commerce clause cases directly implicate both federalism and separation of powers concerns, which also are common tropes in critiques of substantive due process.

In any event, judicial review of executive action based on this "shocks-the-conscience" notion remains a plausibly invoked, though abstract and faintly enforced due process benchmark. It has not been removed altogether from the due process

---

[151] *See, e.g.*, Pennsylvania Coal Co. v. Mahon, 260 U.S. 393, 415 (1922). *Cf.* Penn Central Transportation Co. v. City of New York, 428 U.S. 104 (1978) (balancing the burden of land use regulation against the public benefit). For an exceptionally thoughtful analysis of *Mahon* and its history see William Michael Treanor, *Jam for Justice Holmes: Reassessing the Significance of* Mahon, 86 Geo. L.J. 813 (1998). Most notably, Professor Treanor observes that "*Mahon* is [technically] a substantive due process case. It preceded the Supreme Court's acceptance of incorporation." *Id.* at 856. It also was a case that rejected formalism in favor of a more pragmatic balancing test, but with a strong presumption of government authority. *Id.* at 857–58.

[152] *See, e.g.*, Printz v. United States, 521 U.S. 898 (1997) (invoking structural aspects of the Constitution to strike down federal legislation that "commandeers" state executive officials).

[153] *See, e.g.*, United States v. Morrison, 529 U.S. 598 (2000) (holding that Congress lacked Commerce Clause authority to pass the challenged sections of the Violence Against Women Act, despite congressional evidence of a the substantial, albeit indirect effect of domestic sexual violence on interstate commerce; Congress needed a rational basis for assuming such a link, but the Court need not defer uncritically to that decision by Congress). *See also* United States v. Lopez, 514 U.S. 549 (1995) (overturning a congressional act as beyond its Commerce Clause powers for the first time in nearly sixty years, and signaling a revival of Tenth Amendment and constitutional structure-based limits on federal legislative power).

[154] *See, e.g.*, Pike v. Bruce Church, Inc., 397 U.S. 137 (1970) (defining standard for judicial review of state legislation that burdens interstate commerce but involves no intentional discrimination against out-of-state commerce, in terms that resemble due process rational basis scrutiny). *See* discussion of similarities between due process scrutiny and Dormant Commerce Clause analysis in chapter 5, *infra*.

bundle of protections, perhaps because it is so rarely enforced and reflects an enduring sense that this modest cache of judicial power is worth preserving.

FUNDAMENTAL RIGHTS—ENUMERATED

The third category of liberty-based substantive due process includes rights that have been "selectively incorporated" into the Fourteenth Amendment through judicial interpretation. As noted above, even those who regard substantive due process as an oxymoron view the process of selective incorporation as more textually defensible than more ad hoc and free-floating determinations of liberty drawn from the structure of the Constitution, its "penumbras," or the Ninth Amendment. Justice Black, an ardent opponent of judicial construction of textually ungrounded due process rights, nevertheless believed strongly in the total incorporation of the Bill of Rights into the Fourteenth Amendment.[155]

The incorporation process began in 1897, when the Court concluded that taking of private property for public use without just compensation violated the Due Process Clause of the Fourteenth Amendment.[156] The basis for the opinion was not literally movement of the Fifth Amendment takings clause into the Fourteenth, but rather the notion that a taking violated fundamental principles of civil liberties that the Fourteenth Amendment was adopted to protect. This in turn led to a series of cases in which the Court assessed whether a particular enumerated right was fundamental in this sense and, if so, whether it should apply to the states in every respect as it did to the federal government. In *Twining v. New Jersey*,[157] decided in 1908, the Court stated that the test was not whether a right was enumerated in the Bill of Rights, but whether it was "of such a nature" that it should be included in due process.

Some years later Justice Cardozo elaborated on this concept in *Palko v. Connecticut*,[158] which addressed whether due process included the Double Jeopardy Clause of the Fifth Amendment and prohibited a state from appealing an acquittal after a jury trial. The Court concluded that due process did not include this clause, and attempted to clarify the difference between rights like freedom of expression—which by this time had been deemed to be among the rights protected by substantive due process—and other enumerated rights that were not so protected. The key, said Cardozo, was whether the right in question was "of the very essence of a scheme of ordered liberty."[159] That is, would liberty or justice exist if it were sacrificed?[160]

---

[155] *See Adamson v. California*, 332 U.S. 46, 86–89 (1947) (Black, J., dissenting). *See* chapter 2, *supra*.
[156] Chicago, Burlington & Quincy Railroad Co. v. Chicago, 166 U.S. 226, 241 (1897).
[157] 211 U.S. 78, 98 (1908).
[158] 302 U.S. 319, 325–27 (1937).
[159] *Id.* at 325.
[160] *Id.* at 327.

The justices continued to wrestle thereafter with this notion of some but not all, and not necessarily jot for jot approach of defining substantive due process. Again, Justice Black believed in total incorporation, with every element included. Justice John Marshall Harlan disagreed, and viewed the overlap between the Bill of Rights and the Fourteenth Amendment as a function not of literal incorporation, but of the fact that both promote overlapping notions of fairness and ordered liberty. The Due Process Clause of the Fourteenth Amendment, he maintained, "stands on its own bottom."[161]

In 2010, the Court for the first time in many years returned to the problem of how to assess whether and how an enumerated right under the Bill of Rights should be applied to the states via the Fourteenth Amendment.[162] The specific question was whether the Second Amendment, which recently had been determined to include an individual right to bear arms vis-à-vis the federal government,[163] likewise should apply to state and local governments. A plurality of the Court concluded that due process did include the Second Amendment guarantee,[164] and did so in terms that vindicated the Harlan approach as a general matter, but as a practical matter also nudged forward the Black agenda of total incorporation, "jot for jot." As noted above, Justice Alito described the issue as whether the right to bear arms was "fundamental to *our* scheme of ordered liberty, or … 'deeply rooted in this Nation's history and tradition.'"[165] He then observed that "[u]nless principles of *stare decisis* counsel otherwise, a provision of the Bill of Rights that protects a right that is fundamental from an American perspective applies equally to the Federal Government and the States."[166] In other words, the two clauses should be read symmetrically, even though the Fourteenth Amendment was ratified almost a century after the Bill of Rights, is a federal restraint on state and local power, and was adopted in the midst of a vastly different legal and social context than that of the Bill of Rights. If this is constitutional originalism, it is a self-consciously dynamic form of it.

In any event, the effect of the decades of selective incorporation of the Bill of Rights principles into the Fourteenth Amendment thus now stands as follows: all but the Third Amendment proscription against the quartering of soldiers, the Fifth Amendment requirement of a grand jury indictment for criminal prosecutions, the Seventh Amendment right to trial by jury in civil cases, and the Eighth Amendment proscription of excessive bail and excessive fines have been deemed to be incorporated.

---

[161] *See* Duncan v. Louisiana, 391 U.S. 145, 171–93 (Harlan, J., dissenting).

[162] *McDonald*, 130 S. Ct. 3020 (2010).

[163] District of Columbia v. Heller, 554 U.S. 570 (2008).

[164] Justice Thomas agreed that the right to bear arms constrains state and local government, but argued that the proper textual basis for this right is the Privileges or Immunities Clause of the Fourteenth Amendment. 130 S. Ct. 3020, 3088 (Thomas, J., concurring in part and concurring in the judgment).

[165] 130 S. Ct. 3020, 3036 (emphasis in original) (internal quotations omitted).

[166] *Id.* at 3035.

Finally, the touchstone of incorporation is American tradition—but with considerable respect for *stare decisis*. Indeed, the same touchstone holds for all of due process.

II. Summary

The post-bellum due process case law holds that substantive due process has three parts: nonfundamental rights, fundamental unenumerated rights, and enumerated, "incorporated" rights, which by definition are fundamental. The latter two categories of due process rights proceed from an assessment of whether violation of the right in question would be inimical to basic principles of ordered liberty—as Justice Cardozo suggested decades ago. Less clear is whether nonfundamental rights, now subject solely to toothless rational basis review, will continue to receive even minimal due process protection under this ordered liberty approach.

The better view, as a matter of doctrine and a longer view of constitutional history, is that due process does extend to these nonfundamental liberties. Due process is a general right that polices arbitrary government conduct in all of its forms, but with an eye toward two goals: preservation of liberty and a baseline requirement that government actions promote public ends. In the realm of nonfundamental liberties, the balance will typically tip in favor of public ends, as they are identified and effected via properly functioning legislative and executive processes. But this does not mean that due process principles are not applicable to government conduct *across the board*.

LIBERTY AS EQUALITY AND "REVERSE INCORPORATION"

Another conundrum built into the due process doctrine is whether equal protection—which has its own text and historical backdrop under the Fourteenth Amendment—also constrains the federal government through the Fifth Amendment Due Process Clause. As noted above, the Court has answered this question in the affirmative.[167]

Reverse incorporation applies rights defined in the Fourteenth Amendment through the Fifth Amendment to limit the federal government.[168] Incorporation and reverse incorporation take rights once designated for application to either solely the states or solely the federal government and apply the rights against both.[169] The arguments against incorporation described above find counterparts

---

[167] *See supra* notes 164–66 and accompanying text.

[168] *See supra* notes 164–67 and accompanying text.

[169] *See, e.g.*, Akhil Reed Amar, *Constitutional Rights in a Federal System: Rethinking Incorporation and Reverse Incorporation*, in BENCHMARKS: GREAT CONSTITUTIONAL CONTROVERSIES IN THE SUPREME COURT 71, 71–72 (Terry Eastland ed., 1995).

in reverse incorporation doctrine. Yet despite arguments challenging the validity of incorporation and reverse incorporation, both doctrines have become well-established in American due process jurisprudence.

The application of incorporation and reverse incorporation principles raises the question of whether their application effectively eliminates federalism limits intended by the different language in the Due Process Clauses of the Fifth and Fourteenth Amendments.[170] This concern can only be addressed fully after an exploration of the historical development of the reverse incorporation doctrine.

The Court's recognition of reverse incorporation came in its 1954 decision in *Bolling v. Sharpe*;[171] however, the idea of applying the Equal Protection Clause of the Fourteenth Amendment against the federal government as a means to prevent discrimination predates *Bolling*. Indeed, support for the idea can be found dating back to the nation's beginnings.[172] Despite this, before *Bolling*, the argument that the Due Process Clause of the Fifth Amendment encompassed equal protection rights was frequently disregarded.[173] The Court did recognize, however, that the Due Process Clause of the Fifth Amendment included some equal protection principles, but did not contain as many as the Fourteenth Amendment's Equal Protection Clause.[174]

---

[170] *Id.*

[171] 347 U.S. 497, 498 (1954). *See also* Richard A. Primus, Bolling *Alone*, 104 COLUM. L. REV. 975, 975 (2004).

[172] David E. Bernstein, Bolling, *Equal Protection, Due Process, and Lochnerphobia*, 93 GEO. L.J. 1253, 1261 (2005); *see also* chapter 1 *supra* (discussing how even the early influences on the development of the American due process system, including Lord Coke, thought that the actions of the government should be subjected to review).

[173] *See, e.g.*, Hirabayashi v. United States, 320 U.S. 81, 100, 100–105 (1943) (recognizing that "[t]he Fifth Amendment contains no equal protection clause and it restrains only such discriminatory legislation by Congress as amounts to a denial of due process;" and holding ultimately that the military curfew order applying to Japanese persons was constitutional); Detroit Bank v. United States, 317 U.S. 329, 337–38 (1943) (recognizing that the Fifth Amendment does not contain an equal protection clause in upholding a statute "authorizing an unrecorded tax lien against the property mortgaged to it and withholding such a lien against innocent purchasers of property which a decedent had transferred inter vivos in contemplation of death"); United States v. Carolene Prods. Co., 304 U.S. 144, 145–16, 151 (1938) (recognizing that the Fifth Amendment contains no equal protection clause in upholding a statute that "prohibit[ed] the shipment in interstate commerce of skimmed milk compounded with any fat or oil other than milk fat, so as to resemble milk or cream, transcends the power of Congress to regulate interstate commerce or infringes the Fifth Amendment"); and La Belle Iron Works v. United States, 256 U.S. 377, 392 (1921) (stating that the Fifth Amendment has no equal protection clause in upholding a federal tax provision that was challenged as discriminatory) as cited in Primus, *supra* note 171, at 982 (explaining that all the cited cases rejected the argument that the Fifth Amendment contained "an equal protection clause").

[174] *See* Primus, *supra* note171, at 983 ("Even if constitutional equal protection did not bind the federal government, however, the federal government did face certain requirements of evenhandedness. Every legal system that respects the principle that like cases should be treated alike necessarily answers to some idea of equality, however thin, and the Court accordingly acknowledged that some minimal spirit of 'equality of application of the law' was inherent in the system and specifically in the Due Process Clause.") (footnotes omitted); Bernstein, *supra* note 172, at 1261 ("The Court initially remained agnostic on the matter. However, by 1921, the Court acknowledged in dicta that the concept of due process contained in the Fifth and Fourteenth Amendments included an equal protection component, albeit a weaker one than that contained in the Fourteenth Amendment's Equal Protection Clause.").

In *Truax v. Corrigan*,[175] for example, the Court recognized that there was a certain level of protection for equality inherently in due process:

> The due process clause brought down from Magna Carta was found in the early state constitutions and later in the Fifth Amendment to the federal Constitution as a limitation upon the executive, legislative and judicial powers of the federal government, while the equality clause does not appear in the Fifth Amendment and so does not apply to congressional legislation. The due process clause requires that every man shall have the protection of his day in court, and the benefit of the general law, a law which hears before it condemns, which proceeds not arbitrarily or capriciously, but upon inquiry, and renders judgment only after trial, so that every citizen shall hold his life, liberty, property and immunities under the protection of the general rules which govern society. It, of course, tends to secure equality of law in the sense that it makes a required minimum of protection for every one's right of life, liberty, and property, which the Congress or the Legislature may not withhold.[176]

This general protection of equality under the Fifth Amendment proved insufficient for addressing equal protection issues, as evidenced by the Court's eventual shift in its treatment of equal protection guarantees under the Fifth Amendment.

Early cases seeking to challenge unequal treatment by the federal government tended to focus on discrimination in federal income tax regulations, and resulted in the reiteration that there was no equal protection clause in the Fifth Amendment.[177] A step toward the recognition of equal protection in the Fifth Amendment resulted from challenges to the military's internment of Japanese Americans in the 1940s. Justice Murphy's dissent, in *Korematsu v. U.S.*,[178] observed: "[b]eing an obvious racial discrimination, the order deprives all those within its scope of the equal protection of the laws as guaranteed by the Fifth Amendment."[179]

Despite this racial discrimination by the federal government in the 1940s, it was not until 1954 that the Court began to develop the doctrine of reverse incorporation. In *Bolling v. Sharpe*,[180] the Court faced a Fifth Amendment due process challenge

---

[175] 257 U.S. 318 (1921).

[176] *Id.* at 332. In *Truax*, a labor dispute arose between an employer and a workers' union which eventually prompted the employees to strike and to boycott the employer's business, which caused the employer to suffer a loss of sales. *Id.* at 321. In the course of the action, the employer challenged an Arizona statute protecting striking employees, by alleging that if the statute protected the union employees' conduct it "depriv[ed] plaintiffs [the employer] of their property without due process of law, and by denying to plaintiffs the equal protection of the laws, and was therefore void and of no effect." *Id.* at 322; *see also* Primus, *supra* note 171, at 983 ("[T]he Court ... acknowledged that some minimal spirit of 'equality of application of the law' was inherent in the system and specifically in the Due Process Clause.") (citing *Truax*, 257 U.S. at 332).

[177] Primus, *supra* note 171, at 983–84.

[178] 323 U.S. 214 (1944).

[179] *Id.* at 234–35 (Murphy, J., dissenting); *see also* Primus, *supra* note 171, at 984.

[180] 347 U.S. 497 (1954).

by African American school children of the racial segregation in public schools in the District of Columbia.[181] The Court noted that similar racial segregation by the states in public schools had been deemed prohibited by the Equal Protection Clause of the Fourteenth Amendment.[182] The Court in *Bolling*,[183] however, faced a new challenge in the District of Columbia in which the Fifth Amendment, without an Equal Protection Clause, applied.[184] In discussing how the Equal Protection Clause of the Fourteenth Amendment related to the Due Process Clause of the Fifth Amendment, the Court stated:

> The Fifth Amendment, which is applicable in the District of Columbia, does not contain an equal protection clause as does the Fourteenth Amendment which applies only to the states. But the concepts of equal protection and due process, both stemming from our American ideal of fairness, are not mutually exclusive. The "equal protection of the laws" is a more explicit safeguard of prohibited unfairness than "due process of law," and, therefore, we do not imply that the two are always interchangeable phrases. But, as this Court has recognized, discrimination may be so unjustifiable as to be violative of due process.[185]

The Court explained that liberty was an expansive concept and that racial segregation in District of Columbia schools deprived the African American school children of their due process liberty.[186] The Court concluded that because "the Constitution prohibits the states from maintaining racially segregated public schools, it would be unthinkable that the same Constitution would impose a lesser duty on the Federal Government."[187] Accordingly, the Court held that racial segregation in public schools in the District of Columbia violated the African American students' Fifth Amendment due process rights.[188] The Constitution ensured that the prohibition of racial segregation in state public schools extended to federally run public schools as well.

The Court did not hold that the Fifth Amendment incorporated the Equal Protection Clause of the Fourteenth Amendment.[189] It instead relied on the "liberty" component of due process as encompassing certain prohibitions against "unjustifiable" discrimination.[190] The Court initially stuck to this due process analysis in facing Fifth Amendment equal protection cases, maintaining that the Due

---

[181] Bolling v. Sharpe, 347 U.S. 497, 498 (1954).

[182] *Id.* (citing Brown v. Board of Education, 347 U.S. 483 (1954)).

[183] 347 U.S. 497 (1954).

[184] *Id.* at 498–99.

[185] *Id.* (footnotes omitted).

[186] *Id.* at 499–500.

[187] *Id.* at 500.

[188] *Id.*

[189] Bradford Russell Clark, *Judicial Review of Congressional Section Five Action: The Fallacy of Reverse Incorporation*, 84 Colum. L. Rev. 1969, 1971 (1984).

[190] *See* Bolling v. Sharpe, 347 U.S. 497, 498–500 (1954).

Process Clause of the Fifth Amendment protected against certain "unjustifiable" discrimination, even though it contained no equal protection provision.[191] Over time, however, the Court's discussion changed as to what equal protection principles operate in the context of the Fifth Amendment.

The Court thereafter began to equate the equal protection analysis under the Fifth Amendment with the analysis under the Equal Protection Clause of the Fourteenth Amendment.[192] In *Weinberger v. Wiesenfeld*,[193] the Court explicitly stated the issue in the case was whether there was a violation of the Fifth Amendment's Due Process Clause based on gender differences in Social Security benefits.[194] To support its assertion that this gender discrimination issue correctly fell within the purview of the Fifth Amendment, the Court stated:

> (W)hile the Fifth Amendment contains no equal protection clause, it does forbid discrimination that is "so unjustifiable as to be violative of due process...." This Court's approach to Fifth Amendment equal protection claims has always been precisely the same as to equal protection claims under the Fourteenth Amendment.[195]

The Court thus treated the Fifth Amendment as if it contained an Equal Protection Clause, and performed its analysis accordingly.

This approach has been confirmed in subsequent case law where it has been accepted essentially or assumed by federal courts at all levels that the Fifth Amendment contains equal protection guarantees similar to those contained in the Fourteenth Amendment.[196] The Court itself, in 1997, relegated the issue to a footnote in *Regan v. Taxation With Representation of Wash.*,[197] where the Court held that a tax exemption that was unavailable to an organization that partook in "attempting to

---

[191] *See* Schneider v. Rusk, 377 U.S. 163, 168 (1964) ("[W]hile the Fifth Amendment contains no equal protection clause, it does forbid discrimination that is 'so unjustifiable as to be violative of due process.') (citing Bolling v. Sharpe, 347 U.S. 497, 499 (1954)); U. S. Dep't of Agric. v. Moreno, 413 U.S. 528, 533 n.5 (1973) (citing to the same *Bolling* language as *Schneider*); Frontiero v. Richardson, 411 U.S. 677, 680 n.5 (1973) (citing to the same *Bolling* language as *Schneider*); Shapiro v. Thompson, 394 U.S. 618, 641–42 (1969) (citing to the same *Bolling* language as *Schneider*) as cited in Primus, *supra* note 171, at 988.

[192] *See, e.g.*, Weinberger v. Wiesenfeld, 420 U.S. 636, 638, 639 n.5 (1975) ("The question in this case is whether this gender-based distinction violates the Due Process Clause of the Fifth Amendment.").

[193] 420 U.S. 636 (1975).

[194] *Id.* at 638.

[195] *Id.* at 638 n.2 (modifications in original) (internal citations omitted).

[196] *See, e.g.*, Moran v. U.S., 18 F.3d 412, 413 (7th Cir. 1994) (holding that when a federal statute provides a fee to witnesses testifying in federal cases but the fee was not given to a prisoner, this did not violate the Fifth Amendment under which "the federal government has been held to have the same duty under the due process clause of the Fifth Amendment to avoid arbitrary classifications as the states have under the equal protection clause of the Fourteenth Amendment.");Young v. Hawaii, 548 F. Supp. 2d 1151, 1172 (D. Hawaii 2008) (holding that a Hawaii statute that regulates the ability of certain people to obtain licenses to carry guns did not violate the Fifth Amendment's Due Process Clause or its equal protection guarantee, as to which the court noted "[t]he applicable legal standards under the Fifth Amendment's equal protection component are the same as the legal standards under the Fourteenth Amendment Equal Protection Clause.").

[197] 461 U.S. 540 (1997).

influence legislation" did not violate "the equal protection component of the Fifth Amendment's Due Process Clause."[198] The Court explained that "[t]he Due Process Clause imposes on the Federal Government requirements comparable to those that the Equal Protection Clause of the Fourteenth Amendment imposes on the states."[199] This quick treatment of the Fifth Amendment's lack of an Equal Protection Clause evidences how universal the assumption of "reverse incorporation" has become.

Although the theory of reverse incorporation developed in an attempt to limit racial discrimination, an analysis of subsequent case law shows that the doctrine has expanded to including discrimination based on: gender,[200] birth,[201] citizenship,[202] and residency.[203] In addition, the Court has held that the equal protection guarantee under the Fifth Amendment applies to "any person, of whatever race, [who] has the right to demand that any governmental actor subject to the Constitution justify any racial classification subjecting that person to unequal treatment under the strictest judicial scrutiny."[204] Both racial preferences and racial discrimination are subject to equal protection analysis under the Fifth Amendment.[205]

The historical progression of reverse incorporation case law shows how federalism limits in the text of the Fifth and Fourteenth Amendments have waned as the Court recognized equal protection guarantees in the Fifth Amendment and equated these protections with the protections contained in the Fourteenth Amendment's Equal Protection Clause. A driving force behind the Court's recognition of reverse incorporation[206] principles as noted above comes from concerns for fairness to the individual.[207] Thus, by effectively disregarding the importance of the absence of

---

[198] *Id.* at 542.

[199] *Id.* at 542 n.2.

[200] *See generally* Weinberger v. Wiesenfeld, 420 U.S. 636 (1975) (holding that unequal treatment of men and women under the Social Security Act violated the equal protection right under the Fifth Amendment); Frontiero v. Richardson, 411 U.S. 677 (1973) (holding that the military's differential showings required for the granting of benefits to spouses of military members based on the spouse's sex violated the Due Process Clause of the Fifth Amendment).

[201] *See generally* Jimenez v. Weinberger, 417 U.S. 628 (1974) (holding that the denial of welfare funds to illegitimate children violated the equal protection component of the Fifth Amendment's Due Process Clause).

[202] *See generally* Schneider v. Rusk, 377 U.S. 163 (1964) (holding that classification based on whether one is a native born or naturalized citizen violated the Due Process Clause of the Fifth Amendment). Notably the Court did not mention that equal protection has been treated the same under both the Fifth and Fourteenth Amendments, and instead relied on *Bolling*'s language that the Fifth Amendment, although not containing an Equal Protection Clause prohibited discrimination that was "so unjustifiable as to be violative of due process." *Id.* at 168.

[203] *See generally* Shapiro v. Thompson, 394 U.S. 618 (1969) (holding the denial of welfare benefits to residents of less than one year in violation of the Fifth Amendment's protection against "unjustifiable" discrimination).

[204] Adarand Construction v. Pena, 515 U.S. 200, 224 (1995).

[205] *See id.* at 226, 228–29.

[206] Notably, the Court does not use the term "reverse incorporation."

[207] *See, e.g.*, Amar, *supra* note 169, at 84–85 (arguing that including equal protection guarantees in the Fifth Amendment ensures against the federal government discriminating based on race, as that discrimination would be "a violation of the implicit equal citizenship of all.").

an Equal Protection Clause in the Fifth Amendment and applying the standards contained in the Equal Protection Clause of the Fourteenth Amendment to Fifth Amendment equal protection cases, the Court has elevated fairness concerns over concerns for maintaining federalism principles in the definition of constitutionally protected rights.[208] This general trend toward increased consideration of more abstract notions of fairness in adjudication, which is mirrored in the development of the Court's approach to personal jurisdiction.[209]

Perhaps another justification for the Court's reverse incorporation doctrine comes from rule of law principles. If the Court did not employ reverse incorporation, then the Due Process Clauses in the Constitution would impose different equality mandates. This arguably would contradict the rule of law principle that the higher principles of law should apply universally. Of course, the Court's incorporation of equal rights into due process was a significant constitutional development in and of itself. But the vastly more profoundly important development was the evolution of equal protection theory and doctrine more generally. A full account of the evolution of equal protection since 1868 deserves its own, separate treatment but is beyond the scope of this work. Suffice it to say here that there is no chance that even the most strict constitutional constructionists on the Court are likely to declare that the federal government is not bound by equal protection principles. This in turn means that due process would *not* be restricted to procedural rights, even if substantive due process law were overruled *in toto*—itself a highly unlikely prospect.

Although the textual basis for an equality component to due process is amazingly thin, a core due process value is to protect individuals from arbitrary and capricious government action that burdens important interests. The argument that this due process concern logically extends to freedom from irrational discrimination that affects significant interests therefore is hardly frivolous. Like substantive due process more generally, equal protection requires a baseline of government rationality that ramps up steadily as the affected right becomes more substantial, or "fundamental." Government may justify classifications that burden fundamental rights, but its reasons for doing so must be compelling ones and the measures must be narrowly tailored to those compelling justifications.

Equal protection doctrine also anticipates—for historical reasons as well as liberty-based reasons—that certain forms of discrimination are presumptively odious within a liberal democracy. The quintessential, suspect form of government classification is a race-based classification. For government to distinguish among persons based on race is presumed to be arbitrary and beyond government's

---

[208] *See generally id.* at 84–86 (arguing that the Fourteenth Amendment changed the focus of constitutionally protected rights to principles of general rights applying against both the federal and state governments, while the definition of rights at the time of the founding focused more on principles of federalism).

[209] *See* chapter 5 *infra*.

legitimate regulatory power. Reducing this equal protection guarantee to a mere process-based right would deny the uprooting and reconstituting power of the Civil War, as well as the moral and constitutional significance of emancipation and Reconstruction. It also would ignore the constitutional context of the Fourteenth Amendment, which is surrounded by the neighboring, equally radical Thirteenth and Fifteenth Amendments and "clearly of a piece" with them.[210] The Thirteenth, of course, abolished slavery and involuntary servitude. Distinctively, this amendment binds private actors as well as government. The Fifteenth Amendment provides that the "right of citizens of the United States to vote shall not be denied or abridged by the United States or by any state on account of race, color, or previous condition of servitude." Federal authority to enforce these mandates is included in the amendments, altering forever pre-bellum notions of more limited federal power. And the bold promises of all three amendments are very broadly stated, written by men with "only the dimmest knowledge of events to come."[211]

It may have surprised these nineteenth-century framers to learn that their actions to expand federal authority over the states in the Fourteenth Amendment might one day be read backward, as a reverse gloss on the Bill of Rights that restrains federal power to deny equal rights. But the three amendments, when read together, do suggest they had a vision of constitutional reformation that explicitly included new constraints on the federal government as well as state and local authorities. Indeed, it even reached beyond government action to disrupt traditionally private enclaves, all in the interest of a more democratic and inclusive extension of inalienable rights to all persons. Finally, the amendments established a more expansive account of who is entitled to the special privileges and immunities that flow to United States citizens as such, and of the baseline liberties that personhood triggers.

III. Conclusion

Due process today is part of an astounding mosaic of reconceived constitutional rights, rights that are best read as reconstitutive and interdependent rather than as silos of protection, narrowly understood. Read in this reconstructive spirit, the "relation back" of Fourteenth Amendment "equality" to inform Fifth Amendment "due process" respects constitutional integrity rather than undermining it. In any event—and this theme bears repeating—the imaginative reinterpretation deed is done. The Court *has* read due process thus, and shows no signs of revisiting this interpretation. The arc of due process therefore must include equality.

Likewise, the Court's post-bellum doctrine on substantive due process more generally, which includes more expanded notions of life, liberty, and property, is

[210] Hamilton, *supra* note 1, at 272.

[211] *Id.*

unlikely to be jettisoned. It has become part of our modern expectations of ordered liberty, despite disagreements about some of the specific rights it includes or to which it may one day be extended.

Any account of due process that suggests it is solely about procedural values, such as notice and opportunity to be heard or decisionmaker impartiality, therefore cannot withstand scrutiny unless one scraps the equality strand of Fifth Amendment due process, reads it as an essentially procedural guarantee, or treats it as an analytically distinct appendage that does not draw its life blood from the due process artery. It also would require pitching nearly 125 years of doctrinal practice that created and fortified the substantive due process strand. In our view, all of these moves would defy too much constitutional experience and practice to make them practically sound. They also would represent a theoretically and normatively impoverished view of the due process command and its rule of law roots. Finally, as we explain in chapter 6, it would rest on an insufficiently dynamic view of constitutional evolution, which could compromise the vitality of the document going forward. Consequently, we must add to the set of primary due process values the respect for equality, and for autonomy and individual liberty with respect to important life decisions. Rational government, in this liberal democratic order, is one that recognizes these baseline substantive values as well as one that operates transparently and with procedural integrity.

{5}

Due Process Hybrids

The foregoing chapters have described the basic due process architecture, which has evolved into two primary strands: procedural due process and substantive due process. But just as the post-bellum doctrine demonstrates that American due process is vastly more complex than any simple "notice and opportunity to be heard" summary might suggest, it also shows that the line between procedure and substance is a hazy one. We already have seen that part of the reason for this is that both the trigger for, and the content of, procedural rights depend on the gravity or importance of the "life, liberty, or property" interest at stake: constitutional process is inherently dependent upon constitutional substance. Still another illustration of this interdependence is the "vagueness" doctrine. It seems, and is, inherently unfair for an individual to be subjected to laws that are written is such vague terms that he or she must guess at the meaning, or proceed at his or her legal peril. Given the number of laws, and how difficult it can be to draft them with adequate precision, the due process vagueness objection could doom a lot of them, or require courts to spend considerable time reviewing and refining them. The pattern of successful vagueness objections, not surprisingly, is that they are most successful in high stakes cases: that is, the importance of the right at stake influences the court's willingness to strike down a law on this due process ground. A particularly good illustration of this is the application of due process vagueness principles in cases that involve freedom of expression. Concern about the chilling effect of poorly drafted legislation has prompted courts to strike down legislation that threatens speech more often than they might be inclined to do when other, arguably less compelling, interests are involved.

In this chapter, we introduce still another aspect of due process complexity: entire bodies of due process law exist that are neither procedural fish nor substantive fowl. These hybrid areas of due process law bear procedural and substantive due process markers, yet the courts have spent little time worrying about which due process label best describes the issues involved. Two of the most important hybrids are the personal jurisdiction hybrid, and the punitive damages hybrid.

I. Personal Jurisdiction

Whether a court can claim jurisdiction over a litigant is important for many reasons, perhaps most because a court's final judgment is binding on other forums provided it had proper jurisdiction to hear the case in the first place.[1] The prohibition against relitigating cases places a premium on choosing an advantageous forum for the first instance. Litigants have important interests at stake not only in avoiding the burden of travel to a trial held in a distant state but also in choosing a forum in which key witnesses can attend the hearing, in which the jury or judge is likely to be sympathetic to their case, and in which the laws best support their arguments.[2] States also possess political and economic interests in permitting lawsuits against nonresidents or facilitating the suits of residents within the state's own borders. As is the case with other areas of due process protections, the Court's personal jurisdiction jurisprudence is designed generally to protect the rights of the individual, given the counterbalancing interests of the public and the government. The balance of these interests has been affected by changes in the economy, technology, and society.

The source of restrictions on courts' ability to adjudicate matters that involve parties who are not physically present in the jurisdiction, who do not reside there, or who otherwise have a remote connection to the forum, has been traced to basic notions of territorial sovereignty and horizontal federalism. Courts should be restricted to their own zones of authority and not overreach their geographical and structural limits. These structural and political limits, in turn, protect the liberty of the individual.[3]

---

[1] *See* Milliken v. Meyer, 311 U.S. 457, 462 (1940) (explaining that if a court has proper jurisdiction over a case, "the full faith and credit clause of the Constitution precludes any inquiry into the merits of the cause of action, the logic or consistency of the decision, or the validity of the legal principles on which the judgment is based.") (internal citations omitted). Many of the earliest personal jurisdiction cases dealt with the question whether a decision in one forum was entitled to respect under the Full Faith and Credit Clause in another forum. In *D'Arcey v. Ketchum*, 52 U.S. 165 (1850), for example, a New York ruling was not binding on a Louisiana district court because one of the parties subject to the original case was not a resident of New York at the time and had not been given notice of the proceedings.

[2] For example, in *Keeton v. Hustler Magazine, Inc.*, 465 U.S. 770 (1984), the plaintiff pursued a libel action against the defendant in the only forum—New Hampshire—in which the statute of limitations had not expired despite the fact that neither party was a resident of that state.

[3] *See* P. McIntyre Machinery, Ltd. v. Nicastro, 131 S. Ct. 2780 (2011) (plurality opinion) (noting that "[t]he principal inquiry... is whether the defendant's activities manifest an intention to submit to the power of a sovereign" and adding this is a matter of individual liberty); Insurance Corp. of Ireland v. Compagnie des Bauxites de Guinee, 456 U.S. 694, 702 (1982) (noting that the "personal jurisdiction requirement recognizes and protects an individual liberty interest. It represents a restriction on judicial power not as a matter of sovereignty, but as a matter of individual liberty.") *See* Martin A. Redish, *Due Process, Federalism, and Personal Jurisdiction: A Theoretical Evaluation*, 75 NW. U. L. REV. 1112, 1113–14 (1981) (noting that the Court has inappropriately "infused vague concepts of interstate sovereignty" into its personal jurisdiction jurisprudence while in most other substantive and procedural due process contexts due process "has been construed as a protection of private parties from some form of injustice"). That federalism restrictions on Congress have an individual "liberty" dimension, as well as an intergovernmental respect dimension, is reflected in cases that allow an individual to assert a Tenth Amendment objection to congressional measures that exceed congressional legislative powers. *See, e.g.*, Bond v. United States, 131 S. Ct. 2355 (2011).

Although courts typically speak of those justifications in absolute terms, the content and rhetoric of the Court's decisions over time demonstrate that the two are balanced against each other. Moreover, individual liberty interests may be triggered whenever federal or state actors exceed their legitimate regulatory powers and invade the province of other sovereigns. For example, when the federal government exceeds its limited regulatory power this may not only intrude into so-called states' rights, but also may constitute an invasion of individual liberty rights; a party who suffers injury from this assertion of federal power may have standing to raise the objection.[4]

Although modern personal jurisdiction jurisprudence emphasizes the individual's due process right in analyzing the limits of judicial power, those rights can only be fully understood in the wider context of inter-sovereign relations, and of American federalism.

DOCTRINAL ELEMENTS OF PERSONAL JURISDICTION

A court's ability to assert personal jurisdiction over a party in a lawsuit has two components: the court must have statutory authorization, such as a forum state's long-arm statute, and it must adhere to the limitations of the applicable Due Process Clause of the Constitution.[5] The Court has described the due process limitations of personal jurisdiction as a matter of "fair play and substantial justice," given the relevant connections among the cause of action, the litigants, and the forum, with an emphasis on the defendant's purposeful targeting of the forum. The underlying notion is that government may not assert lawful judicial power over strangers.[6]

A court may claim jurisdiction over residents and entities physically present within the jurisdiction's boundaries.[7] If a litigant is not a resident but has some connection to the forum, as is often the case with corporations, a court may assert personal jurisdiction over the litigant if the litigant has "minimum contacts with [the forum] such that the maintenance of the suit does not offend 'traditional notions of fair play and substantial justice.'"[8]

---

[4] *See Bond*, 131 S. Ct. 2355 (2011).

[5] *See* E. Thomas Sullivan et al., Complex Litigation, 1 (2010); Jack H. Friedenthal et al., Civil Procedure: Cases and Materials 56 (Compact 10th ed. 2010).

[6] Int'l Shoe Co. v. Washington, 326 U.S. 310, 316 (1945) (quoting Milliken v. Meyer, 311 U.S. 457, 463 (1940)). *See also* Sullivan, *supra* note 5, at 2.

[7] *See, e.g.*, McDonald v. Mabee, 243 U.S. 90, 91 (1917) ("The foundation of jurisdiction is physical power, although in civilized times it is not necessary to maintain that power throughout proceedings properly begun, and although submission to the jurisdiction by appearance may take the place of service upon the person.") (internal citations omitted); *Milliken*, 311 U.S. at 462 ("Domicile in the state is alone sufficient to bring an absent defendant within the reach of the state's jurisdiction for purposes of a personal judgment by means of appropriate substituted service."); Burnham v. Superior Court of California, 495 U.S. 604, 610 (1990) ("Among the most firmly established principles of personal jurisdiction in American tradition is that the courts of a State have jurisdiction over nonresidents who are physically present in the State.").

[8] *Int'l Shoe*, 326 U.S. at 316 (quoting Milliken v. Meyer, 311 U.S. 457, 463 (1940)).

Currently, the minimum contacts analysis is divided into two prongs—general and specific jurisdiction.[9] A court can claim general jurisdiction over people or corporations who have such "continuous and systematic" contacts with the forum that they are "at home" there.[10] Even if a person or corporation has only minimum contacts with a forum, however, a court can claim specific jurisdiction if such contacts are related to the action in question and asserting jurisdiction would not be unreasonable given the burden placed on the litigants, the litigants' purposeful submission to the forum, the interests of the forum, and concern for the overall administration of justice.[11] It remains unclear whether the "reasonableness" criteria are applicable to questions of general jurisdiction.[12] Jurisdiction over a litigant

---

[9] *See* Helicopteros Nacionales de Colombia v. Hall, 466 U.S. 408, 413–15 (1984) (noting that personal jurisdiction can be established by specific jurisdiction when a case "arises out of" the defendant's contacts with the forum, or by general jurisdiction when the case is not related to the defendant's contacts with the forum but the connections between the forum and the defendant are of such a nature that the due process is not violated by subjecting the defendant to personal jurisdiction); SULLIVAN, *supra* note 5, at 2; FRIEDENTHAL, *supra* note 5, at 86; Arthur T. von Mehren & Donald T. Trautman, *Jurisdiction to Adjudicate: A Suggested Analysis*, 79 HARV. L. REV. 1121, 1136 (1966) (outlining the definitions of specific and general personal jurisdiction in American law).

[10] *See* Goodyear Dunlop Tires Operations, S.A. v. Brown, 131 S. Ct. 2846 (2011) (holding unanimously that a court may assert general jurisdiction over a foreign (sister-state or foreign-country) corporation when the corporation's affiliations are so continuous and systematic as to render them "essentially at home" in the forum state); Perkins v. Benguet Consolidated Mining Co., 342 U.S. 437, 445–46 (1952) (holding that a corporation with "continuous and systematic corporate activities" is fairly subjected to personal jurisdiction in the forum in "causes of action relating to those very activities or to other activities of the corporation within the state"). In contrast to specific jurisdiction cases, the Supreme Court has ruled infrequently on general jurisdiction grounds, leading to confusion over standards. *See* B. Glenn George, *In Search of General Jurisdiction*, 64 TUL. L. REV. 1097, 1108–19 (1990) (arguing that a lack of clarity of standards for general jurisdiction leads to inconsistent rulings in the lower courts); Mary Twitchell, *The Myth of General Jurisdiction*, 101 HARV. L. REV. 610 (1988) (describing confusion over the distinction between specific and general jurisdiction led to the emergence of "conditional" general jurisdiction). Courts also can claim general jurisdiction over nonresident people, not just corporations. *See* McMurtry v. Botts, 2005 U.S. Dist. LEXIS 22114 (D. Ky. 2005) (holding in an insurance dispute between two Tennessee-based litigants, defendant was subject to general jurisdiction in Kentucky because he was licensed to sell insurance there at the time at which the suit was commenced); Nikolai v. Strate, 922 S.W.2d 229 (Tex. App. 1996) (holding that Texas could claim general jurisdiction over Colorado-based attorney who performed systematic and continuous legal work in Texas). *But see* Kulko v. Superior Court of Cal., 436 U.S. 84 (1978) (holding that a New York resident whose only contacts with California consisted of sending his daughter there to live with his ex-wife did not have sufficient minimum contacts to justify California in claiming personal jurisdiction over him in a child-support payment case). In *Kulko*, Justices Brennan, White, and Powell, in a short dissent asserted that the facts of the case supported California's exercise of personal jurisdiction. *Id.* at 101–102.

[11] *See* SULLIVAN, *supra* note 5, at 2; FRIEDENTHAL, *supra* note 5, at 56–57. *See also* McGee v. Int'l Life Ins. Co., 355 U.S. 220, 223–24 (1957) (considering the burden placed on forum state residents if forced to litigate in a foreign forum, the location of witnesses, and general fairness).

[12] FRIEDENTHAL, *supra* note 5, at 149. *See also* Metro. Life Ins. Co. v. Robertson-Ceco Co., 84 F.3d 560 (2d Cir. 1996) (applying reasonableness test to a case in which the defendant met the minimum contacts test for general jurisdiction); Recent Case, *Civil Procedure—Personal Jurisdiction—Second Circuit Applies "Reasonableness" Test for General Personal Jurisdiction*, Metropolitan Life Ins. Co. v. Robertson-Ceco Corp., 110 HARV. L. REV. 1328, 1332 (1996) (arguing that using the reasonableness standard for general jurisdiction invites the court to "substitute its own 'choice-of law' analysis for the forum state's"). The reasonableness standard also may be redundant because litigants whose contacts were

also can be obtained if his or her intentional conduct caused harmful effects in the forum state[13] or if the litigant consents to a state's exercise of jurisdiction.[14]

Contemporary rules of personal jurisdiction, while sometimes ambiguous, are mostly concerned with the pursuit of fair outcomes as determined by the protection of individual rights and the proper administration of justice. Early American case law in this area was more inflexible and preoccupied with questions of sovereignty and territoriality than more modern cases,[15] though there are signs that the Court may be returning to a more formulaic approach to personal jurisdiction. These early cases were concerned less with whether a litigant had done something to deserve being subject to a court's jurisdiction and more with the horizontal federalism concern that a state should not exercise control over a matter more appropriately dealt with by a sister state.[16] The law later evolved to stress individual autonomy as the primary due process concern and the attempt to protect and advance that autonomy while also respecting the interests of the legal system.[17] The following discussion of the evolution of the Court's approach to personal jurisdiction is organized categorically, first addressing jurisdiction over individuals, then corporations, and finally jurisdiction based on libel and Internet activities. Each section roughly follows the chronological progression of case law.

JURISDICTION OVER INDIVIDUALS

Most of the personal jurisdiction cases up until the mid-twentieth century analyzed questions of jurisdiction in terms of sovereignty and territorial restrictions. That a

---

sufficiently continuous and systematic for claiming general jurisdiction would probably not suffer from unforeseen or unfair burdens if jurisdiction were exercised over the litigant.

[13] *See* Calder v. Jones, 465 U.S. 783, 791 (1984) (holding that Florida-based reporters could be sued in California for libel over story written about a Californian resident and with Californian sources); RESTATEMENT (SECOND) OF CONFLICT OF LAWS § 36 cmt. c (1988).

[14] *See, e.g.*, Nat'l Equipment Rental Ltd. v. Szukhent, 375 U.S. 311, 312–18 (1964) (holding that the appointment of a New York resident, in a lease, as an agent for being served in New York for the out-of-state parties to the lease, who in fact did not know the agent, was sufficient to make the New York resident the out-of-state party's "agent authorized by appointment" when the agent promptly alerted the out-of-state parties of any process served).

[15] *Cf.* Shaffer v. Heitner, 433 U.S. 186, 198–202 (1977) (referring to *Pennoyer's* categories as "rigid"); *see also* Douglas D. McFarland, *Drop the Shoe: A Law of Personal Jurisdiction*, 68 MO. L. REV. 753 (2003) (describing the difficulties in adapting the *Pennoyer* rule into a changing economy).

[16] *See generally* Philip B. Kurland, *The Supreme Court, the Due Process Clause and the* In Personam *Jurisdiction of State Courts. From* Pennoyer *to* Denckla*: A Review*, 25 U. CHI. L. REV. 569 (1958) (discussing the evolution of personal jurisdictional standards from their federalism-based beginnings); *see also* James Weinstein, *The Federal Common Law Origins of Judicial Jurisdiction: Implications for Modern Doctrine*, 90 VA. L. REV. 169, 188–209 (2004).

[17] Authors have argued also that personal jurisdiction analysis does or should represent the principles inherent in a Lockean compact between a litigant and the state (Richard B. Cappalli, *Locke as the Key: A Unifying and Coherent Theory of* in Personam *Jurisdiction*, 43 CASE W. RES. L. REV. 97 (1992)); principles borrowed from criminal law such as desert and social utility (Kevin C. McMunigal, *Desert, Utility, and Minimum Contacts: Towards a Mixed Theory of Personal Jurisdiction*, 108 YALE L.J. 189 (1998)); or principles that stem from interstate federalism (Weinstein, *supra* note 16), to name a few.

state could exercise jurisdiction over its own residents and over litigants within its borders was fairly obvious, but it was not clear to what extent jurisdiction could extend beyond its borders.[18] Early court decisions were concerned less with the effects that such expansive personal jurisdiction would have on litigants and more with the potential that a state could infringe upon the sovereign right of a sister state to resolve a conflict more appropriately handled in its own courts.[19] Tying jurisdiction boundaries to state boundaries was a feasible solution when interstate travel and commerce—and hence interstate legal conflicts—were minimal.[20] But technology, society, and the economy began to diminish the relevance of physical boundaries.[21] As a consequence, the rules of physical jurisdiction were forced to adapt.[22]

In English common law before and during the eighteenth century, jurisdictional issues were similar to today's form of "general jurisdiction" in the sense that they were "dispute blind" and based solely on the presence of the litigant.[23] This can be partly explained by matters of pure practicality and by the fact that more complicated rules were largely unnecessary. It was practical because basing jurisdiction entirely on presence meant that courts did not have to rely on foreign governments or uncooperative sister states to produce the litigant.[24] At the same time, more complicated rules for gaining jurisdiction across borders were unnecessary because the difficulty of travel made it unlikely that individuals would try to avoid litigation by leaving the forum in which the plaintiff resided.[25] As such, there was uniform acceptance among courts during the eighteenth and early nineteenth centuries that the basis of jurisdictional rules was providing service of process to litigants while they were within the territorial limits of the forum in question, and that judgments made consistent with such practices were worthy of respect by other jurisdictions under the Full Faith and Credit Clause.[26]

---

[18] *See infra* notes 23–30 and accompanying text.

[19] *See infra* notes 32–45 and accompanying text.

[20] *See infra* notes 23–30 and accompanying text.

[21] *See infra* notes 46–59 and accompanying text.

[22] *See id.*

[23] Twitchell, *supra* note 10, at 615 n.20.

[24] *Id.* at 615–18.

[25] *See* Joseph J. Kalo, *Jurisdiction as an Evolutionary Process: The Development of* Quasi in Rem *and* in Personam *Principles*, 5 Duke L. J. 1147, 1150–62 (1978) (describing the situation in Colonial America).

[26] *See* Weinstein, *supra* note 16 at 178–80, 191–96; *see also* D'Arcy v. Ketchum, 52 U.S. 165 (1850) ("The foundation of the existing law on this subject will be found in the Constitution, Art. IV. § 1, which provides that 'full faith and credit shall be given in each State to the public acts, records, and judicial proceedings of every other State. And the Congress may, by general laws, prescribe the manner in which such acts, records, and proceedings shall be proved, and the effect thereof.' Congress, by the act of May 26, 1790, did prescribe this mode of authentication, and declare that the records and judicial proceedings of the courts of any State shall be proved or admitted in any other court within the United States, by the attestation of the clerk and the seal of the court annexed, if there be a seal, together with a certificate of the judge, &c., that the said attestation is in due form. In this case there is no seal of court attached.") (internal citations omitted). *But see* Albert A. Ehrenzweig, *The Transient Rule of Personal Jurisdiction: The "Power" Myth and Forum Conveniens*, 65 Yale L. J. 289, 306–309 (1956) (arguing that the sufficiency of service within the forum for personal jurisdiction purposes did not become an established rule until *Pennoyer v. Neff* in 1877).

As the nation developed, social, legal, and economic changes made territorial-based jurisdictional rules less practical. In order to protect residents and pursue litigants outside of the narrowly defined bounds of the forum's jurisdiction, states developed legal strategies to claim jurisdiction over nonresident individuals through the development of related *quasi in rem*-styled doctrines such as the expanded use of writs of attachment;[27] the use of default judgments;[28] and simply claiming jurisdiction over nonresidents' property located within the forum state.[29] Courts sometimes would also claim jurisdiction over nonresident defendants who were temporarily within the forum's borders, a practice known as exercising transient jurisdiction.[30]

The landmark personal jurisdiction case, *Pennoyer v. Neff*,[31] attempted to provide consistency to the rules courts used to claim jurisdiction over nonresidents while also reasserting the appropriate boundaries of a state's jurisdictional authority and the importance of providing adequate notice.[32] The plaintiff, Neff, sued for the return of property located in Oregon that he had lost in an earlier lawsuit.[33] In the earlier suit, the Oregon court had claimed jurisdiction over Neff even though he was a nonresident.[34] In *Pennoyer*, the United States Supreme Court found the lower court had not properly exercised jurisdiction over Neff in the original suit because the jurisdiction exercised was *in personam* (concerning the rights of the person) and not *in rem* (concerning only property rights) and, as Neff was not within the state's territory, the service was inadequate.[35] This pivotal ruling is notable for two thematic threads that are woven through many previous and subsequent cases. First, the Court reaffirmed a formalist approach to determining jurisdiction, one based on actual physical presence of people or property in the forum state.[36] Second, the ruling was largely justified out of a concern for "international law,"

---

[27] *See* Hubbard v. Hamilton Bank, 48 Mass. 340, 342 (1844) ("Originally, an attachment on mesne process seems to have been instituted merely for the purpose of compelling the appearance of the defendant in court to answer to the suit. But as early as 1650, attachments were authorized for the additional purpose of securing the payment of such judgment as might be recovered in the action.") (referring to Massachusetts ordinances from 1650 and 1659); *see also* Kalo, *supra* note 25, at 1160–62.

[28] *See* Geoffrey C. Hazard, *A General Theory of State-Court Jurisdiction*, 1965 SUP. CT. REV. 241, 248–50. *See also* Kalo, *supra* note 25, at 1157 n.65, 1159–62.

[29] *See* Weinstein, *supra* note 16, at 201 (citing Rogers v. Coleman, 3 Ky. 413, 417–18 (1808)).

[30] *See, e.g.*, Barrell v. Benjamin, 15 Mass. 354 (1819) (claiming jurisdiction over nonresident who was in Massachusetts solely for the purpose of boarding a boat bound for a foreign country); *see also* Ehrenzweig, *supra* note 26, at 303–304.

[31] 95 U.S. 714 (1878).

[32] *See generally* Weinstein, *supra* note 16.

[33] Pennoyer v. Neff, 95 U.S. 714, 719–21 (1877).

[34] *Id.* at 719–20.

[35] *Id.* at 726–34. The distinction for jurisdictional purposes between *in personam*, *in rem*, and *quasi in rem* (personal claims satisfied by attachment of the defendant's property) was eliminated in *Shaffer v. Heitner*, 433 U.S. 186, 212 (1977), when the Court ruled that the *International Shoe* "minimum contacts" analysis applied to all three types of actions.

[36] *Id.* at 720–22 ("The authority of every tribunal is necessarily restricted by the territorial limits of the State in which it is established.... [E]very state possesses exclusive jurisdiction and sovereignty over persons and property within its territory.").

or the balance of legal rulings across sovereign and independent regimes.[37] The question was not whether Neff would be unfairly burdened by having to defend his interests in Oregon,[38] but whether Oregon would be overstepping its sovereign bounds by resolving a rights conflict of a nonresident.[39]

Subsequent cases reestablished *Pennoyer's* requirement of physical presence and reaffirmed that "the foundation of jurisdiction is physical power."[40] Thus a person can be subject to the jurisdiction of the state in which they are a resident or are domiciled even if they are absent from the state when notice is given.[41] As a corollary, leaving the state permanently can sever jurisdiction or at least alter the requirements for giving proper notice.[42] *Pennoyer* also reaffirmed a general presumption that a state can exercise jurisdiction over property that is within its own borders even if the owner of that property is not.[43] Courts can assume, according to *Pennoyer*, that property is always in "possession of its owner" and that seizure of a defendant's property is sufficient notice to inform him of a legal proceeding.[44] Thus, a state has wider latitude in exercising jurisdiction in matters that relate solely to rights over property, otherwise known as *in rem* proceedings, than it does when adjudicating the "personal" rights of defendants, otherwise known as *in personam* proceedings.[45]

Proving the physical presence of an individual and tangible property in a given forum is typically a simple task, but jurisdictional questions become more complicated when a forum claims *in rem* jurisdiction over intangible property like stock and other financial instruments that became more prominent as America's economy developed.[46] In *Hanson v. Denckla*,[47] for example, both Delaware and Florida courts passed judgments relating to the same trust assets created through the will of a former Florida resident.[48] The assets were presumed to be located in Delaware, but Florida claimed *in rem* jurisdiction based on its authority over the "probate and construction of its domiciliary's will, under which the assets might pass. . . ."[49] The Court determined that authority over probate of a will does not provide a forum with jurisdiction over all property that might "augment" the estate because

[37] *Id.* at 729–30 (citing D'Arcy v. Ketchum, 52 U.S. 165 (1850)); *see also* Weinstein, *supra* note 16, at 172–75.

[38] Indeed, the Court saw no problem with claiming jurisdiction over Neff's property, stating that "the State, through its tribunals, may subject property situated within its limits owned by non-residents to the payment of the demand of its own citizens against them." *Pennoyer*, 95 U.S. at 723.

[39] *See id.* at 722–23.

[40] McDonald v. Mabee, 243 U.S. 90, 91 (1917).

[41] Milliken v. Meyer, 311 U.S. 457, 462–64 (1940).

[42] *McDonald*, 243 U.S. at 92.

[43] *See* Pennoyer v. Neff, 95 U.S. 714, 727 (1877).

[44] *See id.*

[45] *See id.*

[46] *See* Hanson v. Denckla, 357 U.S. 235, 246–47 (1958).

[47] 357 U.S. 235 (1958).

[48] *Id.* at 238–43.

[49] *Id.* at 247–48.

such a rule would give probate courts "nationwide service of process to adjudicate interests in property with which neither the State nor the decedent could claim any affiliation."[50] The Court thus ruled that there was no *in rem* jurisdiction.[51] The Court also noted that the foundation of *in personam* jurisdiction is the "territorial restrictions" placed upon states and that in order for a state to exercise such jurisdiction a defendant must "purposefully [avail] itself of the privilege of conducting activities within the forum State, thus invoking the benefits and protections of its laws."[52] The contacts between the trustee and Florida were insufficient to claim *in personam* jurisdiction.[53]

Hanson both reaffirmed *Pennoyer* while also recognizing that its formalistic rules regarding *in rem* and *in personam* jurisdiction had evolved in response to changes in commerce and technology.[54] The Court more explicitly parted such distinctions in *Shaffer v. Heitner*[55] when it ruled that property and personal-based jurisdiction should be governed by the same functional "minimum contacts" analysis.[56] In *Shaffer*, the statutory presence of stock in Delaware was an insufficient basis for claiming jurisdiction over corporate officers whose operations were primarily in Arizona.[57] The Court noted that an *in rem* decision affects the owner of the property in question and, because it is in that sense identical to *in personam* decisions, it should be treated just like an action *in personam*.[58] Under the more restrictive *in personam* standards, the Court found that exercising personal jurisdiction violated due process because the action in *Shaffer* did not arise from the statutory presence of stock in Delaware and because the ownership of said stock was the only contact that the defendants had with the forum.[59] The functionalist analysis of *Shaffer* demonstrates a clear shift from *Pennoyer*-era formalism, one that emphasized the activities of the defendant above the concerns or powers of the State.

Although the Court has struggled to determine the jurisdictional relevance of intangible property's location within a forum, it has also had to deal with the

---

[50] *Id.* at 248–49.

[51] *See id.* at 246, 249–50. In so ruling, the Court reaffirmed its holding in *Pennoyer* that states could not claim *in rem* jurisdiction over property located outside its own borders and that the foundation of *in rem* jurisdiction is "physical power."

[52] *See id.* at 251, 253 (internal citations omitted).

[53] *See id.* at 251–54.

[54] *See id.* at 250–51 (discussing how the rigid *Pennoyer* rule has changed over time).

[55] 433 U.S. 186 (1977).

[56] *Id.* at 212 ("We therefore conclude that all assertions of state-court jurisdiction must be evaluated according to the standards set forth in International Shoe and its progeny.") (footnotes omitted).

[57] *Id.* at 213–17.

[58] *Id.* at 206, 212 ("The fiction that an assertion of jurisdiction over property is anything but an assertion of jurisdiction over the owner of the property supports an ancient form without substantial modern justification. Its continued acceptance would serve only to allow state-court jurisdiction that is fundamentally unfair to the defendant.").

[59] *Id.* at 213–17. Contrary to the theme of functional analysis, the Court did imply that if Delaware had a statute that treated acceptance of directorship of a Delaware corporation as consent to jurisdiction in Delaware the result would have been otherwise. *Id.* at 216.

question whether the temporary presence within a forum state gives rise to *in personam* jurisdiction. Doctrines establishing that the temporary physical presence of a defendant in a forum is sufficient justification for claiming personal jurisdiction over him were originally developed in the eighteenth and nineteenth centuries to compensate for the otherwise limiting effects of sovereignty-based jurisdictional rules.[60] Even though the rules of personal jurisdiction became more flexible and less focused on the "territorial restrictions" of states' sovereign power in the twentieth century (as demonstrated by cases like *Shaffer* and, as discussed later, *International Shoe*[61]), the Court retained "transient jurisdiction" as a valid jurisdictional rule. For example, the Court ruled that due process limitations do not prohibit states from acting on the fiction that motorists consent to being subject to a state's jurisdiction by using the state's highways[62] or even from claiming jurisdiction over people that fly over a state in an airplane.[63]

These transient jurisdiction cases remain common, even when the subject of the lawsuit has nothing to do with the defendant's temporary presence in the forum.[64] In *Burnham v. Superior Court of California*,[65] for example, the Court held that when the defendant, a New Jersey resident, was served while physically present in California, this was sufficient to establish personal jurisdiction over him there. In his plurality opinion, Justice Scalia stated as follows:

> [J]urisdiction based on physical presence alone constitutes due process because it is one of the continuing traditions of our legal system that define the due process standard of "traditional notions of fair play and substantial justice." That standard was developed by analogy to "physical presence," and it would be perverse to say it could now be turned against that touchstone of jurisdiction.[66]

Even as the Court moved to a more functional approach to personal jurisdiction—one based more on the actions and liberty interests of the litigants—*Burnham* and other transient jurisdiction cases demonstrated the lingering influence of state sovereignty-based rationales for personal jurisdiction. Yet in an era of ubiquitous and constant travel across state and national boundaries, the decision to visit or even fly over[67] a given forum has become a less meaningful one. To allow a state to base its jurisdiction over someone solely on transient presence thus implicitly acknowledged the jurisdictional relevance of a state's sovereign control over its territorial borders.

Nevertheless, basing rules on something as simple as the physical presence could present other problems. A court may unjustifiably exert jurisdiction based

---

[60] *See supra* notes 25–26 and accompanying text.

[61] *See infra* notes 86–92 and accompanying text.

[62] Hess v. Pawloski, 274 U.S. 352, 356–57 (1927).

[63] Grace v. MacArthur, 170 F. Supp. 442 (D.C. Ark. 1959).

[64] *See* Burnham v. Superior Court of California, 495 U.S. 604, 619 (1990) (plurality opinion, joined by Chief Justice Rehnquist and Justices Kennedy and White).

[65] 495 U.S. 604 (1990).

[66] *Id.* at 619.

[67] *Grace*, 170 F. Supp. at 447.

on the abstracted and meaningless presence of a person or property within its borders,[68] or a court may be precluded from claiming jurisdiction over litigants who have otherwise significant contacts with, but no presence in, the forum.[69] This could privilege respect for state borders over substantive fairness.[70] This problem is particularly clear in the case of corporate litigants for which the concept of physical presence itself is complicated. The historical development of personal jurisdiction for corporations demonstrates this tension.

JURISDICTION OVER CORPORATIONS

Claiming personal jurisdiction over individuals often is fairly straightforward, though the above analysis demonstrates the difficulty of applying the rules to gray areas like transient jurisdiction or intangible property. Basing jurisdiction on the temporary presence of an individual within a forum or on the purported authority over his intangible property brings the balance of state sovereignty versus individual liberty to the forefront of personal jurisdiction doctrines. Personal jurisdiction cases involving corporations further highlight that delicate balance because corporations can temporarily operate in many states simultaneously and are, by their very nature, intangible entities. Jurisdictional doctrines for corporations co-evolved with social and technological forces, and the case law explicitly demonstrates the Court's ongoing struggle with the tension between personal jurisdiction's protection of state sovereignty and its protections of individual liberty.

In the eighteenth and early nineteenth centuries, corporations were closely tied to a given state through legal and physical necessity, which made establishing jurisdiction over them through physical presence relatively simple.[71] Personal jurisdiction rules for corporations typically limited *in personam* suits to the state in which they were chartered and were justified on the grounds that, by taking advantage of the legal power of that state, a corporation had, in turn, consented to being sued there.[72] This did not impose a substantial burden or result in many complications because corporations were, by and large, only active in one state.[73]

---

[68] *See supra* notes 46–66 and accompanying text discussing intangible property and transient jurisdiction.

[69] The Court has recognized this interest, for example, in *McGee v. Int'l Shoe*, 355 U.S. 220, 223 (1957), where the Court wrote that a State "has a manifest interest in providing effective means of redress for its residents" for actions committed by nonresidents.

[70] *See id.* at 223–24 (discussing how forcing forum state residents to litigate claims against insurance companies would "severe[ly] disadvantage" the forum state residents, which may persuade them not to litigate their claims).

[71] Kalo, *supra* note 25, at 1162–76 (describing the situation in late eighteenth- and early nineteenth-century America).

[72] *See id.* at 1166–76 (describing the evolution of the "consent" theory of personal jurisdiction).

[73] *See id.* Corporations that developed railways, canals, or were otherwise involved in commerce that might stretch between states would still often obtain charters in all of the states in which they transacted business in order to take advantage of the state's legal powers like eminent domain and the ability to grant monopolies. *Id.*

As corporations grew and their activities spread into multiple states in which they had no formal charter, courts were forced to pursue new legal theories in order to govern adequately in-state activities.[74] Corporations were said to have impliedly consented to submitting to personal jurisdiction in a state in which they had commercial transactions.[75]

After the Civil War, courts began to develop legal doctrines that were consistent with and even supportive of a national economy in response to prevailing social and political sentiment.[76] The use of the legal fiction that corporations gave "implied consent" to being subject to personal jurisdiction became complicated by the fact that dormant commerce clause jurisprudence limited a state's ability to prohibit a corporation from operating within its borders when this would interfere unduly with the flow of interstate commerce.[77] But if a corporation was not *explicitly* required to consent and could not be said to have *impliedly* consented to being subject to personal jurisdiction in a state, there would be little reason for it to *actually* consent to personal jurisdiction and it could feel free to operate in the state without fear of legal ramifications.[78] Subsequent case law created new rationales like the "presence" or "doing business" doctrines that sought to circumvent this legal conundrum.[79]

In *International Harvester Company of America v. Kentucky*,[80] for example, the Court acknowledged a potential conflict between requiring companies to consent to personal jurisdiction as a condition of operating in a given state if the company in question engaged in interstate commerce.[81] The Court, nonetheless, insisted that

---

[74] *Id.* Residents of a state could sue a foreign corporation using a *quasi in rem* action. But because they would be limited to pursuing only the property that the defendant corporation currently had in the state, these actions often were insufficient. *Id.* at 1168–69.

[75] *Id.* The issue of "implied consent" is complicated by the fact that dormant commerce clause jurisprudence would conceivably limit a state's ability to actually prohibit a corporation from operating within its borders, hence taking away any incentive for a corporation to "consent" to personal jurisdiction when it would be free to operate in the state without facing retribution for refusing such consent. Subsequent case law created new rationales like the "presence" or "doing business" doctrines that more explicitly balanced a state's interests in claiming personal jurisdiction with potential adverse impacts interstate commerce. *Id.* at 1176–82. *See also* Lafayette Ins. Co. v. French, 59 U.S. 404, 407 (1855) ("A corporation created by Indiana can transact business in Ohio only with the consent, express or implied, of the latter state."); St. Clair v. Cox, 106 U.S. 350, 356 (1882) ("A corporation of one state cannot do business in another state without the latter's consent, express or implied.... ").

[76] *See* Kalo, *supra* note 25, at 1176–79.

[77] Kalo, *supra* note 25, at 1179 n.208.

[78] *Cf. id* at 1176–79 (citing the need to create new theories to justify personal jurisdiction).

[79] *See, e.g.*, Kurland, *supra* note 16; Weinstein, *supra* note 16. It has been pointed out that the theories of consent, presence, and doing business significantly overlap with each other and that one was often used to satisfy conditions of another. For example, a corporation that was "doing business" in a forum could then be found to be "present" within that forum or to have impliedly consented to be bound by the jurisdictional rules of that forum. *See* Hutchinson v. Chase & Gilbert, 45 F.2d 139 (2d Cir. 1930) (pointing out that the "presence" or "consent" doctrines are not as analytically helpful as simply considering questions of fairness); Kalo, *supra* note 25, at 1182; Kurland, *supra* note 16, at 578–86.

[80] 234 U.S. 579 (1914).

[81] *Id.* at 587–89.

even if a company's business was purely interstate in nature, if the company was properly "present" within a state then it was not unreasonable to subject it to personal jurisdiction in part because it received protection from that state's laws.[82] To expand on this theme of presence or doing business and how it differs from mere allegations of implied consent, the Court in *Bank of America v. Whitney Cent. Nat'l Bank*[83] highlighted the tangible requirements of the doctrine:

> The jurisdiction taken of foreign corporations, in the absence of statutory requirement or express consent, does not rest upon a fiction of constructive presence.... It flows from the fact that the corporation itself does business in the State or district in such a manner and to such an extent that its actual presence there is established.[84]

The *International Shoe*[85] test that replaced such theories was a natural progression, given its focus on facts as opposed to legal fiction. Although the "minimum contacts" test may not be substantively different than discussion of "presence," it is more flexible and more centered on the corporations' actual activities in comparison to the formal theories of consent, presence, and doing business.[86]

In *International Shoe*, the state attempted to collect unemployment insurance contributions from a Delaware-based company that had no permanent offices or official agents and only a minimal sales presence in Washington.[87] Noting the difficulty of dealing with personal jurisdiction issues involving a legal fiction, the Court determined that a court can still claim *in personam* jurisdiction if the litigant has "certain minimum contacts with [the forum] such that the maintenance of the suit does not offend 'traditional notions of fair play and substantial justice.'"[88] The question depends upon the "quality and nature" of the defendant's activities in the forum.[89] The Court noted that the defendant corporation's conduct was "systematic and continuous" and the suit in question was related to that conduct. The corporation also benefited from the protection of Washington's laws.[90] The case marked a shift away from Civil War-era jurisprudence, as the Court focused on the

---

[82] *Id.* at 588.

[83] 261 U.S. 171 (1923).

[84] Bank of Am. v. Whitney Cent. Nat'l Bank, 261 U.S. 171, 173 (1923).

[85] 326 U.S. 310 (1945).

[86] *See* Int'l Shoe v. Washington, 326 U.S. 310, 316–17 (1945) ("To say that the corporation is so far 'present' there as to satisfy due process requirements ... is to beg the question to be decided.... 'Presence' in the state in this sense has never been doubted when the activities of the corporation there have not only been continuous and systematic, but also give rise to the liabilities sued on, even though no consent to be sued or authorization to an agent to accept service of process has been given."). *See also* Kalo, *supra* note 25, at 1183–84 (arguing that this shift in jurisprudence mirrored a shift in political philosophy from a *laissez-faire* to a social welfare state).

[87] *Int'l Shoe*, 326 U.S. at 311–15 (1945).

[88] *Id.* at 316.

[89] *Id.* at 319.

[90] *Id.* at 320.

company's conduct and whether it availed itself of the privileges and benefits of the state's laws rather than on territory-based distinctions.[91]

Even though the Court would not explicitly use the distinction of general and specific jurisdiction until almost half a century later, the *International Shoe* "minimum contacts" rule clarified the standards of jurisdiction and gave rise to those two lines of relatively stable jurisprudence. And although the factors a court takes into consideration when determining "minimum contacts" vary,[92] the decision at least focused the Court's analysis on the rights of the defendant, the other litigants' interests, and the states' interests. *International Shoe* and its progeny served as an interim step between the purely territory-based cases of *Pennoyer* and its predecessors, and the more rights-oriented cases of the second half of the twentieth century.

The Court's shift from sovereignty-based rationale for personal jurisdiction to the autonomy-based rationale was subtle, but was visible in two cases that explicitly deviated from Civil-War-era formalistic doctrines like "corporate consent." In *Perkins v. Benguet Consolidated Mining Co.*,[93] a company was subject to litigation in Ohio, where it had been conducting business during World War II, even though it was based in the Philippines and the action was unrelated to its activities in Ohio.[94] In its opinion, the Court quoted *International Shoe*'s dismissal of the legal fiction of consent in favor of an analysis that focused on the actual behavior of the corporation.[95] Using this approach, the Court looked at the myriad actions that the company took in Ohio to demonstrate that its contacts were continuous and systematic to the degree that it would not offend the Due Process Clause to claim jurisdiction over it.[96]

Although the shift was evident, several of the Court's cases in this period demonstrate the Court's uneasiness in totally forsaking the territorial sovereignty analysis. This is most clearly shown in those cases dealing with actions against nonresidents that arise from the defendant's conduct in the forum state.[97] In such cases, which are now deemed specific jurisdiction cases, the Court first determines if the litigant's actions are the type that can give rise to jurisdiction before considering questions of fairness and the interests of the state.[98] The first part of this analysis

---

[91] The Court moved away from "*in personam* jurisdiction ... grounded on [the] de facto power over the defendant's person." *Id.* at 316. *See also* David E. Seidelson, *A Supreme Court Conclusion and Two Rationales That Defy Comprehension:* Asahi Metal Indus. Co., Ltd v. Superior Court of California, 53 Brooklyn L. Rev. 563, 569 (1987) (claiming that the *International Shoe* court was attempting to "bury the concept" of territorial sovereignty).

[92] *See* Kevin C. McMunigal, *Desert, Utility, and Minimum Contacts: Toward a Mixed Theory of Personal Jurisdiction*, 108 Yale L.J. 189 (1998) (cataloguing the various factors that have been included in "minimum contacts" analysis over the years).

[93] 342 U.S. 437 (1952).

[94] *Id.* at 438–39.

[95] *Id.* at 446–47.

[96] *Id.* at 447–49.

[97] *See infra* notes 99–103 and accompanying text.

[98] *See infra* notes 99–103 and accompanying text.

focuses on the actions and rights of the defendant, whereas the second part shadows somewhat the justifications behind doctrines of the *Pennoyer* era.

World-Wide Volkswagen Co. v. Woodson[99] is a good example of the limits that the first step in the specific jurisdiction analysis places on a state's ability to reach beyond its borders. In *World-Wide Volkswagen*, a car sold in New York was involved in an accident in Oklahoma and the injured parties brought a products-liability suit against the retail dealer that sold the car.[100] Although it was foreseeable that selling an automobile in New York might result in harm caused in a foreign state, the mere "fortuitous circumstance" was insufficient basis to claim personal jurisdiction.[101] Instead, the Court looked narrowly at the defendant's act of selling the automobile and ruled that foreseeability of a product passing into a foreign jurisdiction was insufficient grounds for claiming jurisdiction and that the real question was whether "the defendant's conduct and connection with the forum State are such that he should reasonably anticipate being haled into court there."[102] In its determination of the first factor of specific jurisdiction analysis, the *World-Wide Volkswagen* Court emphasized the defendant's actions, not the state or the plaintiff's interests. The Court was careful, however, to defend this approach while also paying homage to concerns of interstate federalism, cautioning that the Court has "never accepted the proposition that state lines are irrelevant for jurisdictional purposes. . . . "[103]

Although the Court in *World-Wide Volkswagen* focused on the defendant's acts at the expense of the Oklahoma's interests in resolving the dispute, the Court will sometimes focus on a state's interests in claiming jurisdiction over a dispute involving its residents. In *Mc Gee v. Int'l Life Insurance Co.*,[104] for example, the Court ruled that having one insurance contract in California was sufficient for personal jurisdiction given the interests of the plaintiff and the forum in the litigation.[105] The Court in *McGee* weighed heavily the obvious equity concerns involved, stating that "California has a manifest interest in providing effective means of redress for its residents when their insurers refuse to pay claims. These residents would be at a severe disadvantage if they were forced to follow the insurance company to a distant State in order to hold it legally accountable."[106]

Personal jurisdiction cases post-*International Shoe* thus featured a flexible and less formal approach that was not strictly limited by territorial boundaries. Instead, the fact-based analysis focused more on the behavior of litigants and whether they

---

[99] 444 U.S. 286 (1980).

[100] *See id.* at 288.

[101] *Id.* at 295. The Court was not persuaded by the fact that automobiles were previously ruled to be inherently dangerous and that the value of an automobile is dependent upon a driver's ability to drive it to and in places like Oklahoma. *Id.* at 296 n.11, 298.

[102] *Id.* at 297 (1980).

[103] *See id.* at 293.

[104] 355 U.S. 220 (1957).

[105] *Id.* at 223.

[106] *Id.*

did something to avail themselves of the state's services or protections. Despite this more lenient and individual-focused analysis, however, the Court continued to weigh the state's interests in its personal jurisdiction decisions and continued to rely on the rhetoric and rationale of the older sovereignty analysis and justifications for its decisions.[107]

In *Hanson v. Denckla*, for example, after describing the flexible standards of personal jurisdiction post-*International Shoe*, the Court cautioned that:

> [I]t is a mistake to assume that this trend heralds the eventual demise of all restrictions on the personal jurisdiction of state courts. Those restrictions are more than a guarantee of immunity from inconvenient or distant litigation. They are a consequence of territorial limitations on the power of the respective States.[108]

Even in *World-Wide Volkswagen*, a case famous for limiting the grounds for claiming personal jurisdiction based on the behavior and reasonable expectations of the litigant, the Court stipulated that due process limitations on personal jurisdiction exist to protect litigants rights *and* "it acts to ensure that the States through their courts, do not reach out beyond the limits imposed on them by their status as coequal sovereigns in a federal system."[109] The *International Shoe* decision itself made reference to interstate federalism concerns when the Court wrote that the demands of due process must be considered "in the context of our federal system of government"[110] and later stated that the nature of the defendant's actions must be weighed in relation "to the fair and orderly administration of the laws which it was the purpose of the due process clause to insure."[111]

Remnants of the sovereignty and territory-based jurisdictional rules remained post-*International Shoe*, but the application of formalistic rules undoubtedly waned as the twentieth century progressed. This was due, in part, to changes in technology and the growth and evolution of the national economy.[112] In comparison to the "horse and buggy" commerce of the nineteenth century, multinational corporations had substantial activities across many states and adopted structures that made establishing physical presence in any one place difficult. Similarly, travel

---

[107] *See generally* John N. Drobak, *The Federalism Theme in Personal Jurisdiction*, 68 IOWA L. REV. 1015 (1983); David E. Seidelson, *A Supreme Court Conclusion and Two Rationales That Defy Comprehension:* Asahi Metal Indus. Co., Ltd v. Superior Court of California, 53 BROOKLYN L. REV. 563 (1987) (tracing the territorial sovereignty concept throughout twentieth-century jurisdiction cases).

[108] Hanson v. Denckla, 357 U.S. 235, 251 (1958) (citations omitted). The *Shaffer* court minimized the passage from *Hanson* by saying that the *Hanson* court was "simply mak[ing] the point that the States are defined by their geographical territory." Shaffer v. Heitner, 433 U.S. 186, 205 n.20 (1977). *See also* Harold S. Lewis, *The Three Deaths of "State Sovereignty" and the Curse of Abstraction in the Jurisprudence of Personal Jurisdiction*, 58 NOTRE DAME L. REV. 699, 709–11 (1983).

[109] World-Wide Volkswagen v. Woodson, 444 U.S. 286, 292 (1980).

[110] Int'l Shoe v. Oregon, 326 U.S. 310, 317 (1945).

[111] *Id.* at 319.

[112] *Cf. Shaffer*, 433 U.S. at 202 (discussing the change that automobiles inflicted upon jurisdiction rules); Hanson v. Denckla, 357 U.S. 235, 250–51 (1958) (noting the general influence of technology on personal jurisdiction rulings).

by air and road lessened the burdens of appearing in a foreign jurisdiction. These changes, which decreased the importance of making distinctions between states, were instrumentally important in demonstrating the limitations of jurisdictional rules based only on state borders and helped refocus the jurisprudence on the rights and activities of the litigants in question.

The official and formal recognition of that change was made in 1982.[113] In *Insurance Corp. of Ireland v. Compagnie Des Bauxites de Guinea*,[114] the Court stated that "[t]he personal jurisdiction requirement recognizes and protects an individual liberty interest[;] [i]t represents a restriction on judicial power not as a matter of sovereignty, but as a matter of individual liberty."[115] The defendants in *Insurance Corp. of Ireland* challenged on due process grounds the district court's issuance of a sanction[116] establishing personal jurisdiction over them after they failed to comply with court-ordered jurisdictional discovery.[117] The Court held that the use of the sanction to establish personal jurisdiction did not violate due process.[118] The majority, in upholding jurisdiction, clarified how its liberty-based decision operated in the context of earlier state sovereignty-based personal jurisdiction decisions as follows:

> Contrary to the suggestion of Justice [Powell], ... our holding today does not alter the requirement that there be "minimum contacts" between the nonresident defendant and the forum State. Rather, our holding deals with how the facts needed to show those "minimum contacts" can be established when a defendant fails to comply with court-ordered discovery. The restriction on state sovereign power described in World-Wide Volkswagen Corp., however, must be seen as ultimately a function of the individual liberty interest preserved by the Due Process Clause. That Clause is the only source of the personal jurisdiction requirement and the Clause itself makes

[113] 456 U.S. 694 (1982). *But see* Weinstein, *supra* note 16 (arguing that inconsistencies in current personal jurisdiction jurisprudence stem from the insistence that due process is the principle source of jurisdictional requirements and not at historically based territorial based limitations).

[114] 456 U.S. 694.

[115] *Id.* at 702–03.

[116] The sanction at issue was a Fed. R. Civ. Pro. 37(b)(2)(A) sanction. *Insurance Corp. of Ireland*, 456 U.S. at 699.

[117] *Id.* at 694–96. Jurisdictional discovery refers to plaintiff's attempts to "use discovery in order to establish jurisdictional facts" after certain defendants asserted "the defense of lack of personal jurisdiction." *Id.* at 694.

[118] *See id.* at 709 ("Because the application of a legal presumption to the issue of personal jurisdiction does not in itself violate the Due Process Clause and because there was no abuse of the discretion granted a district court under Rule 37(b)(2), we affirm the judgment of the Court of Appeals."). Also, it is worth noting that the Court in *Insurance Corp. of Ireland* was not attempting to establish personal jurisdiction via the normal minimum contacts and fairness analysis, thus the Court did not employ the balancing tests. *See id.* at 713–14 (Powell, J. concurring) (discussing the majority's decision) ("By finding that the establishment of minimum contacts is not a prerequisite to the exercise of jurisdiction to impose sanctions under Federal Rule of Civil Procedure 37, the Court may be understood as finding that 'minimum contacts' no longer are a constitutional requirement for the exercise by a state court of personal jurisdiction over an unconsenting defendant.").

> no mention of federalism concerns. Furthermore, if the federalism concept operated as an independent restriction on the sovereign power of the court, it would not be possible to waive the personal jurisdiction requirement: Individual actions cannot change the powers of sovereignty, although the individual can subject himself to powers from which he may otherwise be protected.[119]

In further supporting its declaration that "personal jurisdiction represents ... an individual right"[120] the Court explained that "the requirement of personal jurisdiction may be intentionally waived, or for various reasons a defendant may be estopped from raising the issue. These characteristics portray it for what it is—a legal right protecting the individual."[121] In his dissent, Justice Powell argued that "[b]y finding that the establishment of minimum contacts is not a prerequisite to the exercise of jurisdiction to impose sanctions ..., the Court may be understood as finding that 'minimum contacts' no longer are a constitutional requirement for the exercise by a state court of personal jurisdiction over an unconsenting defendant. Whenever the Court's notions of fairness are not offended, jurisdiction apparently may be upheld."[122] Justice Powell also expressed concern over the Court's seeming abandonment of the "'sovereign' limits on state assertions of personal jurisdiction over unconsenting defendants."[123]

The Court's pronouncement of the individual liberty-based personal jurisdiction analysis raised questions as to whether the *Pennoyer* era power over the defendant requirement, based on state sovereignty principles, remained.[124] Nevertheless, the Court stated that its analysis did not change the minimum contacts framework for

---

[119] *Id.* at 702 n.10.

[120] *Id.* at 703.

[121] *Id.* at 704.

[122] *Id.* at 713–14 (Powell, J., dissenting) (footnotes omitted).

[123] *Id.* at 714 (internal citations omitted).

[124] *See* Peter A. Diana & J. Michael Register, *Personal Jurisdiction in Flux:* Insurance Corp. of Ireland v. Compagnie Des Bauxites De Guinee, 69 CORNELL L. REV. 136, 162 (1983) ("The power requirement of the traditional composite test for personal jurisdiction looks only to the relationship of the defendant to the forum. Unless sufficient defendant-forum contacts exist, regardless of the interests of the plaintiff and the forum state, a court cannot exercise jurisdiction. If sufficient forum-defendant contacts are present, a court, under the second component of the composite test, inquires into the reasonableness of a jurisdictional finding. Notions of state sovereignty underlie the power requirement of fourteenth amendment due process, which originally derived from *Pennoyer v. Neff.* The Court's rejection of sovereignty concerns in footnote 10 might suggest a total abandonment of the power requirement and its absolute demand of forum-defendant contacts. Such a reading of the Court's position would leave only a reasonableness standard with which to judge a court's exercise of jurisdiction under the fourteenth amendment. The Court's assertion, however, that its opinion 'does not alter the requirement that there be "minimum contacts" between the nonresident defendant and the forum State' appears incompatible with such an interpretation. Perhaps the Court is suggesting not that it is abandoning the power requirement's absolute demand of forum-defendant contacts, but that it is altering that requirement's theoretical basis. A dual power-reasonableness test may still be required, but the power component of that test, rather than being based on notions of state sovereignty, would now be based, like the reasonableness requirement, on 'individual liberty interests.'") (footnotes omitted).

personal jurisdiction cases established in *International Shoe*.[125] The test for specific jurisdiction cases therefore remained the following: the Court first determines if the litigants' purposeful actions are the type that can give rise to the requisite minimum contacts before considering questions of "fair play and substantial justice."[126] After the Court's *Insurance Corp. of Ireland* holding, it seemed that "reasonableness was the touchstone of personal jurisdiction."[127]

Despite the emphasis on the reasonableness of the exercise of personal jurisdiction over a litigant in specific personal jurisdiction cases, the Court still considered the interests of the state in a fashion reminiscent of *Pennoyer*-era jurisprudence when faced with specific personal jurisdiction cases.[128] In *Burger King Corp. v. Rudzewicz*,[129] for example, the Court began its personal jurisdiction analysis by stating "[t]he Due Process Clause protects an individual's liberty interest in not being subject to the binding judgments of a forum with which he has established no meaningful 'contacts, ties, or relations.'"[130] The Court in *Burger King* resolved a contract dispute between a Michigan-based franchisee and a Florida-based franchisor by establishing, first, that the defendant had sufficient minimum contacts in the forum state,[131] and second, that exercising personal jurisdiction over the defendant would be fair.[132] Notably, the Court specifically considered Florida's interest in the adjudication of the matter and said, "[w]e cannot conclude that Florida had no 'legitimate interest in holding [Rudzewicz] answerable on a claim related to' the contacts he had established in that State."[133]

---

[125] *See id.* (responding to Justice Powell's assertion in his concurrence that the Court's holding is essentially saying minimum contacts are no longer a constitutional requirement for a state court seeking to exercise personal jurisdiction after the Court's decision in *Insurance Corp. of Ireland*).

[126] *See, e.g.*, SULLIVAN ET AL., *supra* note 5, at 2 (outlining the analysis that applies for cases of specific personal jurisdiction); *see also* 4 WRIGHT ET AL., FEDERAL PRACTICE AND PROCEDURE § 1067 (3d ed. 2011) ("As countless cases decided in the years since the *International Shoe* decision demonstrate, the Court's reference to the defendant's 'minimum contacts' with the forum and its invocation of 'traditional notions of fair play and substantial justice' have become centerpieces for the analysis and application of the Constitution's due process limitations on attempts to assert *in personam* jurisdiction over an out-of-state defendant.").

[127] *See Leading Cases*, 125 HARV. L. REV. 311, 316–17 (2011) ("Under the territorial approach of Pennoyer v. Neff, personal jurisdiction was predicated on state power and its controlling rationale was sovereignty. In *International Shoe Co. v. Washington*, the Court seemed to discard *Pennoyer's* emphasis on sovereignty. In announcing the minimum contacts test, the Court placed significant emphasis on 'traditional notions of fair play and substantial justice,' indicating a break with the conceptual underpinnings of *Pennoyer's* rule in favor of reasonableness and fairness considerations. Although in succeeding cases the Court attempted to 'tie[] together the flexible standard of International Shoe and the state sovereignty prong of *Pennoyer*,' by the early 1980s it was clear that reasonableness was the touchstone of personal jurisdiction doctrine.") (footnotes omitted).

[128] *See infra* notes 129–172 and accompanying text.

[129] 471 U.S. 462 (1985).

[130] Burger King Corp. v. Rudzewicz, 471 U.S. 462, 471–72 (1985) (internal citations omitted).

[131] *See id.* at 482 (explaining Rudzewicz's twenty-year relationship with Burger King's Miami headquarters in addition to the choice of law provision in the franchise contract that stated Florida law would govern all disputes).

[132] *Id.* at 485–87.

[133] *Id.* at 482–83.

Similarly, in *Asahi Metal Industry Co. Ltd. v. Superior Court of California*[134] the Court "splintered on how the stream-of-commerce theory would establish minimum contacts, [but] eight Justices agreed that the exercise of jurisdiction would be unreasonable."[135] The Justice O'Connor plurality held that the defendant did not have sufficient purposeful minimum contacts under the first prong of the specific personal jurisdiction test.[136] In support of this conclusion, the O'Connor plurality explained as follows:

> The placement of a product into the stream of commerce, without more, is not an act of the defendant purposefully directed toward the forum State. Additional conduct of the defendant may indicate an intent or purpose to serve the market in the forum State.... But a defendant's awareness that the stream of commerce may or will sweep the product into the forum State does not convert the mere act of placing the product into the stream into an act purposefully directed toward the forum State.[137]

Justice Brennan's concurrence, on the other hand, would not have required more than placing a product into the stream of commerce with the knowledge or reasonable belief that the product would be swept into the forum state to establish the requisite purposeful availment.[138] A majority of the Court stipulated that personal jurisdiction would *also* be unreasonable under the second prong, which considers whether a finding of personal jurisdiction "would offend 'traditional notions of fair play and substantial justice,'"[139] because of the minimal interests of the forum state in comparison to the important international forces in play.[140]

In a recent specific personal jurisdiction case, the Court continued its approach of considering liberty-based interests as well as the forum state's interest in its analysis; however, it may have carved out a more prominent role for sovereignty concerns as they relate to individual liberty in stream of commerce cases.[141] In *J. McIntyre Machinery, Ltd. v. Nicastro*,[142] the plaintiff filed a products liability action in New Jersey state court following injuries he sustained in New Jersey from using

---

[134] 480 U.S. 102 (1987).

[135] *Leading Cases*, *supra* note 127, at 317.

[136] 480 U.S. at 108–13 (1987).

[137] *Id.* at 112.

[138] *Id.* at 116–17 (Brennan, J., concurring in part).

[139] *Id.* at 113 (quoting Int'l Shoe Co. v. Washington, 326 U.S. 310, 316 (1945) (quoting Milliken v. Meyer, 311 U.S. 457, 463 (1940))).

[140] *Id.* at 114–16 (noting that the remaining litigants were both international entities, that the distance and the procedures of a foreign court were severe burdens to Asahi, and that California only had a slight interest in subjecting Asahi to personal jurisdiction in its courts because the Plaintiff was not a California citizen and that state safety standards were not really at issue because Cheng Shin was seeking indemnification). Justice Scalia did not join in the part of the O'Connor plurality opinion that concluded that jurisdiction over Asahi would be unreasonable. Justice Kennedy, who wrote the plurality opinion in J. McIntyre Mach. Ltd. v. Nicastro, 131 S. Ct. 2780 (2011), was not yet on the Court.

[141] *See* J. McIntyre Machinery, Ltd. v. Nicastro, 131 S. Ct. 2780, 2788 (2011).

[142] 131 S. Ct. 2780 (2011).

a machine manufactured by the defendant in England.[143] Notably, the defendant company was both incorporated and operated in England; it challenged the New Jersey state court's ability to exercise personal jurisdiction over it.[144] The New Jersey Supreme Court ruled that it could exercise personal jurisdiction over the defendant under a "stream of commerce" analysis because the defendant knew or should have known that its products would be distributed throughout the United States, which presented the possibility of sales in any state.[145] The New Jersey Supreme Court, in addition, contemplated the state's interest in preventing defective products from reaching its citizens as well as other policy reasons supporting the exercise of personal jurisdiction.[146]

A majority of the United States Supreme Court, however, concluded that New Jersey could not sustain personal jurisdiction though for different reasons that related to the "purposeful availment" requirement.[147] The plurality opinion, written by Justice Kennedy, stated that "[t]he principal inquiry in ... [stream of commerce cases] is whether the defendant's activities manifest an intention to submit to the power of a sovereign[,]" which the Court equated with the purposeful availment test from *Hanson*.[148] There was no personal jurisdiction over the defendant because "[a]t no time did [defendant] engage in any activities in New Jersey that reveal *an intent* to invoke or benefit from the protection of its laws."[149] The plurality characterized personal jurisdiction as "restrict[ing] 'judicial power not as a matter of sovereignty, but as a matter of individual liberty,' for due process protects the individual's right to be subject only to lawful power[,] [b]ut whether a judicial judgment is lawful depends on whether the sovereign has authority to render it."[150] The Court recognized the importance of New Jersey's interest, but stated that despite the strength of the state's interest, "the Constitution commands restraint before discarding liberty in the name of expediency."[151] The four-justice plurality

---

[143] *Id.* at 2786.

[144] *Id.* at 2782.

[145] *Id.* at 2782–83.

[146] *Id.* at 2791.

[147] *Id.* at 2787 (citing Hanson v. Denckla, 357 U.S. at 253). The Court was divided on the reasoning, with four justices joining in the Kennedy plurality opinion and Justices Breyer and Alito concurring in the judgment. Justices Ginsburg, Sotomayor, and Kagan dissented. As one commenter has observed: "*Nicastro* produced a clear result: six justices voted to reject personal jurisdiction over J. McIntyre. But finding a majority holding is more difficult. Four justices tried to heighten the standard for personal jurisdiction, but five justices rejected that attempt. Yet those five justices were not able to agree on an alternative approach." John T. Parry, *Due Process, Borders, and the Qualities of Sovereignty—Some Thoughts on J. McIntyre Machinery v. Nicastro*, 16 Lewis & Clark L. Rev. 827, 848 (2012).

[148] *See id.* at 2788 ("The principal inquiry in cases of this sort is whether the defendant's activities manifest an intention to submit to the power of a sovereign. In other words, the defendant must 'purposefully avai[l] itself of the privilege of conducting activities within the forum State, thus invoking the benefits and protections of its laws.'") (internal citations omitted).

[149] *Id.* (emphasis added).

[150] *Id.* at 2789 (citations omitted) (quoting *Insurance Corp. of Ireland*, 456 U.S. 694, 702 (1982)).

[151] *Id.* at 2791.

was joined by concurring Justices Breyer and Alito in holding that New Jersey could not exercise personal jurisdiction over the defendant.[152]

It has been suggested that *J. McIntyre* represents a return to sovereignty concerns in the personal jurisdiction inquiry, despite the plurality's clear statement that liberty, not sovereignty, is key.[153] The suggestion is that the Court is returning to sovereignty-based concerns by "reformulat[ing] the purposeful availment requirement's underlying rationale to emphasize sovereignty" instead of focusing on fairness, which had become prevalent in the 1980s after the Court announced the purposeful availment requirement.[154] Again, the Court equated the purposeful availment requirement, as set forth in *Hanson*, with asking "whether the defendant's activities manifest an intention to submit to the power of a sovereign."[155]

Yet the heightened concern for sovereignty principles in *J. McIntyre* was joined only by a plurality of the Court, which makes it difficult to say whether this signals a return to *Pennoyer* era personal jurisdiction inquiries, at least insofar as the earlier cases focused more on sovereignty concerns than on notions of reasonableness and fairness. If anything, *Nicastro* only makes the case law in this area murkier. If it does signal greater attention to horizontal sovereignty concerns, however, an area in which the case could have a major impact would be in cases that assert personal jurisdiction based on Internet activity.[156]

The Court's liberty-based minimum contacts analysis is also muddy in the general jurisdiction cases, where the forum state has an important interest in adjudication of the suit. In *Helicopteros Nacionales de Colombia, S.A. v. Hall*,[157] a Columbian corporation, Helicol, challenged Texas's ability to exercise personal jurisdiction over it in a wrongful death suit.[158] In consideration of Helicol's contacts with Texas, the Court stated:

---

[152] *Id.* Justice Breyer's concurring opinion rejected the stricter approach of the plurality, on the ground that "modern concerns" may make such an approach impracticable. *Id.* at 2791–94 (Breyer, J., concurring in the judgment).

[153] *See Leading Cases*, *supra* note 127, at 316–18 (arguing that the Court's *J. McIntyre* opinion increases emphasis on sovereignty).

[154] *Id.* at 317–18 (noting that "The Court's decision in *Nicastro*, specifically the reasoning embodied in the plurality opinion, signals a shift in this trend [of reasonableness concerns trumping sovereignty concerns].... In *Hanson's* initial conception, purposeful availment operated to protect state sovereignty. However, as reasonableness became the touchstone of jurisdiction in the 1980s, purposeful availment was reinterpreted to guard against a defendant's being haled into a forum solely as a result of 'random,' 'fortuitous,' or 'attenuated' contacts." But "the *Nicastro* plurality's appeal to *Hanson's* purposeful availment requirement took on a strikingly different rationale. Instead of characterizing the test as a way to determine reasonableness, the plurality asserted that purposeful availment occurs when a defendant 'submit[s] to a State's authority.' In doing so, the plurality elevated purposeful availment—as well as the values that it was initially created to protect—to a 'general rule' that would trump any appeal to '[f]reeform notions of fundamental fairness.' ") (footnotes omitted)

[155] *See supra* note 153 and accompanying text.

[156] *See Leading Cases*, *supra* note 127, at 319–21 (discussing how elevating sovereignty concerns over reasonableness and fairness could have major impacts on Internet cases).

[157] 466 U.S. 408 (1984).

[158] *Id.* at 409–10, 412.

> It is undisputed that Helicol does not have a place of business in Texas and never has been licensed to do business in the State. Basically, Helicol's contacts with Texas consisted of sending its chief executive officer to Houston for a contract-negotiation session; accepting into its New York bank account checks drawn on a Houston bank; purchasing helicopters, equipment, and training services from Bell Helicopter for substantial sums; and sending personnel to Bell's facilities in Fort Worth for training.[159]

The Court ultimately held that these contacts were insufficient to satisfy due process requirements because the action did not arise from the defendant's contacts with the forum, as specific jurisdiction rules require, and because the defendant's general contacts with the forum state, while extensive, were insufficient for general jurisdiction purposes.[160] The extensive contacts Helicol had with Texas as well as Texas's interest in adjudicating the suit were not sufficient for the Court to find general jurisdiction, which raises the question of how helpful the doctrine is for states seeking to assert personal jurisdiction over a foreign corporation.[161]

In a more recent general personal jurisdiction case, a unanimous Court refined its prior holdings and helped clarify this doctrine, though many questions still remain. In *Goodyear Dunlop Tires Operations, S.A., v. Brown,*[162] parents of two young boys who were killed in a bus accident in Paris, France, filed a wrongful death action against Ohio-incorporated Goodyear USA and three of its subsidiaries, respectively doing business in "Luxembourg, Turkey, and France," citing tire failure as the cause of the accident.[163] Goodyear USA submitted to personal jurisdiction because of its ties with North Carolina, but its three foreign subsidiaries sought dismissal of the suit for lack of personal jurisdiction.[164] The Court held

---

[159] *Id.* at 416.

[160] *See id.* at 418–19 ("This Court in *International Shoe* acknowledged and did not repudiate its holding in *Rosenberg*. In accordance with *Rosenberg*, we hold that mere purchases, even if occurring at regular intervals, are not enough to warrant a State's assertion of *in personam* jurisdiction over a nonresident corporation in a cause of action not related to those purchase transactions. Nor can we conclude that the fact that Helicol sent personnel into Texas for training in connection with the purchase of helicopters and equipment in that State in any way enhanced the nature of Helicol's contacts with Texas. The training was a part of the package of goods and services purchased by Helicol from Bell Helicopter. The brief presence of Helicol employees in Texas for the purpose of attending the training sessions is no more a significant contact than were the trips to New York made by the buyer for the retail store in *Rosenberg*. We hold that Helicol's contacts with the State of Texas were insufficient to satisfy the requirements of the Due Process Clause of the Fourteenth Amendment. Accordingly, we reverse the judgment of the Supreme Court of Texas.") (citations omitted).

[161] *See, e.g.*, Earl M. Maltz, *Unraveling the Conundrum of the Law of Personal Jurisdiction: A Comment on* Asahi Metal Industry Co. v. Superior Court of California, 1987 DUKE L.J. 669, 674–75 (1987) ("Several commentators have suggested that different standards should be applied when dealing with alien defendants. Prior to Asahi, the Supreme Court never explicitly addressed the question. The issue had, however, been potentially relevant in two earlier decisions—*Perkins v. Benguet Consolidated Mining Co.* and Helicopteros Nacionales de Colombia, S.A. v. Hall (Helicol).") (footnotes omitted).

[162] 131 S. Ct. 2846 (2011).

[163] *Id.* at 2851–52.

[164] *Id.*

that Goodyear USA's three foreign subsidiaries had only "attenuated contacts" with North Carolina, because "[s]ome of the tires made abroad … had reached North Carolina through 'the stream of commerce.'"[165] The Court ruled that these contacts did not constitute the requisite "continuous and systematic" connection necessary for North Carolina to be a "home" for the corporation that would justify the exercise of general jurisdiction.[166] In reversing the North Carolina court's finding of personal jurisdiction, the Court repudiated the state court's approach as "[c]onfusing or blending general and specific jurisdictional inquiries," and reaffirmed that a showing of "'continuous and systematic' affiliation" is necessary for the exercise of general personal jurisdiction.[167] Because the Court failed to find the requisite minimum contacts, it did not have to reach the lingering question of whether the reasonableness element of specific jurisdiction cases is applicable in cases of general jurisdiction. In fact, the debate over the applicability of reasonableness to general jurisdiction was not even mentioned in the Court's unanimous but more restrictive decision.[168] The Court also did not resolve whether a corporation can have multiple "homes" for general jurisdiction purposes.

Although the Court never *explicitly* weighed the forum state's interests in resolving the dispute within its borders in *Helicopteros*,[169] some commentators have noted that the very distinction between general and specific jurisdiction is "difficult to justify without direct or indirect reference to the allocation of sovereign authority between states."[170] Requiring more extensive contacts in establishing jurisdiction over unrelated causes of action (general jurisdiction cases) than required in related causes of action (specific jurisdiction cases) arguably can only be explained as a means of

> prevention of the illegitimate intrusion of one state into another's regulatory sphere. When the defendant's contacts are related to the cause of action, the state's assertion of jurisdiction vindicates a legitimate interest in intrastate regulation. When the contacts are unrelated, the state must possess equivalent authority to that which it possesses over its own citizens.[171]

The Court's handling of personal jurisdiction cases relating to corporations mirrors its struggles with similar cases applying to individuals. The proliferation

---

[165] *Id.* at 2851.

[166] *Id.* at 2856–57.

[167] *Id.* at 2851.

[168] 131 S. Ct. 2846 (2011).

[169] Allan R. Stein, *Styles of Argument and Interstate Federalism in the Law of Personal Jurisdiction*, 65 Tex. L. Rev. 689, 724–25 (1987) ("The first effects of Bauxites were evident the following term in *Helicopteros Nacionales de Colombia, S.A. v. Hall.* In keeping with the new doctrine, *Helicopteros* made no reference to inter-sovereign relations. The sole focus was whether the defendant, Helicol, had sufficient contacts with Texas to constitute voluntary affiliation with the forum and to justify 'general jurisdiction'—jurisdiction over a claim unrelated to the defendant's contacts with the forum.") (footnotes omitted).

[170] *See, e.g.*, *Id.* at 726.

[171] *Id.*

and expansion of corporations and corporate activity makes rules based on physical presence difficult, as some corporations can be said to exist almost everywhere and nowhere at the same time. Thus Court was forced to abandon doctrines based on fictions of corporate consent or where the corporation was "doing business" in favor of a more functional approach that assesses corporate activities. *International Shoe* and its progeny attempt to hold corporations accountable only in those forums in which they have certain "minimum contacts," but whether this and the Court's related general jurisdiction doctrine is designed to protect states' or the corporation's rights is an open question. Despite the strong language of *Insurance Corp. of Ireland* that established the defendant's liberty interests and the primary animator of personal jurisdiction rules, more recent cases, like *J. McIntyre*, demonstrate that the Court still considers the state's sovereign control over its territory a relevant factor in ensuring that "substantial justice" has been done.

CORPORATIONS, PERSONAL JURISDICTION, AND THE DORMANT COMMERCE CLAUSE

Still another complexity of the personal jurisdiction cases and of the horizontal federalism trope within them is the conceptual overlap between the Dormant Commerce Clause and the Court's personal jurisdiction jurisprudence.[172] This overlap is most visible when states tax out-of-state corporations. The Due Process Clause limits a state's ability to tax people and corporations that lack sufficient contacts with the state.[173] Similarly, the "negative implications of the Commerce Clause" limit state taxes that discriminate against or unduly burden interstate commerce, and may be triggered when an out-of-state corporation that lacks significant contacts with the forum state is taxed by a state.[174] The two clauses apply to the same behavior, but the constitutional principles that animate them are different and hence the results can be different as well.

In cases dealing with taxes on out-of-state corporations, the Court has set forth a four-part, functionalist test to determine whether the tax runs afoul of the Commerce Clause. The Court considers whether "the 'tax [1] is applied to an activity with a substantial nexus with the taxing State, [2] is fairly apportioned, [3] does not discriminate against interstate commerce, and [4] is fairly related to the services provided by the State.'"[175] This approach is generally consistent with the Court's general Dormant Commerce Clause jurisprudence,[176] but the first prong is quite

---

[172] *See* Quill Corp. v. North Dakota, 504 U.S. 298, 305–306 (1992) (quoting Int'l Harvester Co. v. Dept. of Treasury, 322 U.S. 340, 353 (1944) (Rutledge, J., concurring in part and dissenting in part)).

[173] *See id.* at 312.

[174] *See id.*

[175] *See id.* at 311 (quoting Complete Auto Transit v. Brady, 430 U.S. 274, 279 (1977)).

[176] *See, e.g.*, Dep't of Rev. of Kentucky v. Davis, 553 U.S. 328, 338–39 (2008) ("Under the resulting protocol for Dormant Commerce Clause analysis, we ask whether a challenged law discriminates against interstate commerce.... A discriminatory law is 'virtually per se invalid,' and will survive only if it

similar to the Court's analysis in personal jurisdiction cases.[177] Looking back at the evolution of the Court's approach to this overlap helps to demonstrate its views on personal jurisdiction and the general function of the Due Process Clause.

In *Lawrence v. State Tax Commission of Mississippi*,[178] a citizen of Mississippi was forced to pay Mississippi taxes on income from building roads in Tennessee.[179] The Court ruled that domicile within a state was sufficient to "establish[] a basis for taxation" and that "[e]njoyment of the privileges of residence within the state, and the attendant right to invoke the protection of its laws, are inseparable from the responsibility for sharing the costs of government."[180] The Due Process Clause is not violated when a tax is based on property or privileges enjoyed within the state and the tax is not itself unreasonable or arbitrary.[181] Even though the state was taxing income earned beyond its borders, the tax was constitutional because it was effectively levied on Lawrence's ability to enjoy that income in Mississippi.[182]

Lawrence indicates, however, that a tax on out-of-state income or property may be unconstitutional if it is unreasonable or arbitrary. In a simplified version of this analysis, the Court asked whether "the state has given anything for which it can ask return."[183] Such a rule is consistent with the foundational purpose of the Due Process Clause: to ensure some amount of fairness and protect against arbitrary government abuses.[184] At the same time, the Court has stipulated that for Commerce Clause purposes a tax on interstate commerce "can only be justified as designed to make such commerce bear a fair share of the cost of the local government whose protection it enjoys."[185] Thus both rules seem to apply similar tests—requiring that there be a "substantial nexus" or "minimum contacts"[186]—and both of the tests are designed to ensure there is some degree of fairness and that the taxed individual or company is bearing only a reasonable share of costs.[187]

'advances a legitimate local purpose that cannot be adequately served by reasonable nondiscriminatory alternatives[.]' Absent discrimination for the forbidden purpose, however, the law 'will be upheld unless the burden imposed on [interstate] commerce is clearly excessive in relation to the putative local benefits.' State laws frequently survive this Pike scrutiny, though not always, as in Pike itself.") (citations omitted).

[177] *See, e.g.*, Int'l Shoe Co. v. Washington, 326 U.S. 310, 316 (1945) (noting that, for personal jurisdiction cases, due process requires that the defendant "have certain minimum contacts with [the forum] such that the maintenance of the suit does not offend 'traditional notions of fair play and substantial justice.'") (quoting Milliken v. Meyer, 311 U.S. 457, 463 (1940)).

[178] 286 U.S. 276 (1932).

[179] *Id.* at 279.

[180] *Id.* at 279.

[181] *See id.* at 280.

[182] *See id.* at 280–81 (noting that the tax was "founded upon the protection afforded to the recipient of the income by the state, in his person, in his right to receive the income, and in his enjoyment of it when received").

[183] *See* Wisconsin v. J.C. Penney Co., 311 U.S. 435, 444 (1940).

[184] *See* chapter 1.

[185] Nat'l Bellas Hess, Inc. v. Dept. of Rev. of Ill., 386 U.S. 753, 756 (1967) (quoting Freeman v. Hewit, 329 U.S. 249, 253 (1946)).

[186] *See supra* footnotes 174–75 and accompanying text.

[187] *See supra* footnotes 183 and 185 and accompanying text.

But despite the facial similarity of the tests employed, the Court has emphasized that the tests are distinct because of the different functions of the relevant constitutional clauses.[188] The due process minimum contacts test is a "proxy" for ensuring that an individual or corporation has "notice" and "fair warning" that their activities will give rise to tax-liabilities in a given state.[189] In this sense, the due process test is concerned with the "fundamental fairness of government activity"[190] because it establishes an absolute protection against state's power to tax property except in situations where the individual has actually done something to warrant the tax.[191] This is in contrast to the Commerce Clause and its nexus requirement, "which are informed not so much by concerns about fairness for the individual defendant as by structural concerns about the effects of state regulation on the national economy."[192] Citing the structural defects of the Articles of the Confederation as applied to economic competition among the states, the Court emphasized that the Commerce Clause's nexus requirement is designed to protect against burdens on commerce, not burdens on individuals.[193] As such, an individual's activities can meet the "minimum contacts" threshold for due process purposes and yet not be "substantial" enough to warrant the burden on commerce that a tax may impose.[194]

From a policy perspective, the distinction makes sense. Personal jurisdiction creates more subtle and indirect costs that can be better managed through the courts than is true of "legislative jurisdiction" or jurisdiction based on taxes on interstate commerce.[195] For example, a company in one of Missouri's eight neighboring states has a decent chance of being subject to a lawsuit there, especially if Missouri has aggressive long-arm statutes. It can hedge against that risk by purchasing slightly more expensive insurance and passing a portion of that cost off to consumers.[196] More importantly, due process protections can effectively protect a defending company's interests by limiting suits to only those situations where the company would have fair notice that it would likely be haled into court in Missouri. If, however, Missouri has extremely aggressive laws taxing out-of-state commerce, it creates more uniform, constant, and severe impacts on its neighboring states. Companies cannot adapt to these laws so much as they are forced to conform to them,[197] and the question of whether the burden that this places on

---

[188] *See generally* John A. Swain, *Cybertaxation and the Commerce Clause: Entity Isolation or Affiliate Nexus*, 75 S. CAL. L. REV. 419, 425–32 (2002) (describing the difference between the Commerce Clause and Due Process Clause as applied to taxing out-of-state sellers).

[189] *See* Quill Corp. v. North Dakota, 504 U.S. 298, 312–13 (1992). *See generally The Supreme Court, 1991 Term—Leading Cases*, 106 HARV. L. REV. 163 (1992) (discussing *Quill Corp. v. North Dakota*).

[190] *Quill Corp.*, 504 U.S. at 312.

[191] *See id.* at 305.

[192] *Id.* at 312.

[193] *See id.* at 312–13.

[194] *See id.* at 313.

[195] *See* Allan R. Stein, *Personal Jurisdiction and the Internet: Seeing Due Process Through the Lens of Regulatory Precision*, 98 NW. U. L. REV. 411, 428–29 (2004).

[196] *See id.*

[197] *See id.*

interstate commerce is justified is likely better left to Congress than to the legislators of an individual state.[198]

Yet the analysis in Dormant Commerce Clause cases demonstrates many of the same principles displayed in the Court's traditional personal jurisdiction analysis, especially post-*Ireland*. Like personal jurisdiction's sovereignty-based protection of liberty, the Dormant Commerce Clause preserves the balance of interests among the states. Just as the Court has demonstrated historically a concern that states may impermissibly exert legal authority over nonresidents and thus infringe upon the coequal authority of sister states, the Court is also concerned that states may tax out-of-state corporations or income in a way that burdens interstate commerce and threatens the union's prosperity. The Court has come to recognize that the Due Process Clause is designed to protect individual liberty from abusive or arbitrary government practices that include overreaching their sovereign powers. Although that rationale might not often produce significantly different outcomes than one based more directly on horizontal federalism and interstate cooperation concerns, it is a similarity worth noting.[199]

THE EXTENDED FRONTIERS OF PERSONAL JURISDICTION: LIBEL AND THE INTERNET

The previous sections demonstrate ways in which personal jurisdiction rules can quickly become complicated by novel contexts. The physical presence of a person or property within a forum may be sufficient for claiming personal jurisdiction, but it is a more difficult question if the person is literally flying over the forum or the property in question is intangible. It may be easy to claim that a corporation that is chartered and does a substantial portion of its business within a state should be subject to personal jurisdiction there, but modern businesses that lack brick and mortar operations and do business all over the world present more complicated issues.

In cases like *Perkins, Helicol*, and *Goodyear*, the Court defined the boundaries of what counts as continuous and systematic contacts within a forum such that a corporation can reasonably be expected to be "haled" into court there. But in these cases, the Court focused on specific, tangible factors like the presence of employees or equipment. Cases that involve the reputation harm of libel or lawsuits

---

[198] *See Quill Corp.*, 504 U.S. at 305.

[199] *See id.* at 305–306 ("'[A]lthough the two notions cannot always be separated, clarity of consideration and of decision would be promoted if the two issues are approached, where they are presented, at least tentatively as if they were separate and distinct, not intermingled ones.'") (quoting Int'l Harvester Co. v. Dept. of Treasury, 322 U.S. 340, 353 (1944) (Rutledge, J., concurring in part and dissenting in part)); *see also* Robert H. Abrams & Paul R. Dimond, *Toward a Constitutional Framework for the Control of State Jurisdiction*, 69 MINN. L. REV. 75, 83–87 (1984) (describing the problems with using the Due Process Clause to regulate interstate federalism issues and noting that Congress is better suited to handle those issues through constitutional provisions like the Commerce Clause).

stemming from Internet activity provide an additional level of abstraction to the Court's personal jurisdiction analysis. In these cases, the Court (and for Internet cases, the lower courts) attempts to strike a balance between the liberty interests of defendants and the need to hold people accountable where harms are committed.

The paucity of modern Supreme Court decisions on point has left lower courts with the difficult task of extrapolating how the doctrine should be applied in the context of libel,[200] The Court provided some guidance in two companion cases, *Keeton v. Hustler Magazine, Inc.*[201] and *Calder v. Jones.*[202] In *Keeton v. Hustler Magazine, Inc.*,[203] a New York resident brought a diversity suit in New Hampshire alleging libel against Hustler, an Ohio corporation.[204] The Court reversed the lower courts by finding the existence of personal jurisdiction over the defendant because the defendant had "continuously and deliberately exploited the New Hampshire market, [so] it must reasonably anticipate being haled into court there in a libel action based on the contents of its magazine."[205] In *Calder v. Jones*[206] the Jones brought a libel suit in California against the *National Enquirer*, alleging libel caused by an article written and edited by defendants in Florida and subsequently published in the magazine and widely distributed in California.[207] The Court found that defendants had sufficient minimum contacts for specific jurisdiction[208] based on what later courts would identify as a three-pronged test:

> (a) an intentional action (writing, editing, and publishing the article), that was (b) expressly aimed at the forum state (the article was about a California resident and her activities in California; likewise it was drawn from California sources and widely distributed in that state), with (c) knowledge that the brunt of the injury would be felt in the forum state (defendants knew Ms. Jones was in California and her career revolved around the entertainment industry there).[209]

---

[200] *See*, for example, Inset Systems, Inc. v. Instruction Set, Inc., 937 F. Supp. 161 (D. Conn. 1996) and Zippo Mfg. Co. v. Zippo Dot Com, Inc. 952 F. Supp. 1119, 1124 (W.D. Pa. 1997), wherein the courts came to fundamentally different conclusions regarding how minimum contacts analysis should be employed in the context of Internet contacts.

[201] 465 U.S. 770 (1984).

[202] 465 U.S. 783 (1984).

[203] 465 U.S. 770 (1984).

[204] *See id.* at 772. Plaintiff brought the suit in New Hampshire because its favorable statute of limitations made it the only jurisdiction in which she could still sue. *Id.* at 778. The Court found no problem in using this litigation strategy, likening it to other plaintiffs' forum shopping for a favorable jurisdiction in which to bring their actions and noting that the defendant likely would have taken advantage of the same law if it had a complaint against someone. *Id.* at 779.

[205] *Id.* at 781.

[206] 465 U.S. 783 (1984).

[207] *See id.* at 784–85. About 600,000 copies of the magazine were sold in California and the state with the next highest total was New York with about 300,000 copies. *Id.* at 785 n.2.

[208] *See id.* at 788–91.

[209] Dudnikov v. Chalk & Vermilion Fine Arts, Inc., 514 F.3d 1063, 1072 (10th Cir. 2008) (distilling the *Calder* test); *see also Calder*, 465 U.S. at 791 ("We hold that jurisdiction over petitioners in California is proper because of their intentional conduct in Florida calculated to cause injury to respondent in California.").

The Court continued to emphasize the "relationship among the defendant, the forum, and the litigation" and the importance of determining whether the focal point of the "harm" was effectuated in the forum.[210] These cases represent an adaption of the *Pennoyer*-era requirement of physical presence in the forum state as the requisite purposeful acts to overcome the nonresident defendant's liberty interests and to establish personal jurisdiction.

After the Court's definitive statement regarding personal jurisdiction's protection of personal liberty, it has continued in subsequent cases to frame its personal jurisdictional analysis in terms of individual liberty interests.[211] The Court in *Insurance Corp. of Ireland*[212] stated that state sovereignty interests are recognized implicitly through the Court's protection of individual liberty. Consequently, a court is not precluded from considering matters of state sovereignty or federalism in a personal jurisdiction analysis.[213] Yet the sovereignty analysis is not easily mapped onto the new and unexplored frontier of the Internet.

Lower courts have struggled mightily to adapt the existing minimum contacts framework to a technological medium that blurs traditional territorial notions of personal jurisdiction.[214] Due to the worldwide accessibility and interconnectedness of Internet services, websites now have a near ubiquitous electronic presence that is not proscribed by jurisdictional borders.[215] Increasing economic globalization and technological advances have further tested traditional conceptions of personal jurisdiction.[216] The rapid proliferation of Internet-based transactions and communications and the absence of a Supreme Court precedent pertaining to personal jurisdiction over the Internet has left lower courts with the task of addressing how jurisdictional doctrine should be applied to this novel landscape.[217]

---

[210] *Calder*, 465 U.S., at 788–89.

[211] Although the Court's analysis has placed considerable emphasis on the affected liberty interests at stake, the Court has not completely deviated from past decisions and at times continues to consider state sovereignty and federalism concern, often times under the umbrella of liberty itself. *See supra* notes 151–69 and accompanying text.

[212] 456 U.S. 694 (1982).

[213] *See supra* notes 113–23 and accompanying text.

[214] *See* Allan R. Stein, *Personal Jurisdiction and the Internet: Seeing Due Process Through the Lens of Regulatory Precision*, 98 Nw. U. L. Rev. 411, 411 (2004).

[215] *See id.*

[216] The spread of the Internet and e-commerce has made the outcome of this legal question even more important. *See* The World Bank, World Bank Development Indicators 20 (April 15, 2011) *available at* http://issuu.com/world.bank.publications/docs/9780821387092 (stating that, as of 2009, an estimated 78.1 percent of the United States had access to the Internet.); *U.S. Census Bureau E-Stats*, U.S. Census Bureau, 2 (May 26, 2011), http://www.census.gov/econ/estats/2009/2009reportfinal.pdf (noting that in 2009, e-commerce accounted for approximately $3.3 trillion, or 16.8 percent of total U.S. shipments).

[217] *See* Todd David Peterson, *The Timing of Minimum Contacts*, 79 Geo. Wash. L. Rev. 101, 101 (2010) (noting that the Supreme Court had not decided any personal jurisdiction cases since 1990 and that courts and scholars were left guessing how personal jurisdiction doctrine should apply to the Internet); *see also* Eric C. Hawkins, Note, *General Jurisdiction and Internet Contacts: What Role, if any, Should the* Zippo *Sliding Scale Test Play in the Analysis?*, 74 Fordham L. Rev. 2371, 2385–412 (2006) (documenting disagreement in lower courts over the appropriate analysis for personal jurisdiction Internet cases).

Early Internet Jurisdiction

An early attempt to reconcile existing personal jurisdiction doctrine with Internet-based activities came in 1996 with *Inset Systems, Inc. v. Instruction Set, Inc.*[218] The plaintiff, a developer of computer software, registered the trademark name "Inset" and subsequently sued the defendant in Connecticut for using an identical name in its Internet address and toll-free telephone number.[219] The defendant was not incorporated nor did it conduct regular business in Connecticut.[220] The district court ruled that the defendant's advertising activities through its website were directed "toward not only the state of Connecticut, but to all states" and held that 1) the record established minimum contacts in Connecticut and 2) the defendant purposefully availed itself of the privilege of doing business within the state.[221]

The court effectively found that a website on the Internet is directed to all fifty states and is a sufficient basis to uphold jurisdiction, portending the possibility of a universal personal jurisdiction when engaging in Internet-based activities. An Internet user's actions might be subject to jurisdictional consequences in nearly any location where those actions could be viewed.[222] This low threshold required to establish meaningful contacts over the Internet appeared to place greater emphasis on allowing states the ability to vindicate a sovereign interest in protecting their residents from harm, at the expense of providing a robust protection of the defendant's liberty interest in not being subject to binding judgments from forums with which they lack purposeful ties.

One notable deviation from the *Inset* reasoning was the seminal case of *Zippo Manufacturing Co. v. Zippo Dot Com, Inc.*,[223] which established the now widely adopted framework for analyzing Internet contacts based on the "nature and quality of commercial activity that an entity conducts over the Internet."[224] Zippo Manufacturing filed a complaint against Zippo Dot Com in Pennsylvania alleging a series of claims under the Federal Trademark Act.[225] The defendant, located in

---

[218] 937 F. Supp. 161 (D. Conn. 1996).

[219] *See id.* at 162–63.

[220] *Id.*

[221] *Id.* at 164–65.

[222] *See* Michael A. Geist, *Is There a There There? Toward Greater Certainty for Internet Jurisdiction*, 16 Berkeley Tech. L.J. 1345, 1362 (2001) ("The court's decision was problematic for several reasons. First, its conclusion that creating a website amounts to a purposeful availment of every jurisdiction distorts the fundamental principle of jurisdiction. Second, the court did not analyze the Internet itself, but merely drew an analogy between the Internet and a more traditional media form, in this case a continuous advertisement. If the court was correct, every court, everywhere, could assert jurisdiction where a website was directed toward its forum. This approach would stifle future Internet growth, as would-be Internet participants would be forced to weigh the advantages of the Internet with the potential of being subject to legal jurisdiction throughout the world. Third, the court did not assess Instruction Set's actual activity on the Internet. The mere use of the Internet was sufficient for this court to establish jurisdiction. In fact, the court acknowledged that Instruction Set did not maintain an office in Connecticut nor did it have a sales force or employees in the state.") (footnotes omitted).

[223] 952 F. Supp. 1119, 1124 (W.D. Pa. 1997).

[224] *See id.* at 1124.

[225] *Id.* at 1121

California, sought to dismiss for lack of personal jurisdiction.[226] Zippo Dot Com's contacts with Pennsylvania were almost exclusively advertising that involved "posting information about its service on its Web page, which is accessible to Pennsylvania residents via the Internet."[227]

As compared with the prior *Inset* decision, the *Zippo* Court's analysis appeared to balance both the liberty-based interests of the defendant and its burden in defending against a suit in Pennsylvania, as well as the sovereign interests of the state of Pennsylvania in adjudicating disputes involving resident corporations and providing state residents with relief.[228] The Court employed a sliding scale test to assess the "interactivity" of the defendant's website and assist in the determination of whether the defendant's actions suggested the purposeful availment necessary to permit the exercise of personal jurisdiction.[229] Although the *Zippo* decision ultimately affirmed the decision to claim jurisdiction over the defendant in Pennsylvania,[230] the Court's analysis of the nature of the website and its level of interactivity was a step toward raising the threshold necessary to constitute sufficient contacts over the Internet and seemingly placed greater emphasis on protecting the defendant's liberty interests in litigation stemming from Internet-based activities than the *Inset* decision. The Court's sliding scale analysis was an attempt to retain the foundational principles of personal jurisdiction while simultaneously addressing Internet-specific issues.[231]

Some critics, however, have argued that the *Zippo* test is not consistent with the traditional due process and minimum contacts doctrine in that it fails "to encapsulate the critical requirement of minimum contacts, which [demands] deliberate action in the forum state or conduct directed at forum residents" such that bringing a suit would not offend "traditional notions of fair play and substantial justice."[232] The operation of an Internet site does not by itself satisfy the purposeful availment requirement, even if the website is interactive, and because the sliding scale *Zippo* test assesses websites in a relatively limited fashion, it "ultimately reveals

---

[226] *Id.*

[227] *Id.*

[228] *Id.* at 1127 (noting that Zippo Dot Com "conspicuously chose to conduct business in Pennsylvania" and that Pennsylvania "has a strong interest in adjudicating disputes involving the alleged infringement of trademarks owned by resident corporations").

[229] *See id.* at 1124. The Court indicated that personal jurisdiction is clearly appropriate where defendants repeatedly and knowingly enter into contracts or exchanges with residents of a foreign jurisdiction via the Internet. On the other end of the spectrum in which defendants merely operate "passive" websites accessed by residents of foreign jurisdictions, it would be inappropriate to exercise personal jurisdiction. "The middle ground" is occupied by defendants that operate interactive websites and here the appropriateness of exercising personal jurisdiction is dictated by the level of interactivity. *See id.*

[230] *See id.* at 1128.

[231] *See id.* at 1123–24 (noting that personal jurisdiction rules must change with technological progress and elaborating the ways in which the Internet is a qualitatively different innovation that requires a novel approach to personal jurisdiction issues).

[232] *See* Hawkins, *supra* note 217, at 2386, (referring to Millennium Enterprises, Inc. v. Millennium Music, LP, 33 F. Supp. 2d 907 (D. Or. 1999), and noting that many scholars and courts have criticized *Zippo* on multiple grounds).

only a defendant's ability to create contacts with the forum, not the defendant's actual contacts."[233] Others have suggested that the "interactive" or "passive" traits measured in the sliding scale of *Zippo* represent a reversion back to thinking about jurisdiction in *Pennoyer*-like physical terms rather than the purposeful availment inquiry articulated in *World-Wide Volkswagen*.[234] Despite these criticisms and any potential shortcomings, the *Zippo* test has been widely applied in many jurisdictions, often in slightly modified forms, including the five federal circuit courts.[235]

The court's concerns in *Zippo* were in many ways comparable to those in *International Shoe*; both courts were faced with "commercial environment[s] that tested the limits of existing jurisdictional doctrine..., and that, therefore, demanded a new way of evaluating jurisdictional issues."[236] As the nature and quality of "minimum contacts" were essential in ascertaining personal jurisdiction in *International Shoe*, these same concerns are reflected in *Zippo*. The *Zippo* decision sought to fashion a test that was responsive to the novel issues created by Internet activity, while anchoring itself in traditional due process and jurisdictional principles.[237] Although Internet activities may in many instances establish contacts with various jurisdictions, it must be reasonably foreseeable that those contacts may lead to litigation in order for jurisdiction to comport with due process protections.[238] *Zippo* reflects this attempt to extend the principles of "the minimum contacts model to a new technology."[239]

Although *Zippo* has been lauded for rejecting the "notion of universal jurisdiction emanating from the *Inset* line of cases,"[240] it also has been criticized as being "difficult to apply and incapable of consistent application,"[241] particularly with respect to websites that fall within the broad middle area between "passive" and "interactive."[242] This is especially problematic because there are few websites on the *Zippo* scale that are amenable to categorization as either completely passive or completely active, creating "a black hole of doubt and confusion" for courts

---

[233] *See id* at 2418.

[234] Stein, *supra* note 214, at 429 (1998).

[235] *See* Hawkins, *supra* note 217, at 2392–406 (citing Toys "R" Us, Inc. v. Step Two, S.A., 318 F.3d 446 (3rd Cir. 2003)) (discussing a hybrid *Zippo* test); ALS Scan, Inc. v. Digital Serv. Consultants, Inc., 293 F.3d 707 (4th Cir. 2002) (applying a hybrid *Zippo* test); Mink v. AAAA Dev. LLC, 190 F.3d 333, 336–37 (5th Cir. 1999) (holding that the defendant's website was nothing more than a "passive advertisement, which is not grounds for the exercise of personal jurisdiction"); Soma Med. Int'l v. Standard Chartered Bank, 196 F.3d 1292 (10th Cir. 1999); Cybersell, Inc. v. Cybersell, Inc., 130 F.3d 414 (9th Cir. 1997) (supporting the *Zippo* approach). *Cf.* Revell v. Lidor, 317 F.3d 467 (5th Cir. 2002) (noting that the *Zippo* sliding scale approach to websites is not well adapted to a general jurisdiction inquiry).

[236] Dennis T. Yokoyama, *You Can't Always Use the* Zippo *Code: The Fallacy of a Uniform Theory of Internet Personal Jurisdiction*, 54 DePaul L. Rev. 1147, 1163 (2005).

[237] *See supra* note 231 and accompanying text.

[238] *See* Zippo Mfg., Co. v. Zippo Dot Com, Inc., 952 F. Supp 1119, 1122–24 (W.D. Pa. 1997).

[239] Yokoyama, *supra* note 236, at 1164.

[240] *Id.* at 1160.

[241] *See id.* at 1167.

[242] *See* Illinois v. Hemi Group LLC, 622 F.3d 754, 758–59 (7th Cir. 2010) (noting that the *Zippo* test is merely "short-hand" for minimum contacts analysis and that an "easy-to-apply categorical test" is unnecessary); Howard v. Mo. Bone & Joint Ctr., Inc., 373 Ill. App. 3d 738, 742–43 (Ill. App. Ct. 2007)

attempting to resolve Internet jurisdiction issues strictly with the *Zippo* test.[243] Since *Zippo*, many courts have acknowledged the need to address potential deficiencies of the test by adopting hybrid frameworks, some of which require an "intentionality requirement."[244] Moreover, in his concurring opinion in *Nicastro*, Justice Breyer criticized the plurality opinion for announcing "a rule of broad applicability without full consideration of the modern-day consequences,"[245] which include the conduct of business and communication on the Internet.

General Jurisdiction and the Internet

Most courts have been reluctant to exercise general jurisdiction based exclusively on the operation of a website, apprehensive that general jurisdiction based on an Internet site alone would "render any individual or entity that created such a web site subject to personal jurisdiction in every state," with the result that it "would eviscerate the personal jurisdiction requirement as it currently exists."[246] In addition, there has been uncertainty as to whether courts should apply the *Zippo* test, originally a test for specific jurisdiction, to general jurisdiction cases.[247]

(concluding that the *Zippo* sliding scale approach is "arbitrary" and a web page's level of interactivity is "irrelevant" in determining personal jurisdiction); Hy Cite Corp. v. Badbusinessbureau.com, L.L.C., 297 F. Supp. 2d 1154, 1160 (W.D. Wis. 2004) ("I am reluctant to fall in line with these courts for two reasons. First, it is not clear why a website's level of interactivity should be determinative on the issue of personal jurisdiction. As even courts adopting the *Zippo* test have recognized, a court cannot determine whether personal jurisdiction is appropriate simply by deciding whether a website is 'passive' or 'interactive' (assuming that websites can be readily classified into one category or the other).... Moreover, regardless how interactive a website is, it cannot form the basis for personal jurisdiction unless a nexus exists between the website and the cause of action or unless the contacts through the website are so substantial that they may be considered 'systematic and continuous' for the purpose of general jurisdiction. Thus, a rigid adherence to the Zippo test is likely to lead to erroneous results.") (questioning the need for a special test for determining personal jurisdiction over the Internet); *see also* C. Douglas Floyd & Shima Baradaran-Robison, *Toward a Unified Test of Personal Jurisdiction in an Era of Widely Diffused Wrongs: The Relevance of Purpose and Effects*, 81 IND. L.J. 601, 657–58 (2006) (arguing that "a unique test of personal jurisdiction should not be adopted for cases involving wrongs committed by means of the Internet").

[243] *See* Hawkins, *supra* note 217, at 2388–89, (citing Yokoyama, *supra* note 236, at 1166–67).

[244] *See, e.g.*, Toys "R" Us, Inc. v. Step Two, S.A., 318 F.3d 446, 451–53 (3rd Cir. 2003) (recognizing that "an 'intentionality' requirement when fashioning a test for personal jurisdiction in the context of the Internet" is necessary to comport with the spirit of personal jurisdiction and due process); ALS Scan, Inc. v. Digital Serv. Consultants, Inc., 293 F.3d 707, 714 (4th Cir. 2002) ("Thus, adopting and adapting the *Zippo* model, we conclude that a State may, consistent with due process, exercise judicial power over a person outside of the State when [that person] ... manifested intent of engaging in business or other interactions within the State....").

[245] *Nicastro*, 131 S. Ct. at 2791 (Breyer, J., concurring).

[246] Hawkins, *supra* note 217, at 2391 (quoting Dagesse v. Plant Hotel N.V., 113 F. Supp. 2d 211, 221 (D.N.H. 2000)).

[247] *See* Hawkins, *supra* note 217 (citing cases that using the *Zippo* test for general jurisdiction cases, including Gorman v. Ameritrade Holding Corp., 293 F.3d 506, 513(D.C. Cir. 2002); Mink v. AAAA Development LLC, 190 F.3d 333 (5th Cir. 1999); Soma Medical International v. Standard Chartered Bank, 196 F.3d 1292 (10th Cir. 1999); and cases that declined to follow the *Zippo* approach, including Revell v. Lidov, 317 F.3d 467, 471 (5th Cir. 2002) and Bell v. Imperial Palace Hotel/Casino, Inc., 200 F. Supp. 2d 1082, 1091–92 (E.D. Mo. 2001).

The concerns expressed are that *Zippo* is "under-protective of due process rights" in the general jurisdiction context because it is inconsistent with *Helicopteros* and sets a lower threshold to establish general jurisdiction.[248]

Of the general jurisdiction cases that have applied the *Zippo* sliding scale test, there is one notable case in which the court exercised general jurisdiction based on Internet activities alone. In *Gator.com Corp. v. L.L. Bean, Inc.*,[249] a trademark dispute case, the Ninth Circuit asserted that L.L. Bean's business activities over the Internet were sufficient to allow general jurisdiction over the corporation in California, despite the fact that it was not incorporated there and had no official agents present in California.[250]

The *Gator.com* court, which chose to apply the *Zippo* sliding scale test in conjunction with conventional minimum contacts analysis, determined that L.L. Bean's Internet transactions were suitably "substantial or continuous and systematic" to satisfy general jurisdiction and effectively had created a constructive presence within the state.[251] The court stated that even if "the only contacts L.L. Bean had with California were through its virtual store, a finding of general jurisdiction in the instant case would be consistent with the 'sliding scale' test.... "[252] The Court's analysis, following the existence of sufficient contacts, also weighed reasonableness factors that included the following:

> [t]he extent of purposeful interjection, the burden on the defendant to defend the suit in the chosen forum, the extent of conflict with the sovereignty of the defendant's state, the forum state's interest in the dispute; the most efficient forum for judicial resolution of the dispute; the importance of the chosen forum to the plaintiff's interest in convenient and effective relief; and the existence of an alternative forum.[253]

Alternatively, other courts have avoided applying *Zippo* in the context of general jurisdiction cases; they have opted for more conventional minimum contacts analysis.[254] The Fifth Circuit, for example, originally applied *Zippo* in the context

---

[248] Hawkins, *supra* note 217, at 2418–19 ("Had *Helicol* established the same or similar contacts with Texas over the Internet, the *Zippo* test would likely have authorized jurisdiction" and "Because it would confer general jurisdiction over out of state defendants in situations where the Supreme Court's minimum contacts framework would not, the *Zippo* test is under-protective of due process rights.")

[249] 341 F.3d 1072 (9th Cir. 2003), *vacated as moot*, 398 F.3d 1125 (9th Cir. 2005) (ruling that a settlement made the case moot). Although the Ninth Circuit declared that the original holding regarding personal jurisdiction should not be construed as binding precedent in the Ninth Circuit, other courts have cited it for its holding on personal jurisdiction. *See, e.g.*, Lakin v. Prudential Securities, Inc., 348 F.3d 704, 708 n.7 (8th Cir. 2003); Shrader v. Biddinger, 633 F.3d 1235, 1243 (10th Cir. 2011).

[250] *See id.* at 1074–75, 1081–82.

[251] *Id.* at 1078–80.

[252] *Id.* at 1079.

[253] *See id.* at 1080–81.

[254] *See, e.g.*, Revell v. Lidov, 317 F.3d 467 (5th Cir. 2002); *See also* Bird v. Parsons, 289 F.3d 865, 873–74 (6th Cir. 2002) (applying conventional general jurisdiction case law of *Helicopteros*, as well as *Cybersell, Inc. v. Cybersell, Inc.*, to find that a website alone cannot establish general jurisdiction); Hawkins, *supra*

of general jurisdiction in *Mink v. AAAA Development LLC*.[255] Three years later, it rejected its application to general jurisdiction cases in *Revell v. Lidov*.[256] More commonly, courts have begun advancing various hybrid forms of analysis for Internet-based general jurisdiction cases.[257]

Summary

Whether or not personal jurisdiction rules are founded solely upon the autonomy of the individual, territorial sovereignty issues matter to the due process inquiry. Early cases emphasized sovereignty limitations in part because geographical-based line-drawing was simpler then, and, in part, because economic and social forces made the approach practical. People and corporations rarely traveled to foreign jurisdictions, and sovereignty-based analysis protected individual liberty as a byproduct: if you neither owned property nor traveled to a foreign jurisdiction, you were protected against attempts by foreign courts to claim jurisdiction over you. As the economy developed and the burdens of travel lessened, however, the formalistic and sovereignty-based jurisdictional rules that made the older distinctions sensible became increasingly complicated and unworkable. The Court thus was faced with the challenge of redefining personal jurisdiction rules to better suit a modern world.

The mid-twentieth century saw a shift to a more functionalist approach to personal jurisdiction that examined the activities the defendant had undertaken to justify haling her into a foreign court, instead of just considering what interests the forum state had in hearing the case. By basing the analysis on the choices made by an individual, the Court privileged the individual's autonomy over the state's interest, and also more comfortably fit personal jurisdiction doctrine into a due process frame. Notably, the Court now claimed to consider state sovereignty interests merely as a byproduct of its liberty-based analysis. But even the most affirmative

---

note 217, at 2407 ("At least one scholar sees *Bird* as an indication that *Zippo* is on the way out.") (citing Bunmi Awoyemi, Zippo *Is Dying, Should It Be Dead?: The Exercise of Personal Jurisdiction by U.S. Federal Courts Over Non-Domiciliary Defendants in Trademark Infringement Lawsuits Arising Out of Cyberspace*, 9 Marq. Intell. Prop. L. Rev. 37, 55 (2005)).

[255] 190 F.3d 333 (5th Cir. 1999).

[256] 317 F.3d 467, 471 (5th Cir. 2002).

[257] *See, e.g.*, Lakin v. Prudential Securities, Inc., 348 F.3d 704, 712 (8th Cir. 2003) (applying hybrid test for general jurisdiction over the Internet which, first, analyzes the nature and quality of the Internet activities under the *Zippo* framework and, second, assesses the quantity of those contacts); ALS Scan, Inc. v. Digital Serv. Consultants, Inc., 293 F.3d 707, 714–15(4th Cir. 2002) (applying hybrid *Zippo* test in the context of specific jurisdiction when a "person (1) directs electronic activity into the State, (2) with the manifested intent of engaging in business or other interactions within the State, and (3) that activity creates, in a person within the State, a potential cause of action cognizable in the State's courts"). The *ALS Scan* court also made note of potential implications toward general jurisdiction and based its decision, in part, on landmark personal jurisdiction cases of *Calder* and *Burger King*. *See id.*

pronouncements of a liberty- and autonomy-based rule did not advance particularly robust notions of liberty and autonomy. Allowing a state to claim jurisdiction over people who temporarily use its airspace during travel[258] or who post messages on websites accessible to the state's citizens[259] may not protect people from being haled into a foreign court based solely on their conscious and intentional acts. At the same time, the judicially constructed standards for general jurisdiction may be so high as to prevent a state from claiming jurisdiction over a company that has substantial ties to a forum but is not incorporated within its territory.[260] Taken in that light, the Court's liberty-based jurisprudence protects state interests as a byproduct because its analysis is flexible enough to ensure that the interests of the state and its citizens are at least functionally represented by the outcomes of many decisions.

Personal jurisdiction jurisprudence thus represents a microcosm of the Court's larger thematic approach to due process questions. The Court attempts to protect the autonomy and liberty interests of citizens within an ordered, liberal democratic system. This necessarily entails balancing the rights-based interests of individuals against the practical interests of the state and society at large. At the same time, the Court's analysis shows its deference to concerns of democracy and the separation of powers, at least by implication, because its jurisprudence so carefully maps onto changes in the economy and society. The doctrine is inherently procedural, in the sense of worrying about transparency and the ability to plan one's affairs with advance notice of government requirements, but also is substantive in its attention to ordered liberty and territorial restrictions on government reach over basic human affairs. Notably, the legal concept of restrictions on state courts predated the Fourteenth Amendment. Yet the move to due process as the constitutional home for personal jurisdiction-based limits on state court power occurred fairly seamlessly. As it has for other fundamental rights, due process here became the textual anchor for notions of fairness that may be less easily cabined or defined as the exclusive or primary concern of this constitutional provision. Yet the notions are enduring ones, even if they have roamed more freely across the constitutional, structural terrain. The much-derided argument that substantive due process rights derive from "penumbras" of the Constitution is therefore not limited to the privacy cases, and has a deeper and wider scope than *Griswold* and its progeny recognized.

II. Punitive Damages

A second hybrid category of due process concerns punitive damages, which are extra-compensatory damages used by courts to simultaneously punish defendants

[258] *See, e.g.*, Grace v. MacArthur, 170 F. Supp. 442, 447 (D.C.Ark. 1959).

[259] *See, e.g.*, Silver v. Brown, 382 Fed. Appx. 723 (10th Cir. 2010) (ruling that postings on a blog can be sufficient basis for personal jurisdiction).

[260] *See* Helicopteros Nacionales de Colombia, S.A. v. Hall, 466 U.S. 408, 416–19 (1984).

for conduct that was particularly blameworthy or egregious and to deter similar behavior in the future.[261] Since the goal of punitive damages, like that of criminal law, is to punish and deter offenders, the specter of constitutionality and due process protections looms over what appears to be functionally similar to criminal punishment.[262] As we will see, and as one author has noted, the "obvious objection to punitive damages is that it seems clearly unconstitutional to punish a defendant with a sanction that the Supreme Court concedes is conceptually and functionally indistinguishable from a criminal punishment without affording the procedural safeguards that the Constitution guarantees to criminal defendants."[263]

Punitive damages have long been utilized for the purposes of punishing and deterring reprehensible behavior. Although punitive damages have been used within American jurisprudence since the eighteenth century, the legal doctrine of punitive damages has an ancient origin and can be found in many earlier systems of law, including the Code of Hammurabi (2000 B.C.), Hittite law (1400 B.C.), and the Hindu Code of Manu (200 B.C.).[264] In English common law, the doctrine took root when courts espoused certain applications of punitive damages, for occasions where the actions of the defendant were particularly blameworthy, by refusing to reduce damages that exceeded the apparent value of harm.[265] Over the years, courts have struggled to develop a coherent set of principles governing the proper application of punitive damages.[266] In an attempt to provide clearer guidance on when the application of punitive damages may impinge upon constitutionally protected

---

[261] Punitive damages generally are thought to facilitate two social goals: (1) retribution against the defendant for a severe violation of a defendant's right and (2) deterrence against future offenses by the same or different parties through a clear financial disincentive. *See, e.g.*, City of Newport v. Fact Concerts, Inc., 453 U.S. 247, 266–67 (1981) ("Punitive damages by definition are not intended to compensate the injured party, but rather to punish the tortfeasor whose wrongful action was intentional or malicious, and to deter him and others from similar extreme conduct.").

[262] Thomas B. Colby, *Clearing the Smoke from* Philip Morris v. Williams: *The Past, Present, and Future of Punitive Damages*, 118 YALE L.J. 392, 395 (2008).

[263] *Id.*

[264] James B. Sales & Kenneth B. Cole, Jr., *Punitive Damages: A Relic That Has Outlived Its Origins*, 37 VAND. L. REV. 1117, 1119 (1984). *See also* William Schubert, *Simplifying Punitive Damages in the U.S.: Due Process and the Pursuit of Manageable Words and Procedures* (2011) (working paper) (on file with Inst. for Consumer Antitrust Stud. at Loy. U. Chi. Sch. of L.) *available at* http://www.luc.edu/law/academics/special/center/antitrust/pdfs/punitive_damages_09242010.pdf.

[265] Schubert, *supra* note 264, at 5–6 (discussing Wilkes v. Wood, 98 Eng. Rep. 489 (C.P. 1763), where a law enforcement officer broke into the home of the defendant and searched and seized property under an unlawfully-issued warrant. The Court of King's Bench found the conduct to be so egregious that the damages should serve as a punishment and deterrence, and "as a proof of the detestation of the jury to the action itself." *Wilkes*, 98 Eng. Rep. 489, 498–99). See Exxon Shipping Co. v. Baker, 554 U.S. 471, 490–93, for a general overview of evolution of the modern Anglo-American doctrine of punitive damages.

[266] *See* A. Mitchell Polinsky & Steven Shavell, *Punitive Damages: An Economic Analysis*, 111 HARV. L. REV. 870, 870 n.1 (1998) (delineating many of the "skeptical views expressed by various Justices on the rationality of punitive damages").

rights, the Court in recent years has addressed the substantive and procedural due process limitations on punitive damages.[267]

The Court first held that punitive damages would be subject to due process limitations roughly two decades ago.[268] Due process "imposes certain limits, in respect both to procedures for awarding punitive damages and to amounts forbidden as 'grossly excessive.'"[269] The Due Process Clause of the Fourteenth Amendment provides both procedural and substantive protections against state deprivation by punitive damages.[270] States that impose punitive damages violate the due process clause when the court (1) fails to provide defendants with adequate procedures to protect against excessive awards or (2) administers a "grossly excessive" award in violation of substantive due process.[271]

The first clear consideration of due process protections that safeguard against punitive damages was examined by the Court in *Pacific Mutual Life Insurance Co. v. Haslip*.[272] The case involved an insurance agent who misappropriated premiums paid by city employees, causing their health coverage to lapse.[273] One of the employees, Haslip, was hospitalized and unable to make full payment of her bill due to a lack of coverage, which adversely affected her credit.[274] Haslip was awarded

---

[267] *See, e.g.*, State Farm Mut. Auto. Ins. Co. v. Campbell, 538 U.S. 408, 425 (2003) ("We decline again to impose a bright-line ratio which a punitive damages award cannot exceed. Our jurisprudence and the principles it has now established demonstrate, however, that, in practice, few awards exceeding a single-digit ratio between punitive and compensatory damages, to a significant degree, will satisfy due process.").

[268] Since the late 1980s, the Court has issued nine cases that examined constitutional limitations on punitive damages, seven of which were analyzed under the ambit of due process. *See* Schubert, *supra* note 264, at 17. However, the Court, as early as 1919, indicated that some constitutional limitations may limit the doctrine of punitive damages. *See* St. Louis, I. M. & S. Ry. Co. v. Williams, 251 U.S. 63, 66–67 (1919).

[269] Philip Morris USA v. Williams, 549 U.S. 346, 353 (2007) (quoting Honda Motor Co. v. Oberg, 512 U.S. 415, 432 (1994)). See also Colby, *supra* note 262, at 401–402 (suggesting that the Court's motivation for basing the due process analysis on procedural rather than substantive grounds in *Williams* stems from its reluctance to expand the "much-maligned" doctrine of substantive due process).

[270] *See, e.g.*, *Williams*, 549 U.S. at 353. *See also* Schubert, *supra* note 264, at 18.

[271] Schubert, *supra* note 264, at 18; *Williams*, 549 U.S. at 353; Colby, *supra* note 262, at 404 (arguing that the Court's preference for issuing holdings based on procedural due process over substantive is to ward off "unwelcome analogies to the *Lochner* era," despite that the majority of the Court's analysis appears to be quintessentially substantive in nature.).

[272] 499 U.S. 1 (1991). However, the possibility that a due process challenge against punitive damages may exist had been previously stated by the Court in *Browning-Ferris Industr. of Vt., Inc. v. Kelco Disposal, Inc.*, 492 U.S. 257 (1989), suggesting that future challenges to punitive damages may find some support from these protections.

> There is some authority in our opinions for the view that the Due Process Clause places outer limits on the size of a civil damages award made pursuant to a statutory scheme .... but we have never addressed the precise question presented here: whether due process acts as a check on undue jury discretion to award punitive damages in the absence of any express statutory limit.... That inquiry must await another day.
>
> *Haslip*· 499 U.S. at 10 (quoting *Kelco Disposal*, 492 U.S. at 276–77).

[273] *Haslip*, 499 U.S. at 4–5.

[274] *Id.* at 5.

$1,040,000 in undifferentiated damages.[275] Because the insurance company had prior notice that the agent was "engaged in a pattern of fraud identical to those perpetrated against respondents" the corporation could be held liable for both compensatory and punitive damages caused by the employee's actions, the Court ruled.[276]

Haslip held that "[i]mposing exemplary damages on the corporation ... creates a strong incentive for vigilance by those in a position 'to guard substantially against the evil to be prevented'" and rationally furthers the State's goal of deterring fraud; therefore, there was no violation of due process protections.[277] The Court provided additional historical support for administering punitive damages, noting that it "has been practiced for two hundred years by common consent, [and] will need a strong case for the Fourteenth Amendment to affect it."[278] Further, the common law method for applying punitive damages was extant before the creation of the Fourteenth Amendment, yet the Amendment does not appear to contemplate any intention to modify or overturn the practice.[279]

The historical practice of administering punitive damages, however, was not per se sufficient to support the contention that their application is always constitutional.[280] The Court examined the procedural safeguards in place to protect the defendant against these "quasi-criminal" damages.[281] The Court determined that the jury was instructed adequately to understand the function of punitive damages as punishment and deterrence, a required post-verdict hearing was provided, and the court specifically found that the conduct in question "evidenced intentional malicious, gross, or oppressive fraud ... and found the amount of the award to be reasonable in light of the importance of discouraging ... similar conduct."[282]

Considering the substantive due process grounds, even though the "punitive damages award in this case is more than four times the amount of compensatory damages, is more than 200 times the out-of-pocket expenses of respondent Haslip ... [and] is much in excess of the fine that could be imposed for insurance fraud," the Court found sufficient objective criteria to support the damages.[283]

---

[275] Haslip's counsel argued for compensatory damages of $200,000 and punitive damages of $3,000,000. The Court stated, therefore, that "it is probable that the general verdict for respondent Haslip contained a punitive damages component of not less than $840,000." *Id.* at 6 & n.2.

[276] *Id.* at 14.

[277] *Id.* (citations omitted).

[278] *Id.* at 17 (quoting Sun Oil Co. v. Wortman, 486 U.S. 717, 730 (1988)).

[279] *Id.* at 17–18.

[280] *Id.* at 18.

[281] *Id.* at 19.

[282] *Id.* at 19, 23. Under *Hammond v. Gadsden*, 493 So. 2d. 1374 (Alabama 1986), trial courts must explicate in the record their reasons for interfering, or not, on grounds of excessiveness of damages. The Court determined that the *Hammond* test was appropriated applied in *Haslip*. *Haslip*, 499 U.S. at 20.

[283] *Haslip*, 499 U.S. at 18, 23.

It refused to "draw a mathematical bright line between the constitutionally acceptable and the constitutionally unacceptable [punitive damages] that would fit every case."[284]

Four years later, in *TXO Production Corp. v. Alliance Resources Corp.*,[285] the Court held that punitive damages arising from a slander-of-title action,[286] over 500 times greater than the actual damages, were not so grossly excessive as to violate substantive due process protections.[287] In determining whether a particular punitive damage award is so grossly excessive that it violates the Due Process Clause of the Fourteenth Amendment, the Court reiterated its refusal to "draw a mathematical bright line" between what values may be constitutionally acceptable and those which are not, instead choosing to proceed with a "general concer[n] of reasonableness."[288]

The Court in *TXO* underlined the importance of taking into account the "potential harm that might result from a defendant's conduct" in determining whether the punitive damages were reasonable in light of the circumstances, and refusing to focus entirely on the relationship the actual damages incurred and the punitive damages awarded.[289] It found that given the amount of money at stake, the bad faith by TXO, and the larger pattern of fraud, the disparity between actual damages and the punitive award were not controlling in this case and were not so grossly excessive so as to be arbitrary deprivation and violative of due process.[290]

---

[284] *Id.* at 18. The fixing of punitive damages "may invite extreme results that jar one's constitutional sensibilities." *Id.* The Court did note, however, that "general concerns of reasonableness and adequate guidance from the court when the case is tried to a jury properly enter into the constitutional calculus." *Id.*

[285] 509 U.S. 443 (1993).

[286] A slander of title action is one in which a party falsely claims ownership of another party's property. TXO Production Corp. knew that the respondent, Alliance Resources Corp., had good title to the oil and gas development rights on a particular tract of land and TXO acted in bad faith to misrepresent its ownership of that land in an effort to favorably renegotiate its royalty arrangements with Alliance. *Id.* at 447–49

[287] The jury's verdict provided $19,000 in actual damages for litigation expenses and $10,000,000 "based on other evidence." *Id.* at 451.

[288] *Id.* at 458 (citations removed). "Legal standards need not be precise in order to satisfy [due process] concern[s] … [b]ut they must offer some kind of constraint upon a jury or court's discretion, and thus protection against purely arbitrary behavior." BMW of N. Am. v. Gore, 517 U.S. 559, 588 (1986) (Breyer, J., concurring).

[289] *TXO Production Corp.*, 509 U.S. at 460 ("It is appropriate to consider the magnitude of the *potential harm* that the defendant's conduct would have caused to its intended victim if the wrongful plan had succeeded, as well as the possible harm to other victims that might have resulted if similar future behavior were not deterred.").

[290] *Id.* at 462. The Court proceeded to consider whether the punitive damages were the result of a "fundamentally unfair procedure" due to inadequate jury instructions, inadequate review by the trial or appellate court, or because TXO had not received advance notice that such a substantially large ward might have issued. The Court declined to address the issue of whether the jury was adequately instructed and found the other issues to be without merit. *Id.* at 462–63. However, in the dissent, Justices O'Connor, White and Souter expressed concern that the court system's administration of punitive damages was fostering "arbitrary and oppressive" outcomes and that the procedures provided were "wholly

In contrast with the holding of *TXO*, in *BMW of North America, Inc. v. Gore*,[291] the Court refused to uphold punitive damages "500 times" the amount of actual harm.[292] In *Gore*, the state court issued an award of $2,000,000 to a customer who purchased a car from a BMW dealer, pursuant to the manufacturer's nationwide policy that damaged cars would be repaired and sold as new without notifying dealers that such repairs had been made.[293] BMW sold 983 cars that had been misrepresented as new prior to the action brought by the plaintiff.[294]

In determining that the punitive award was "grossly excessive" and "transcend[ed] the constitutional limit," the Court laid out three "guideposts" or indicia that can provide guidance to future cases, including (1) the degree of reprehensibility of the defendant's actions, (2) the ratio of punitive awards to the actual harm inflicted on the plaintiff, and (3) comparison of the punitive damages to civil or criminal penalties that could be imposed for comparable misconduct.[295]

The Court suggested that the "most important indicium" of reasonability in assessing punitive damages may be the level of reprehensibility of the defendant's actions, reflecting the underlying principle of utilizing punitive damages for the purpose of punishing and deterring particularly egregious or blameworthy actions.[296] In *Gore*, the Court found that none of the aggravating factors that might be associated with reprehensible conduct existed.[297] Instead, the damages incurred

---

inadequate." *Id.* at 473 (O'Connor, J., dissenting). The "vague and amorphous guidance" provided to juries leads to "caprice, passion, bias, and prejudice [that] are antithetical to the rule of law" and contrary "to the fixture of due process." *Id.* at 474–75 (O'Connor, J., dissenting).

[291] 517 U.S. 559 (1986).

[292] *Id.* at 582, 584–86. Although the Court appeared to at least nominally rely on procedural concepts of "fair notice" in determining that a due process violation occurred, the majority of the Court's analysis appears to be concerned with the grossly excessive nature of the sanction, typically a substantive inquiry. *See* Colby, *supra* note 262, at 403–404 (arguing that Court's reliance on procedural concepts was illusory and "[i]f the state had previously enacted a law publicly declaring that any company that commits a tort like the one committed by BMW can be punished by punitive damages in an amount up to $1 billion—thus taking the issue of inadequate notice off the table—it is hard to believe that the Court's decision would have come out any differently. The Court's real problem with the punitive damages award in *BMW* was that it was too large, not that it was unexpected").

[293] *Gore*, 517 U.S. at 563–64. The trial court awarded damages of $4,000,000, which were subsequently reduced to $2,000,000 upon remittitur by the Alabama Supreme Court, finding that the jury had improperly computed the amount of punitive damages. *Id.* at 567.

[294] *Id.* at 564. The plaintiff argued for punitive damages of $4,000,000 based on the actual damage estimate of $4,000 per car, and approximately 1,000 cars were sold.

[295] *Id.* at 575–86.

[296] *Id.* at 575. The Court noted, "We have instructed courts to determine the reprehensibility of a defendant by considering whether: the harm caused was physical as opposed to economic; the tortious conduct evinced an indifference to or a reckless disregard of the health or safety of others; the target of the conduct had financial vulnerability; the conduct involved repeated actions or was an isolated incident; and the harm was the result of intentional malice, trickery, or deceit, or mere accident." State Farm Mut. Auto. Ins. Co. v. Campbell, 538 U.S. 408, 419 (2003) (citing *Gore*, 517 U.S. 559, 575 (1986)). Moreover, "[t]he existence of any one of these factors weighing in favor of a plaintiff may not be sufficient to sustain a punitive damages award; and the absence of all of them renders any award suspect." *Id.*

[297] *Gore*, 517 U.S. at 575–76.

on the plaintiff were "purely economic in nature."[298] Importantly, the Court, however, stated that purely economic damages could warrant significant punitive awards if "done intentionally through affirmative acts of misconduct, or when the target is financially vulnerable ... [b]ut this observation does not convert all acts that cause economic harm into torts that are sufficiently reprehensible to justify a sanction in addition to compensatory damages."[299]

The ratio of the punitive damages to the actual harm sustained by the plaintiff emphasizes the importance that "exemplary damages must bear a 'reasonable relationship' to compensatory damages...."[300] The proper inquiry into this reasonable relationship is the level of punitive damages awarded and both "the harm likely to result" from the conduct of the defendant and the "harm that actually occurred."[301] Other considerations may have an important role in determining whether the ratio for a particular award is appropriate, such as the level of the compensatory damages—low compensatory awards may support higher ratios[302]—or cases where the injury is difficult to detect or determine.[303]

Comparing punitive damages to those imposed by civil or criminal penalties may provide further guidance in determining whether an award is reasonable and complies with due process. Considerable deference should be accorded to judgments made by the legislature concerning the level of sanctions necessary to punish and deter certain conduct. A sanction "cannot be justified on the ground that it was necessary to deter future misconduct without considering whether less drastic remedies could be expected to achieve that goal."[304]

Seven years later, in *State Farm Mutual Automobile Insurance Co. v. Campbell*,[305] the Court again struck down on due process grounds a punitive damages award, this time $145,000,000, of which $1,000,000 was compensatory.[306] The state court in *Campbell* issued the award against State Farm Insurance for bad faith, fraud, and intentional infliction of emotional distress in failing to reasonably settle claims against the insured, Campbell, stemming from a wrongful death and tort action.[307]

---

298 *Id.* at 576.

299 *Id.* (citation omitted).

300 *Id.* at 580.

301 *Id.* at 581. The Court examined the harm which would have been inflicted onto the plaintiff had defendant's plan actually succeeded and determined that the "relevant ratio was not more than 10 to 1." *Id.*

302 *Id.* at 582. "[F]or example, a particularly egregious act [that] result[s] in only a small amount of economic damages."

303 *Id.*

304 *Id.* at 584 ("The fact that a multimillion dollar penalty prompted a change in policy sheds no light on the question whether a lesser deterrent would have adequately protected the interests of Alabama consumers."). In the present case, the $2,000,000 punitive damages imposed on the defendant were substantially larger than statutory penalties imposed for similar malfeasance. *Id.*

305 538 U.S. 408 (2003).

306 *Id.* at 412, 428; *see also* Colby, *supra* note 262, at 404 (stating that the Court "again paid lip service to the procedural notion of inadequate notice, and it again failed to acknowledge explicitly that it was relying on substantive due process").

307 *Campbell*, 538 U.S. at 412–15.

The Court argued that the present case was inappropriately "used as a platform to expose, and punish, the perceived deficiencies of State Farm's operations throughout the country," specifically the nationwide policy goal of capping payouts on claims company-wide.[308] While

> [l]awful out-of-state conduct may be probative when it demonstrates the deliberateness and culpability of the defendant's action in the State where it is tortious ... that conduct must have a nexus to the specific harm suffered by the plaintiff. A jury must be instructed, furthermore, that it may not use evidence of out-of-state conduct to punish a defendant for action that was lawful in the jurisdiction where it occurred.[309]

The court determined that acts "independent from the acts upon which liability was premised, may not serve as the basis for punitive damages."[310]

The Court in *Campbell* continued to decline "to impose a bright-line ratio which a punitive damages award cannot exceed."[311] It suggested, however, that "few awards exceeding a single-digit ratio between punitive and compensatory damages, to a significant degree, will satisfy due process."[312] Ratios, therefore, that do not exceed double digits are more likely to simultaneously achieve the state's goals while complying with due process protections.[313]

In 2007, in *Philip Morris USA v. Williams*,[314] the Court again examined the requisite due process protections afforded when punitive damages are to be administered, holding that punitive damages could not be awarded "to *punish* the defendant for harming persons who are not before the court ... [and] that such an award would amount to a taking of 'property' from the defendant without due process."[315] The widow of a smoker filed suit against the tobacco company, Philip Morris, for negligence and deceit, ultimately receiving $821,000 in compensatory damages and $79,500,000 in punitive damages.[316] The Court chose to consider, exclusively, whether a procedural due process violation had occurred; it declined to engage in substantive inquiry as to whether the award was grossly excessive.[317]

Although left open in previous cases, the Court in *Williams* held that utilizing punitive damages to punish a defendant for injuries inflicted upon nonparties

---

[308] *Id.* at 420.

[309] *Id.* at 422. The Court's refusal to use evidence of out-of-state conduct is at least partly based on concerns of state sovereignty. "A basic principle of federalism is that each State may make its own reasoned judgment about what conduct is permitted or proscribed within its borders, and each State alone can determine what measure of punishment, if any, to impose on a defendant who acts within its jurisdiction." *Id.* (citing *Gore*, 517 U.S. at 572–73).

[310] *Id.*

[311] *Id.* at 425.

[312] *Id.*

[313] *Id.*

[314] 549 U.S. 346 (2007).

[315] *Id.* at 349.

[316] *Id.* at 350.

[317] *Id.* at 353.

would violate due process.[318] Such damages would effectively permit the state to punish individuals without providing them with an adequate opportunity to present every available defense, since the defendant would be provided no opportunity to demonstrate that these nonparties were not entitled to damages.[319] Further, the indeterminate nature of nonparties and their injuries forces the jury to engage in significant speculation, creating a "standardless" and arbitrary dimension to the calculation of punitive damages.[320]

The Court qualified its holding that a defendant cannot be punished for injuries inflicted onto nonparties by stating that the plaintiff could introduce evidence of harm that may assist the jury in assessing the reprehensibility of the defendant's actions.[321] Some scholars have argued that this qualification is contrary to the rationale on which the Court based its holding, asserting

> The problem with the plaintiff's jury instructions in Philip Morris, according to the Court, was that they allowed the jury to decide whether the defendant had legally harmed smokers who had not sued and whose cases were not properly presented to the jury. But how could that problem be cured by an instruction that allowed the jury to enhance its punishment of the defendant for what it did to the plaintiff on the basis of its conduct towards others? Wouldn't that require making a judgment about hypothetical cases—e.g., cases that involved claims of legal wrongs by the defendant in relation to persons who were not part of the case?[322]

Along similar lines, Justice Stevens argued in the dissent that no procedural due process deficiency existed and Philip Morris did not need to be provided with individualized defenses against nonparty victims because such victims were not being awarded compensatory damages, nor did the punitive damages go toward that purpose.[323] Instead, the punitive damages served the sole purpose of retribution and deterrence. These damages were unrelated to the injuries inflicted on nonparties but instead facilitated the aforementioned social goals.[324] Some scholars argue that the Court's conclusion that the defense is being punished for harm to nonparties without being afforded the ability to prevent individualized defenses is

---

[318] *Id.*

[319] *Id.* at 353–54. The plaintiff may show that harm occurred to others as a means of demonstrating the reprehensibility of the defendant's conduct but the jury must not be allowed to use punitive damages as a means for punishing the defendant for these nonparty injuries. *Id.* at 355.

[320] *Id.* at 354.; *see also* Colby, *supra* note 262, at 409–10 (noting that "Our law has long accepted the fact that even in the criminal law—where due process concerns are at their apex—the magnitude of a sentence for harming large numbers of persons can be calculated through just this type of approximation. How can it violate due process to calculate civil punitive damages in the same manner?").

[321] *Williams*, 549 U.S. at 355; *see also* Colby, *supra* note 262, at 410–11.

[322] Anthony J. Sebok, *Punitive Damages: From Myth to Theory*, 92 Iowa L. Rev. 957, 999 (2007) (footnote omitted); *see also* Colby, *supra* note 262, at 410–11.

[323] *Williams*, 549 U.S. at 358–59 (Stevens, J., dissenting).

[324] *Id.* at 359 (Stevens, J., dissenting).

predicated on the "notion that punitive damages are a form of individualized sanction, rather than a form of punishment for public wrongs; yet the Court reached that conclusion in an opinion that elsewhere suggests that punitive damages are indeed punishment for the harm to the public. . . ."[325]

The puzzle arising from the quasi-criminal nature of punitive damages has led to concerns about the overall "risk of unfairness that arises as a result of the fact that 'defendants subjected to punitive damages in civil cases have not been accorded the protections applicable in a criminal proceeding.'"[326] At least one scholar has argued that punitive damages, absent criminal procedural safeguards, escape unconstitutionality because of its "civil-criminal duality," wherein the damages contain both "subjective and objective senses of punitiveness."[327]

> When the punitive damages are justified only as objective punishment, then it is untenable to deny that the state is imposing punishment, and the criminal protections available should, at least prima facie, be applicable. However, if the damages award represents something else—if it is really something distinct from the imposition of punishment by the state, if it is essentially civil—then it is not appropriate to plug in criminal procedural safeguards. The problem is explaining what that "something else" could be. The subjective aspect of punishment provides an explanation. For if a punitive damages award is grounded in the state's judgment that the plaintiff is entitled to be punitive in exacting a remedy from the defendant, then the award is being granted within the context of the state's empowering action among private parties, as a matter of the plaintiff's right of redress. The state might be happy about the consequences of such an award, and might even maintain its regime in part because of these recognized consequences. But if the state is imposing punitive damages out of respect for a right of private redress, then the reasons for providing criminal procedural protections are not necessarily implicated.[328]

However, the dual nature of punitive damages alone, according to some scholars, is not justification for imposing sanctions with criminal goals in the absence of criminal procedural safeguards.[329]

Although *Williams* helped further develop constitutional law and due process issues associated with punitive damages, the Court left several questions, perhaps

---

[325] Colby, *supra* note 262, at 414. For a detailed discussion of punitive damages as punishment for private wrongs, see *id.* at 414–66.

[326] *Id.* at 444.

[327] Benjamin C. Zipursky, *A Theory of Punitive Damages*, 84 TEX. L. REV. 105, 155 (2005).

[328] *Id.* at 156.

[329] Colby, *supra* note 262, at 446 ("The death penalty also serves the victim's family's interest in exacting private revenge, but that does not mean that it can be imposed on behalf of society without regard to the constraints demanded by the Bill of Rights."). Instead, the Constitution "mandates that, absent criminal procedural safeguards, punitive damages may be employed as punishment for private wrongs, but not as punishment for public wrongs." *Id.* at 455.

purposefully, unresolved.[330] For example, the decision provides lower courts with little guidance on how to instruct juries to consider nonparties' harm in assessing reprehensibility, without simultaneously punishing the defendant based on that consideration.[331] How the Court should facilitate the separation of a juror's determination of reprehensibility and the amount of punitive damages awarded is unclear.[332]

The retributive nature of punitive awards continues to engender significant due process problems. The ostensibly dual nature of punitive damages and its similarity to criminal punishment have complicated questions regarding what due process safeguards should be provided, and the Court has had further difficulties in establishing a clear metric for determining the appropriate value to be applied for the purposes of punishment and deterrence. However, the Court's holdings in *Williams*, *BMW*, and *State Farm* have acted to constrain the role of juries in determining punitive damages and have limited some of the arbitrariness that inheres in the process of calculating the optimal punitive awards for protecting the public, while simultaneously hinting at the Court's desire to continue protecting the economic substantive due process rights of corporations from excessive state punishment.[333]

III. Conclusion

The hybrid due process cases are important to the due process story in several ways. First, they show the fluid nature of "process" and "substance," as well as their interdependence. Second, they show that the Court again has not stood still: the doctrine is ever in motion, and has moved here—as elsewhere—away from formalism and toward multi-faceted tests that allow contextual nuance. Third, the personal jurisdiction materials in particular vividly display how structural, geographical, and political boundaries matter to due process liberty. Finally, the punitive damage cases may give the lie to claims that *Lochner* era anxieties about government regulation of socioeconomic interests have no modern reference.

---

330 Benjamin J. Robinson, Case Comment, *Distilling Minimum Due Process Requirements for Punitive Damages Awards*, 60 Fla. L. Rev. 991, 1002 (2008).

331 *Id.* (speculating that "[t]rial courts will likely meet *Philip Morris*'s charge by changing existing jury instructions, and then releasing the panel to perform whatever mental gymnastics are needed to return a constitutional punitive damages award" and that, "[a]rguably, the surest method for a court to avoid review under *Philip Morris* is to say nothing more than the punitive award it has imposed is a proper response to the defendant's reprehensible conduct toward the victim. Either way, the practical effect of any additional jury instructions will be de minimis and the immediate effect will be to muddy the waters until the Court revisits this issue again.") (footnotes omitted).

332 Daniel Sulser Agle, Comment, *Working the Unworkable Rule Established in* Philip Morris: *Acknowledging the Difference Between Actual and Potential Injury to Nonparties*, 2007 B.Y.U. L. Rev. 1317, 1349 (2007) (arguing that the rule established in *Williams* is "unworkable, critically flawed, and will lead to future constitutional problems.").

333 *See* Schubert, *supra* note 264, at 32.

Taken together, the cases in this chapter also show that the arc of due process is not only long, but wide. If the jurisdiction and damages cases are proper subjects for due process attention, then theories about the meaning of modern due process must take their subtleties and underlying premises into account. In our view, the cases unquestionably belong in the due process story, and they fortify our ultimate conclusions about the importance of substance to due process, as well as about the inherently dynamic nature of American constitutional interpretation as it has been traditionally understood and practiced under the due process runs.

{6}

A Theory Runs Through It

The foregoing chapters have outlined the long and broad arc of due process, stemming from its rule of law and Magna Carta roots, to its early American formulations, to its expansive and controversial judicial interpretations during the post-bellum period. Given the juris-centric nature of American constitutional law—which gives courts primary, though not exclusive, authority to interpret its mandates—this judge-made doctrine offers the most important source of the modern meaning of due process. There is little reason to doubt that this will continue to be true, despite the many criticisms of the contemporary judiciary, or concerns about excessive judicial power.

As we have seen, some constitutional historians claim that the proper and original intention of the nineteenth-century framers of the Fourteenth Amendment was to provide for fundamental rights under the Privileges or Immunities Clause. Regardless of the historical strength of this claim, however, the Court in 2010 was unwilling to jettison the large body of case law that instead locates such rights under the Due Process Clause.[1] Notwithstanding the rise of constitutional originalism, which emphasizes original text, framers' intent, and the public meaning of constitutional language, the Court bowed deeply to its own past decisions as a guide to the scope and content of particular clauses.

Likewise, despite the forceful critiques of due process jurisprudence on other grounds, including that its focus on individual privacy and autonomy is excessive,[2] that it pays inadequate attention to collective responsibility and communitarian ends,[3] or that it has created some constitutional rights out of judicial whole cloth,[4] due process today imposes an important check on government power over public policy.

Consequently, a central task for anyone seeking to understand or shift the course of American due process is to first analyze the judicial constructions of

---

[1] *See* McDonald v. Chicago, 130 S. Ct. 3020 (2010). *See also* Toni M. Massaro, *Substantive Due Process, Black Swans and Innovation*, 2011 UTAH L. REV. 987.

[2] *See, e.g.*, AMITAI ETZIONI, THE LIMITS OF PRIVACY (1999) (critique of aspects of privacy law on communitarian grounds).

[3] *See, e.g.*, MARY ANN GLENDON, RIGHTS TALK (1993) (arguing that framing issues in terms of rights can direct attention away from responsibility and community).

[4] *See* discussion of unenumerated rights in chapter 4 *supra*.

that concept over time. No doubt, research and voices external to doctrine will remain important to a deeper understanding of the doctrine itself. Scholarship that re-plumbs the history of the constitutional provisions will continue to matter, as will scholarship that analyzes and critiques particular aspects of the doctrine from other theoretical perspectives. Historical, sociopolitical, economic, cultural, intellectual, scientific and technological developments too will continue to influence the Court's understanding of "life, liberty and property." Nevertheless, no successful argument for changes in the due process architecture is likely to prevail without dealing with the body of law that we already have, because this body of law itself is part of the reasonable expectations of ordered liberty and justice that shape our due process intuitions. Moreover, revisions or retreats in one part of the due process edifice always have implications for other parts, in ways that reformers focused solely on one area may not anticipate. In particular, critiques that zero in on subcategories of substantive due process such as reproductive or family rights can obscure or altogether ignore ways in which theoretical arguments for or against an interpretation strategy in one due process arena are logically inconsistent with the interpretation approach that governs in another context. Such context-specific analyses are useful, of course, and in many respects essential for making sense of this sprawling doctrine. Yet if—as we have shown is the case—all of the due process veins flow from one constitutional artery, then interpretive integrity and theoretical coherence may require, at most, that the various interpretation approaches be reconciled. At a minimum, they require that internal contradictions and departures be noted and explained.

Finally, no abstract or static theory about due process ever has trumped or likely ever will trump the perceived urgencies or specific tensions between collective and individual interests of the time and place in which due process is applied. The process due, the liberty constrained, and the exercise of government power denied all depend on a balance of interests effected by the courts and other government actors within the larger political process that molds their decisions.

This leads us to a paradoxical conclusion. It makes sense to assert, from a panoptic perspective, that a theory does run through the full span of the due process cases. Yet it also makes sense, given the broad terrain that due process law traverses, to note that the words "'substance' and 'procedure' [here] are the same key-words to very different problems. Neither ... represents the same invariants. Each implies different variables depending upon the particular problem for which it is used."[5] In short: due process context matters—a lot—to due process theory. The nuances of even the most basic due process concepts are not constant across all settings, let alone across generations.

Nevertheless, there are general, cross-contextual concepts that bind this area of law together. This is so despite the many contextual variations and shadings and

[5] *See* Guaranty Trust Co. of New York v. York, 326 U.S. 99, 108 (1945).

despite the dramatic evolution of due process law. These common cords become visible when one looks at "due process of law" from a panoramic, doctrinal, and temporal perspective.

We believe that the fuller, doctrinal picture that we have painted here reveals nine core principles that constitute the baseline of due process, or what counts as "rationality" within a liberal democratic order. This baseline, however, is general enough to accommodate substantial variations across the due process spectrum, and across generations of due process evolution. We outline these nine principles below, offer a response to the primary critiques of an evolutionary approach to due process, and close with a look at the future of due process.

I. The Common Cords

Due process doctrine today reflects an expectation, imperfectly satisfied, that government action that burdens life, liberty, or property will be limited by the following core principles that define constitutional "rationality":

- fair procedures, especially notice and opportunity to be heard, but also political processes
- respect for settled expectations and traditions
- impartial decisionmakers
- prospective rather than retrospective, lawmaking
- proportionality, in terms of avoiding excessive government measures
- transparency and accessibility of government processes
- respect for individual autonomy and liberty in making fundamental life decisions
- respect for individual equality
- respect for separation of powers, geographical limits, and other structural and jurisdictional limits on government authority

These principles are interdependent as well as context sensitive. Taken together, the principles anticipate a system that advances collective goals in a nonarbitrary manner, that respects individual autonomy, procedural regularity and equal treatment, and that observes structural restraints on official power.

Courts have applied these basic principles in order to help preserve the conditions under which members of the constitutional community will be willing to accept the many burdens imposed by government. The *judicially-reinforced* due process baseline, however, is very "thin" in most contexts. Minimum due process constraints are triggered when (1) the individual interests at stake are perceived as non-essential to personhood and autonomy; (2) government burdens on the interest are relatively indirect (such as denial of government funding to support it) versus direct (such as criminal prohibitions of or civil sanctions on the individual activity); (3) the public interest in burdening the interest is at least reasonable, if not important or compelling; (4) the burdens imposed by government are widely shared; (5) the process that produced the burdens, and the methods by which they are enforced, are neither arbitrary nor capricious, or otherwise so distorted that they violate baseline expectations of procedural and political regularity; (6) any untoward consequences of the regulation are likely to be noticed and capable of correction without judicial intervention; and (7) the responsible government actors have not strayed from their legitimate structural, geographical, and jurisdictional limits in adopting the applicable policies.

This minimum due process baseline for government rationality includes an impressive set of restraints. But these restraints are policed in a manner that gives to government actors nearly every benefit of the due process doubt. Courts intone the "thin" rationality command, yet typically defer deeply to government's judgment about how the command is respected in the countless settings to which it applies.

"Thicker" due process brakes on government power apply when the burdened interests become more powerful and the fear of arbitrary government power escalates. This continuum is reflected in the *Mathews v. Eldridge* test for procedural due process,[6] the *International Shoe* test for personal jurisdiction,[7] the *Glucksberg/Lawrence* test for substantive due process,[8] and the *McDonald* test for selective incorporation of Bill of Rights provisions into the Fourteenth Amendment.[9] All involve context-dependent notions about when the due process right becomes fundamental. Once a "fundamental" right is identified, courts will begin to impose more formidable, judicially enforceable restraints on the government. Yet even then, government reserves "play in the policy joints."[10]

Allowing the judiciary to develop due process "specifics" from these core due process generalities makes enduring practical sense, despite the reasonable ever-present concern that the judiciary may exceed its legitimate sphere of powers by overturning government action that it dislikes on policy, rather than constitutional grounds. The doctrine offers courts bounded discretion to enforce constitutional rights, which allows them to shape the contours of the rights in response to changing conditions;[11] it does not confer unbridled power to second-guess the

---

[6] *See* chapter 3, *supra*.

[7] *See* chapter 5, *supra*.

[8] *See* chapter 4, *supra*.

[9] *See id.*

[10] Likewise, the equal treatment principle that "there is no more effective practical guaranty against arbitrary and unreasonable government than to require that the principles which officials would impose upon a minority must be imposed generally" is applied in highly contextual ways. Yet the principle is no less fundamental or judicially enforceable for this complexity; the core due process principles are inherently general and aspirational.

[11] *See* E. Thomas Sullivan and Richard S. Frase, Proportionality Principles in American Law: Controlling Excessive Government Actions (2009). The American due process principles in this respect echo what other nations express through what is described as "proportionality" principles.

representative branches. Post-1937, the doctrine actually limits due process "activism" significantly: substantive due process, in most circumstances, triggers only rational basis review.

Rational basis review is a safety valve that is theoretically available to check on the most excessive or outrageous government actions, but it is *very* rarely invoked. Even "thick" due process rights—what the Court calls "fundamental" rights—develop in a gradual way that takes emerging cultural consensus and other social transformations into account, within a common-law-like process of doctrinal growth. Courts proceed by analogy to past doctrinal practices, though are not utterly tethered to them.

Finally, the foregoing historical analysis of the post-bellum case law shows that the "thick" rights often began as "thin" rights, subject to the strong presumption in favor of government power, and protected first from only the most excessive burdens on the rights, such as criminal prohibitions. This gradual development of a set of thick rights occurred even though it has produced some constitutional rights that neither the eighteenth-century nor the nineteenth-century Framers likely could have imagined.[12] Yet this evolutionary *process*, if not all of the specific *results*, was something the Framers could well have foreseen when they drafted a constitution designed to live for the ages.

As we also have seen, due process protection in American law is scaled by several so-called "tiers" of judicial review. These ostensibly formal and distinct tiers blur considerably at their edges, and within each tier there is considerable doctrinal "float." In fact, this float has triggered complaints that the tiers are *insufficiently* formalist. The Court may invoke "strict scrutiny"—the highest tier of review—yet uphold the government action in question.[13] It also may strike down government action under the rational basis test, though very rarely.[14]

This float is both inevitable and healthy. Due process problems entail "reconciling the expansion of protected individual autonomy with the rule of law principle that individual autonomy should be preserved insofar as it does not harm others or inhibit the normal functioning of human society."[15] Formal tiers of review may establish useful presumptive ways of reconciling these interests, but these presumptions should be rebuttable because judges occasionally must rebalance the competing concerns to consider evolving conditions relevant to due process rights.

---

[12] See Nathan S. Chapman & Michael W. McConnell, *Due Process as Separation of Powers* forthcoming 121 Yale L.J. 1672 (2012) (describing due process as "the oldest phrase and the oldest idea in our constitution, but ... the most unrecognizable in modern interpretation" and "not at all about judicial creation of fundamental rights outside the reach of legislature amendment, and only secondarily about notice and opportunity to be heard.... ").

[13] *See, e.g.*, Grutter v. Bollinger, 539 U.S. 306–26 (2003) (citations omitted) (although decided on equal protection grounds, the analysis would be the same under due process as applied to the federal government)

[14] *See, e.g.*, Lawrence v. Texas, 539 U.S. 558 (2003).

[15] Sullivan & Frase, *supra* note 11, at 66.

Once a particular right has been assigned to a tier, of course, the judicial analysis may become more formalistic. Yet the analytical process that leads to location of a right under a particular tier itself is a balancing process, not a matter of pure formulaic reasoning. In the early stages of a fundamental right's evolution, the Court often conducts the balance of applicable interests quite transparently. Thereafter, this part of the analysis becomes less transparent, and more assumed than explained. But this does not mean balancing is not involved in the due process calculus.

At the lower end of the due process spectrum—conventional, "rational basis" review—the balance of relevant interests typically is conducted by the applicable rule-making body or actor, not by the courts. Even here, however, the core due process values described above properly should and likely do inform the government process, and may impose self-policed limits on government power.

It may well be, as one of us has argued elsewhere,[16] that a more accurate way of capturing this balancing process across legal contexts would be for judges to openly adopt a "proportionality test," similar to that used by some European nations. European proportionality analysis includes a multifactored investigation into government procedural and substance rationality and fairness that resembles American due process analysis but is more openly fluid and nonformalistic.

Nevertheless, the United States Supreme Court is unlikely to pitch its existing doctrinal structure and vocabulary in favor of this arguably more transparent proportionality approach to due process review of government action.[17] Consequently, even if it is compatible with a proportionality theory, American due process doctrine is best understood in terms of the elements of the nine principles described above.

II. The Common Objections to Due Process Doctrine

We have argued that due process doctrine is a major factor in defining "due process," and have shown that the doctrine has undergone dramatic evolution over time. What due process means today thus is quite different from how the right was first conceived, or how it may appear in the ever-changing future. We also have shown that the doctrine covers extensive territory, and is subject to important contextual variations that have led to quite divergent branches from the due process clause trunk. Finally, we have identified common themes that run throughout the case law, which are cords that bind due process problems but at a quite high level of abstraction.

---

[16] *See* SULLIVAN & FRASE, *supra* note 11.

[17] Similarly, emerging international principles of human rights captured under some "rules of law" theories of justice also are consistent with the doctrine-specific concept of due process outlined here. *See, e.g.*, TOM BINGHAM, THE RULE OF LAW (2010) (outlining the Rule of Law and its basic requirements in terms that correspond well to the due process core values principles described herein).

Our last task is to engage the most powerful critiques of the due process doctrine, as the doctrine has evolved. In particular, we address the claim that the Court has occasionally overturned government acts under due process in the absence of plain text, clear and uninterrupted historical practices that recognize the right, or other steadfast anchors of judicial interpretation. Critics of evolutionary due process doctrine, for example, argue that cases like *Lawrence v. Texas*[18] fell outside of all established categories of fundamental rights or suspect classes, yet overturned government policy. Can due process cases like *Lawrence* that identified "new" due process liberties be justified?

The answer, we assert, is yes. The play in the doctrinal joints that permits judges to expand substantive liberties is justified—by past judicial practice, by the imperfect nature of government, by the shortcomings of existing categories, and by the Court's special role in the evolution of liberty.[19] In the following sections, we offer responses to the most compelling arguments against judicially conceived "new" liberties.

PAST JUDICIAL PRACTICE JUSTIFIES "NEW" DUE PROCESS RIGHTS

Constitutional doctrine is a human creation, not a divine emanation arising unambiguously from the text or framers' intent. Due process doctrine is no exception. The outcomes inevitably are shaped by human judgment and human experience, both of which defy formalist conventions. For example, the due process cases that first identified "fundamental rights" entailed a dynamic and fluid approach to these rights, under which the Court accommodated changed perspectives on government power, on affected private interests, and on the delicate balance between them. The Court attached the analytically significant label of "fundamental" *after* it considered a complex set of factors, which included sociopolitical phenomena external to text and doctrine.

So-called "selective incorporation" of rights into the Fourteenth Amendment occurred over time and entailed judgment calls not clearly dictated by text. The Court did not deem freedom of speech to be incorporated into Fourteenth Amendment due process until 1925,[20] and did so even though the Fourteenth Amendment nowhere mentions freedom of speech. The phrase "due process" was hardly an obvious or uncontroversial signal that the Framers of the Fourteenth Amendment intended to incorporate any specific part of the Bill of Rights, including freedom of speech. Moreover, even after the Court deemed freedom of speech to be fundamental to ordered liberty and thus part of substantive due process, it

---

[18] 539 U.S. 558 (2003).

[19] The following arguments are drawn in substantial part from Toni M. Massaro, *Substantive Due Process, Black Swans, and Innovation*, 2011, Utah L. Rev. 987; and Toni M. Massaro, *Constitutional Law as "Normal Science,"* 21 Const. Commentary 547 (2004), and used with permission.

[20] Gitlow v. New York, 268 U.S. 652 (1925).

first used "reasonableness" as the test of state-imposed burdens on expression.[21] "Strict scrutiny" of state action in this arena occurred much later.[22]

In any event, whether the Court analyzes freedom of expression under a flaccid "rational basis" test, the most demanding version of "strict scrutiny" test, or under "intermediate" scrutiny, it weighs multiple factors in the inquiry that arguably should instead be weighed by legislators or other nonjudicial actors. The burden on speech, the potential harms or "secondary effects" of speech, the comparative value of speech, and whether reasonable alternative methods of expression exist, all entail judgments that defy formalist methods of determining them. Yet few people claim that the Court violates separation of powers or unduly usurps democratic will whenever it makes First Amendment decisions that turn on these assessments.

First Amendment law is not unique in this regard. The Court engages in a common-law-like process of doctrinal development in countless other areas of constitutional law as well. In each area, the Court slowly accommodates changes on the margins of accepted law. This growth occurs because the Court finds it impossible to uphold government acts that defy constitutional "reason." Constitutional "reason," in turn, is informed by the foregoing core due process principles, and their extensions to specific contexts. Judicial applications rely upon analogy to past cases, and reference to evolving cultural norms of "reason."

Lawrence is an excellent, if controversial, example of the Court's embrace of evolving notions of due process. As we have explained, the majority struck down the Texas law in light of precedent regarding the scope of sexual autonomy, changed attitudes about the alleged social harms of homosexuality, and a growing sense that criminalizing this behavior is illiberal, even cruel.[23] Missing from the opinion, of course, were key phrases—especially "fundamental right"—that the Court in recent decades has linked to outcomes that struck down government acts otherwise well within its regulatory powers. But the basic task was a familiar one. The Court spoke of liberty, privacy, equality,[24] and human dignity, and it chose to act to protect them, despite the political firestorm it surely knew would follow.

If *Lawrence* is condemned over time as poorly crafted or analytically shaky, but correctly decided as a matter of policy and justice, it will be in superb constitutional company, as *Brown v. Board of Education*[25] proves. Breakthrough decisions *typically* are analytically imperfect because they rearrange relationships between and among the existing categories, and because the categories themselves are analytically imperfect.

In any event, analytical purity is virtually unattainable in the highly abstract and ever-evolving realm of constitutional law. Unless constitutional doctrine

---

[21] *Id.* at 670.

[22] Brandenburg v. Ohio, 395 U.S. 444 (1969).

[23] *See* chapter 4, *supra*.

[24] *Lawrence*, 539 U.S. at 579–85, (O'Connor, J., concurring).

[25] 347 U.S. 483 (1954).

today has achieved perfection—a ludicrous notion for any generation of judges to embrace—then these occasional doctrinal fractures may signal healthy growth, not doctrinal chaos or dissolution. Recognizing this, a majority of the Court has never favored the death of doctrinal development—even in the highly contested arena of substantive due process—and has continued to apply doctrine to new terrain in an evolutionary manner.

IMPERFECT GOVERNMENT AND THE SHORTCOMINGS OF EXISTING CATEGORIES JUSTIFY "NEW" DUE PROCESS RIGHTS

A second justification for the evolutionary dynamism within due process doctrine is that government action can confound "reason" in remarkably extensive ways that cannot be captured by any fixed set of outcomes or even fixed categories.[26] A single government act might be irrational in multiple ways, though people may disagree about *which* types of reason it violates and why. Consequently, it would be astoundingly complex for the Court to draft a finite set of rules for all potential applications of due process principles. The "common law" method thus is actually well-suited to the task of deciding these due process cases.

A simple series of examples shows just how complex assessments of "rationality"—a primary due process concern—can become. Assume, for example, that the Congress or a state legislature adopts measure *A*, to promote end *E*. How might this act be irrational? A *non*-exhaustive list of due process flaws might include the following:

- *A* does not actually serve *E*.
- Government officials did not reasonably believe *A* served *E* when they enacted the measure, but it does in fact further that end. *E* is a good end.
- *A* does serve *E*, but *E* is not a good end.
- *A* serves *E*, a good end, but is trumped by weightier good end *F*, which is substantially thwarted by *A*.
- *A* serves *E*, a good end, but also promotes *F*, a bad end (corollary of 4).
- *A* does serve good end *E*, but far less well than other means that serve *E* better.
- *A* does serve good end *E*, but government officials actually sought to promote *E* only in order to promote good end *F*, and *A* does not promote *F*.
- Government adopted *A* in order to serve *E*, a bad end, which *A* does serve, but it turns out to also serve end *F*, a good end.

---

[26] *Cf.* H.L.A. Hart, The Concept of Law 128 (1994) (noting that flexibility in rules is necessary because lawmakers cannot anticipate all consequences or contexts in advance); Robert C. Post, *Foreward: Fashioning the Legal Constitution: Culture, Courts, and Law*, 117 Harv. L. Rev. 4, 8 (2003) (concluding that "constitutional law and culture are locked in a dialectical relationship, so that constitutional law both arises from and in turn regulates culture").

- Government adopted *A* in order to serve *E*, a good end, but it did so knowing it would have a much harsher impact on a minority of citizens than others, but did it anyway.
- Government adopted *A* in order to serve *E*, but defined the class of individuals regulated by *A* in a manner that exempts some citizens but not others, with no "rational" basis for doing so.
- Same as above, but government acted out of "animus" toward the burdened class of citizens, where burden on them is disproportionate to any harm to others that the regulation seeks to prevent.
- Government followed a nondemocratic process to determine whether to do *E*, though *E* is a good end, and the process does serve *E*.

This series is obviously and intentionally incomplete: other flaws also might render government action "irrational."[27] This list also does not explain how courts should evaluate government rationality where reliable evidence relevant to the regulatory inquiry is unavailable or inconclusive. But the list does help to explain why due process cases inevitably require judicial balancing. In every due process decision, the judge must distinguish garden-variety government "irrationality" (and uphold the government action), from government "irrationality" *on stilts* (and strike the government action down). Whatever categories the judiciary develops to capture the process of distinguishing these types of cases, that process will defy easy summary given the wide variety of government acts that are subject to due process review. The "tier" approach crudely separates cases into "exacting review"—"intermediate review"—"little or no review" categories, but the actual and ongoing process of funneling cases into these categories is a matter of balance, pragmatism, and judicial judgment. If this is judicial "activism," then activism is inescapable.

THE SPECIAL ROLE OF THE COURT JUSTIFIES "NEW" DUE PROCESS RIGHTS

Of course, to say that government may act irrationally, in multiple ways, does not prove that the judiciary should be given broad discretion to correct for these abuses as it sees fit. Instead, the wide variety of potential government errors may lead one to conclude that judicial flexibility should be curtailed, not expanded.

Justice Antonin Scalia, for one, likely would point to the foregoing list of potential government follies as an excellent argument *against* overturning government action, absent very explicit textual or historical indications that the action is

[27] In general, the Court has decided that a legislative act that serves a good end should be upheld, even if it was adopted for bad reasons. But this is *not* always, or even so literally, so. "Purpose" matters to constitutional analysis in many ways, and a *very* bad purpose may well influence a court's estimation of the gravity of the harms it produces. *See, e.g.*, United States v. O'Brien, 391 U.S. 367, 383 (1968) ("It is a familiar principle of constitutional law that this Court will not strike down an otherwise constitutional statute on the basis of an alleged illicit legislative motivation.").

improper.[28] He might concede that these decisions entail complex judgment calls, but would argue that they nevertheless should be made through the political process as far as possible. As imperfect and illogical as the political process might be, it should trump the judicial process—*not* because the government, acting through the people, acts rationally in any self-proving sense, but because "rationality" is *never* self-proving and may not even be the point of legislation. Consequently, all of these policy decisions should be left to the wider democratic process, and certainly should not be made by a "law trained elite."[29] That is, the Court should talk the formalist talk *and* walk the formalist walk—all the way to doctrine's edge.

We disagree, respectfully, with Justice Scalia. To be sure, intervention by unelected federal judges is not a proper vehicle for bottom-up policy formulation. But, the courts intervene only *after* government officials have acted, and their actions have been challenged by citizens as cruel, captured, clueless, or corrupt. This intervention is not necessarily a disruption of "democracy," and may even be described as a vehicle for perfecting it. A worse alternative would be for judges to align themselves with government officials and refuse to ever act on their power of review, even in when litigants insist they have been seriously mistreated.[30] Government officials include members of Congress, state legislators, state attorneys general, university faculty committees, police officers, public librarians, park officials, municipal planning boards, border patrol agents, city council members, prison guards, parole officers, and child protective services investigators. Robust, horizontal, and

---

[28] *See* Antonin Scalia, A Matter of Interpretation: Federal Courts and the Law, 37–41 (1997); Antonin Scalia, *The Rule of Law as the Law of Rules*, 56 U. Chi. L. Rev. 1175, 1186–87 (1989) (acknowledging that balancing modes of analysis are inevitable, but should be avoided when possible).

[29] *See* United States v. Virginia, 518 U.S. 515, 567 (1996) (Scalia, J., dissenting). *Cf.* John F. Manning, *The Absurdity Doctrine*, 116 Harv. L. Rev. 2387, 2395 (2003) (noting that "a statute's apparently odd contours may reflect unknowable compromises or legislators' behind-the-scenes strategic maneuvers" so that "a legislative classification can seem absurd (in a policy sense) but still be rational (in a process sense) as a means of assuring the passage of the overall legislation"). That is, close examination of how laws actually are made undermines notions of "rational legislation" in ways that may point against judicial interventions. Of course, the "irrationality" of the process may prompt others to argue that judicial interventions are necessary.

[30] Many commentators, of course, already have made similar observations, with varying degrees of force and sophistication. Among the most famous of these is the late John Hart Ely's account of judicial review, which too anticipates a modest corrective role for the judiciary to play in assuring that the democratic process remains participation-oriented and representation-reinforcing. Countless others have critiqued or expanded upon Ely's theory, and many have focused on the complexities of defining a process defect, or of identifying the type of "democracy" one hopes to protect through constitutional law. John Hart Ely, Democracy and Distrust: A Theory of Judicial Review (1980). *See also* Alexander M. Bickel, The Least Dangerous Branch: The Supreme Court at the Bar of Politics 16 (1962) (describing the "counter-majoritarian" difficulty); Christopher L. Eisgruber, Constitutional Self-Government 78 (2001) (arguing that judicial review is not inconsistent with self-governance); Jed Rubenfeld, Freedom and Time: A Theory of Constitutional Self-Government 168, 172 (2002) (arguing that "constitutionalism is not *counter* to democracy," that constitutionalism "is *required* by democracy" and a written Constitution demands judicial review); Mark V. Tushnet, Taking the Constitution Away from the Courts 129–53 (1999) (questioning the courts' capabilities); Jeremy Waldron, Law and Disagreement 296–98 (1999) (arguing that the judiciary supplants popular values).

vertical deference to all of these government officials would be contrary to our experience and our post-bellum history.

Moreover, there is no *cross*-contextual reason to assume that all or even most government action—whether at the local, state, or federal level—necessarily reflects any true "majority's" will. In many contexts, the opposite assumption is warranted.[31] In what sense, then, are all of the foregoing government officials part of a "democratic" process? Many likely are not, and thus do not see themselves as such, or as constrained by democratic principles when they execute their duties.

There also is no reason to condemn a judicial decision as "undemocratic" simply because it emerges from a body composed of legally trained people. Judges are not immune from cultural or political influences that affect government decision makers in other realms. In several states, judges are elected,[32] and the process of appointing federal and state court judges is far from apolitical. Few if any judges operate unaware of or heedless of politics, despite respect for the limiting principles of judicial independence, textual constraint, and *stare decisis*, among other powerful curbs on judicial excess.

Nor would the *absence* of judges in constitutional decision making, in particular, necessarily promote better substantive outcomes. Legally trained judges have received an education that typically includes instruction in constitutional decision making over time, discussion of alternative methods of constitutional interpretation, and critiques of *Lochner v. New York, Korematsu v. United States, Dred Scott v. Sandford,* and *Plessy v. Ferguson*. Law-trained judges also get a close look at the actual impact of government policy on the governed. Granting judges authority to mitigate the harshest, cruelest, or most unintended consequences of these law—especially when the consequences are felt only by a small minority of citizens—is a sensible, reasonably efficient, even democracy-enhancing corrective to a sometimes wooden and unfeeling legislative process. Recall that due process nullification power is exercised infrequently, is subject to further review, proceeds on the basis of analogies to past decisions, and is conducted in public.[33] This modest check on public officials may be especially important as applied to policies that are adopted by the countless low-visibility decision makers whose actions otherwise would *never* pass through a public, deliberative body.

We are not arguing that judges are inherently better than nonprofessionals at making policy decisions for the nation. Rather, we are asserting that judges play an important structural role in constitutional assessments of the *reasons* underlying policy decisions that burden individual liberties. We also are asserting that sweeping condemnations of judicial discretion as "antidemocratic" are inconsistent with

---

[31] *See* Eisgruber, *supra* note 30, at 78.

[32] *See* Daniel Isaacs & Sandra Newman, *Historical Overview of the Judicial Selection Process in the United States: Is the Electoral System in Pennsylvania Unjustified?*, 49 Vill. L. Rev. 1 (2004).

[33] For a particularly compelling development of this argument, with which we concur, see Eisgruber, *supra* note 30.

our constitutional structure. In their broadest forms, the arguments would make it difficult to justify judicial review in nearly any form.

Similarly unpersuasive is the claim that courts rely solely on "personal predilection" in resolving substantive due process cases.[34] Judges' personal predilections surely do influence how they interpret facts and apply the principles, given the nature of judicial review. As Justice Scalia himself recognized, in *Republican Party of Minnesota v. White*,[35] any well-qualified judicial candidate will have "predilections."[36]

But due process doctrine is not the only constitutional doctrine vulnerable to the critique of subjectivity or contextualism. Government classifications often require "important" government reasons, "compelling" government reasons, or "exceedingly persuasive" government reasons. In *United States v. Virginia*,[37] for example, the Court demanded "exceedingly persuasive" justifications for gender-based classifications—placing these classifications in a gray zone above "intermediate" and just below "strict" scrutiny terminology.[38]

In the free speech area, where First Amendment text explicitly protects the right in question, the case law too is exceedingly muddy. The general claim that content-based government regulations of speech trigger "strict scrutiny" is subject to several categorical and other qualifications.[39] In short, the practice of balancing complex interests is well-ingrained, inescapable, and deeply embedded in the very process of interpreting and applying imperfectly drafted laws to fact patterns often not anticipated by the rule makers.

One might instead argue that that Court should at least do a better job of matching its words with its deeds. The Court should openly state that it follows a dynamic, pragmatic, and context-driven approach to due process and jettison talk of categories or tiers of review.[40] It should simply ask in each case whether government has

---

[34] Planned Parenthood of Southeastern Pennsylvania v. Casey, 505 U.S. 833, 1002 (1992) (Scalia, J., dissenting).

[35] 536 U.S. 765 (2002).

[36] Justice Scalia concluded a candidate should be allowed to talk about these views when running for an elected judicial post, even though he or she also must act "impartially" if elected. 536 U.S. 765, 784 (2002). Justice Scalia must believe, as we do, that bending *to* facts, as one perceives them through the lens of one's life experiences, is not the same as *bending* facts. We thus must consider the wider implications of the insight about judicial predilections for constitutional doctrine, rhetoric, and interpretation.

[37] 518 U.S. 515 (1996).

[38] *Id.*

[39] In one freedom of expression case involving congressional conditions on federal funds for public libraries, Justice Breyer suggested that the Court use "heightened, but not 'strict scrutiny.'" United States v. American Library Association, Inc., 539 U.S. 194, 217 (2003) (Breyer, J., concurring). This approach, Judge Breyer continued, "is more flexible [than more speech-protective forms of 'strict scrutiny'] but nonetheless provides the legislature with less than ordinary leeway in light of the fact that constitutionally protected expression is at issue." *Id.* at 218.

[40] This is essentially the approach favored by Justice Stevens and by Justice Thurgood Marshall. *See* Craig v. Boren, 429 U.S. 190, 212 (1976) (Stevens, J. concurring) ("the two-tiered analysis ... actually appl[ies] a single standard"); San Antonio Indep. School Dist. v. Rodriguez, 411 U.S. 1, 110 (1973) (Marshall, J., dissenting) (arguing for a method that considers the "invidiousness" of the classification and the "importance of the interest adversely affected by it").

convincing reasons for acts that significantly burden liberty, property, or life, and identify a nonexhaustive cluster of concerns for lower courts to consider that go beyond *stare decisis* and text. Examples would include the significance of the interest affected, the democratic and deliberative nature of the body that produced the rule, the nature of the group burdened, the nature of the harm the rule produces, alternative avenues for overcoming the rule's harsh consequences, the nature of the harm to others if the rule is voided, and the role of empirical unknowns.

The Court could assert a simple presumption against disruption of truly democratic procedures that allow for meaningful participation by the citizens most affected by the rule in question, but insist that other rules—especially ones that burden a minority of citizens with respect to important interests—be examined more closely. Or, it might abandon formalism altogether, in favor of an approach that pays closer attention to consequences, and less to abstract principles.[41] Perhaps the Court could begin constitutional cases with the following reminder of the anti-majoritarian virtues of judicial review: *"[s]o long as the Court exercises the power of judicial review ..., it should not only protect 'safe' or orthodox views which rarely need its protection."*[42] This incantation would reinforce that the Court properly corrects government excesses and preserves substantive and procedure values, as a matter of institutional design and purpose. Existing due process case law would continue to frame the Court's analysis of future cases in much the same way it now does, but under a "tier free," nonformulaic rubric. The primary advantage of such an open-ended, legal realist approach would be its transparency: it may better describe what the Supreme Court actually does when it develops and extends doctrine to new settings.

Nevertheless, the drawbacks of adopting this approach across the full spectrum of due process cases are overwhelming, for at least four reasons. First, the work of the lower courts is not the same as the work of the Supreme Court. Lower courts likely are better guided and constrained by the Court's blunt categories than by a fluid, multifactored test. Second, the Court itself relies on the blunt categories in many cases. Third, as we have explained, domestic law is best understood using familiar doctrinal vocabulary and conventions. Finally, if the Court were to justify its power in such openly realist terms, this could further obscure the Court's inherent conservatism. Rhetoric that emphasizes the Court's discretion and balancing methods may fuel modern overblown claims about judicial activism.

One thing has been clear from the beginning: the task has fallen to "courts of justice, whose duty it must be to declare all acts contrary to the *manifest tenor* of the Constitution void ... [Otherwise] all the reservations of particular rights or privileges would amount to nothing."[43] Judges are not superior beings—they too

---

[41] *See, e.g.*, Richard A. Posner, Law, Pragmatism and Democracy *passim* (2003).

[42] Dennis v. United States, 341 U.S. 494, 580 (1951) (Black, J., dissenting).

[43] The Federalist No. 78 (Alexander Hamilton). For recent analyses of the history of due process see sources cited in note 11, *supra*. For an in-depth new look at the roots of liberty of contract and due process, *see* David E. Bernstein, Rehabilitating Lochner: Defending Individual Rights Against Progressive Reform (2011).

may violate "notions of fair play and substantial justice."[44] But fear of judicial arbitrariness, bias, irrationality, or indifference to basic liberties does not, and should not, compel us to jettison judicially enforced due process limits on the arbitrariness, bias, and irrationality of public actors who craft and administer our laws.

On the contrary, preserving judicial power to police substantive irrationality preserves the rule of law. If arbitrary official acts could not be undone, except through political responses from the very same bodies that produced the arbitrariness in the first place, this could foster a destabilizing sense of lawlessness. If there were no principled, *judicially enforceable* distinction between a rational act and an irrational one, then people might legitimately ask: "Why obey the law?" Judicial review of irrational acts thus fortifies the rule of law because it imposes an external check on tyrannical or abusive legislative or executive power, especially as it pertains to evolving conceptions of fundamental rights. The due process umbrella also covers the full range of government acts—including those that do not currently trigger fundamental rights,[45] but that nevertheless may be wildly irrational, procedurally unsound, or simply arbitrary. It brings "ordered liberty" principles to bear over governing. It reins in legislators and governors by providing a reasonably independent, public, and procedurally distinctive means of reviewing their work.

Finally, the due process principles preserve constitutional integrity. Due process interposes a cooling mechanism—a "stop and think" brake—on government actors. This may douse occasional conflagrations, increase transparency of low visibility government decision making, impose minimal levels of political accountability, afford aggrieved individuals and other entities the right to be heard, restore baseline procedural and substantive rationality, and thereby best preserve the constitutional parchment. Insofar as the Constitution presupposes, as is commonly believed, "a government of laws, not men,"[46] it presupposes laws that transcend the whims of politicians and government officials. Due process of *law* thus requires that judges help uphold and define what counts as "law."

In many respects, due process doctrine therefore resembles Anglo-American "equity"—the place where litigants seek relief from the harshness of a wooden application of legal rules and standards. The bottom tier of rational basis analysis provides comparable space for appeals to decision makers to modify more

---

[44] International Shoe Co. v. Washington, 326 U.S. 310, 316 (1945) (quoting Milliken v. Meyer, 311 U.S. 457, 463 (1940)).

[45] This includes socioeconomic rights, post 1937. *See* NLRB v. Jones & Laughlin Steel Corp., 307 U.S. 1 (1937); United States v. Darby, 312 U.S. 100 (1941). *Cf.* Kermit Roosevelt III, *Forget the Fundamentals: Fixing Substantive Due Process*, 8 U. PA. J. CONST. L., 983, 1000 (2006) (arguing that "The focus on fundamentality is not a plausible due process approach because the operative proposition behind the Due Process Clause ... is not about fundamental rights at all. Instead, it is about government's duty to act in the public interest—to promote the general welfare, either through laws whose benefits are available at all, or at least through laws whose benefits exceed their costs").

[46] The phrase has deeper roots, but in the United States often is attributed to John Adams. *Novanglus Papers*, no. 7. *See* 4 THE WORKS OF JOHN ADAMS, 230 (Charles Francis Adams, ed. 1856).

generally applicable laws or conventions by relieving their harshest consequences, as applied to specific cases or persons. To suggest that such acts are "political" and therefore not "judicial" because they are guided by fluid maxims, not rigid formulas, is to ignore the tradition of equity in American jurisprudence. To suggest that they are not important complements to judicial formalism also is belied by domestic experience—past and especially present.

We recognize that judicial review itself may ignore the limiting principles of due process, which could put us at the mercy of a judiciary captured by particular economic or political interests and perspectives.[47] Unchecked judicial review could lead to judicial "mission creep" or to unduly wooden enforcement of constitutional rights that could threaten other worthy ends.[48] Yet despite this concern, the post-bellum due process doctrine that grants judges bounded power to define due process liberties is worth preserving. This doctrine provides the courts with authority to step in when government goes *wildly* off the rails, and when no other body is willing or able to check—or even subject to public light—actions that are "cruel, captured, clueless, or corrupt."[49] It also provides, in effect, a constitutional laboratory where new liberties slowly can emerge and be tested before they are elevated to the higher standards of a so-called "fundamental right." Preservation of the due process continuum is responsible constitutional stewardship. Holding on to the *possibility* of new or revised substantive due process constraints on government power makes sense, even

---

[47] As Justice Black observed, "it is up to the legislatures, not courts, to decide on the wisdom and utility of legislation. There was a time when the Due Process Clause was used by this Court to strike down laws which were thought unreasonable, that is, unwise or incompatible with some particular economic or social philosophy.... [That doctrine] has long since been discarded." Ferguson v. Skrupa, 372 U.S. 726, 729 (1963). For recent, especially powerful arguments against broad judicial review see LARRY D. KRAMER, THE PEOPLE THEMSELVES: POPULAR CONSTITUTIONALISM AND JUDICIAL REVIEW (2004); MARK TUSHNET, TAKING THE CONSTITUTION AWAY FROM THE COURTS (1999); Cass R. Sunstein, ONE CASE AT A TIME: JUDICIAL MINIMALISM ON THE SUPREME COURT 24–60 (1999). *Cf.* Lawrence Gene Sager, *Fair Measure: The Legal Status of Underenforced Constitutional Norms* 91 HARV. L. REV. 1212, 1213 (1978) (discussing the institutional characteristics that limit the judiciary's enforcement of the Constitution "to its full conceptual boundaries.").

[48] It makes practical, normative sense to reject ostensibly "neutral" structural or substantive approaches to law that produce normatively undesirable outcomes in the times in which one lives. As stated by Justice Jackson, though not in these precise words, our Constitution is not a suicide pact. See Terminiello v. City of Chi., 337 U.S. 1, 36, (1949) (Jackson, J., dissenting) ("There is danger that, if the court does not temper its doctrinaire logic with a little practical wisdom, it will convert the constitutional Bill of Rights into a suicide pact."). Though Justice Jackson was not the first to express a similar notion. Lincoln, among others, reflected on the tension between strict constitutional principles and the exigencies of war. JAMES M. MCPHERSON, TRIED BY WAR: ABRAHAM LINCOLN AS COMMANDER IN CHIEF 29–30 (Penguin ed. 2008) (discussing Lincoln's justifications for suspending the writ of habeas corpus during the Civil War).

[49] *See* Toni M. Massaro, *Constitutional Law as "Normal Science,"* 21 CONST. COMMENT. 547, 580 (2004). As Cardozo put it, in much more optimistic terms, "By conscious or subconscious influence, the presence of this restraining power, aloof in the background, but none the less always in reserve, tends to stabilize and rationalize the legislative judgment, to infuse it with the glow of principle, to hold the standard aloft and visible for those who must run the race and keep the faith." BENJAMIN N. CARDOZO, THE NATURE OF THE JUDICIAL PROCESS, 93 (1921).

if in a given constitutional era the power lies dormant or is applied incorrectly, by one's lights.[50] Finally, American due process protects fundamental rights—ones that have become "self-evident" and now form part of a baseline expectation of ordered liberty.

THE LIMITS OF "TRADITIONALISM" DUE PROCESS AND HISTORY JUSTIFY "NEW" DUE PROCESS RIGHTS

A final critique of due process doctrine argues that the meaning of due process rights should be hooked primarily—if not exclusively—to traditional practices and historical understandings. Judges should rely on settled legal practices, rather than engage in a more open-ended and evolutionary approach to due process. Under this view, constitutional limits on government power should be narrowly construed, especially when they are derived from the substantive due process strand of the doctrine.

We believe that traditionalism and history should matter to contemporary due process, but that an evolutionary dimension is essential to liberty. As Justice Cardozo put it, "Somewhere between worship of the past and exaltation of the present, the path of safety will be found."[51] We also agree with an especially illuminating critique of due process traditionalism by Professor Cass Sunstein, who challenges the best defenses to the tradition-based theories.[52] Specifically, he identifies,

> three families of explanations. The first, and most ambitious points to the fact that traditions have been supported by many minds across long periods of time. The second sees traditionalism as a second-best substitute for more radical restrictions on substantive uses of the due process clause. The third justifies traditionalism on rule-consequentialist grounds.[53]

The first set of arguments is based upon the ideas of Edmund Burke and Friedrich Hayek, who argued that traditions have the virtue of being accepted by many minds.[54] The theory is that time is a crucible that leaves as its residue practices that tend to serve useful social ends. Moreover, the voices of the many have "epistemic credentials"[55] and may reflect democratic principles better than affording judges the power to develop liberty notions.

The second set of arguments is premised on the notion that due process should be restricted to procedure, not substance.[56] Rather than jettisoning the entire body

---

[50] *See* Robert G. McCloskey, *Economic Due Process and the Supreme Court: An Exhumation and Reburial*, 1962 Sup. Ct. Rev. 34, 43 (suggesting that the extremes of the past generated the extreme deference of post-*Lochner*).

[51] Cardozo, *supra* note 49, at 160.

[52] Cass R. Sunstein, *Due Process Traditionalism*, 106 Mich. L. Rev. 1543 (2008).

[53] *Id.* at 1546.

[54] *Id.*

[55] *Id.*

[56] John Hart Ely, Democracy and Distrust: A Theory of Judicial Review 18 (1980). *See also* chapter 4, *supra.*

of substantive due process, this version of "procedure rights only" due process traditionalism offers the Court a way to at least cabin the expansion of these textually dubious substantive rights.

The third set of arguments relies on the pragmatic notion that "whatever its faults, due process traditionalism produces better results than the likely alternatives."[57] That is, judges are not likely to be better at developing notions of liberty than are more organic sources of norm development outside the judiciary.

We have already addressed the second set of arguments—that due process is about process and not substance. The notion that due process is solely about process rights is simply too difficult to square with the vast body of constitutional doctrine that provides for substantive rights. *Lawrence and McDonald* are particularly good recent examples of the modern Court's unwillingness to limit due process to process-based rights, or to even reject the doctrinal elaborations on due process that may contradict historical evidence. Moreover, this judge-made law on substantive due process now has become part of our sense of "ordered liberty."[58] Constitutional rights advocates inevitably will invoke past case law to make arguments based on analogy and underlying principles that advance "new" rights as plausible extensions of past practice. They do so out of a traditional expectation that "like cases be treated alike,"[59] and in reliance on the inherently evolutionary common law approach to legal argumentation.

The first and third sets of tradition and history-based arguments are more challenging: why shouldn't courts defer to the "wisdom of crowds?"[60] Even if crowds occasionally (or often) lack wisdom, why imagine that the judiciary possesses this elusive quality in ways that make "dynamic due process" better than the judicial restraint of due process traditionalism?

As Sunstein notes, knowing what "judgment" a "tradition" reflects is vastly more complex than this deceptively comforting interpretation tool suggests. The underlying factual propositions that animate a tradition may be difficult or impossible to discern. The tradition also may not shed light on a particular outcome as circumstances change because "traditions apply only to the circumstances in which they governed, and when circumstances have changed, it is not clear that many minds have decided in favor of a particular tradition that is being invoked."[61]

---

[57] See Antonin Scalia, *Originalism: The Lesser Evil*, 57 U. Cinn. L. Rev. 849, 861–62 (1989) (describing relative values of originalism, though describing himself as a "faint-hearted originalist").

[58] It is difficult to imagine, for example, that the judge-made doctrine of selective incorporation of the Bill of Rights into the Fourteenth Amendment will be reversed. It was central to *McDonald*, which applied the Second Amendment to state and local government.

[59] The notion has been traced back to the Nicomachean Ethics. *See, e.g.*, H.L.A. Hart, The Concept of Law, ch. VIII (1961).

[60] *See* James Surowiecki, The Wisdom of Crowds: Why The Many Are Smarter Than the Few and How Collective Wisdom Shapes Business, Economics, Societies, and Nations 57 (2004) (discussing why collective decisions of cognitively diverse groups of people can be good decisions when the people reach "independent conclusions, relying primarily on their private information").

[61] Sunstein, *Due Process Traditionalism*, *supra* note 52 at 1552.

Another problem with deference to past practices is that bias may infect past thinking. Prejudice can be, as Sunstein notes, a "wisdom without reflection"[62] that may produce more errors in our thinking, not fewer ones. This insight is especially relevant to whether courts should defer to the traditions when addressing issues of equality, but it also bears on due process more generally, because systematic biases even can infect the way people think about laws that burden *themselves*, not just ones that burden others. Our capacity for rational thinking is limited: we can and do follow practices that are, upon reflection, "silly or harmful."[63] Judicial review compels reflection and requires the production of reasons as well as procedures designed to prevent arbitrary imposition of burdens on liberty.

We also are prone to simply "follow the herd." Traditions may persist because of what Sunstein calls a "cascade effect,"[64] rather than due to sound thinking.[65] Additionally, there is a stickiness to some social norms or traditions that is not necessarily rational. For all of these reasons, the "group judgment" reflected in traditional legal practices may be impaired.

One nevertheless might respond that the legal norms that emerge over time are the product of evolutionary forces that benefit society in ways that "reason cannot replace."[66] A different but related point is that there may be a value in deference to traditional practices that lies not in their inherent wisdom, but in resolving social issues—which have no objective answer—through democratic processes.[67]

Sunstein replies that this assumption about the positive attributes of legal norms that emerge over time must "offer some kind of account by which we can judge outcomes to be good."[68] He also notes that most problems with which substantive due process must deal—such as same-sex marriage, informational privacy, or the right to use medical marijuana—do not literally endanger the species, and thus cannot be judged by their ability to promote survival.[69]

Nor can many of them even be defended on the basis of "economic efficiency" or the wisdom of an "invisible hand."[70] Market competition may be desirable in the commercial domain, but it is not so clearly beneficial in the moral domain, where most substantive due process issues arise. In any event, democratic processes may be "inefficient" yet still be upheld against more efficient mechanisms.[71]

---

[62] *Id.* at 1553.

[63] *Id.* at 1555.

[64] *Id.* at 1556.

[65] Indeed, the cascade can become a stampede when people respond to "moral panic." *Id.* (quoting Stanley Cohn, Folk Devils and Moral Panics (3d ed., Routledge 2002) (1972)).

[66] *Id.* at 1558 (quoting F.A. Hayek, *The Origins and Effects of Our Morals*, Address at the Hoover Institution (Nov. 1 1983)).

[67] Surowiecki, *supra* note 60, at 270–71.

[68] Sunstein, *Due Process Traditionalism*, *supra* note 52, at 1559.

[69] *Id.*

[70] *Id.* at 1560.

[71] *Id.*

Most fundamentally, saying that "the people have spoken" is not the same thing as saying "*tradition* should trump current understandings, because this furthers *democracy*."[72] Democratic processes can and occasionally do reject long-standing traditions, and there is nothing *non-democratic* about this. This is especially true when the traditions themselves are not democratic.[73]

Another set of traditionalism arguments echoes the concerns articulated above about "judicial activism" and skepticism about judicial wisdom The institutional competencies of courts, the nature of judicial selection, and the inherently incrementalist nature of judicial decisionmaking itself already provide brakes on judicial innovation. If anything, the conservative nature of judges and judging suggests "[w]e are better off if traditions are a place to start but not to end, and if courts occasionally deploy a more critical approach, testing whether the tradition is sensible in principle."[74]

In other words, due process doctrine is inherently and substantially informed by traditional notions of fair play and substantial justice—the "common law" constitutional method is necessarily retrospective in ways that support traditionalism. But the reference to tradition should not be the final word.[75] A related criticism of evolutionary due process is that historical understandings of due process are more faithful to the text, to its public meaning at the time it was adopted, and to the core notion of a democratic government "by the People." Unelected judges should not supplant this democratic process.

Again, however, the invocation of history is deceptively comforting.[76] For one thing—as good historians know—our accounts of the legal past can deceive us. "Presentism"—using contemporary perspectives to explain the past—often infects our efforts at historical analysis. Invoking constitutional history also can become selective and distorted.[77] History may be "abused when people try to ignore or

---

[72] *Id.*

[73] *Id.* at 1570.

[74] *Id.* at 1569.

[75] For a recent discussion of the proper role of tradition in constitutional analysis, see Kim Forde-Mazrui, *Tradition as Justification: The Case of Opposite-Sex Marriage*, 78 U. CHI. L. REV. 281 (2011).

[76] In her slim and well-written book *Dangerous Games: The Uses and Abuses of History*, Margaret MacMillan patiently outlines for a general audience what professional historians understand about the perils of looking to history to understand the present. MARGARET MACMILLAN, DANGEROUS GAMES: THE USES AND ABUSES OF HISTORY (2009). Just a few of her points are worth underscoring here. First, she notes that people dislike uncertainty, and some turn to history "when the present seems bewildering and chaotic." *Id.* at 15. History serves as a kind of "comfort." *Id.* at 13. She notes that we sometimes "call on the past to help us with our values at least in part because we no longer trust the authorities of today." *Id.* at 19. It even can, in a secular world, substitute for a common religion. *Id.* at 20. The current fascination with history and its popularization occur at an especially worrisome moment. MacMillan notes that professional historians have "abandon[ed] the field to amateurs," *Id.* at 36, who make "sweeping generalizations for which there is not adequate evidence and ignore[] awkward facts that do not fit." *Id.* Professional historians need to reenter the fray, she argues, and assume their proper role, which is to "challenge and even explode national myths." *Id.* at 39.

[77] *Id.* at 53–58 (discussing how history can be involved for political ends).

even suppress evidence that might challenge their preferred view of the past."[78] Moreover, such misuse of history is hardly a rare occurrence; it is a fairly common response to political histories, and occasionally may be a conscious political strategy.[79]

A better use of history is to alert us to what we do *not* know.[80] History lessons can help to amend "lazy generalizations" and assist in "self-knowledge."[81]

Used judiciously, then, our constitutional history and legal traditions are a compass, not a blueprint. They can help us to frame due process questions and may offer cautions about past examples of arbitrary or unreasonable assertions of government power, which may make us better at seeing and responding to contemporary conflicts and how our actions likewise may be arbitrary or unreasonable.[82] Past understandings of due process may shed useful light on how to apply due process to our current affairs, but they cannot—by themselves—offer a complete guidebook. For all of these reasons, we believe that the common critiques of the Court's evolutionary approach to due process fall short. Judges play an important role in defining due process liberties, despite the risks of judicial overreaching.

III. Conclusion

We have identified common cords that we believe bind the Court's due process decisions, which are best seen by reviewing the full arc of the cases over time. We also have shown that the judicial practice in most due process cases is to defer to government actors, not to second-guess their policy choices. Finally, we have defended the Court's expansion of due process to include rights that protect liberty in ever-evolving ways.

On the thin end of the due process spectrum, due process allows *considerable* breathing room for government discretion. Yet it also offers a place for emerging rights to be considered, defined, and applied to an ever-evolving world. Candidates for inclusion under the thick end of due process protection begin here—but they do so with all bets against them. This "rational basis," tier preserves limited judicial flexibility to police cases of *exceptionally* arbitrary, cruel, or excessive government intrusions into liberty. But the power is exercised very sparingly. As the power actually has been applied by the Court—especially post-*Lochner*—it therefore

---

[78] *Id.* at 69.

[79] Invoking history selectively can also be a weapon. Political opponents may use history to "label or diminish" each other. *Id.* at 94. The results can be very grim ones—even genocide—and the aftermath may be covered with more false narratives, as the particularly horrific example of Holocaust deniers proves. *Id.*

[80] For example, knowing the history of other people and cultures may help us to better grasp what otherwise would escape us: "their values, their fears, and their hopes or how they are likely to react to something you do." *Id.* at 144.

[81] *Id.* at 146.

[82] *Id.* at 154.

respects the "passive virtues" that commentators concerned about judicial activism have extolled.[83] It is very mindful of the admonition that "[r]ecognizing a new liberty right is a momentous step [because] [i]t takes that right, to a considerable extent, 'outside the arena of public debate and legislative action.'"[84] Consequently, striking something down as "irrational" is a rare occurrence, and typically done "slowly and incrementally, building on what came before"[85] with implications that are designed very contextually.

We believe this room for new rights should be preserved. As Justice Stevens has observed, "[j]ust because there may not be a categorical right to physician-assisted suicide, for example, does not foreclose the possibility that an individual seeking to hasten her death, or a doctor whose assistance was sought, could succeed in a more particularized challenge."[86] This gradual movement of something from the "particularized" to the "categorical" column of rights is only possible if a "rational basis" starting point exists, and if due process is seen as an open-ended and dynamic concept. Nevertheless, a new right must undergo testing of its feasibility, its scope, its urgency, and its relationship to other rights before it can earn "fundamental," or "thicker" right status.

This evolutionary but cautious approach to rights is a sound constitutional practice for a liberal democratic order. Excessive reliance on traditionalism when interpreting contemporary notions of fundamental fairness is less likely to preserve a living liberty, or even an ordered liberty. Indeed, a wholly backward-referential approach to constitutional law may be ruinous. To quote Alexander Bickel, "[n]o good society can be unprincipled; and no viable society can be principle-ridden."[87]

Bickel's insight remains a compelling one. The modern world places unprecedented demands on government, even as cynicism about government seems to be mounting. New economic, technological, environmental, and other pressures *inevitably* will prompt novel legislation that pushes the boundaries of past constitutional thinking. Courts then *inevitably* will be tasked with determining the fate of these governmental innovations. When this occurs, a familiar interpretative question will arise: should the courts invoke the dogmas of the quiet past, or acknowledge the imperatives of a stormy present?

Finally, as our world changes, even our *selves* will evolve. The constitutional home of "personhood," and its relationship to the state, is due process. Consequently, judges charged with interpreting due process must do more than cast a nostalgic glance back through the vapors of centuries past as they puzzle through the due

---

[83] Alexander M. Bickel, The Least Dangerous Branch: The Supreme Court at the Bar of Politics, 111–83 (2d ed. 1986).

[84] McDonald v. City of Chicago, 130 S. Ct. 3020, 3102 (2010) (Stevens, J., dissenting) (quoting Washington v. Glucksberg, 521 U.S. 702, 720 (1997) (Stevens, J., concurring in judgments)).

[85] *Id.*

[86] *Id.* at 3103 (quoting Washington v. Glucksberg, 521 U.S. 702, 735, n.24, 742 (1997) (Stevens, J., concurring in judgments)).

[87] Bickel, *supra* 84, at 64.

process concept of "personhood," not just the due process concepts of "property" or "liberty."

The central constitutional question is this: how might we best fashion *era-appropriate* constitutional practices and theories? We have explained why modern due process notions of personhood, property, and liberty should not be derived solely from the notions that made sense in an eighteenth- or even nineteenth-century face-to-face political and legal culture. We should begin with these historical insights, and with the fundamental constitutional principles established in earlier eras. But we should not *end* there. Rather, American judges, policy makers, and citizens in this century and the next should be wary of the appearance of inevitability and reasonableness that can come from ideas that are "handed down" and not critically reexamined, as they seek to protect rapidly evolving "persons" from new forms of government intrusion into "life, liberty, and property." The Reconstruction and Founding era Framers likely would have understood the paradox that we have identified here. For our constitutional fundamentals to *endure*, our constitutional practices must be *revised*. In other words, hewing to our constitutional history means grasping the revolutionary spirit of that history. We might, for example, recall the words of forefathers like Benjamin Franklin, who famously said that he signed the original Constitution "because I am not sure, that it is *not* the best."[88] He then added that, with "better Information, or fuller Consideration,"[89] he might have found it to be otherwise. Franklin believed in bending his constitutional thinking to embrace new evidence and changed circumstances. In our own age, we would do well to express comparable humility and provisional faith in our current notions of "ordered liberty" as we continue to define this enduring cornerstone of our liberal democracy: due process of law.

---

[88] *See* Jill Lepore, *The Commandments*, THE NEW YORKER, Jan 17, 2001, at 70 (emphasis added).

[89] *Id.*

{INDEX}

www.ingramcontent.com/pod-product-compliance
Ingram Content Group UK Ltd.
Pitfield, Milton Keynes, MK11 3LW, UK
UKHW020926180926
475595UK00034B/144